D1247856

Official Catholic Teachings

christ our lord

Amanda G. Watlington

Manufactured in the United States of America

Library of Congress Card Catalog Number: 78-53844
ISBN: 0-8434-0714-X
ISBN: 0-8434-0720-4 paper

The publisher gratefully acknowledges permission to quote from the following copyrighted publications.

AMERICA PRESS
DIVINUM ILLUD MUNUS, Reprinted in "The Catholic Mind", May, 1938
LUX VERITATIS, Reprinted in "The Catholic Mind", February, 1932

AMERICAN CATHOLIC QUARTERLY REVIEW
ANNUM SACRUM, Volume XXIV, July, 1899.
TAMETSI FUTURA PROSPICIENTIBUS, Volume XXVI, January to October, 1901.
MIRAE CARITATIS, Volume XXVII, January to October, 1902.
E SUPREMI, Volume XXIX, January to October, 1904.
PASCENDI DOMINICI GREGIS, Volume XXXII, January to October, 1907.

CATHOLIC TRUTH SOCIETY, LONDON
ORIENTALIS ECCLESIAE DECUS, ©1944. From selected letters and addresses of Pius XII.

COSTELLO PUBLISHING COMPANY, INC. & REV. AUSTIN FLANNERY, OP
SACROSANCTUM CONCILUM; DEI VERBUM; GAUDIUM ET SPES; "Vatican Council II, The Conciliar and Post Conciliar Documents", ©1975.

DAUGHTERS OF ST. PAUL
EPHESINAM SYNODUM, LETTER TO CARDINAL SINCERO, "Our Lady", ©1961.

EASTERN CHURCHES QUARTERLY
SEMPITERNUS REX CHRISTUS, Volume IX, Spring, ©1952.

IRISH ECCLESIASTICAL RECORD
QUAS PRIMAS, Volume XXVII, January to June, ©1926.

NATIONAL CATHOLIC WELFARE CONFERENCE NEWS SERVICE
MISERENTISSIMUS REDEMPTOR, Reprinted in "The Catholic Mind", June 1928.
HAURIETIS AQUAS, ©1956.

OUR SUNDAY VISITOR
CHRISTMAS MESSAGE OF POPE PIUS XII, "The Pope Speaks", ©Winter 1955.
AETERNA DEI SAPIENTIA, "The Pope Speaks", Volume 8, Number 1, ©1962.

LUMEN GENTIUM: THE DOGMATIC CONSTITUTION ON THE CHURCH, (CHAPTER I), "The Pope Speaks", Volume 10, Number 4, © 1965.

MYSTERIUM FIDEI, "The Pope Speaks", Volume 10, Number 4, © 1965.

SOLEMN PROFESSION OF FAITH, "The Pope Speaks", Volume 13, Number 3, ©1968.

ADDRESS OF POPE PAUL VI TO A GENERAL AUDIENCE, January 13, 1971, "The Pope Speaks", Volume 16, Number 1, ©1971.

ADDRESS OF POPE PAUL VI TO A GENERAL AUDIENCE, January 27, 1971, "The Pope Speaks", Volume 16, Number 1, © 1971.

ADDRESS OF POPE PAUL VI TO A GENERAL AUDIENCE, February 3, 1971, "The Pope Speaks", Volume 16, Number 1, ©1971.

ADDRESS OF POPE PAUL VI TO A GENERAL AUDIENCE, February 10, 1971, "The Pope Speaks", Volume 16, Number 1, ©1971.

ADDRESS OF POPE PAUL VI TO A GENERAL AUDIENCE, February 17, 1971, "The Pope Speaks", Volume 16, Number 1, ©1971.

DECLARATION OF THE SACRED CONGREGATION FOR THE DOCTRINE OF THE FAITH, "The Pope Speaks", Volume 17, Number 1, ©1972.

HOMILY OF POPE PAUL VI ON THE 16TH CENTENARY OF ST. ATHANASIUS' DEATH, "The Pope Speaks", Volume 18, Number 1, ©1972.

ADDRESS OF POPE PAUL VI TO A GENERAL AUDIENCE, February 6, 1974, "The Pope Speaks", Volume 19, Number 1, ©1974.

ADDRESS OF POPE PAUL VI TO A GENERAL AUDIENCE, February 13, 1974, "The Pope Speaks", Volume 19, Number 1, ©1974.

TIPOGRAFIA POLIGLOTTA VATICANA

MYSTICI CORPORIS, Reprinted by "National Catholic Welfare Conference", 1943.

Table of Contents

DOCUMENTS	PAGE
Introduction	xi
Subject Index	xxiii
DIVINUM ILLUD MUNUS: Encyclical Letter of Pope Leo XIII on the Holy Ghost, May 9, 1897	1
ANNUM SACRUM: Encyclical Letter of Pope Leo XIII on the Consecration of Mankind to the Sacred Heart of Jesus, May 25, 1899	18
TAMETSI FUTURA PROSPICIENTIBUS: Encyclical Letter of Pope Leo XIII on Jesus Christ Our Redeemer, November 1, 1900	25
MIRAE CARITATIS: Encyclical Letter of Pope Leo XIII on the Most Holy Eucharist, May 23, 1902	39
E SUPREMI: Encyclical Letter of Pope Pius X on Restoration of All Things in Christ, October 4, 1903	54
PASCENDI DOMINICI GREGIS: Encyclical Letter of Pope Pius X on the Doctrine of the Modernists, September 8, 1907	66

QUAS PRIMAS: Encyclical Letter of Pope Pius XI on the Feast of Christ the King, December 11, 1925. 122

MISERENTISSIMUS REDEMPTOR: Encyclical Letter of Pope Pius XI on the Reparation Due to the Sacred Heart, May 9, 1928 140

Ephesinam Synodum, Letter to Cardinal Sincero, December 25, 1930 155

LUX VERITATIS: Encyclical Letter of Pope Pius XI on the Light of Truth, December 25, 1931 157

MYSTICI CORPORIS: Encyclical Letter of Pope Pius XII on the Mystical Body of Christ and Our Union in It with Christ, June 29, 1943 179

ORIENTALIS ECCLESIAE DECUS: Encyclical Letter of Pope Pius XII on St. Cyril, Patriarch of Alexandria, April 9, 1944 228

SEMPITERNUS REX CHRISTUS, Encyclical Letter of Pope Pius XII on the Ecumenical Council of Chalcedon on the Occasion of its Fifteen Hundredth Anniversary, September 8, 1951 243

The Christmas Message of Pope Pius XII to the Whole World, December 24, 1955 261

HAURIETIS AQUAS: Encyclical Letter of Pope Pius XII on Devotion to the Sacred Heart, May 15, 1956 279

AETERNA DEI SAPIENTIA: Encyclical Letter of Pope John XXIII Commemorating the Fifteenth Centenary of the Death of St. Leo the Great, Pope and Doctor of the Church, November 11, 1961 318

SACROSANCTUM CONCILIUM: General Principles for the Restoration and Promotion of the Sacred Liturgy, December 4, 1963 335

LUMEN GENTIUM: The Dogmatic Constitution on the Church, November 21, 1964 349

MYSTERIUM FIDEI: Encyclical Letter of Pope Paul VI on the Doctrine and Worship of the Holy Eucharist, September 3, 1965 358

DEI VERBUM: Dogmatic Constitution on Divine Revelation, November 18, 1965 380

GAUDIUM ET SPES: Selections from Pastoral Constitution on the Church in the Modern World, December 7, 1965 394

Solemn Profession of Faith by Pope Paul VI at the Closing of the Year of Faith, June 30, 1968 404

Address of Pope Paul VI to a General Audience, January 13, 1971 414

Address of Pope Paul VI to a General Audience, January 27, 1971 418

Address of Pope Paul VI to a General Audience, February 3, 1971 422

Address of Pope Paul VI to a General Audience, February 10, 1971 426

Address of Pope Paul VI to a General Audience, February 17, 1971 431

Declaration of the Sacred Congregation for the Doctrine of the Faith, March 8, 1972 435

Homily of Pope Paul VI on the 16th Centenary of St. Athanasius' Death, May 6, 1973 440

Address of Pope Paul VI to a General Audience, February 6, 1974 445

Address of Pope Paul VI to a General Audience, February 13, 1974 448

References 452

Introduction

Christ Our Lord, the current volume in the Official Catholic Teaching series, presents in English translation the major twentieth century papal pronouncements on the Christological question. The material in this volume has been selected to give a balanced impression of the problems and twentieth century concerns relative to this important area of theology. The documents are set out in chronological order so that developments in thought and treatment will be visible and easily traceable. The subject index at the front of the volume is set up to aid the reader desiring a topical treatment.

The reader might question why in the last quarter of the twentieth century do we need a retrospective view of the Christological question and its interpretation in this century. No significant challenges to the definition of Chalcedon have been raised during this century. The only brief flurry of controversy was during the early part of the century when Pope Pius X dealt with the Modernists. Similarly, new Christological definitions, treatment, research, and interpretation did not develop out of Vatican II, the great twentieth century Catholic Church Council. The Christological question, however, is so central to Christian faith that any formulation of doctrine on any topic during any century is done with the question, its definition, and contemporary interpretation in the background.

The Catholic Church in this century has been a dynamic rather than a static being. As Church history shows, theologians have never been content with simply going over the Chalcedon definition. They continue to seek insights by examining the definition and its implications relative to their own time and place in history. Because Christology is so basic to Christian faith and is indeed reviewed by each generation of theologians, a survey of twentieth century pronouncements on the topic is a must in a series such as Official Catholic Teachings.

Although this volume represents the output of a century without serious conflict, even the briefest survey of the contents shows that there has been considerable evaluation, interpretation, and reaffirmation of the beliefs affecting the life of the Church. Further, a complete collection, such as the one presented here, offers the reader the opportunity to see for himself the background and development of contemporary trends within the Church. A new way of thinking simply does not burst out overnight. It is almost always the product of gradual change.

At present the Church faces a small group of theologians who want the Church's Christological interpretation to focus more on Christ's full humanity and concern itself less with the abstract concept of divinity. Any shift in emphasis such as this runs counter to Chalcedon which gave equal emphasis to Christ's divinity and humanity. Challenges such as this contemporary one force the Church to review the Chalcedon decision. As the documents in this volume show, the Church has recently done this and has reaffirmed without hesitation the 451 A.D. Chalcedon decision. This church council decreed that Jesus Christ had two natures, a divine and a human, which were merged unchanged and unconfused in one Person of the Trinity. The 1972 Declaration of the Faith, included in this collection, met head-on the question of Christ's humanity and reaffirmed the traditional definition.

The so-called new Christology, which has posed this most recent challenge to traditional Christological interpretation, is actually a development of the Church which itself is seeking to place more emphasis on man and his place in the world.

This is in keeping with the direction of Vatican II. From the collection of documents presented here, the reader can trace the development of a man-centered Church as reflected in the Christological treatment. The official position is firmly rooted in the past. Although emphasizing man, it does not lose sight of the Chalcedon definition which gave equal weight to the two natures of Christ.

The documents selected for inclusion in this volume were carefully chosen from the papal encyclicals, conciliar documents, papal addresses, and letters. All the material was reviewed for its relevance to the Christological theme. It was neither possible nor desirable to screen out soteriological material. Christology and soteriology are generally regarded by theologians as intertwined so no effort was made to avoid material dealing with Christ's salvific role. It should, however, be noted that there are no specifically Mariological documents in this volume. The Blessed Virgin and her role in the Incarnation has been a fascination of twentieth century theologians. A collection of contemporary Mariological documents would in itself fill an entire volume.

The variety of sources represented by the documents was in part the product of intentional selection. Although the volume is basically comprised of encyclicals, other materials are given in an effort to view the Christological question and contemporary interpretation in light of the entire life of the Church. Informal messages to various types of audiences furnish a more pastoral view and give an idea of how the doctrinal material of the encyclicals relates to other areas of the Church's life.

A brief analysis of the contents shows that all the material can be divided into several loose categories. Aligning and discussing the material by topic will show a balance in the twentieth century treatment. There are roughly twelve doctrinal statements, eight pastoral addresses, six documents that peer into the historical background of the Christological definition, four documents from Vatican II, and a single topical encyclical dealing with the Modernist controversy that does not fit into any of the other categories. An examination of the documents by category will give the reader a clearer view of the papal treatment of the Christological question during the twentieth century.

As the analysis shows, the bulk of the material presented in this collection is dogmatic doctrinal statements. Although the volume purports to contain twentieth century thought, two of the doctrinal statements are from the closing years of the nineteenth century. They were both issued by Pope Leo XIII whose reign (1878-1902) spanned the nineteenth and twentieth centuries. Leo issued fifty encyclicals during his pontificate and was particularly concerned in them with fostering the life of Catholic devotion. Another of his primary concerns was the study of the gifts and functions of Jesus Christ. The four documents selected for this volume, two from the nineteenth and two from the twentieth centuries, reflect this pope's concerns.

Divinum Illud Munus, issued May 9, 1897, discussed the doctrine of the Holy Trinity. It focused on the Holy Ghost and his role in both the Incarnation and the Church. Although actually from the nineteenth century this document is much too important a doctrinal statement to omit for chronological reasons.

Leo in his efforts to foster devotion consecrated the entire human race to the Sacred Heart in 1900, for the Jubilee year. *Annum Sacrum*, dated May 25, 1899, not only called for devotion to the Sacred Heart but also placed mankind under Christ's dominion as the only begotten Son of God.

Leo's concern with Christ's gifts and functions is witnessed to by the last two encyclicals from his reign selected for inclusion in this collection. *Tametsi Futura Prospicientibus*, issued November 1, 1900, took up the redemptive qualities of Jesus; whereas, *Mirae Caritatis*, issued May 28, 1902, treated the Holy Eucharist.

Two Christological statements are included from the pontificate of Pius X, Leo's successor. Pius X took as his motto, "To restore all things in Christ." The October 4, 1903, encyclical *E Supremi* called for increased faith in Christ and restoration of all things in Christ. Unfortunately for Pius X fulfillment of this avowed goal was not to be his only task as pontiff, for it was his misfortune to have to proscribe the

Modernist movement. *Pascendi Dominici Gregis*, the other Christological statement in this volume from Pius X's pontificate, took this task in hand. Because of its unique topical nature, this encyclical letter is treated in a special category as a separate type of pronouncement.

There are no Christological statements in the volume from the reign of Pius X's successor Benedict XV (1914-1922). Pius XI who followed Benedict XV, however, is well represented with three encyclicals and a personal letter. Only two of these documents discuss doctrinal subjects. The others commemorate historical events. Pius XI reawakened Leo XIII's concerns, for *Quas Primas*, issued on December 11, 1925, took up the question of Christ's jurisdiction, a subject which Leo had treated in *Annum Sacrum*. Pius carefully spelled out in *Quas Primas* that the kingship of Christ belongs to Christ the man who received the power, glory, and kingdom from the Father and shared in it through the Hypostatic Union. This view represented a development from Leo's position. Although Leo noted that Christ's dominion is through the Father, he did not explicitly note that it was given to Christ the man.

In the 1928 encyclical *Miserentissimus Redemptor* Pius like Leo discussed the Sacred Heart. Again, as in *Quas Primas*, Pius developed Leo's interpretation. Whereas, Leo stressed mankind's consecration to the Sacred Heart, Pius wanted the faithful to console Christ in spite of the fact that Christ's suffering more than paid for our offences and that he is already glorified in heaven.

Two Christological statements are included from the pontificate of Pius XII. *Mystici Corporis*, issued June 29, 1943, is a major statement on Christ's relationship with the Mystical Body, the Church. Pius stated that Christ must be acknowledged as Head of the Church since the supernatural gifts have found their supreme fullness and perfection in Him and since by His Incarnation He has exceptional knowledge of his Mystical Body.

Pius XII, like Leo XIII and Pius XI, also took up the Sacred Heart. His encyclical *Hauretis Aquas* is on the devotion due to the Sacred Heart. In this encyclical Pius ably countered the movement which wanted a more metaphorical understanding of the Sacred Heart. Using scripture and tradition, Pius focused on the humanity of Christ. Pius left no doubt that the physical heart itself must in some way be included as an object of devotion.

This collection also contains three pronouncements issued during the current pontiff's reign. On September 3, 1965, Paul VI issued the encyclical *Mysterium Fidei* on the doctrine and worship of the Holy Eucharist. This is similar to Leo XIII's *Mirae Caritatis* issued more than fifty years earlier. The 1968 *Solemn Profession of Faith* issued by Paul at the closing of the year of Faith also touches on the subject of the Eucharist, but it did not take this as its main subject matter. The 1968 document is primarily a discussion of the Church's position on the Trinity. It, however, touches on a number of different related topics: the Blessed Virgin, original sin, the Church, and several other areas.

The most recent Christological document and perhaps the most important for contemporary students is the 1972 *Declaration of the Sacred Congregation for the Doctrine of the Faith.* This is the culmination of recent official Christological interpretation. This pronouncement came face-to-face with the challenge to the Chalcedon definition posed by a small group of contemporary theologians who want to place greater emphasis on Christ's full humanity. The 1972 Declaration specifically took issue with errors regarding the Son of God and the Trinity; herein, the challenge was met and dealt with. Pope Paul VI reaffirmed the Chalcedon definition as the Church's official position. This *Declaration* and the 1968 *Profession of Faith* clearly reaffirm Chalcedon and spell out decisively the Church's official contemporary position on this central issue.

As this brief review of the volume's array of dogmatic pronouncements suggests, the twentieth century has been an era for reaffirmation of the Chalcedon decision. It has also been a period during which the Eucharist, the Sacred Heart, and Christ's relationship to the Mystical Body have been reviewed and reinterpreted.

The eight pastoral documents were selected from the past twenty-five or so years. They are included to show how the dogmatic statements are used in the life of the Church. The earliest pastoral message is Pius XII's 1955 Christmas radio message. In this message the pontiff used the Nativity and the mystery of the Incarnation as a springboard for a call for peace among mankind. He stated that the Incarnation was man's basis for the support of social order and peace.

All the other informal messages are from the current pontiff's reign. In the five 1971 addresses to general audiences Pope Paul examined Christ as He is presented in the Gospels. He considered the questions raised by Christians: How do we picture Christ for ourselves; who was He; and what did He do? Although these addresses focused on the human aspects of Christ, they always interplayed his divinity. In these addresses the divine Christ's human life showed through as an example for how modern man might life his life.

In 1974 Pope Paul again dealt with man's relationship with Christ in two addresses to general audiences. In these he first discussed man's encounter with Christ and secondly the mystery of Jesus.

These eight informal pastoral addresses give a vitality to the interpretation of Christ's person in the Church. It should be noted that although they are not in themselves doctrinal statements, they all have the dogmatic treatment as a backdrop.

The twentieth century marked the fifteen hundredth anniversary of the great councils of Ephesus and Chalcedon; wherein, the Christological definition used by the Church since that time was wrought. These anniversaries have engendered papal pronouncements reflecting on these councils which have shaped Christian belief. The twentieth century popes have seen fit to reaffirm the decisions of these councils as a means of strengthening Catholic faith.

The Church's early history was filled with controversies which were resolved by councils. The Christological work of the councils built on one another until the 351 A.D. definition of Chalcedon. The Council of Nicea, for example, in 325 defined the perfect divinity and full equality of Jesus, the Son, with God, the Father. It, however, did not fully define Christ's nature. Ephesus and Chalcedon sorted out how Christ could have both a divine and human nature and yet be one part of the Trinity.

Pius XI's letter to Cardinal Sincero, *Ephesinam Synodum*, offers a short interesting summary of the historical background of the Council at Ephesus. It is included in this collection as a backdrop for the encyclical *Lux Veritatis.*

On Christmas of 1931 Pius XI issued the encyclical *Lux Veritatis* to commemorate the fifteen hundredth anniversary of the Council of Ephesus. The Council was called to counter Nestorius who held that the divinity and humanity of Christ existed as two distinct natures and were not unified into a single personality. The Council defended the unity of Christ through the Hypostatic Union. The encyclical recalls this council and praises the work of Cyril of Alexandria, one of the prime forces in working out the Council's decision. Pius XI in commemorating the conciliar decision also uses it as a forum to spell out the Church's belief on the Incarnation.

Just as 1931 marked the fifteenth centenary for the Council of Ephesus, 1944 marked the fifteenth centenary of the death of Cyril of Alexandria, a major figure at the Council. The success of this council has often been heavily attributed to Cyril. He was such a powerful figure that his thinking strongly influenced the Council of Chalcedon which was held after his death. On April 9, 1944, Pius XII commemorated Cyril and his work in an encyclical *Orientalis Ecclesiae Decus.* The issuance of this encyclical to commemorate the fifteenth centenary of the saint's death is particularly significant since in recent years Cyril's reputation has suffered somewhat at the hands of those wanting to rehabilitate our estimation of Nestorius. By so highly praising and honoring Cyril, Pius XII reestablished him as a major figure to whom a large measure of respect is due.

At first glance it seems that Ephesus should have laid to rest the argument over Christ's person, but Eutyches, a monk of Constantinople, and Dioscurus of Alexandria sought to hedge from the Ephesus Formula of Union. They held that after the union the divine and human natures became blended so as to constitute one nature. The Roman pontiff Leo I was the leading figure of the Chalcedon Council. The Council condemned Eutyches and developed the definition of Christ's nature as we know it: Christ has two natures, divine and human, which are merged unchanged and without confusion into one person of the Trinity.

On September 8, 1951, Pius XII issued an encyclical *Sempiternus Rex* to commemorate the fifteen hundredth anniversary of the Council of Chalcedon. In this encyclical Pius reviewed the history of the Council and the import of its decision. He also took the opportunity while reaffirming the Catholic position of rejecting the Protestant kenotic theories which overstress the humanity of Christ. This encyclical is a major Christological statement reaffirming one of the profoundest of Catholic beliefs.

John XXIII issued a 1961 encyclical to commemorate the fifteenth centenary of the death of Pope Leo the Great. Leo was a major figure in the Chalcedon Council. *Aeterna Dei Sapientia* recalled Leo's role and offered insights into the controversy and the Council. The five documents relating to the Councils at Ephesus and Chalcedon all carry the same theme: reaffirmation of basic beliefs and respect due to the great thinkers of the Early Church.

The most recent commemorative pronouncement issued to honor an early figure in the Christological controversy is Paul VI's homily on the sixteenth centenary of St. Athanasius' death. Athanasius was a defender of the Church against the early heresy Arianism. Arius, a fourth century Alexandrian, taught that Jesus Christ was not of the same substance as God but was simply the best of created things. Athanasius championed the consubstantiality of the Son with the Father. Pope Paul's homily recalled Athanasius' role in Christian thinking and reaffirmed the Church's position on consubstantiation.

The popes issuing the six documents commemorating the councils and great figures of the Early Church had three basic reasons for issuing the encyclicals. First, they offered an opportunity for the pontiffs to remember and in essence interpret the events of the councils and the respective roles of the great theologians. Second, the pontiffs were able to use the anniversaries to reaffirm and redirect Catholic thinking on the major issue of Christ's divinity. Third, by recollecting these important events and figures the popes hoped to renew and strengthen the faith on this very basic belief.

Although the documents from the Second Vatical Council (1962-1965) frequently mention Christ, there is little of Christological importance in this material. Vatican II was primarily pastoral and ecumenical in outlook. The documents in this collection selected from the Vatican II pronouncements were chosen because they give an overview or perspective on how Christ emerged from the Council.

In *Sacrosanctum Concilium* Christ was shown as the redeemer. He was prefigured in the Old Testament and came as the Savior in the New. As Savior he serves as a mediator between God and Man. *Lumen Gentium* showed Christ as the center of the Church just as *Mystici Corporis* did in 1943. By reaffirming this central position of Christ within the Church, Vatican II had little need for elaborate treatment of Christ and his role in the Church and society today. The rest of the century's interpretation stood in the background for theologians to draw from.

In *Dei Verbum*, another Vatican II document, Christ was recognized as the souce of revelation. He was chosen by God to serve as a mediator between God and Man. This document also depicted Christ as the source of truth about salvation and showed that it is through him that the task of salvation was completed. In *Gaudium et Spes* Christ was shown as the key, the focal point and goal of all human existence and history. Christ is depicted as the consummation of God's love at work in human history.

As this brief summary shows Christ emerged from Vatican II as the center of the Church, the mediator, and guide for human existence. Vatican II considered Christ's relationship with mankind and reaffirmed the position of Christ as center of the Church.

As mentioned earlier the twentieth century had a brief flurry of theological controversy at the beginning of the century. In 1907 Pius X issued *Pascendi Dominici Gregis*, an encyclical condemning the errors of Modernism. Due to its unique topical nature and inasmuch as it attacks a specific error, for the purposes of this discussion it is dealt with as a separate entity.

The Modernists claimed that they saw in the Gospels evidence and ignorance on Christ's part. They also saw fit to question his divinity and messianic character. They sharply distinguished between the Christ of Faith and the Christ of History. This particular distinction has remained a source of debate for recent decades. The questioning by theologians of Christ's divinity and messianic character struck so hard at the bedrock of Christian belief that the Church was forced to officially condemn the Modernists. The encyclical is couched in very negative terms and does not give any sense of the positive questioning which the controversy evoked. The encyclical is included in this volume because of what it says relative to erroneous twentieth century thought and the official Catholic Church position on the divinity and nature of Christ.

As this brief review of the contents of this volume shows, each document speaks to a specific area of twentieth century Christological thought. It is hoped that the reader aided by the subject index will be able to get a full insight into the dimensions of the twentieth century Christological research and interpretation.

Subject Index

AGNOSTICISM 102, 107, 133–140, 146

ANGER OF GOD 71, 82, 211–212, 335, 598

ANTICHRIST 81, 616

APOSTLES 1, 6, 7, 17, 23, 178, 204, 263, 335, 338, 343, 345, 361, 370, 510, 649, 808–816, 827, 850, 926, 957, 963, 1024, 1083, 1089, 1091, 1108

APOSTOLIC SUCCESSION 7, 345, 347, 808–810, 829–830, 1023, 1108

APPROPRIATION (THEOLOGY) 4

ARIANISM 235, 278, 1213

ATHANASIUS, SAINT, PATRIARCH OF ALEXANDRIA d. 373 1204–1222

ATHEISM 102, 146

AUTHORITY (RELIGION) 150

BAPTISM 5, 10, 322–323, 327, 332, 335, 805, 850–851, 858, 924, 1105, 1229–1234

BELIEF AND DOUBT 96, 113

BIBLE, NEW TESTAMENT 607–608, 610, 1022–1023, 1031, 1040–1045, 1125–1133, 1135–1145

BIBLE, OLD TESTAMENT 596–604, 606, 849, 918, 1031, 1037–1039

BLESSED SACRAMENT, FEAST OF THE 999

CELESTINE I, SAINT, POPE, d. 432 253–265, 269, 272, 283, 420, 448–449, 451–453

CENSORSHIP (CANON LAW) 158–164

CHALCEDON, COUNCIL OF 271, 420, 461, 466–511, 784, 821

CHARITY 42, 61, 63–65, 91, 329, 375, 378–380, 402–403, 437–438, 643, 656, 841, 970

CHRISTIAN LIFE 42–47, 68, 92, 411, 530–545, 547–551, 579, 745, 861, 1122–1124, 1220

CHURCH 42, 65, 67, 86–88, 125–131, 190, 198–199, 241–242, 281–282, 306–308, 310–311, 318–332, 334–339, 341–352, 354–382, 385–420, 427, 569, 625, 634, 648, 656, 670–672, 849, 851–852, 856–858, 911–936, 970–975, 1028–1029, 1106–1111

CHURCH – UNITY 64, 65, 67, 186, 282–283, 297, 310–311, 313, 319, 327, 347, 408, 426–427, 434, 441–442, 456, 458, 460, 463, 468, 493, 502–506, 776–778, 785, 789–790, 801–803, 806–808, 829–841, 843–846, 978, 1006–1007

CHURCH AND SOCIAL PROBLEMS 529–534, 1054–1082, 1115–1117

CHURCH AND STATE 29, 43, 126-127, 184, 198, 788

CLERGY 48, 88–89, 92, 144, 150, 154

COLONIALISM 563

COMMUNION, HOLY 219, 389, 394, 1000

COMMUNION OF SAINTS 65, 394

COMMUNISM AND RELIGION 537–541

CONDUCT OF LIFE 41–47, 55–57, 61, 92, 525–531, 541–542, 1220

CONFESSION 393

CONFIRMATION 10, 323, 805

CONSTANTINOPLE, COUNCIL OF. 4th, 869–870 150, 420

COUNCILS AND SYNODS, ECUMENICAL 271, 989, 1171

CREATION 46, 912

CYRIL, SAINT, PATRIARCH OF ALEXANDRIA, ca. 370–444 180, 236–237, 252–253, 255–259, 264–265, 269–272, 286, 288, 297, 419–465, 482, 487, 492

DOCETISM 494

DOGMA 110–112, 123, 128, 131, 142, 144, 245, 958–960, 1085

EASTERN CHURCHES 443–445, 468, 491, 502, 1010, 1203–1205

END OF THE WORLD 81, 142

EPHESUS, COUNCIL OF 235, 238–305, 422–423, 435, 451, 466–467, 488–489, 496

ERROR 89, 96–98, 151–152, 155, 164, 188, 206, 314, 346, 370, 390, 392, 438–440, 616, 699

EUCHARIST 16, 52–54, 56–62, 64–65, 67–73, 214, 324–325, 332, 386–389, 394, 634, 648–650, 657, 753–754, 805, 850, 858–859, 913, 925, 936–1013

EUCHARIST – CONFRATERNITES 53, 72

EUCHARISTIC CONGRESSES 53

EUTYCHIANS 271, 468–471, 473–475, 477, 482, 485, 488–489, 492, 782

FAITH 104–105, 107, 109, 116–117, 128, 371, 375–376, 429–431, 433, 610, 703–704, 858, 938, 970, 1083–1120

FAITH AND REASON 315

FALL OF MAN 212, 317, 912, 1103

FEAST OF PENTECOST 3, 15

FORGIVENESS OF SIN 14, 275

GOD 1–13, 44–46, 69–70, 82–83, 85, 87, 117, 142, 146, 510, 600, 608, 916, 1016, 1092–1093

GOD – CREATOR 46, 85, 912, 1016, 1092

GOD – FATHERHOOD 85, 608

GOD – GOODNESS 87

GOD – KINGSHIP 82–83, 916

GOD – MERCY 93

GOD – OMNIPOTENCE 516, 600, 1093

GOD – PERSONALITY 146, 1093

GOD – SOVEREIGNTY 82–83, 85

GOOD AND EVIL 310, 371

GRACE (THEOLOGY) 317, 323, 608, 656–657, 940–941, 1019

GREGORY I, THE GREAT, SAINT, POPE, 540 (ca.)–604 271, 348, 467

HOLY ORDERS 89, 157, 322, 325

HOLY SPIRIT 1–15, 17, 142, 270, 275, 328, 331, 336, 338, 347, 373–374, 383, 392, 571–572, 634, 662–667, 914, 1019, 1100

HOLY YEAR 20, 37, 171, 173–174, 194, 209

HOPE 375–377

IMMANENCE (PHILOSOPHY) 103, 108, 121–122, 135, 143, 146

IMMORTALITY 62, 849–850, 1118–1120

IGNORANCE 48, 149–150

INDULGENCES 16

INSPIRATION 124, 1031–1032

JESUS CHRIST 3–9, 22–28, 30–32, 36–44, 56–57, 60, 63–65, 85, 87–88, 133–134, 142, 166, 169–187, 190–200, 207–210, 215, 217–222, 227–233, 235, 245–246, 250–251, 271–278, 280–281, 286–288, 317, 333–337, 341, 351, 353, 355–356, 359, 360–361, 370, 372, 380, 391, 395, 422, 461, 467, 469–471, 473–474, 483, 485–490, 492, 494–500, 502, 509, 512–513, 517–520, 523–524, 528, 542, 544, 569, 573–575, 585, 588, 593, 594, 605, 616–632, 634–638, 640–641, 643–666, 670, 679, 700, 704–705, 707–709, 748, 779–782, 784, 803, 848–849, 913, 917, 928, 932, 934, 974–975, 1003, 1015, 1073–1077, 1093–

1099, 1102, 1127–1133, 1137–1145, 1148–1154, 1160–1174, 1178–1180, 1187–1196, 1211–1217, 1224–1229, 1235–1241

JESUS CHRIST – ASCENSION 660–662, 849

JESUS CHRIST – CRUCIFIXION 333–337, 361, 646–647, 653, 655, 658–659, 913

JESUS CHRIST – DIVINITY 3–4, 22, 38, 44, 85, 133–134, 173, 175–176, 178, 184, 195, 235, 245–246, 250–251, 271, 273–278, 280–281, 286–288, 336, 341, 351, 355–356, 360–361, 395, 485, 499, 544, 616–617, 626, 638, 656, 775, 1096, 1161–1173, 1187–1196, 1211–1217

JESUS CHRIST – EXAMPLE 88, 186, 207, 215, 353, 370, 528, 928, 934, 974, 1003, 1073–1077, 1127–1133

JESUS CHRIST – HUMANITY 176, 351, 359, 471, 495–498, 617–623, 625–627, 630, 640–641, 1075, 1128, 1133, 1137–1145, 1148–1153, 1160–1174, 1224–1229, 1237–1241

JESUS CHRIST – HYPOSTATIC UNION 180, 273–274, 278, 286, 353, 372, 380, 422, 467, 473–474, 485–490, 492, 499, 593, 605, 616, 618, 624, 707, 848, 1187–1188

JESUS CHRIST – INCARNATION 3–5, 60, 273, 275, 278, 280, 317, 336, 380, 483, 485, 494, 497–498, 512–513, 517–518, 542, 622–625, 779–780, 782, 803, 1102

JESUS CHRIST – KINGSHIP 22–23, 37, 42–44, 169–187, 190–200, 209, 231–232, 1099, 1148–1154

JESUS CHRIST – MIRACLES 641

JESUS CHRIST – NATIVITY 519–520, 523–524, 1235–1236

JESUS CHRIST – PARABLES 642

JESUS CHRIST – PASSION 634, 647, 653, 679, 849, 1098, 1178–1180

JESUS CHRIST – PERSON 173, 175–176, 271–274, 277–278, 351, 391, 395, 461, 469–470, 490, 492, 496, 499–500, 502, 509, 617, 619, 625, 670, 704–705, 708–709, 779, 781, 784, 932, 975, 1015, 1093–1099

JESUS CHRIST – RESURRECTION 178, 341, 636, 849, 917, 1098

JESUS CHRIST – SACRED HEART 21, 27–28, 31–32, 195, 206–208, 210, 217–222, 227–233, 569, 573–575, 585, 588, 594, 628–632, 635–637, 643–666, 700, 748

JESUS CHRIST THE KING, FEAST OF 174, 187–188, 190, 192–199, 209–210

JOSEPH, SAINT 299, 641

JUSTICE 71, 84, 233, 501, 612, 613

KENOSIS 494, 1224

KINGDOM OF GOD 916–922, 1097, 1115, 1151–1155

LATERAN COUNCIL, 4th, 1215 68

LEO I, THE GREAT, SAINT, POPE, d. 461 271, 334, 420, 473–477, 482, 496, 499, 767–847

LITANY OF THE SACRED HEART 33

LITURGY 848–910, 937, 1046

LOVE (THEOLOGY) 42, 571–574, 590, 594–595, 599, 601–612, 615, 618, 622, 630–631, 634–637, 641, 644–656, 659–677, 694, 703–706, 711–713, 718, 720–721, 725, 743–746, 752, 1097

LOVE OF GOD 13, 42, 80, 211, 220–221, 379, 598–599, 755

MARGARET MARY ALACOQUE, SAINT, 1647–1690 21, 205, 208, 218, 231, 685, 690, 762

MARRIAGE (SACRAMENT) 299–300, 322, 325

MARY, BLESSED VIRGIN 5, 17, 93, 166, 178, 188, 233, 235, 237–240, 245, 251, 271, 275, 286–297, 299–300, 341, 361, 415–416, 419, 422, 424–425, 458, 471, 510, 616, 632, 634, 640, 641, 648, 651–652, 757–760, 775, 804, 1011, 1096, 1101–1102

MARY, BLESSED VIRGIN – ANNUNCIATION 178, 640 755

MARY, BLESSED VIRGIN – IMMACULATE CONCEPTION 5, 275, 341, 361, 471, 632, 1096, 1101

MARY, BLESSED VIRGIN – MOTHERHOOD 235, 237–240, 245, 251, 271, 286–296, 299–300, 422, 424–425, 616, 641, 775, 1011

MARY, BLESSED VIRGIN – QUEENSHIP 297, 300

MASS 884, 939–942, 945–946, 966–969, 1112

MATERIALISM (THEOLOGY) 523–524, 531–535, 580, 741, 1072

MERCY 501, 612–614, 970

MISSIONS 171, 932–935

MODERNISM 96–168

MONOPHYSITES 490, 508

MONOTHELISM 420

MORTIFICATION 215–216, 411

MYSTICAL BODY OF CHRIST 6, 7, 11, 223, 283–284, 306, 310–311, 318, 323, 328, 330, 335, 339, 344–346, 349, 354, 356, 358, 364–365, 367, 369, 380, 382, 393–394, 398, 402, 502, 835, 853, 923–931, 975, 1006, 1106, 1232

NATIONALISM 562–564

NESTORIANS 235–237, 245, 248–257, 265–266, 269–271, 273, 278, 281, 288–289, 297, 422, 432–433, 435, 438, 442, 447–449, 451–452, 461–462, 468–469, 473, 482, 485, 487–489, 492, 508, 771, 775

NICAEA, COUNCIL OF, 325 173, 194, 235, 433, 466–467, 1213

NICAEA, COUNCIL OF, 787 150

NOVATIONISTS 422

NOVENAS 16

NUCLEAR WEAPONS 554–560

OBEDIENCE 42–45, 185, 611, 1019

PANTHEISM 146

PEACE 84, 169, 186, 301–302, 410, 434, 503, 552–554, 561–564, 746, 785

PELAGIANISM 212, 273, 775

PENANCE 16, 323, 393

PENTECOST 331, 338, 361, 850, 914

PENTECOST SEASON 2, 16

PERFECTION, CHRISTIAN 88, 108, 344, 349, 351–352, 550, 734, 842

PERSECUTION 506–508

PHILOSOPHY, SCHOLASTIC 145–150, 153–154, 157, 340

PIETY 313, 583, 586, 591

POPES – AUTHORITY 245, 254, 257, 263, 267, 272, 282–283, 347, 422, 446, 456, 468, 481, 786, 808–810, 812–820, 828

PRAYER 394–395, 406–407, 458–459, 531, 861, 892, 970

PREACHING 48, 115, 895, 971

PRECIOUS BLOOD 38, 607, 611

PRIDE AND VANITY 55, 61, 148, 309

PROPHETS 177, 278–279, 570, 599, 601, 603, 606, 1017

PURGATORY 16, 65, 406

REDEMPTION 1, 9, 24, 38–39, 56–57, 180–182, 185, 212–214, 274–276, 278, 280, 293, 317, 336, 349, 370, 494, 501, 611, 619–623, 625, 633, 640, 659, 670–671, 677, 758, 849–850, 913, 931, 1016, 1075–1076, 1102, 1104, 1219

RELICS AND RELIQUARIES 164

RELIGIOUS EDUCATION 89–90, 153–156, 299

REVELATION 102, 105–107, 131, 1014–1053, 1074–1079, 1194

ROSARY 93

SACRAMENTS 122–123, 323–325, 336, 356, 371, 657, 851, 924, 1107

SACRED BOOKS 124, 135–137, 141–142, 178–179, 319, 334–335, 595, 879, 1024, 1027, 1031–1053

SACRED HEART – CULTUS 207–208, 217–222, 575–579, 581–587, 591–592, 668, 675–690, 700, 710–734, 743–744, 749–751, 753, 755, 759–760, 763–765

SACRED HEART, FEAST OF THE 21, 230, 568, 589, 683–684, 690, 692, 761

SALVATION 28, 30, 38–41, 60, 69–70, 85–87, 170, 184, 204, 278, 282, 308, 356, 364, 414, 565–567, 609, 612–613, 626–627, 640, 648, 848, 850, 934, 969, 1015–1016, 1037–1045, 1080–1082, 1111

SCHISM – EASTERN AND WESTERN CHURCH 789

SECULARISM 190

SEMINARIES, THEOLOGICAL 89, 153–154, 156, 868–870

SIN 13–14, 38, 41, 224–226, 317, 328, 613–614

SIN, ORIGINAL 38, 41, 212, 280, 317, 1103, 1233

SOUL 60, 62

SPIRITUAL LIFE 520–528, 861, 974

SUFFERING 307, 645–646

TRADITION (THEOLOGY) 150, 164, 372, 1023–1030

TRANSUBSTANTIATION 945–946, 981–987, 990, 1112–1114

TRENT, COUNCIL OF, 1545–1563 65, 67, 89, 938, 946, 959, 976, 980–981, 990, 1008, 1103

TRINITY 2–11, 383, 385, 571, 591, 611, 677, 1093–1096, 1185–1201

UNIVERSITIES AND COLLEGES, CATHOLIC 157–158

WORSHIP 128, 144, 701–702

DIVINUM ILLUD MUNUS

Encyclical Letter of Pope Leo XIII
on the Holy Ghost
May 9, 1897

That Divine office which Jesus Christ received from His Father for the welfare of mankind, and most perfectly fulfilled, had for its final object to put men in possession of the eternal life of glory, and proximately during the course of ages to secure to them the life of divine grace, which is destined eventually to blossom into the life of heaven. Wherefore, our Saviour never ceases to invite, with infinite affection, all men, of every race and tongue, into the bosom of His Church: "Come ye all to Me," "I am the Life," "I am the Good Shepherd." Nevertheless, according to His inscrutable counsels, He did not will to entirely complete and finish this office Himself on earth, but as He had received it from the Father, so He transmitted it for its completion to the Holy Ghost. It is consoling to recall those assurances which Christ gave to the body of His disciples a little before He left the earth: "It is expedient to you that I go. for if I go not, the Paraclete will not come to you. but if I go, I will send Him to you" (1 *John* xvi. 8). In these words He gave as the chief reason of His departure and His return to the Father, the advantage which would most certainly accrue to His followers from the coming of the Holy Ghost, and, at the same time, He made it clear that the Holy Ghost is equally sent by–and therefore proceeds from–Himself and the Father; that He would complete, in His office of Intercessor, Consoler, and Teacher, the work which Christ Himself had begun in His mortal life. For, in the redemption of the world, the completion of the work was by Divine Providence reserved to the manifold power of that Spirit, who, in the creation, "adorned the heavens" (*Job* xxvi, 13), and "filled the whole world" (*Wisdom* i, 7).

2 Now We have earnestly striven, by the help of His grace, to follow the example of Christ, our Saviour, the Prince of Pastors, and the Bishop of our Souls, by diligently carrying on His office, entrusted by Him to the Apostles and chiefly to Peter, "whose dignity faileth, not, even in his unworthy successor" (St. Leo the Great, Sermon ii, On the Anniversary of his Election). In pursuance of this object We have endeavored to direct all that We have attempted and persistently carried out during a long pontificate towards two chief ends: in the first place, towards the restoration, both in rulers and peoples, of the principles of the Christian life in civil and domestic society, since there is no true life for men except from Christ; and, secondly, to promote the reunion of those who have fallen away from the Catholic Church either by heresy or by schism, since it is most undoubtedly the will of Christ that all should be united in one flock under one Shepherd. But now that We are looking forward to the approach of the closing days of Our life, Our soul is deeply moved to dedicate to the Holy Ghost who is the life-giving Love, all the work We have done during Our pontificate, that He may bring it to maturity and fruitfulness. In order the better and more fully to carry out this Our intention, We have resolved to address you at the approaching sacred season of Pentecost concerning the indwelling and miraculous power of the Holy Ghost; and the extent and efficiency of His action, both in the whole body of the Church and in the individual souls of its members, through the glorious abundance of His Divine graces. We earnestly desire that, as a result, faith may be aroused in your minds concerning the mystery of the adorable Trinity, and especially that piety may increase and be inflamed towards the Holy Ghost, to whom especially all of us owe the grace of following the paths of truth and virtue;

for, as St. Basil said, "Who denieth that the dispensations concerning man, which have been made by the great God and our Saviour, Jesus Christ, according to the goodness of God, have been fulfilled through the grace of the spirit?" (*Of the Holy Ghost*, c. xvi, v.39.)

3 Before We enter upon this subject, it will be both desirable and useful to say a few words about the Mystery of the Blessed Trinity. This dogma is called by the doctors of the Church "the substance of the New Testament," that is to say, the greatest of all mysteries, since it is the fountain and origin of them all. In order to know and contemplate this mystery, the angels were created in Heaven and men upon earth. In order to teach more fully this mystery, which was but foreshadowed in the Old Testament, God Himself came down from the angels unto men: "No man hath seen God at any time; the only begotten Son, who is in the bosom of the Father, He hath declared Him" (*John* i, 18). Whosoever then writes or speaks of the Trinity must keep before His eyes the prudent warning of the Angelic Doctor: "When we speak of the Trinity, we must do so with caution and modesty, for, as St. Augustine saith, nowhere else are more dangerous errors made, or is research more difficult, or discovery more fruitful" *(Summa. Th.* 1, p. xxxi, Art. 2). The danger that arises is lest the Divine Persons be confounded one with the other in faith or worship, or lest the one Nature in them be separated: for "This is the Catholic Faith, that we should adore one God in Trinity and Trinity in Unity." Therefore Our predecessor Innocent XII absolutely refused the petition of those who desired a special festival in honor of God the Father. For, although the separate mysteries connected with the Incarnate Word are celebrated on certain fixed days, yet there is no special feast on which the Word is honored according to His Divine Nature alone. And even the Feast of Pentecost was instituted in the earlier times, not simply to honor the Holy Ghost in Himself, but to commemorate His coming, or His external mission. And all this has been wisely ordained, lest from distinguishing the Persons men should be led to distinguish the Divine Essence. Moreover

the Church, in order to preserve in her children the purity of faith, instituted the Feast of the Most Holy Trinity, which John XXII afterwards extended to the Universal Church. He also permitted altars and churches to be dedicated to the Blessed Trinity, and, with the Divine approval, sanctioned the Order for the Ransom of Captives, which is specially devoted to the Blessed Trinity and bears Its name. Many facts confirm its truths.

4 The worship paid to the saints and angels, to the Mother of God, and to Christ Himself, finally redounds to the honor of the Blessed Trinity. In prayers addressed to one Person, there is also mention of the others: in the litanies after the individual Persons have been separately invoked, a common invocation of all is added: all psalms and hymns conclude with the doxology to the Father, Son, and Holy Ghost; blessings, sacred rites, and sacraments are either accompanied or concluded by the invocation of the Blessed Trinity. This was already foreshadowed by the Apostle in those words: "For of Him, and by Him, and in Him, are all things: to Him be glory for ever" (*Rom.* xi, 36), thereby signifying both the Trinity of Persons and the Unity of Nature: for as this is one and the same in each of the Persons, so to each is equally owing supreme glory, as to one and the same God. St. Augustine commenting upon this testimony writes: "The words of the Apostle, *of Him, and by Him, and in Him*, are not to be taken indiscriminately; *of Him* refers to the Father, *by Him* to the Son, *in Him* to the Holy Ghost" (*De Trin.* 1. vi, c. 10; 1. i, c. 6). The Church is accustomed most fittingly to attribute to the Father those works of the Divinity in which power excels, to the Son those in which wisdom excels, and those in which love excels to the Holy Ghost. Not that all perfections and external operations are not common to the Divine Persons; for "the operations of the Trinity are indivisible, even as the essence of the Trinity is indivisible" (St. Aug. *De Trin.*, 1. I, cc. 4-5); because as the three Divine Persons "are inseparable, so do they act inseparably" (St. Aug., *ib*). But by a certain comparison, and a kind of affinity between the operations and the properties of the Persons, these operations are attributed or, as

it is said, "appropriated" to One Person rather than to the others. "Just as we make use of the traces of similarity or likeness which we find in creatures for the manifestation of the Divine Persons, so do we use Their essential attributes; and this manifestation of the Persons by Their essential attributes is called *appropriation*" (St. Th. I, q. 39, xxxix, a. 7). In this manner the Father, who is "the principle of the whole Godhead" (St. Aug. *De Trin.* 1, iv, c. 20) is also the efficient cause of all things, of the Incarnation of the Word, and the sanctification of souls; "of Him are all things": *of Him,* referring to the Father. But the Son, the Word, the image of God, is also the exemplar cause, whence all creatures borrow their form and beauty, their order and harmony. He is for us the Way, the Truth, and the Life; the Reconciler of Man with God. "By Him are all things": *by him* referring to the Son. The Holy Ghost is the ultimate cause of all things, since, as the will and all other things finally rest in their end, so He, who is the Divine Goodness and the Mutual Love of the Father and Son, completes and perfects, by His strong yet gentle power, the secret work of man's eternal salvation. "In Him are all things": *in Him*, referring to the Holy Ghost.

5 Having thus paid the due tribute of faith and worship owing to the Blessed Trinity, and which ought to be more and more inculcated upon the Christian people, we now turn to the exposition of the power of the Holy Ghost. And, first of all, we must look to Christ, the Founder of the Church and the Redeemer of our race. Among the external operations of God, the highest of all is the mystery of the Incarnation of the Word, in which the splendor of the divine perfections shines forth so brightly that nothing more sublime can even be imagined, nothing else could have been more salutary to the human race. Now this work, although belonging to the whole trinity, is still appropriated especially to the Holy Ghost, so that the Gospels thus speak of the Blessed Virgin: "She was found with child of the Holy Ghost," and "that which is conceived in her is of the Holy Ghost" (*Matt.* i, 18, 20). And this is rightly attributed to Him who is the love of the Father and the Son, since this

"great mystery of piety" (1 *Tim.* iii, 16) proceeds from the infinite love of God towards man, as St. John tells us: "God so loved the world as to give His only begotten Son" (*John* iii, 16). Moreover, human nature was thereby elevated to a *personal* union with the Word, and this dignity is given, not on account of any merits, but entirely and absolutely through grace, and therefore, as it were, through the special gift of the Holy Ghost. On this point St. Augustine writes: "This manner in which Christ was born of the Holy Ghost, indicates to us the grace of God, by which humanity, with no antecedent merits, at the first moment of its existence, was united with the Word of God, by so intimate a personal union, that He, who was the Son of Man, was also the Son of God, and He who was the Son of God, was also the Son of man" (*Enchir.*, c. x]; *St. Th.*, 3, q. xxxii, a I). By the operation of the Holy Spirit, not only was the conception of Christ accomplished, but also the sanctification of His soul, which, in Holy Scripture, is called His "anointing" (*Acts* x, 38). Wherefore all His actions were "performed in the Holy Ghost" (St. Basil *de Sp. S.*, c. xvi), and especially the sacrifice of Himself: "Christ, through the Holy Ghost, offered Himself without spot to God" (*Heb.* ix, 14). Considering this, no one can be surprised that all the gifts of the Holy Ghost inundated the soul of Christ. In Him resided–the absolute fulness of grace, in the greatest and most efficacious manner possible; in Him were all the treasures of wisdom and knowledge, graces *gratis datae*, virtues, and all other gifts foretold in the prophecies of Isaias (*Is.* iv, 1; xi, 23), and also signified in that miraculous dove which appeared at the Jordan, when Christ, by His baptism, consecrated its waters for a new sacrament. On this the words of St. Augustine may appropriately be quoted: "It would be absurd to say that Christ received the Holy Ghost when He was already thirty years of age, for He came to His baptism without sin, and therefore not without the Holy Ghost. At this time, then (this is, at His baptism), He was pleased to prefigure His Church, in which those especially who are baptized receive the Holy Ghost" (*De Trin.* 1, xv, c. 26). Therefore, by the conspicuous apparition of the Holy Ghost over Christ and by

His invisible power in His soul, the twofold mission of the Spirit is foreshadowed, namely His outward and visible mission in the Church, and His secret indwelling in the souls of the just.

6 The Church which, already conceived, came forth from the side of the second Adam in His sleep on the Cross, first showed herself before the eyes of men on the great day of Pentecost. On that day the Holy Ghost began to manifest His gifts in the Mystical Body of Christ, by that miraculous outpouring already foreseen by the prophet Joel (ii, 28, 29), for the Paraclete "sat upon the Apostles as though new spiritual crowns were placed upon their heads in tongues of fire" (St. Cyril Hier, *Catech.* 17). Then the Apostles "descended from the mountain," as St. John Chrysostom writes, "not bearing in their hands tables of stone like Moses, but carrying the Spirit in their mind, and pouring forth the treasure and the fountain of doctrines and graces" (*In Matt.* Hom. I, 2 *Cor.* iii, 3). Thus was fully accomplished that last promise of Christ to His Apostles of sending the Holy Ghost, who was to complete and, as it were, to seal the deposit of doctrine committed to them under His inspiration. "I have yet many things to say to you, but you cannot bear them now; but when He, the Spirit of Truth, shall come, He will teach you all truth" (*John* xvi, 12, 13). For He who is the Spirit of Truth, inasmuch as He proceedeth both from the Father, who is the eternally True, and from the Son, who is the substantial Truth, receiveth from each both His essence and the fulness of all truth. This truth He communicates to His Church, guarding her by His all powerful help from ever falling into error, and aiding her to foster daily more and more the germs of Divine doctrine and to make them fruitful for the welfare of the peoples. And since the welfare of the peoples, for which the Church was established, absolutely requires that this office should be continued for all time, the Holy Ghost perpetually supplies life and strength to preserve and increase the Church. "I will ask the Father, and He will give you another Paraclete, that He may abide with you for ever, the Spirit of Truth" (*John* xiv, 16, 17).

7 By Him the Bishops are constituted, and by their ministry are multiplied not only the children but also the fathers—that is to say, the priests—to rule and feed the Church by that Blood wherewith Christ has redeemed Her. "The Holy Ghost hath placed you bishops to rule the Church of God, which He hath purchased with His own Blood" (*Acts* xx, 28). And both bishops and priests, by the miraculous gift of the Spirit, have the power of absolving sins, according to those words of Christ to the Apostles: "Receive ye the Holy Ghost; whose sins you shall forgive they are forgiven them, and whose you retain they are retained" (*John* xx, 22, 23). That the Church is a divine institution is most clearly proved by the splendor and glory of those gifts and graces with which she is adorned, and whose Author and Giver is the Holy Ghost. Let it suffice to state that, as Christ is the Head of The Church, so is the Holy Ghost her soul. "What the soul is in our body, that is the Holy Ghost in Christ's body, the Church" (St. Aug., *Serm.* 187, *de Temp.*) This being so, no further and fuller "manifestation and revelation of the Divine Spirit" may be imagined or expected; for that which now takes place in the Church is the most perfect possible, and will last until that day when the Church herself, having passed through her militant career, shall be taken up into the joy of the saints triumphing in heaven.

8 The manner and extent of the action of the Holy Ghost in individual souls is no less wonderful, although somewhat more difficult to understand, inasmuch as it is entirely invisible. This outpouring of the Spirit is so abundant, that Christ Himself, from whose gift it proceeds, compares it to an overflowing river, according to those words of St. John: "He that believeth in Me, as the Scripture saith, out of his midst shall flow rivers of living water"; to which testimony the Evangelist adds the explanation: "Now this He said of the Spirit which they should receive who believed in Him" (*John* vii, 38, 39). It is indeed true that in those of the just who lived before Christ, the Holy Ghost resided by grace, as we read in the Scriptures concerning the prophets, Zachary, John the Baptist, Simeon, and Anna; so that on Pentecost the Holy Ghost did not communicate Himself in such a way

"as then for the first time to begin to dwell in the saints, but by pouring Himself forth more abundantly; crowning, not beginning His gifts; not commencing a new work, but giving more abundantly" (St. Leo the Great, Hom. iii, *de Pentec.*). But if they also were numbered among the children of God, they were in a state like that of servants, for "as long as the heir is a child he differeth nothing from a servant, but is under tutors and governors" (*Gal.* iv, 1, 2). Moreover, not only was their justice derived from the merits of Christ who was to come, but the communication of the Holy Ghost after Christ was much more abundant, just as the price surpasses in value the earnest and the reality excels the image. Wherefore St. John declares: "As yet the Spirit was not given, because Jesus was not yet glorified" (*John* vii, 39). So soon, therefore, as Christ, "ascending on high," entered into possession of the glory of His Kingdom which He had won with so much labor, He munificently opened out the treasures of the Holy Ghost: "He gave gifts to men" (*Eph.* iv, 8). For "that giving or sending forth of the Holy Ghost after Christ's glorification was to be such as had never been before; not that there had been none before, but it had not been of the same kind" (St. Aug., *De Trin.* 1, iv, c. 20).

9 Human nature is by necessity the servant of God: "The creature is a servant; we are the servants of God by nature" (St. Cyr. Alex., *Thesaur.* 1, v, c. 5). On account, however, of Original Sin, our whole nature had become enemies to God. "We were by nature the children of wrath" (*Eph.* ii, 3). There was no power which could raise us and deliver us from this ruin and eternal destruction. But God, the Creator of mankind and infinitely merciful, did this through His only begotten Son, by whose benefit it was brought about that man was restored to that rank and dignity whence he had fallen, and was adorned with still more abundant graces. No one can express the greatness of this work of divine grace in the souls of men. Wherefore, both in Holy Scripture and in the writings of the Fathers, men are styled regenerated, new creatures, partakers of the Divine Nature, children of God, godlike, and similar epithets. Now these

great blessings are justly attributed as especially belonging to the Holy Ghost. He is "the Spirit of adoption of sons, whereby we cry: Abba, Father." He fills our hearts with the sweetness of paternal love: "The Spirit Himself giveth testimony to our spirit that we are the sons of God" (*Rom.* viii, 15, 16). This truth accords with the similitude observed by the Angelic Doctor between both operations of the Holy Ghost; for through Him "Christ was conceived in holiness to be by nature the Son of God," and "others are sanctified to be the sons of God by adoption" (St. Th. 3a, q. xxxii, a. 1). This spiritual generation proceeds from love in a much more noble manner than in the natural: namely, from the uncreated Love.

10 The beginnings of this regeneration and renovation of man are by Baptism. In this sacrament when the unclean spirit has been expelled from the soul, the Holy Ghost enters in and makes it like to Himself. "That which is born of the Spirit, is spirit" (*John* iii, 6). The same Spirit gives Himself more abundantly in Confirmation, strengthening and confirming Christian life; from which proceeded the victory of the martyrs and the triumph of the virgins over temptations and corruptions. We have said that the Holy Ghost gives Himself: "The charity of God is poured out into our hearts by the Holy Ghost who is given to us" (*Rom.* v, 5). For He not only brings to us His Divine gifts, but is the author of them and is Himself the supreme Gift, who, proceeding from the mutual love of the Father and the Son, is justly believed to be and is called "Gift of God most High." To show the nature and efficacy of this gift it is well to recall the explanation given by the Doctors of the Church of the words of Holy Scripture. They say that God is present and exists in all things, "by His power, in so far as all things are subject to His power; by His presence, inasmuch as all things are uncovered and open to His eyes; by His essence, inasmuch as He is present to all as the cause of their being" (St. Th. 1a, p. viii, a. 3). But God is in man, not only as in inanimate things, but because he is more fully known and loved by him, since even by nature we spontaneously love, desire and seek after the good. Moreover God by grace re-

sides in the just soul as in a temple, in a most intimate and peculiar manner. From this proceeds that union of affection by which the soul adheres most closely to God, more so than the friend is united to his most loving and beloved friend, and enjoys God in all fulness and sweetness. Now this wonderful union, which is properly called "indwelling," differing only in degree or state from that which God beatifies the saints in Heaven, although it is most certainly produced by the presence of the whole Blessed Trinity—"We will come to Him and make our abode with Him" (*John* xiv, 23) nevertheless is attributed in a peculiar manner to the Holy Ghost. For, whilst traces of Divine power and wisdom appear even in the wicked man, charity, which, as it were, is the special mark of the Holy Ghost, is shared in only by the just. In harmony with this, the same spirit is called Holy, for He, the first and supreme Love, moves souls and leads them to sanctity, which ultimately consists in the love of God. Wherefore the apostle when calling the Just the temple of God, does not expressly mention the Father or the Son, or the Holy Ghost: "Know ye not that your members are the temple of the Holy Ghost, who is in you, whom you have from God?" (1 *Cor* vi, 19).

11 The fulness of divine gifts is in many ways a consequence of the indwelling of the Holy Ghost in the souls of the just. For, as St. Thomas teaches, "when the Holy Ghost proceedeth as love, He proceedeth in the character of the first gift; whence Augustine saith that through the gift which is the Holy Ghost, many other special gifts are distributed among the members of Christ" (*Summ. Th.,* 1a. p. xxxviii, a. 2. St. Aug. *de Trin.,* xv, c. 19). Among these gifts are those secret warnings and invitations, which from time to time are excited in our minds and hearts by the inspiration of the Holy Ghost. Without these there is no beginning of a good life, no progress, no arriving at eternal salvation. And since these words and admonitions are uttered in the soul in an exceedingly secret manner, they are sometimes aptly compared in Holy Writ to the breathing of a coming breeze, and the Angelic Doctor likens them to the movements of the heart which are wholly hidden in the

living body. "Thy heart has a certain hidden power, and therefore the Holy Ghost, who invisibly vivifies and unites the Church, is compared to the heart" (*Summ. Th.* 3a, q. vii, a. 1, ad 3). More than this, the just man, that is to say he who lives the life of Divine grace, and acts by the fitting virtues as by means of faculties, has need of those seven *gifts* which are properly attributed to the Holy Ghost. By means of them the soul is furnished and strengthened so as to be able to obey more easily and promptly His voice and impulse. Wherefore these gifts are of such efficacy that they lead the just man to the highest degree of sanctity; and of such excellence that they continue to exist even in Heaven, though in a more perfect way. By means of these gifts the soul is excited and encouraged to seek after and attain the evangelical beatitudes, which, like the flowers that come forth in the springtime, are the signs and harbingers of eternal beatitude. Lastly, there are those blessed fruits, enumerated by the Apostle (*Gal.* v, 22), which the Spirit, even in this mortal life, produces and shows forth in the just; fruits filled with all sweetness and joy, inasmuch as they proceed from the Spirit, "who is in the Trinity the sweetness of both Father and Son, filling all creatures with infinite fulness and profusion" (St. Aug. *de Trin.* 1, vi, c. 9). The Divine Spirit, proceeding from the Father and the Word in the eternal light of sanctity, Himself both Love and Gift, after having manifested Himself through the veils of figures in the Old Testament, poured forth all his fulness upon Christ and upon His Mystical Body, the Church; and called back by his presence and grace men who were going away in wickedness and corruption with such salutary effect that, being no longer of the earth earthy, they relished and desired quite other things, becoming of Heaven heavenly.

12 These sublime truths, which so clearly show forth the infinite goodness of the Holy Ghost towards us, certainly demand that we should direct towards Him the highest homage of our love and devotion. Christians may do this most effectually if they will daily strive to know Him, to love Him, and to implore Him more earnestly; for which reason may this Our exhortation, flowing spontaneously

from a paternal heart, reach their ears. Perchance there are still to be found among them, even nowadays, some, who if asked, as were those of old by St. Paul the Apostle, whether they have received the Holy Ghost, might answer in like manner: "We have not so much as heard whether there be a Holy Ghost" (*Acts* xix, 2). At least there are certainly many who are very dificient in their knowledge of Him. They frequently use His name in their religious practices, but their faith is involved in much darkness. Wherefore all preachers and those having care of souls should remember that it is their duty to instruct their people more diligently and more fully about the Holy Ghost—avoiding, however, difficult and subtle controversies, and eschewing the dangerous folly of those who rashly endeavor to pry into divine mysteries. What should be chiefly dwelt upon and clearly explained is the multitude and greatness of the benefits which have been bestowed, and are constantly bestowed, upon us by this divine Giver, so that errors and ignorance concerning matters of such moment may be entirely dispelled, as unworthy of "the children of light." We urge this, not only because it affects a mystery by which we are directly guided to eternal life, and which must therefore be firmly believed; but also because the more clearly and fully the good is known the more earnestly it is loved.

13 Now We owe to the Holy Ghost, as We mentioned in the second place, love, because He is God: "Thou shalt love the Lord thy God with thy whole heart, and with thy whole soul, and with thy whole strength" (*Deut.* vi, 5). He is also to be loved because He is the substantial, eternal, primal Love, and nothing is more lovable than love. And this all the more because He has overwhelmed us with the greatest benefits, which both testify to the benevolence of the Giver and claim the gratitude of the receiver. This love has a twofold and most conspicuous utility. In the first place it will excite us to acquire daily a clearer knowledge about the Holy Ghost; for, as the Angelic Doctor says, "the lover is not content with the superficial knowledge of the beloved, but striveth to inquire intimately into all that appertains to the beloved, and thus to penetrate into the interior;

as is said of the Holy Ghost, who is the Love of God, that He searcheth even the profound things of God" (1 *Cor.* ii, 10; *Summ. Theol.*, 1a. 2ae., q. 28, a. 2). In the second place it will obtain for us a still more abundant supply of heavenly gifts, for whilst a narrow heart contracts the hand of the giver, a grateful and mindful heart causes it to expand. Yet we must strive that this love should be of such a nature as not to consist merely in dry speculations or external observances, but rather to run forward towards action, and especially to fly from sin, which is in a more special manner offensive to the Holy Spirit. For whatever we are, that we are by the divine goodness, and this goodness is specially attributed to the Holy Ghost. The sinner offends this his Benefactor, abusing His gifts; and taking advantage of His goodness becomes more hardened in sin day by day. Again, since He is the Spirit of Truth, whosoever faileth by weakness on ignorance may perhaps have some excuse before Almighty God; but he who resists the truth through malice and turns away from it, sins most grievously against the Holy Ghost. In our days this sin has become so frequent that those dark times seem to have come which were foretold by St. Paul, in which men, blinded by the just judgment of God, should take falsehood for truth, and should believe in "the prince of this world," who is a liar and the father thereof, as a teacher of truth: "God shall send them the operation of error, to believe lying (2 *Thess.* ii, 10). In the last times some shall depart from the faith, giving heed to spirits of error and the doctrines of devils" (1 *Tim.* iv, 1). But since the Holy Ghost, as We have said, dwells in us as in His temple, We must repeat the warning of the Apostle: "Grieve not the Holy Spirit of God, whereby you are sealed" (*Eph.* iv, 30). Nor is it enough to fly from sin; every Christian ought to shine with the splendor of virtue so as to be pleasing to so great and so beneficent a guest; and first of all with chastity and holiness, for chaste and holy things befit the temple. Hence the words of the Apostle: "Know you not that you are the temple of God, and that the Spirit of God dwelleth in you? But if any man violate the temple of God, him shall God destroy. For the temple of God is holy, which you are" (1 *Cor.* iii, 16, 17): a terrible, indeed, but a just warning.

14 Lastly, we ought to pray to and invoke the Holy Spirit, for each one of us greatly needs His protection and His help. The more a man is deficient in wisdom, weak in strength, consolation, and holiness. And chiefly that first requisite of man, the forgiveness of sins, must be sought for from Him: "It is the special character of the Holy Ghost that He is the Gift of the Father and the Son. Now the remission of sins is given by the Holy Ghost as by the Gift of God" *(Summ. Th.* 3a, q. iii, a. 8, ad 3m). Concerning this Spirit the words of the Liturgy are very explicit: "For He is the remission of all sins" (*Roman Missal,* Tuesday after Pentecost). How He should be invoked is clearly taught by the Church, who addresses Him in humble supplication, calling upon Him by the sweetest of names: "Come, Thou Father of the poor! Come, Thou Giver of gifts! Come, Light of our hearts! O, best of Consolers, sweet Guest of the soul, our refreshment!" (Hymn, *Veni Sancte Spiritus*). She earnestly implores Him to wash, heal, water our minds and hearts, and to give to us who trust in Him "the merit of virtue, the acquirement of salvation, and joy everlasting." Nor can it be in any way doubted that He will listen to such prayer, since we read the words written by His own inspiration: "The Spirit Himself asketh for us with unspeakable groanings" (*Rom.* viii, 26). Lastly, we ought confidently and continually to beg of Him to illuminate us daily more and more with His light and inflame us with His charity: for, thus inspired with faith and love, we may press onward earnestly towards our eternal reward, since He "is the pledge of our inheritance" (*Eph.* i, 14).

15 Such, Venerable Brethren, are the teachings and exhortations which We have seen good to utter, in order to stimulate devotion to the Holy Ghost. We have no doubt that, chiefly by means of your zeal and earnestness, they will bear abundant fruit among Christian peoples. We Ourselves shall never in the future fail to labor towards so important an end; and it is even Our intention, in whatever ways may appear suitable, to further cultivate and extend his admirable

work of piety. Meanwhile, as two years ago, in Our Letter *Provida Matris,* We recommended to Catholics special prayers at the Feast of Pentecost for the Reunion of Christendom, so now We desire to make certain further decrees on the same subject.

16 Wherefore, We decree and command that throughout the whole Catholic Church, this year and in every subsequent year, a Novena shall take place before Whit Sunday, in all parish churches, and also, if the local Ordinaries think fit, in other churches and oratories. To all who take part in this Novena and duly pray for Our intention, We grant for each day an Indulgence of seven years and seven quarantines; moreover, a Plenary Indulgence on any one of the days of the Novena, or on Whit Sunday itself, or on any day during the Octave; provided they shall have received the Sacraments of Penance and the Holy Eucharist, and devoutly prayed for Our intention. We will that those who are legitimately prevented from attending the Novena, or who are in places where the devotions cannot, in the judgment of the Ordinary, be conveniently carried out in church, shall equally enjoy the same benefits, provided they make the Novena privately and observe the other conditions. Moreover, We are pleased to grant, in perpetuity, from the Treasury of the Church, that whosoever, daily during the Octave of Pentecost up to Trinity Sunday inclusive, offer again publicly or privately any prayers, according to their devotion, to the Holy Ghost, and satisfy the above conditions, shall a second time gain each of the same Indulgences. All these Indulgences We also permit to be applied to the suffrage of the souls in Purgatory.

17 And now Our mind and heart turn back to those hopes with which We began, and for the accomplishment of which We earnestly pray, and will continue to pray, to the Holy Ghost. Unite, then, Venerable Brethren, your prayers with Ours, and at your exhortation let all Christian peoples add their prayers also, invoking the powerful and ever-acceptable intercession of the Blessed Virgin. You know well the intimate and wonderful relations existing between her and the Holy Ghost, so that she is justly called His Spouse. The

intercession of the Blessed Virgin was of great avail both in the mystery of the Incarnation and in the coming of the Holy Ghost upon the Apostles. May she continue to strengthen our prayers with her suffrage, that, in the midst of all the stress and trouble of the nations, those divine prodigies may be happily revived by the Holy Ghost, which were foretold in the words of David: "Send forth Thy Spirit and they shall be created, and Thou shall renew the face of the earth" (*Ps.* ciii, 30).

18 As a pledge of Divine favor and a testimony of Our affection, Venerable Brethren, to you, to your Clergy and people, We gladly impart in the Lord the Apostolic Benediction.

19 Given at St. Peter's in Rome, on the 9th day of May, 1897, in the 20th year of Our Pontificate.

ANNUM SACRUM

Encyclical Letter of Pope Leo XIII
on the Consecration of Mankind
to the Sacred Heart of Jesus
May 25, 1899

But a short time ago, as you well know, We, by letters apostolic, and following the custom and ordinances of Our predecessors, commanded the celebration in this city, at no distant date, of a Holy Year. And now to-day, in the hope and with the object that this religious celebration shall be more devoutly performed, We have traced and recommended a striking design from which, if all shall follow it out with hearty good will, We not unreasonably expect extraordinary and lasting benefits for Christendom in the first place and also for the whole human race.

21 Already more than once We have endeavored, after the example of Our predecessors Innocent XII., Benedict XIII., Clement XIII., Pius VI., and Pius IX., devoutly to foster and bring out into fuller light that most excellent form of devotion which has for its object the veneration of the Sacred Heart of Jesus; this We did especially by the Decree given on June 28, 1889, by which We raised the Feast under that name to the dignity of the first class. But now We have in mind a more signal form of devotion which shall be in a manner the crowning perfection of all the honors that people have been accustomed to pay to the Sacred Heart, and which We confidently trust will be most pleasing to Jesus Christ, our Redeemer. This is not the first time, however, that the design of which We speak has been mooted. Twenty-five years ago, on the approach of the solemnities of the second

centenary of the Blessed Margaret Mary Alacoque's reception of the Divine command to propagate the worship of the Sacred Heart, many letters from all parts, not merely from private persons but from Bishops also were sent to Pius IX. begging that he would consent to consecrate the whole human race to the Most Sacred Heart of Jesus. It was thought best at the time to postpone the matter in order that a well-considered decision might be arrived at. Meanwhile permission was granted to individual cities which desired it thus to consecrate themselves, and a form of consecration was drawn up. Now, for certain new and additional reasons, We consider that the plan is ripe for fulfilment.

22 This world-wide and solemn testimony of allegiance and piety is especially appropriate to Jesus Christ, who is the Head and Supreme Lord of the race. His empire extends not only over Catholic nations and those who, having been duly washed in the waters of holy baptism, belong of right to the Church, although erroneous opinions keep them astray, or dissent from her teaching cuts them off from her care; it comprises also all those who are deprived of the Christian faith, so that the whole human race is most truly under the power of Jesus Christ. For He who is the Only-begotten Son of God the Father, having the same substance with Him and being the brightness of His glory and the figure of His substance (Hebrews i., 3) necessarily has everything in common with the Father, and therefore sovereign power over all things. This is why the Son of God thus speaks of Himself through the Prophet: "But I am appointed king by him over Sion, his holy mountain. . . . The Lord said to me, Thou art my son, this day have I begotten thee. Ask of me and I will give thee the Gentiles for thy inheritance and the utmost parts of the earth for thy possession" (Psalm, ii.). By these words He declares that He has power from God over the whole Church, which is signified by Mount Sion, and also over the rest of the world to its uttermost ends. On what foundation this sovereign power rests is made sufficiently plain by the words, "Thou art My Son." For by the very fact that He is the Son of the King of all, He is also the heir of all His Father's power: hence the words—"I will give thee the

Gentiles for thy inheritance," which are similar to those used by Paul the Apostle, "whom he hath appointed heir of all things" (Hebrews i., 2).

23 But we should now give most special consideration to the declarations made by Jesus Christ, not through the Apostles or the Prophets but by His own words. To the Roman Governor who asked Him, "Art thou a king then?" He answered unhesitatingly, "Thou sayest that I am a king" (John xviii, 37). And the greatness of this power and the boundlessness of His kingdom is still more clearly declared in these words to the Apostles: "All power is given to me in heaven and on earth" (Matthew xxviii., 18). If then all power has been given to Christ it follows of necessity that His empire must be supreme, absolute and independent of the will of any other, so that none is either equal or like unto it: and since it has been given in heaven and on earth it ought to have heaven and earth obedient to it. And verily he has acted on this extraordinary and peculiar right when He commanded His Apostles to preach His doctrine over the earth, to gather all men together into the one body of the Church by the baptism of salvation, and to bind them by laws, which no one could reject without risking his eternal salvation.

24 But this is not all. Christ reigns not only by natural right as the Son of God, but also by a right that He has acquired. For He it was who snatched us "from the power of darkness" (Colossians i., 13). and "gave Himself for the redemption of all" (I Timothy ii., 6). Therefore not only Catholics, and those who have duly received Christian baptism, but also all men, individually and collectively, have become to Him "a purchased people" (I Peter ii., 9). St. Augustine's words are therefore to the point when he says: "You ask what price He paid? See what He gave and you will understand how much He paid. The price was the blood of Christ. What could cost so much but the whole world, and all its people? The great price He paid was paid for all" (T. 120 on St. John).

25 How it comes about that infidels themselves are subject to the power and dominion of Jesus Christ is clearly shown by St. Thomas, who gives us the reason and its explanation. For having put the question whether His judicial power extends

to all men, and having stated that judicial authority flows naturally from royal authority, he concludes decisively as follows: "All things are subject to Christ as far as His power is concerned, although they are not all subject to Him in the exercise of that power" (3a., p., q. 59, a. 4). This sovereign power of Christ over men is exercised by truth, justice, and above all, by charity.

26 To this twofold ground of His power and domination He graciously allows us, if we think fit, to add voluntary consecration, Jesus Christ, our God and our Redeemer, is rich in the fullest and perfect possession of all things: we, on the other hand, are so poor and needy that we have nothing of our own to offer Him as a gift. But yet, in His infinite goodness and love, He in no way objects to our giving and consecrating to Him what is already His, as if it were really our own; nay, far from refusing such an offering, He positively desires it and asks for it: "My son, give me thy heart." We are, therefore, able to be pleasing to Him by the good will and the affection of our soul. For by consecrating ourselves to Him we not only declare our open and free acknowledgment and acceptance of His authority over us, but we also testify that if what we offer as a gift were really our own, we would still offer it with our whole heart. We also beg of Him that He would vouchsafe to receive it from us, though clearly His own. Such is the efficacy of the act of which We speak, such is the meaning underlying Our words.

27 And since there is in the Sacred Heart a symbol and a sensible image of the infinite love of Jesus Christ which moves us to love one another, therefore is it fit and proper that we should consecrate ourselves to His most Sacred Heart—an act which is nothing else than an offering and a binding of oneself to Jesus Christ, seeing that whatever honor, veneration and love is given to this divine Heart is really and truly given to Christ Himself.

28 For these reasons We urge and exhort all who know and love this divine Heart willingly to undertake this act of piety; and it is Our earnest desire that all should make it on the same day, that so the aspirations of so many thousands who are performing this act of consecration may be borne to the

temple of heaven on the same day. But shall We allow to slip from Our remembrance those innumerable others upon whom the light of Christian truth has not yet shined? We hold the place of Him who came to save that which was lost, and who shed His blood for the salvation of the whole human race. And so We greatly desire to bring to the true life those who sit in the shadow of death. As we have already sent messengers of Christ over the earth to instruct them, so now, in pity for their lot with all Our soul we commend them, and as far as in Us lies We consecrate them to the Sacred Heart of Jesus. In this way this act of devotion, which We recommend, will be a blessing to all. For having performed it, those in whose hearts are the knowledge and love of Jesus Christ will feel that faith and love increased. Those who knowing Christ, yet neglect His law and its precepts, may still gain from His Sacred Heart the flame of charity. And lastly, for those still more unfortunate, who are struggling in the darkness of superstition, we shall all with one mind implore the assistance of heaven that Jesus Christ, to whose power they are subject, may also one day render them submissive to its exercise; and that not only in the life to come when He will fulfil His will upon all men, by saving some and punishing others, (St. Thomas, *ibid*), but also in this mortal life by giving them faith and holiness. May they by these virtues strive to honor God as they ought, and to win everlasting happiness in heaven.

29 Such an act of consecration, since it can establish or draw tighter the bonds which naturally connect public affairs with God, gives to States a hope of better things. In these latter times especially, a policy has been followed which has resulted in a sort of wall being raised between the Church and civil society. In the constitution and administration of States the authority of sacred and divine law is utterly disregarded, with a view to the exclusion of religion from having any constant part in public life. This policy almost tends to the removal of the Christian faith from our midst, and, if that were possible, of the banishment of God Himself from the earth. When men's minds are raised to such a height of insolent pride, what wonder is it that the greater part of the

human race should have fallen into such disquiet of mind and be buffeted by waves so rough that no one is suffered to be free from anxiety and peril? When religion is once discarded it follows of necessity that the surest foundations of the public welfare must give way, whilst God, to inflict on His enemies the punishment they so richly deserve, has left them the prey of their own evil desires, so that they give themselves up to their passions and finally wear themselves out by excess of liberty.

30 Hence that abundance of evils which have now for a long time settled upon the world, and which pressingly call upon us to seek for help from Him by whose strength alone they can be driven away. Who can He be but Jesus Christ the Only-begotten Son of God? "For there is no other name under heaven given to men whereby we must be saved" (Acts iv., 12). We must have recourse to Him who is the Way, the Truth and the Life. We have gone astray and we must return to the right path: darkness has overshadowed our minds, and the gloom must be dispelled by the light of truth: death has seized upon us, and we must lay hold of life. It will at length be possible that our many wounds be healed and all justice spring forth again with the hope of restored authority; that the splendors of peace be renewed, and "Every tongue shall confess that our Lord Jesus Christ is in the glory of God the Father" (Philippians ii, 11).

31 When the Church, in the days immediately succeeding her institution, was oppressed beneath the yoke of the Caesars, a young Emperor saw in the heavens a cross, which became at once the happy omen and cause of the glorious victory that soon followed. And now, to-day, behold another blessed and heavenly token is offered to our sight—the most Sacred Heart of Jesus, with a cross rising from it and shining forth with dazzling splendor amidst flames of love. In that Sacred Heart all our hopes should be placed, and from it the salvation of men is to be confidently besought.

32 Finally, there is one motive which We are unwilling to pass over in silence, personal to Ourselves it is true, but still good and weighty, which moves Us to undertake this celebration. God, the author of every good, not long ago preserved Our

life by curing Us of a dangerous disease. We now wish, by this increase of the honor paid to the Sacred Heart, that the memory of this great mercy should be brought prominently forward, and Our gratitude be publicly acknowledged.

33 For these reasons, we ordain that on the ninth, tenth and eleventh of the coming month of June, in the principal church of every town and village, certain appointed prayers be said, and on each of these days there be added to the other prayers the Litany of the Sacred Heart approved by Our authority. On the last day the form of consecration shall be recited which, Venerable Brethren, We sent to you with these letters.

34 As a pledge of divine benefits, and in token of Our paternal benevolence, to you, and to the clergy and people committed to your care We lovingly grant in the Lord the Apostolic Benediction.

35 Given in Rome at St. Peter's on the 25th day of May, 1899, the twenty-second year of Our Pontificate.

TAMETSI FUTURA PROSPICIENTIBUS

Encyclical Letter of Pope Leo XIII
on Jesus Christ Our Redeemer
November 1, 1900

The outlook on the future is by no means free from anxiety; on the contrary, there are many serious reasons for alarm, on account of numerous and long-standing causes of evil, of both a public and a private nature. Nevertheless, the close of the century really seems in God's mercy to afford us some degree of consolation and hope. For no one will deny that renewed interest in spiritual matters and a revival of Christian faith and piety are influences of great moment for the common good. And there are sufficiently clear indications at the present day of a very general revival or augmentation of these virtues. For example, in the very midst of worldly allurements and in spite of so many obstacles to piety, what great crowds have flocked to Rome to visit the "Threshold of the Apostles" at the invitation of the Sovereign Pontiff! Both Italians and foreigners are openly devoting themselves to religious exercises, and, relying upon the undulgences offered by the Church, are most earnestly seeking the means to secure their eternal salvation. Who could fail to be moved by the present evident increase of devotion towards the person of Our Saviour? The ardent zeal of so many thousands, united in heart and mind, "from the rising of the sun to the going down thereof," in venerating the Name of Jesus Christ and proclaiming His praises, is worthy of the best days of Christianity. Would that the outburst of these flames of antique faith might be followed by a mighty conflagration! Would that the splendid example of so many might kindle the enthusiasm of all! For what so necessary for our times as a widespread renovation among the nations of Christian principles and old-fashioned virtues? The great misfortune is that too many turn a deaf ear and will not listen to the teachings of this revival of piety. Yet, "did they but know the gift of God," did they but realize that the greatest of all misfortunes is to fall away from the World's Redeemer and to abandon Christian faith and practice, they would be only too eager to turn back, and so escape certain destruction.

37 The most important duty of the Church, and the one most peculiarly her own, is to defend and to propagate throughout the world the Kingdom of the Son of God, and to bring all men to salvation by communicating to them the divine benefits, so much so that her power and authority are chiefly exercised in this one work. Towards this end we are conscious of having devoted our energies throughout our difficult and anxious Pontificate even to the present day. And you too, Venerable Brethren, are wont constantly, yea daily, to give your chief thoughts and endeavors together with ourselves to the self-same task. But at the present moment all of us ought to make still further efforts, more especially on the occasion of the Holy Year, to disseminate far and wide the better knowledge and love of Jesus Christ by teaching, persuading, exhorting, if perchance our voice can be heard; and this, not so much to those who are ever ready to listen willingly to Christian teachings, but to those most unfortunate men who, whilst professing the Christian name, live strangers to the faith and love of Christ. For these we feel the profoundest pity: these above all would we urge to think seriously of their present life and what its consequences will be if they do not repent.

38 The greatest of all misfortunes is never to have known Jesus Christ: yet such a state is free from the sin of obstinacy and ingratitude. But first to have known Him, and afterwards to deny or forget Him, is a crime so foul and so insane that it seems impossible for any man to be guilty of it. For Christ is the fountain-head of all good. Mankind can no more be saved

without His power, than it could be redeemed without His mercy. "Neither is there salvation in any other. For there is no other name under heaven given to men whereby we must be saved" (Acts iv., 12). What kind of life that is from which Jesus Christ, "the power of God and the wisdom of God," is excluded; what kind of morality and what manner of death are its consequences, can be clearly learnt from the example of nations deprived of the light of Christianity. If we but recall St. Paul's description (Romans i., 24-32) of the mental blindness, the natural depravity, the monstrous superstitions and lusts of such peoples, our minds will be filled with horror and pity. What we here record is well enough known, but not sufficiently realized or thought about. Pride would not mislead, nor indifference enervate, so many minds, if the Divine mercies were more generally called to mind and if it were remembered from what an abyss Christ delivered mankind and to what a height He raised it. The human race, exiled and disinherited, had for ages been daily hurrying into ruin, involved in the terrible and numberless ills brought about by the sin of our first parents, nor was there any human hope of salvation, when Christ Our Lord came down as the Saviour from Heaven. At the very beginning of the world, God had promised Him as the conqueror of "the Serpent," hence, succeeding ages had eagerly looked forward to His coming. The prophets had long and clearly declared that all hope was in Him. The varying fortunes, the achievements, customs, laws, ceremonies and sacrifices of the Chosen People had distinctly and lucidly foreshadowed the truth, that the salvation of mankind was to be accomplished in Him who should be the Priest, Victim, Liberator, Prince of Peace, Teacher of all Nations, Founder of an Eternal Kingdom. By all these titles, images and prophecies, differing in kind though like in meaning, He alone was designated who "for His exceeding charity wherewith He loved us," gave Himself up for our salvation. And so, when the fullness of time came in God's Divine Providence, the only-begotten Son of God became man, and in behalf of mankind made most abundant satisfaction in His Blood to the outraged majesty of His Father, and by this infinite price He redeemed man for His own. "You were not redeemed with corruptible things as gold or silver . . . but with the precious Blood of Christ, as of a lamb, unspotted and undefiled" (I. Peter i., 18-19). Thus all men, though already subject to His kingly power, inasmuch as He is the Creator and Preserver of all, were over and above made His property by a true and real purchase. "You are not your own: for you are bought with a great price" (II. Corinthians vi., 19-20). Hence in Christ all things are made new. "The mystery of His will, according to His good pleasure which He hath purposed to Him in the dispensation of the fullness of times to reestablish all things in Christ: (Ephesians i., 9-10). When Jesus Christ had blotted out the handwriting of the decree that was against us, fastening it to the cross, at once God's wrath was appeased, the primeval fetters of slavery were struck off from unhappy and erring man, God's favor was won back, grace restored, the gates of Heaven opened, the right to enter them revived, and the means afforded of doing so. Then man, as though awakening from a long-continued and deadly lethargy, beheld at length the light of the truth, for long ages desired, yet sought in vain. First of all, he realized that he was born to much higher and more glorious things than the frail and inconstant objects of sense which had hitherto formed the end of his thoughts and cares. He learnt that the meaning of human life, the supreme law, the end of all things was this: that we come from God and must return to Him. From this first principle the consciousness of human dignity was revived: Men's hearts realized the universal brotherhood: as a consequence, human rights and duties were either perfected or even newly created, whilst on all sides were evoked virtues undreamt of in pagan philosophy. Thus men's aims, life, habits and customs received a new direction. As the knowledge of the Redeemer spread far and wide and His power, which destroyeth ignorance and former vices, penetrated into the very life-blood of the nations, such a change came about that the face of the world was entirely altered by the creation of a Christian civilization. The remembrance of these events, Venerable Brethren, is full of infinite joy, but it also teaches us the lesson that we must both feel and render with our whole hearts gratitude to our Divine Saviour.

We are indeed now very far removed in time from the first beginnings of Redemption; but what difference does this make when the benefits thereof are perennial and immortal? He who once hath restored human nature ruined by sin the same preserveth and will preserve it forever. "He gave Himself a redemption for all" (I Timothy ii., 6). "In Christ all shall be made alive" (I. Corinthians xv., 22). "And of His Kingdom there shall be no end" (Luke i., 33). Hence by God's eternal decree the salvation of all men, both severally and collectively, depends upon Jesus Christ. Those who abandon Him become guilty by the very fact, in their blindness and folly, of their own ruin; whilst at the same time they do all that in them lies to bring about a violent reaction of mankind in the direction of that mass of evils and miseries from which the Redeemer in His mercy had freed them. 39

Those who go astray from the road wander far from the goal they aim at. Similarly, if the pure and true light of truth be rejected, men's minds must necessarily be darkened and their souls deceived by deplorably false ideas. What hope of salvation can they have who abandon the very principle and fountain of life? Christ alone is the Way, the Truth and the Life (John xiv., 6). If He be abandoned the three necessary conditions of salvation are removed. 40

It is surely unnecessary to prove, what experience constantly shows and what each individual feels in himself, even in the very midst of all temporal prosperity—that in God alone can the human will find absolute and perfect peace. God is the only end of man. All our life on earth is the truthful and exact image of a pilgrimage. Now Christ is the "Way," for we can never reach God, the supreme and ultimate good, by this toilsome and doubtful road of mortal life, except with Christ as our leader and guide. How so? Firstly and chiefly by His grace; but this would remain "void" in man if the precepts of His law were neglected. For, as was necessarily the case after Jesus Christ had won our salvation, He left behind Him His Law for the protection and welfare of the human race, under the guidance of which men, converted from evil life, might safely tend towards God. "Going, teach ye all nations . . . teaching them to observe all things whatso- 41 ever I have commanded you" (Matthew xxviii., 19-20). "Keep My commandments" (John xiv., 15). Hence it will be understood that in the Christian religion the first and most necessary condition is docility to the precepts of Jesus Christ, absolute loyalty of will towards Him as Lord and King. A serious duty, and one which oftentimes calls for strenuous labor, earnest endeavor and perseverance! For although by Our Redeemer's grace human nature hath been regenerated, still there remains in each individual a certain debility and tendency to evil. Various natural appetites attract man on one side and the other; the allurements of the material world impel his soul to follow after what is pleasant rather than the law of Christ. Still we must strive our best and resist our natural inclinations with all our strength "unto the obedience of Christ." For unless they obey reason they become our masters, and carrying the whole man away from Christ, make him their slave. "Men of corrput mind, who have made shipwreck of the faith, cannot help being slaves. . . . They are slaves to a threefold concupiscence: of will, of pride, or of outward show" (St. Augustine, *De Vera Religione, 37*). In this contest every man must be prepared to undergo hardships and troubles for Christ's sake. It is difficult to reject what so powerfully entices and delights. It is hard and painful to despise the supposed goods of the senses and of fortune for the will and precepts of Christ Our Lord. But the Christian is absolutely obliged to be firm, and patient in suffering, if he wish to lead a Christian life. Have we forgotten of what Body and of what Head we are the members? "Having joy set before Him, He endured the Cross," and He bade us deny ourselves. The very dignity of human nature depends upon this disposition of mind. For, as even the ancient pagan philosophy perceived, to be master of oneself and to make the lower part of the soul obey the superior part, is so far from being a weakness of will that it is really a noble power, in consonance with right reason and most worthy of a man. Moreover, to bear and to suffer is the ordinary condition of man. Man can no more create for himself a life free from suffering and filled with all happiness than he can abrogate the decrees of his Divine Maker, who has willed that the consequences of original sin should be perpetual. It is reasonable, therefore, not to expect an end to troubles in this world, but rather to steel one's soul to bear troubles, by which we are taught to look forward with certainty to supreme happiness. Christ has not promised eternal bliss in heaven to riches, nor to a life of ease, to honors or to power, but to long-suffering and to tears, to the love of justice and to cleanness of heart.

42 From this it may clearly be seen what consequences are to be expected from that false pride which, rejecting our Saviour's Kingship, places man at the summit of all things and declares that human nature must rule supreme. And yet this supreme rule can neither be attained nor even defined. The rule of Jesus Christ derives its form and its power from Divine Love: a holy and orderly charity is both its foundation and its crown. Its necessary consequences are the strict fulfilment of duty, respect of mutual rights, the estimation of the things of heaven above those of earth, the preference of the love of God to all things. But this supremacy of man, which openly rejects Christ, or at least ignores Him, is entirely founded upon selfishness, knowing neither charity nor self-devotion. Man may indeed be king, through Jesus Christ; but only on condition that he first of all obey God, and diligently seek his rule of life in God's law. By the law of Christ we mean not only the natural precepts of morality and the Ancient Law, all of which Jesus Christ has perfected and crowned by His declaration, explanation and sanction; but also the rest of His doctrine and His own peculiar institutions. Of these the chief is His Church. Indeed, whatsoever things Christ has instituted are most fully contained in His Church. Moreover, He willed to perpetuate the office assigned to Him by His Father by means of the ministry of the Church so gloriously founded by Himself. On the one hand He confided to her all the means of man's salvation; on the other He most solemnly commanded men to be subject to her and to obey her diligently, and to follow her even as Himself: "He that heareth you, heareth Me; and he that despiseth you, despiseth Me" (Luke x., 16). Wherefore the law of Christ must be sought in the Church. Christ is man's

"Way;" the Church also is his "Way"—Christ of Himself and by His very nature, the Church by His commission and the communication of His power. Hence all who would find salvation apart from the Church are led astray and strive in vain.

43 As with individuals, so with nations. These, too, must necessarily tend to ruin if they go astray from "The Way." The Son of God, the Creator and Redeemer of mankind, is King and Lord of the earth, and holds supreme dominion over men, both individually and collectively. "And He gave Him power, and glory, and a kingdom: and all peoples, tribes and tongues shall serve Him" (Daniel vii., 14). "I am appointed King by Him. . . . I will give Thee the Gentiles for Thy inheritance, and the uttermost parts of the earth for Thy possession" (Psalm ii., 6, 8). Therefore the law of Christ ought to prevail in human society and be the guide and teacher of public as well as of private life. Since this is so by divine decree, and no man may with impunity contravene it, it is an evil thing for the common weal wherever Christianity does not hold the place that belongs to it. When Jesus Christ is absent, human reason fails, being bereft of its chief protection and light, and the very end is lost sight of for which, under God's providence, human society has been built up. This end is the obtaining by the members of society of natural good through the aid of civil unity, though always in harmony with the perfect and eternal good which is above nature. But when men's minds are clouded, both rulers and ruled go astray, for they have no safe line to follow nor end to aim at.

44 Just as it is the height of misfortune to go astray from the "Way," so is it to abandon the "Truth." Christ Himself is the first, absolute and essential "Truth," inasmuch as He is the Word of God, consubstantial and co-eternal with the Father, He and the Father being One. "I am the Way and the Truth." Wherefore if the Truth be sought by the human intellect, it must first of all submit it to Jesus Christ, and securely rest upon His teaching, since therein Truth itself speaketh. There are innumerable and extensive fields of thought, properly belonging to the human mind, in which it may have free

scope for its investigations and speculations, and that not only agreeably to its nature, but even by a necessity of its nature. But what is unlawful and unnatural is that the human mind should refuse to be restricted within its proper limits, and throwing aside its becoming modesty, should refuse to acknowledge Christ's teaching. This teaching, upon which our salvation depends, is almost entirely about God and the things of God. No human wisdom has invented it, but the Son of God hath received and drunk it in entirely from His Father: "The words which thou gavest me, I have given to them"(John xvii., 8). Hence this teaching necessarily embraces many subjects which are not indeed contrary to reason—for that would be an impossibility—but so exalted that we can no more attain them by our own reasoning than we can comprehend God as He is in Himself. If there be so many things hidden and veiled by nature which no human ingenuity can explain, and yet which no man in his senses can doubt, it would be an abuse of liberty to refuse to accept those which are entirely above nature, because their essence cannot be discovered. To reject dogma is simply to deny Christianity. Our intellect must bow humbly and reverently "unto the obedience of Christ," so that it be held captive by His divinity and authority: "bringing into captivity every understanding unto the obedience of Christ" (II. Corinthians x., 5). Such obedience Christ requires, and justly so. For He is God, and as such holds supreme dominion over man's intellect as well as over his will. By obeying Christ with his intellect man by no means acts in a servile manner, but in complete accordance with his reason and his natural dignity. For by his will he yields not to the authority of any man, but to that of God, the author of his being, and the first principle to Whom he is subject by the very law of his nature. He does not suffer himself to be forced by the theories of any human teacher, but by the eternal and unchangeable truth. Hence he attains at one and the same time the natural good of the intellect and his own liberty. For the truth which proceeds from the teaching of Christ clearly demonstrates the real nature and value of every being; and man, being endowed with this knowledge, if he but obey the truth as perceived, will make all things subject to himself, not himself to them; his appetites to his reason, not his reason to his appetites. Thus the slavery of sin and falsehood will be shaken off, and the most perfect liberty attained: "You shall know the truth, and the truth shall make you free" (John viii., 32). It is, then, evident that those whose intellect rejects the yoke of Christ are obstinately striving against God. Having shaken off God's authority, they are by no means freer, for they will fall beneath some human sway. They are sure to choose some one whom they will listen to, obey and follow as their guide. Moreover, they withdraw their intellect from the communication of divine truths, and thus limit it within a narrower circle of knowledge, so that they are less fitted to succeed in the pursuit even of natural science. For there are in nature very many things whose apprehension or explanation is greatly aided by the light of divine truth. Not unfrequently, too, God, in order to chastise their pride, does not permit men to see the truth, and thus they are punished in the things wherein they sin. This is why we often see men of great intellectual power and erudition making the grossest blunders even in natural science.

45 It must, therefore, be clearly admitted that in the life of a Christian the intellect must be entirely subject to God's authority. And if, in this submission of reason to authority our self-love, which is so strong, is restrained and made to suffer, this only proves the necessity to a Christian of long-suffering not only in will, but also in intellect. We would remind those persons of this truth who desire a kind of Christianity such as they themselves have devised, whose precepts should be very mild, much more indulgent towards human nature, and requiring little if any hardships to be borne. They do not properly understand the meaning of faith and Christian precepts. They do not see that the Cross meets us everywhere, the model of our life, the eternal standard of all who wish to follow Christ in reality and not merely in name.

46 God alone is Life. All other beings partake of life, but *are* not life. Christ from all eternity and by His very nature of "the Life," just as He is the Truth, because He is God of God.

From Him, as from its most sacred source, all life pervades and ever will pervade creation. Whatever is, is by Him; whatever lives, lives by Him. For by the Word "all things were made; and without Him was made nothing that was made." This is true of the natural life; but, as We have sufficiently indicated above, we have a much higher and better life, won for us by Christ's mercy, that is to say, "the life of grace," whose happy consummation is "the life of glory," to which all our thoughts and actions ought to be directed. The whole object of Christian doctrine and morality is that "we being dead to sin, should live to justice"(I. Peter ii., 24)—that is, to virtue and holiness. In this consists the moral life, with the certain hope of a happy eternity. This justice, in order to be advantageous to salvation, is nourished by Christian faith. "The just man liveth by faith" (Galatians iii., 11). "Without faith it is impossible to please God"(Hebrews xi., 6). Consequently Jesus Christ, the creator and preserver of faith, also preserves and nourishes our moral life. This He does chiefly by the ministry of His Church. To her, in His wise and merciful counsel, He has entrusted certain agencies which engender the supernatural life, protect it, and revive it if it should fail. This generative and conservative power of the virtues that make for salvation is therefore lost whenever morality is dissociated from divine faith. A system of morality based exclusively on human reason robs man of his highest dignity and lowers him from the supernatural to the merely natural life. Not but that man is able by the right use of reason to know and to obey certain principles of the natural law. But through life—and even this is impossible without the aid of the grace of our Redeemer—still it in vain for any one without faith to promise himself eternal salvation. "If any one abide not in Me, he shall be cast forth as a branch, and shall wither, and they shall gather him up and cast him into the fire, and he burneth" (John xv., 6). "He that believeth not shall be condemned" (Mark xvi., 16). We have but too much evidence of the value and result of a morality divorced from divine faith. How is it that in spite of all the zeal for the welfare of the masses, nations are in such straits and even distress, and that the evil is daily on the increase? We are told that society is quite able to help itself; that it can flourish without the assistance of Christianity, and attain its end by its own unaided efforts. Public administrators prefer a purely secular system of government. All traces of the religion of our forefathers are daily disappearing from political life and administration. What blindness! Once the idea of the authority of God as the Judge of right and wrong is forgotten, law must necessarily lose its primary authority and justice must perish: and these are the two most powerful and most necessary bonds of society. Similarly, once the hope and expectation of eternal happiness is taken away, temporal goods will be greedily sought after. Every man will strive to secure the largest share for himself. Hence arise envy, jealousy, hatred. The consequences are conspiracy, anarchy, nihilism. There is neither peace abroad nor security at home. Public life is stained with crime.

47 So great is this struggle of the passions and so serious the dangers involved that we must either anticipate ultimate ruin or seek for an efficient remedy. It is, of course, both right and necessary to punish malefactors, to educate the masses, and by legislation to prevent crime in every possible way: but all this is by no means sufficient. The salvation of the nations must be looked for higher. A power greater than human must be called in to teach men's hearts, awaken in them the sense of duty and make them better. This is the power which once before saved the world from destruction when groaning under much more terrible evils. Once remove all impediments and allow the Christian spirit to revive and grow strong in a nation and that nation will be healed. The strife between the classes and the masses will die away; mutual rights will be respected. If Christ be listened to, both rich and poor will do their duty. The former will realize that they must observe justice and charity, the latter self-restraint and moderation, if both are to be saved. Domestic life will be firmly established by the salutary fear of God as the Lawgiver. In the same way the precepts of the natural law, which dictates respect for lawful authority and obedience to the laws, will exercise their influence over the people. Seditions and conspiracies will cease. Wherever Christianity rules over all without let or hin-

drance, there the order established by Divine Providence is preserved, and both security and prosperity are the happy result. The common welfare, then, urgently demands a return to Him from whom we should never have gone astray; to Him who is the Way, and the Truth and the Life—and this on the part not only of individuals, but of society as a whole. We must restore Christ to this His own rightful possession. All elements of the national life must be made to drink in the Life which proceedeth from Him—legislation, political institutions, education, marriage and family life, capital and labor. Every one must see that the very growth of civilization which is so ardently desired depends greatly upon this, since it is fed and grows not so much by material wealth and prosperity, as by the spiritual qualities of morality and virtue.

48 It is rather ignorance than ill-will which keeps multitudes away from Jesus Christ. There are many who study humanity and the natural world; few who study the Son of God. The first step, then, is to substitute knowledge for ignorance, so that He may no longer be despised or rejected because He is unknown. We conjure all Christians throughout the world to strive all they can to know their Redeemer as He really is. The more one contemplates Him with sincere and unprejudiced mind, the clearer does it become that there can be nothing more salutary than His law, more divine than His teaching. In this work your influence, Venerable Brethren, and the zeal and earnestness of the entire clergy can do wonders. You must look upon it as a chief part of your duty to engrave upon the minds of your people the true knowledge, the very likeness of Jesus Christ; to illustrate His charity, His mercies, His teaching, by your writings and your words, in schools, in universities, from the pulpit; wherever opportunity is offered you. The world has heard enough of the so-called "rights of man." Let it hear something of the rights of God. That the time is suitable is proved by the very general revival of religious feeling already referred to, and especially that devotion towards Our Saviour of which there are so many indications, and which, please God, we shall hand on to the New Century as a pledge of happier times to come. But as this consummation cannot be hoped for except by the aid of divine grace,

let us strive in prayer, with united heart and voice, to incline Almighty God unto mercy, that He would not suffer those to perish whom He had redeemed by His Blood. May He look down in mercy upon this world, which has indeed sinned much, but which has also suffered much in expiation! And embracing in His loving-kindness all races and classes of mankind, may He remember His own words: "I, if I be lifted up from the earth, will draw all things to Myself" (John xii., 32).

49 As a pledge of the Divine favors and in token of Our fatherly affection, We lovingly impart to you, Venerable Brethren, and to your Clergy and People, the Apostolic Blessing.

50 Given at St. Peter's in Rome, the first day of November, 1900, in the twenty-third year of Our Pontificate.

MIRAE CARITATIS
Encyclical Letter of Pope Leo XIII
on the Most Holy Eucharist
May 23, 1902

The wonderful zeal for the salvation of men of which Jesus Christ has given us so bright an example we, in accordance with the sanctity of our office, strive to study and imitate unceasingly, and, with His help, we shall continue to follow the same Divine model as long as life remains in us. As it is our lot to live in times bitterly hostile to truth and justice, we have endeavored to supply abundantly as far as lay in our power, by teaching, admonishing and working, whatsoever might seem likely to avert the contagion of error in its various forms or strengthen the energies of Christian life. In this connection there are two things within the memory of the faithful, intimately connecting one with the other, the accomplishment of which fills us with consolation in the midst of so many sorrows. One is that we declared it most desirable that the whole human race should be consecrated in a special manner to the Sacred Heart of Jesus Christ the Redeemer; the other that we most earnestly exhorted all bearing the Christian name to adhere steadfastly to Him who by divine authority is for all men the Way, the Truth and the Life.

52 And now, in truth, watching with vigilance over the fortunes of the Church in these evil days, we are impelled by the same apostolic love to add something which will crown and finish the project we had in mind; namely, to recommend to

the Christian world by a special act of our authority the Most Holy Eucharist.

53 The Blessed Eucharist is the most divine gift, given to us clearly from the inmost heart of the Redeemer, with the desire of one desiring this singular union with man and instituted chiefly for the generous disposal of the fruits of His redemption. In this matter we have hitherto manifested by our authority and zeal not a little solicitude. And it is pleasant to remember among other things, that we, by legitimate approval and privileges, largely increased the number of institutes and sodalities devoted to the perpetual adoration of the Divine Host: that we also took care to have Eucharistic congresses held with suitable splendor and corresponding usefulness, and that we made patron of those and similar works, the heavenly Paschal Baylon, who stood out in his day as a most devout worshiper of the Eucharistic mystery.

54 Therefore, venerable brethren, it is well to fix our minds on certain features of this mystery in defending and illustrating which the zeal of the Church has constantly been manifested and not infrequently crowned by the palm of martyrdom, whilst the doctrine itself has called forth the learning and eloquence of the greatest men and the most noble masterpieces in various arts. Here it will be our duty to point out clearly and expressly the power that is in this mystery to cure the evils and meet the necessities of the present age. And surely, as Christ, at the close of His mortal life, left this sacrament as the great monument of His love for men, as the greatest support "for the life of the world" (St. John vi., 52), so we, who are likewise soon to depart, can desire nothing more eagerly than to excite and nourish in the minds of all men feelings of grateful love and religious devotion towards this most wonderful sacrament, in which, we believe, are to be found the hope and assurance of salvation and peace.

55 It may be a cause of surprise to some that we should think this age, so universally disturbed and groaning under so great a burden, should be best aided by such remedies and helps, and persons shall not be wanting, perhaps, who will treat our utterances with fastidious indifference. This comes chiefly from pride, and pride is a vice which weakens Christian faith

and produces such a terrible darkness about divine things that of many it is said: "Whatever things they know not, they blaspheme." (Judea x). But so far are we from being averted from the purpose we have in view that we believe more firmly than ever that it will bring light to those who are well disposed and obtain, by the brotherly intercession of the devout, pardon from God for those who revile holy things.

56 To know with full and perfect faith what is the virtue of the Most Holy Eucharist is to know what God, made Man, accomplished for the salvation of the human race in His infinite mercy. For as it is a duty of true faith to proclaim our belief in Christ and worship the Supreme Author of our salvation, who by His wisdom, laws, example and the shedding of His blood renewed all things, it is a duty of equal obligation to worship Him who is really present in the Eucharist, that so He may abide among men to the end of the world, and by the perennial communication of Himself make them sharers in the blessings of His redemption.

57 Now, he who studiously and religiously considers the blessings flowing from the Holy Eucharist sees at once that in it are contained in the most eminent degree all other blessings of every kind; for from it that life flows which is truly life: "The bread which I will give is My flesh for the life of the world." Not in one way alone is Christ the life—Christ, who assigned as the cause of His coming among men that He might bring them a sure fullness of life that was more than human: "I come that they may have life and have it more abundantly." For as soon as "the goodness and compassion of God our Saviour" appeared upon earth, a power at once came forth that almost created a new order of things and influenced every department of civil and domestic society. Thence new relations between man and man; new rights, public and private; new duties; a new direction given to institutions, laws, arts and sciences. The thoughts and studies of men were drawn towards the truth of religion and the sanctity of morals, and hence a life given to men truly heavenly and divine. All this is frequently commemorated in the sacred writings; the tree of life, the word of life, the book of life, the crown of life, and, expressly, the bread of life.

58 But this life about which we are speaking bears an express resemblance to the natural life of men, and so, just as the one is nourished by food and grows strong, so does the other likewise require to be supported and strengthened by food. And here it is well to recall the time and manner in which Christ moved the minds of men and excited them to receive suitably and righteously the living bread which He was about to give them. For where the fame had spread abroad of the miracle of the multiplication of the loaves which He had wrought on the shore of Tiberias, many people followed Him so that their hunger, too, might be appeased. Then Jesus, seizing the opportunity, just as when He infused into the Samaritan woman at the well a thirst for the water "springing up into life everlasting," similarly disposes the minds of the eager multitude to desire more eagerly another bread, the bread "which endureth unto life everlasting." But this bread, as Jesus continues to show, is not that heavenly manna given to their fathers wandering through the desert, nor is it that which they themselves had lately received from Him in astonishment; but He Himself is the true bread which He gives: "I am the bread of life." He inculcates still further the same lesson both by council and by precept: "If any man eat of this bread, he shall live forever: and the bread that I will give is My flesh for the life of the world." And the gravity of the command He thus shows clearly: "Amen, amen, I say unto you: Except you eat the flesh of the Son of Man and drink His blood, you shall not have life in you." Away, therefore, with that common and most pernicious error of those who believe that the Holy Eucharist is only for those who, free from business and troubled in mind, resolve to seek repose in some design of a more religious life. For the Holy Eucharist, than which there is nothing more excellent or salutary, is for all, whatsoever their employment or dignity, who wish (and there is no one who should not wish) to nourish in themselves the life of Divine Grace, of which the ultimate end is the attainment of life eternal.

59 Would that those whose genius or industry or authority could do so much to guide the men and affairs of the age would think rightly of eternal life and impart the knowledge

of it to others. But, alas! we see with regret that most of these arrogantly believe that they have given to the world a life prosperous and almost new, because they urge it forward to strive in its excited course for utilitarian objects and the mere gratification of curiosity. Look where you will, human society, alien though it is from God, far from enjoying that tranquility of affairs which it seeks, labors in great anguish and trepidation like one tossing in a fever; it strives vainly to obtain that prosperity in which alone it puts its trust, ever vainly pursuing it and clinging desperately to what is slipping from its grasp. For men and states come necessarily from God, and therefore in no other can they live or move or do good but in God through Jesus Christ, from whom men have received and still receive the best and choicest gifts. But the chief source and fountain head of all these gifts is the Holy Eucharist, which, while it nourishes and supports that life for which we strive so ardently, exalts in the highest degree that dignity of human nature which seems to be so highly valued in these days. For what can be greater or more desirable than to be made as far as possible participators and partners in the Divine nature? But this is what Christ does in the Eucharist, raising man up to divine things by the aid of grace and uniting Himself to him by bonds so close. For there is this difference between the food of the body and the food of the soul, that the former is converted into us, but the latter converts us into itself, and it is to this that Augustine refers when he puts the words into the mouth of Christ: "You shall not change Me into thee as food of thy flesh, but thou shalt be changed into Me."

60 But this most excellent sacrament, which renders men participators of the Divine nature, also enables the soul of man to advance in every class of the higher virtues. And first in faith. At all times faith has had its assailants; for although it exalts the minds of men with knowledge of the most lofty things, yet, while it has revealed that there exist things above nature, it conceals their precise character, and so seems to depress the human mind. Formerly only this or that article of faith was attacked; afterwards war was waged much more widely, until it finally came to be affirmed that there was

nothing at all above nature. Now, for renewing in the mind the vigor and fervor of faith there is nothing more suitable than the mystery of the Eucharist, which is properly called the mystery of faith; for truly in this one mystery, by reason of its wonderful abundance and variety of miracles, is contained the whole supernatural order. "He has made a remembrance of His wonderful works, being a merciful and gracious Lord. He hath given food to them that fear Him." For if God acknowledged what He wrought above nature as due to the incarnation of the word, through whom the salvation of the human race was restored, according to that word of the Apostle: "He hath purposed . . . to reestablish all things in Christ, that are in heaven and on earth, in Him;" the Eucharist, according to the testimony of the Holy Fathers, is a continuation and an expansion of the incarnation. For by it the substance of the incarnate word is united to men, and the supreme sacrifice of Calvary is renewed in a manner that is full of mystery. This the prophet Malachy signified in the words: "In every place there is sacrifice, and there is offered to My name a clean oblation." And this miracle, the greatest of all, is accompanied by innumerable others, for here all the laws of nature are suspended; the whole substance of the bread and wine is changed into the Body and Blood of Christ; the species of bread and wine are sustained without a subject by Divine power; the Body of Christ dwells at the same time in as many places as the sacrament is consecrated. But human reason is enabled the better to reverence so great a mystery by the prodigies which have been performed in its glory in past ages and in our own days, of which, indeed, there still exist renowned and public proofs, and that not in one place merely. We see, therefore, that by this sacrament faith is fostered, the soul nourished, the falsehoods of rationalists dissipated and the whole order of the supernatural made clear to our eyes.

61 But it is not pride alone, but depravity of mind as well, that makes faith in Divine things grow weak. For if it happens that the better the morals the clearer the intelligence, if even the prudence of the Gentiles perceived that the mind is blunted by the pleasures of the body, as Divine wisdom has

already borne testimony, then so much more in Divine things do the pleasures of the body obscure the light of faith, and even extinguish it altogether in God's just punishment. And for these pleasures there is burning in those days an insatiable cupidity, a cupidity which, like the contagion of disease, widely infects all even from their first tender years. There is a remedy for this terrible evil in the Divine Eucharist. For, first of all, by increasing charity it checks voluptuous desire; as Augustine says: "The nourishment (of charity) is the lessening of lust; perfection, no lust." Besides, the most chaste flesh of Jesus restrains the luxury of our flesh, as Cyril of Alexandria has said: "For Christ existing in us calms the law of the flesh raging in our members." But even more the peculiar and most precious fruit of the Eucharist is that signified in the saying of the prophet: "What is the good thing of Him (Christ), and what is His beautiful thing but the corn of the elect, and wine springing forth virgins?"—namely, the strong and constant resolve of sacred virginity, which, while the age slips away in pleasures, flourishes in the Catholic Church more widely and more fruitfully from day to day, and, indeed, what a great advantage and ornament this is everywhere to religion and even to ordinary human intercourse is well known. Moreover, this sacrament strengthens beyond conception the hope of immortal blessings and the confidence of Divine aid. For the desire of happiness which is in the minds of all is more and more sharpened and strengthened by the emptiness of all earthly goods, by the unjust violence of wicked men and by all the other troubles of mind and body.

62 Now the august Sacrament of the Eucharist is at once the cause and pledge of happiness and glory not only for the soul, but also for the body. For while it enriches the soul with an abundance of heavenly gifts, it also fills it with joys so sweet that they far surpass every thought and hope of man; in adversity it sustains; in strife of virtue it confirms; it leads to everlasting life as by an open pathway. But to the frail and perishable body that Divine Host gives a future resurrection, for the immortal Body of Christ implants the seed of immortality which is some time to bud forth. This

advantage, both to soul and body, the Church has at all times taught, following Christ, who said: "He that eateth My flesh and drinketh My blood hath everlasting life; and I will raise him up on the last day." And here it is of great importance to consider that the Eucharist, being instituted by Christ as a "perennial memorial of His passion," declares to all Christian men the necessity of mortifying themselves. For Jesus said to His first priests: "Do this for a commemoration of Me," that is, do this to commemorate My sorrows, griefs, tortures and death on the cross. Hence this sacrament, which is also a sacrifice, is a ceaseless exhortation, for all time, to penance and every spiritual effort; it is also a solemn and severe reproof of those pleasures which shameless men praise and exalt so highly. "As often as you shall eat this bread, and drink this chalice, you shall show the death of the Lord until He come."

63 Moreover, if you diligently examine into the causes of the present evils, you will find that they arise from the fact that the charity of men towards one another has grown faint according as the love of God grew cold. They have forgotten that they were sons of God and brothers in Jesus Christ; they think of nothing but themselves; the rights of others they not only disregard, but attack and invade. Hence the frequent quarrels and contentions among the various classes of citizens; the arrogance, harshness, dishonesty among the more powerful; the misery, envy and spirit of revolt among the weaker. For these evils it is vain to seek a remedy from the enactments of law, the fear of punishment or the plans of human prudence. What must be aimed at, as we ourselves have more than once recommended, is to reconcile the various orders of citizens by a mutual union of duties, a union which would come from God and give birth to works stamped with the true spirit and charity of Christ. This union Christ brought upon earth; by it He wished all things to be inspired, as being the one thing that could bring some happiness, even in the present, not only to the soul, but also to the body, restraining as it does man's immoderate love of himself, and repressing the passion for riches, which is "the root of all evils."

But although it is necessary that all just rights should be well protected, it is nevertheless lawful to establish and preserve in society that salutary "equality" which St. Paul recommended. This, therefore, is what Christ wished in instituting this august sacrament—to excite love toward God and to foster charity among men. For the one flows, as is evident, of its very nature and almost spontaneously, from the other; nor can men live without it at all; nay, it must even burn and flourish in their hearts, if they consider the charity of Christ towards them in this sacrament, in which He has maintained His marvenlous power and wisom, and also "poured forth the riches of His divine love for men." And as Christ has given us such an example of love, how we should love and help each other, bound together as we are still more closely by the needs of our common brotherhood! Moreover, the outward symbols of this sacrament are in a special manner calculated to incite us to union. For St. Cyprian says: "The very sacrifices of redemption themselves proclaim the necessity of Christian concord in the firm and inseparable bonds of charity. For when the Lord calls His body bread which is made up of the union of many grains, He indicates the union of that people whose sins He bore; and when He calls His blood wine which is drawn from many ripe grapes, again He signifies a flock made one by the union of the multitude." Similarly the Angelic Doctor following St. Augustine says: "Our Lord, commended His body and blood in those things which are moulded in unity; for the first, the bread, namely, is made one from many grapes." And therefore Augustine elsewhere says: "O Sacrament of piety, O sign of unity, O bond of charity." 64

All this is confirmed by the declaration of the Council of Trent, that Christ left the Eucharist to the Church "as a symbol of that union and love with which He wished all Christians to be bound together—a symbol of that body of which He is head, and to which He wished us to be united as members by the most firm bonds of faith and hope and charity." And this St. Paul himself had declared: "For we, being many, are one bread, one body, all that partake of one bread." Yes, truly, here is a most beautiful example of Christ- 65 ian brotherhood and of social equality, that all should approach the same altars without distinction; the nobility and the people, the rich and the poor, the learned and the unlearned, are equally sharers in the same heavenly banquet. And if it has been the glory of the Church that, in the first ages, "the multitude of believers had but one heart and one soul," it cannot be doubted that such a wonderful blessing was due to the custom of approaching the holy table; for of them we find it recorded, "And they were persevering in the doctrine of the Apostles, and in the communication of the breaking of bread." Moreover, the grace of mutual charity among the living, so much strengthened and increased as it is by the Sacrament of the Eucharist, flows out unto all who are in the communion of saints particularly through the power of the Holy Sacrifice. For the communion of saints, as all know, is nothing else than the mutual communication of aid, expiation, prayer and benefits among the faithful, whether in heaven or enduring the expiatory fires of Purgatory, or still abiding upon earth, but all forming one state, whose head is Christ, and whose life-giving principle is love. It is also a matter of faith that while to God alone the Holy Sacrifice may be offered, yet it can also be celebrated in honor of the saints reigning in heaven with God "Who crowned them "to obtain their patronage and protection, and also to blot out the stains of the brethren who had died in the Lord, but who had not yet made full atonement. That true charity, therefore, which is wont to do and endure all things for the salvation and utility of all, leaps and burns into life from the Most Holy Eucharist, in which Christ is really present, in which He gives way to His love for us in the highest form, and under the impulse of His divine love, perpetually renews His sacrifice. It is from this that the arduous labors of apostolic men, as well as the various institutions that have had their origin among Catholics and deserve so well of the human race, derive their influence, strength, constancy and successful results.

66 These few things written by us on a great subject will, we doubt not, produce much fruit if you, venerable brethren, seasonably expound and commend them to the faithful.

At the same time this sacrament is so great and so abounding in virtue that no one has ever yet adequately praised it by his eloquence or worshiped it by his adoration. Whether you meditate upon it or rightly worship it, or better still, purely and worthily receive it, it is to be regarded as the great centre round which turns the whole Christian life; to it all other forms of piety lead; in it they end. In the self-same mystery that gracious invitation and still more gracious promise of Christ: "Come to Me all you that labor and are burdened, and I will refresh you," are renewed and daily fulfilled. Lastly, it is, as it were, the soul of the Church, towards which is directed the fulness of sacerdotal grace through the various grades of orders. From the very same source does the Church draw all her power and glory, all the ornaments of her Divine ritual, and all the efficacy of her blessings. Therefore, she takes the greatest care to instruct the faithful and lead them to this intimate union with Christ by the Sacrament of His Body and Blood; and for the same reason she adorns it and makes it more worthy of reverence by means of the most sacred ceremonies. The constant care of our Holy Mother the Church in this matter is summed up in the exhortation of the Council of Trent; an exhortation breathing forth wonderful charity and piety, and worthy of being entirely recalled again by us to the Christian world: "With paternal affection the Holy Synod admonishes, exhorts, demands and, by the bowels of God's mercy, entreats all, without exception, who are called Christians, to sometimes meet and find peace in this sign of unity, in this bond of charity, in this symbol of concord; to be mindful of that immense majesty and of that wonderful love of Jesus Christ, our Lord, who gave His life as price of our salvation, and His flesh to be our food; to believe and venerate those sacred mysteris of His Body and Blood with such constancy and firmness of faith, such devotion of mind and piety and zeal, that they may be able to frequently receive that supersubstantial bread, so that He may be truly to them the life of their soul and the perpetual health of their mind, and thus that strengthened by its vigor, they may be able, after the journey of this miserable exile, to reach their heavenly country and eat without any veil upon their eyes the very same bread of angels which they now eat concealed under the sacred species."

68 Now history bears witness that Christian life flourished better in the times when the reception of the Blessed Eucharist was more frequent. On the other hand, it is not less certain that when men began to neglect and almost despise this heavenly bread the vigor of the Christian profession sensibly diminished. Lest it should some time pass away altogether, Innocent III., in the Council of Lateran, imposed the most solemn precept that, at the very least, no Christian should abstain at Paschal time from receiving the Body of the Lord. This precept, however, was imposed with reluctance, and, it is clear, only as the last remedy; for it has been always the wish of the Church that the faithful should approach the holy table at every sacrifice. "The most Holy Synod would wish the faithful attending each Mass to communicate not only spiritually, but even sacramentally, so that they might receive more abundantly the fruits of the sacrifice."

69 And this most sacred mystery contains as a sacrifice the plenitude of salvation not only for individuals, but for all men; hence the Church is accustomed to offer it unceasingly "for the salvation of the whole world." It is fitting, therefore, that by the common zeal of the devout there should be greater love and esteem for this sacrifice; in this age particularly there is no more pressing necessity. Accordingly, we desire that its efficacy and power should be remembered more widely and even more diligently proclaimed. Principles evident from the very light of reason tell us that God, the creator and preserver of all things, has a supreme and absolute dominion over men, both privately and publicly; that all that we have and are in every sphere has come from His bounty; and that we, in turn, are bound to give Him the highest reverence as our Master and the greatest gratitude as our most generous benefactor. And yet how few are there to-day who fulfil those duties with suitable piety.

70 This age, if any, surely manifests the spirit of rebellion against God; in it that impious cry against Christ again grows strong: "We will not have this man to reign over us," and

that impious resolve, "Let us cut Him off." Nor, indeed, is anything urged more vehemently by very many than this, that they should banish and separate God from all intercourse with men. This criminal madness is not universal, we joyfully admit; yet it is lamentable how many have forgotten the Divine Majesty and His benefits, and the salvation that was obtained chiefly through Christ. Now, this wickedness and folly must be resisted by an increase of general devotion and zeal in the worship of the Eucharistic Sacrifice. Nothing could of itself be more full of sweetness and consolation to the Christian soul. For the Victim that is immolated is Divine, and, accordingly, the honor that we render through it to the Holy Trinity is in proporton to its infinite dignity; we offer also to the Father His only-begotten Son—an offering that is infinite in value and infinitely acceptable; hence it is that we not only give Him thanks for His goodness, but even make Him a return. There is also another two-fold and wonderful fruit which may and ought to be derived from this great sacrifice.

71 The mind grows sad when it reflects on the fearful multitude of crimes which abounds on all sides, God, as we have said, being neglected and the Divine Majesty despised. The human race in great part seems to call upon the Divine anger, although indeed that harvest of evil which has been reaped contains in itself the ripeness of a just punishment. The zeal of the faithful should be roused to appease God, the avenging Judge of crime, and obtain from Him the reform of a sinful age. This is to be done chiefly by the aid of this holy sacrifice. For it is by virtue alone of Christ's death that men can fully satisfy the demand of Divine justice, and abundantly obtain mercy and pardon. But this power of expiation or of entreaty Christ wished to remain wholly in the Eucharist, which is not a mere commemoration of His death, but a real and wonderful, although unbloody and mystic, renewal of it.

72 At the same time let us confess we have not a little joy knowing that in those last years the minds of the faithful seem to have been renewed in love and reverence for the Sacrament of the Eucharist; and this gives us a better hope for the future. For, as we said in the beginning, ingenious

piety has done much in this direction, especially in sodalities, either by increasing the splendor of our Eucharistic rites, or worshiping the Holy Sacrament constantly by day and night, and making atonement for the insults and injuries it receives. But, venerable brethren, it is not lawful for us or for you to stop here; for yet many more things remain to be done or undertaken, so that this, the most Divine work of all, may be put in a clearer light and held in greater honor among those who practice the duties of the Christian religion, that so great a mystery may be honored in a manner worthy of its greatness. Hence the works that have been undertaken are to be urged on more vigorously from day to day; old institutions, where they have disappeared, are to be renewed, as, for example, the Sodalities of the Eucharist, the supplications poured forth to the holy sacrament exposed for adoration, all the solemnity of pomp with which it was surrounded, the pious salutations before the tabernacles, and other holy and most profitable practices of the same nature; in fine, everything is to be done that prudence and piety could dictate. But, above all, endeavor should be made to revive widely again among Catholic nations the frequent use of the Holy Eucharist. To this the example of the early Church, the decrees of councils, the authority of the fathers and of the holy men in every age exhort us; for as the body needs its own food, so does the soul, and the most life-giving nourishment is given by the Holy Eucharist. Therefore, condemn before hand the opinions of those who oppose such frequent communions. Banish the idle fears of many and the spacious excuses or reasons for abstaining from the Body of the Lord; for nothing could be more effective in rescuing the world from its anxiety about perishable things, and in bringing back and perpetually preserving the Christian spirit. Here the exhortations and examples of the higher orders, and still more the zeal and industry of the clergy, will be of great value. For priests to whom Christ, the Redeemer, has given the office of consecrating and administering the mysteries of His Body and Blood, can surely make no greater return for the high honor they have received than to do all in their power to promote His glory in the Eucharist, and by following the desire of His Most Sacred Heart to invite and draw the souls of all to the saving fountains of so great a sacrament and sacrifice.

73 Thus may the surpassing fruits of the Eucharist become, as we ardently desire, more fruitful from day to day, with abundant growth, also, in faith, hope, charity, and in every virtue; may this revival of piety tend to the peace and advantage of the State, and may the designs of God's most provident love in instituting such a perpetual mystery for the life of the world be made manifest to all men.

74 Buoyed up with such a hope, venerable brethren, and as a pledge of Divine gifts as well as of our affection, we lovingly impart to each one of you, and to your clergy and people, our Apostolic Benediction.

75 Given at Rome, near St. Peter's, on this 23d day of May, on the approach of the solemnity of Corpus Christi, in the year 1902, the twenty-fifth of our Pontificate.

E SUPREMI

Encyclical Letter of Pope Pius X
on Restoration of All Things in Christ
October 4, 1903

In addressing you for the first time from the chair of the supreme apostolate to which we have, by the inscrutable disposition of God, been elevated, it is not necessary to remind you with what tears and earnest prayers we exerted ourselves to evade this formidable burden of the Pontificate. Unequal in merit though we be, with St. Anselm, it seems to us that we may with truth make our own the words in which he lamented when he was constrained against his will and in spite of his struggles to receive the honor of the episcopate. For to show with what dispositions of mind and will we subjected ourselves to the most serious charge of feeding the flock of Christ, we can well adduce those same proofs of grief which he invokes in his own behalf. "My tears are witnesses," he wrote, "and the sounds and moanings issuing from the anguish of my heart, such as I never remember before to have come from me for any sorrow, before that day on which there seemed to fall upon me that great misfortune of the archbishopric of Canterbury. And those who fixed their gaze on my fact that day could not fail to see it. . . . I, in color more like a dead than a living man, was pale for amazement and alarm. Hitherto I have resisted as far as I could, speaking the truth, my election or rather the violence done me. But now I am constrained to confess, whether I will or no, that the judgments of God oppose greater and greater resistance to my efforts, so that I see no way of escaping them. Wherefore vanquished as I am by the violence not so much of men as of God, against which there is no providing, I realize that nothing is left for me, after having prayed as much as I could and striven that this chalice should if possible pass from me without my drinking it, but to set aside my feeling and my will and resign myself entirely to the design and the will of God."

77 In truth, reasons both numerous and most weighty were not lacking to justify this resistance of ours. For beside the fact that we deemed ourselves altogether unworthy through our insignificance of seeing himself designated to succeed him who, ruling the Church the honor of the Pontificate, who would not have been disturbed at with supreme wisdom for nearly twenty-six years, showed himself adorned with such sublimity of mind, such lustre of every virtue, as to attract to himself the admiration even of adversaries and to leave his memory consecrated by glorious achievements?

78 Then, again, to omit other motives, we were terrified beyond all else by the disastrous state of human society to-day. For who can fail to see that society is at the present time, more than in any past age, suffering from a terrible and deep-rooted malady which, developing every day and eating into its inmost being, is dragging it to destruction? You understand, Venerable Brethren, what this disease is—apostasy from God than which in truth nothing is more allied with ruin, according to the word of the prophet: "For behold they that go far from Thee shall perish" (Ps. lxxii., 17). We saw, therefore, that in virtue of the ministry of the Pontificate which was to be entrusted to us, we must hasten to find a remedy for this great evil, considering as addressed to us that Divine command: "Lo, I have set thee this day over the nations and over kingdoms, to root up, and to pull down, and to waste, and to destroy, and to build and to plant" (Jerem. i., 10.) But cognizant of our weakness, we recoiled in terror from a task as urgent as it is arduous.

79 Since, however, it has been pleasing to the Divine Will to raise our lowliness to such sublimity of power, we take courage in Him who strengthens us, and setting ourselves to work, relying on the power of God, we proclaim that we have no

other programme in the Supreme Pontificate but that "of restoring all things in Christ" (Ephes. i., 10), so that "Christ may be all and in all" (Coloss. iii., 2). Some will certainly be found who, measuring Divine things by human standards, will seek to discover secret aims of ours, distorting them to an earthly purpose and to political designs. To eliminate all vain delusions for such, we say to them with emphasis that we do not wish to be and with the Divine assistance never shall be aught before human society but the minister of God, of whose authority we are the depository. The interests of God shall be our interests, and for these we are resolved to spend all our strength and our very life. Hence, should any one ask us for a symbol as the expression of our will, we will give this and no other: "To renew all things in Christ."

80 In undertaking this glorious task we are greatly quickened by the certainty that we shall have all of you, Venerable Brethren, as generous cooperators. Did we doubt it, we should have to regard you, unjustly, as either unconscious or heedless of that sacrilegious war which is now almost everywhere stirred up and fomented against God. For in truth "the nations have raged and the peoples imagined vain things" (Ps. ii., 1) against their Creator; so frequent is the cry of the enemies of God: "Depart from us" (Job xxi., 14). And as might be expected, we find extinguished among the majority of men all respect for the Eternal God and no regard paid in the manifestations of public and private life to the Supreme Will—nay, every effort and every artifice is used to destroy utterly the memory and the knowledge of God.

81 When all this is considered, there is good reason to fear lest this great perversity may be, as it were, a foretaste and perhaps the beginning of those evils which are reserved for the last days, and that there may be already in the world the "Son of Perdition" of whom the Apostle speaks (II. Thess. ii., 4). Such, in truth, is the audacity and the wrath employed everywhere in persecuting religion, in combating the dogmas of the faith, in resolute effort to uproot and destroy all relations between man and the Divinity. While, on the other hand, and this according to the same apostle is the distinguishing mark of Antichrist, man has with infinite temerity

put himself in the place of God, raising himself above all that is called God; in such wise that although he cannot utterly extinguish in himself all knowledge of God, he has contemned God's majesty and, as it were, made of the universe a temple wherein he himself is to be adored. "He sitteth in the temple of God, showing himself as if he were God" (II. Thess. ii., 2).

Verily, no one of sound mind can doubt the issue of this contest between man and the Most High. Man, abusing his liberty, can violate the right and the majesty of the Creator of the Universe; but the victory will ever be with God—nay, defeat is at hand at the moment when man, under the delusion of his triumph, rises up with most audacity. Of this we are assured in the holy books by God Himself. Unmindful, as it were, of His strength and greatness, He "overlooks the sins of men" (Wisd. xi., 24), but swiftly, after these apparent retreats, "awakened like a mighty man that hath been surfeited with wine" (Ps. lxxvii., 65), "He shall break the heads of his enemies" (Ps. lvxii., 22), that all may know "that God is the king of all the earth" (Ib. lxvi., 8), "that the Gentiles may know themselves to be men" (Ib. ix., 20). 82

All this, Venerable Brethren, we believe and expect with unshakable faith. But this does not prevent us also, according to the measure given to each, from exerting ourselves to hasten the work of God—and not merely by praying assiduously: "Arise, O Lord, let no man be strengthened" (Ib., ix., 19), but, more important still, by affirming both by word and deed and in the light of day, God's supreme dominion over man and all things, so that His right to command and His authority may be fully realized and respected. 83

This is imposed upon us not only as a natural duty, but by our common interest. For, Venerable Brethren, who can avoid being appalled and afflicted when he beholds, in the midst of a progress in civilization which is justly extolled, the greater part of mankind fighting among themselves so savagely as to make it seem as though strife were universal? The desire for peace is certainly harbored in every breast, and there is no one who does not ardently invoke it. But to want peace without God is an absurdity, seeing that where God is absent 84 thence, too, justice flies, and when justice is taken away it is vain to cherish the hope of peace. "And the work of justice shall be peace." (Is. xxxii., 17). There are many, we are well aware, who, in yearning for peace, that is to say, the tranquility of order, band themselves into societies and parties which they style parties of order. Hope and labor lost! For there is but one party of order capable of restoring peace in the midst of all this turmoil, and that is the party of God. It is this party, therefore, that we must advance, and to it attract as many as possible, if we are really urged by the love of peace.

85 But, Venerable Brethren, we shall never, however much we exert ourselves, succeed in calling men back to the majesty and empire of God except by means of Jesus Christ. "No one," the Apostle admonishes us, "can lay other foundation than that which has been laid, which is Jesus Christ" (I Cor. iii., 11). It is Christ alone "whom the Father sanctified and sent into this world" (Is. x., 36), "the splendor of the Father and the image of His substance" (Hebr. i., 3), true God and true man; without whom nobody can know God with the knowledge for salvation, "neither doth any one know the Father but the Son, and he to whom it shall please the Son to reveal him" (Matt. xi., 27). Hence it follows that to restore all things in Christ and to lead men back to submission to God is one and the same aim. To this, then, it behooves us to devote our care—to lead back mankind under the dominion of Christ; this done, we shall have brought it back to God. When we say to God, we do not mean to that inert being heedless of all things human which the dream of materialists has imagined, but to the true and living God, one in nature, triple in person, Creator of the world, most wise ordainer of all things, Lawgiver most just, who punishes the wicked and has reward in store for the virtuous.

86 Now, the way to reach Christ is not hard to find: it is the Church. Rightly does Chrysostom inculcate: "The Church is thy hope, the Church is thy salvation, the Church is thy refuge" (Hom. de capto Eutropio," n. 6). It was for this that Christ founded it, gaining it at the price of His blood, and made it the depository of His doctrine and His laws, bestow-

ing upon it at the same time an inexhaustible treasury of graces for the sanctification and salvation of men.

87 You see, then, Venerable Brethren, the duty that has been imposed alike upon us and upon you of bringing back to the discipline of the Church human society now estranged from the wisdom of Christ; the Church will then subject it to Christ, and Christ to God. If we, through the goodness of God Himself, bring this task to a happy issue, we shall be rejoiced to see evil giving place to good and hear for our gladness "a loud voice from heaven saying: Now is come salvation, and strength, and the kingdom of our God and the power of His Christ" (Apoc. xii., 10). But if our desire to obtain this is to be fulfilled, we must use every means and exert all our energy to bring about the utter disappearance of that enormous and detestable wickedness so characteristic of our time—the substitution of man for God; this done, it remains to restore to their ancient place of honor the most holy laws and counsels of the Gospel; to proclaim aloud the truths taught by the Church, as her teachings on the sanctity of marriage, on the education and discipline of youth, on the possession and use of property and the duties that men owe to those who rule the State, and, lastly, to restore equilibrium between the different classes of society according to Christian precept and custom. This is what we, in submitting ourselves to the manifestations of the Divine will, purpose to aim at during our Pontificate, and we will use all our industry to attain it. It is for you, Venerable Brethren, to second our efforts by your holiness, knowledge and experience, and above all by your zeal for the glory of God, with no other aim than that Christ may be formed in all.

88 As to the means to be employed in attaining this great end, it seems superfluous to name them, for they are obvious of themselves. Let your first care be to form Christ in those who are destined from the duty of their vocation to form Him in others. We speak of the priests, Venerable Brethren. For all who bear the seal of the priesthood must know that they have the same mission to the people in the midst of whom they live as that which Paul in these tender words proclaimed that he received: "My little children, of whom I am in labor

again until Christ be formed in you" (Gal. iv., 19). But how will they be able to perform this duty if they be not first clothed with Christ themselves? and so clothed with Christ as to be able to say with the Apostle: "I live, yet not I, but Christ lives in me" (Ibid, ii., 20). "For me to live is Christ" (Philip. i., 21). Hence although all are included in the exhortation "to advance towards the perfect man, in the measure of the age of the fullness of Christ" (Ephes. iv., 3), it is addressed before all others to him who exercises the sacerdotal ministry; who is therefore called another Christ not merely by the communication of power, but by reason of the imitation of His works; and he should therefore bear stamped upon himself the image of Christ.

89 This being so, Venerable Brethren, of what nature and magnitude is the care that must be taken by you in forming the clergy to holiness! All other tasks must yield to this one. Wherefore the chief part of your diligence will be directed to governing and ordering your seminaries aright so that they may flourish equally in the soundness of their teaching and in the spotlessness of their morals. Regard your seminary as the delight of your hearts, and neglect on its behalf none of those provisions which the Council of Trent has with admirable forethought prescribed. And when the time comes for promoting the youthful candidates to holy orders, ah! do not forget what Paul wrote to Timothy: "Impose not hands lightly upon any man" (I. Tim. v., 22), bearing carefully in mind that as a general rule the faithful will be such as are those whom you call to the priesthood. Do not, then, pay heed to private interests of any kind, but have at heart only God and the Church and the eternal welfare of souls, so that, as the Apostle admonishes, "you may not be partakers of the sins of others" (Ibid). Then, again, be not lacking in solicitude for young priests who have just left the seminary. From the bottom of our heart we urge you to bring them often close to your breast, which should burn with celestial fire—kindle them, inflame them, so that they may aspire solely after God and the salvation of souls. Rest assured, Venerable Brethren, that we on our side will use the greatest diligence to prevent the members of the clergy from being drawn to the snares of

a certain new and fallacious science, which savoreth not of Christ, but with masked and cunning arguments strives to open the door to the errors of rationalism and semi-rationalism, against which the Apostle warned Timothy to be on his guard when he wrote: "Keep that which is committed to thy trust, avoiding the profane novelties of words and oppositions of knowledge falsely so called which some promising have erred concerning the faith" (I. Tim. vi., 20 s.). This does not prevent us from esteeming worthy of praise those young priests who dedicate themselves to useful studies in every branch of learning the better to prepare themselves to defend the truth and to refute the calumnies of the enemies of the faith. Yet we cannot conceal, nay, we proclaim in the most open manner possible that our preference is, and ever will be, for those who, while cultivating ecclesiastical and literary erudition, dedicate themselves more closely to the welfare of souls through the exercise of those ministries proper to a priest zealous of the Divine glory. "It is a great grief and a continual sorrow to our heart" (Rom. ix., 2) to find Jeremiah's lamentation applicable to our times: "The little ones asked for bread, and there was none to break it to them" (Lam. iv., 4). For there are not lacking among the clergy those who adapt themselves according to their bent to works of more apparent than real solidity—but not so numerous, perhaps, are those who, after the example of Christ, take to themselves the words of the prophet: "The Spirit of the Lord hath anointed me, hath sent me to evangelize the poor, to heal the contrite of heart, to announce freedom to the captive and sight to the blind" (Luke iv., 18, 19).

90 Yet who can fail to see, Venerable Brethren, that while men are led by reason and liberty, the principal way to restore the empire of God in their souls is religious instruction? How many there are who hate Christ and abhor the Church and the Gospel more through ignorance than through badness of mind, of whom it may well be said: "They blaspheme whatever things they know not" (Jude ii., 10). This is found to be the case not only among the people at large and among the lowest classes, who are thus easily led astray, but even among the more cultivated and those enriched in other

respects with great erudition. The result is for a great many the loss of the faith. For it is not true that the progress of knowledge extinguishes the faith; rather is it ignorance; and the more ignorance prevails the greater is the havoc wrought by incredulity. And this is why Christ commended the Apostles: "Going forth teach all nations" (Matt. xxviii., 19).

91 But in order that the desired fruit may be derived from this apostolate and this zeal for teaching, and that Christ may be formed in all be it remembered, Venerable Brethren, that no means is more efficacious than charity, "For the Lord is not in the earthquake" (III. Kings xix., 11)–it is vain to hope to attract souls to God by a bitter zeal. On the contrary, harm is done more often than good by taunting men harshly with their faults and reproving their vices with asperity. True, the Apostle exhorted Timothy: "Accuse, beseech, rebuke," but he took care to add: "With all patience" (II. Tim. iv., 2). Jesus has certainly left us examples of this. "Come to me," we will find Him saying, "Come to me all ye that labor and are burthened and I will refresh you" (Matt. xi., 28). And by those that labor and are burthened He meant only those who are slaves of sin and error. What gentleness was that shown by the Divine Master! What tenderness, what compassion towards all kinds of misery! Isaias has marvelously described His heart in the words: "I will set my spirit upon him; he shall not contend, nor cry out; the bruised reed he will not break, he will not extinguish the smoking flax" (Is. xlii., 1 s.). This charity, "patient and kind" (I Cor. xiii., 4), will extend itself also to those who are hostile to us and persecute us. "We are reviled," thus did St. Paul protest, "and we bless; we are persecuted, and we suffer it; we are blasphemed, and we entreat" (I. Cor. iv., 12 s). They perhaps seem to be worse than they really are. Their associations with others, prejudice, the counsel, advice and example of others, and finally an ill-advised shame have dragged them to the side of the impious; but their wills are not so depraved as they themselves would seek to make people believe. Who will prevent us from hoping that the flame of Christian charity may dispel the darkness from their minds and bring to them light and the peace of God? It may be that the fruits of our labors

may be slow in coming, but charity wearies not with waiting, knowing that God prepares His rewards not for the results of toil, but for the good will shown in it.

92 It is true, Venerable Brethren, that in this arduous task of the restoration of the human race in Christ neither you nor your clergy should exclude all assistance. We know that God recommended every one to have a care for his neighbor (Eccli. xvii., 12). For it is not priests alone, but all the faithful without exception who must concern themselves with the interests of God and souls—not, of course, according to their own views, but always under the direction and orders of the bishops; for to no one in the Church except you is it given to preside over, to teach, to "rule the Church of God wherein the Holy Ghost has placed you bishops" (Acts xx., 28). Our predecessors have long since approved and blessed those Catholics who have banded together in societies of various kinds, but always religious in their aim. We, too, have no hesitation in awarding our praise to this great idea, and we earnestly desire to see it propagated and flourish in town and country. But we wish that all such associations aim first and chiefly at the constant maintenance of Christian life among those who belong to them. For truly it is of little avail to discuss questions with nice subtelty, or to discourse eloquently of rights and duties, when all this is unconnected with practice. The times we live in demand action—but action which consists entirely in observing with fidelity and zeal the divine laws and the precepts of the Church, in the frank and open profession of religion, in the exercise of every kind of charitable works, without regard to self-interest or worldly advantage. Such luminous examples given by the great army of soldiers of Christ will be of much greater avail in moving and drawing men than words and sublime dissertations; and it will easily come about that when human respect has been driven out, and prejudices and doubting laid aside, large numbers will be won to Christ, becoming in their turn promoters of His knowledge and love which are the road to true and solid happiness. Oh! when in every city and village the law of the Lord is faithfully observed, when respect is shown for sacred things, when the sacraments are frequented and the ordinan-

ces of Christian life fulfilled, there certainly will be no more need for us to labor further to see all things restored in Christ. Nor is it for the attainment of eternal welfare alone that this will be of service—it will also contribute largely to temporal welfare and the advantage of human society. For when these conditions have been secured, the upper and wealthy classes will learn to be just and charitable to the lowly, and these will be able to bear with tranquillity and patience the trials of a very hard lot; the citizens will obey not lust, but law; reverence and love will be deemed a duty towards those that govern, "whose power comes only from God" (Rom. xiii., 1). And then? Then at last it will be clear to all that the Church, such as it was instituted by Christ, must enjoy full and entire liberty and independence from all external dominion; and we, in demanding that same liberty, are defending not only the sacred rights of religion, but are also consulting the common weal and the safety of nations. For it continues to be true that "piety is useful for all things" (I. Tim. iv., 8)—when this is strong and flourishing "the people will" truly "sit in the fullness of peace" (Is. xxxii., 18).

93 May God, "who is rich in mercy" (Ephes. ii., 4), benignly speed this restoration of the human race in Jesus Christ, for "it is not of him that willeth, or of him that runneth, but of God that showeth mercy" (Rom. ix., 16). And let us, Venerable Brethren, "in the spirit of humility" (Dan. iii., 39), with continuous and urgent prayer ask this of Him through the merits of Jesus Christ. Let us turn, too, to the most powerful intercession of the Divine Mother—to obtain which we, addressing to you this letter of ours on the day appointed especially for commemorating the Holy Rosary, ordain and confirm all our predecessor's prescriptions with regard to the dedication of the present month to the august Virgin by the public recitation of the Rosary in all churches; with the further exhortation that as intercessors with God, appeal be also made to the most pure Spouse of Mary, the Patron of the Catholic Church, and the holy Princes of the Apostles, Peter and Paul.

94 And that all this may be realized in fulfillment of our ardent desire, and that everything may be prosperous with you,

we invoke upon you the most bountiful gifts of divine grace. And now in testimony of that most tender charity wherewith we embrace you and all the faithful whom Divine Providence has entrusted us, we impart with all affection in the Lord the Apostolic blessings to you, Venerable Brethren, to the clergy and to your people.

95 Given at Rome at St. Peter's on the fourth day of October, 1903, in the first year of our Pontificate.

PASCENDI DOMINICI GREGIS
Encyclical Letter of Pope Pius X
on the Doctrine of the Modernists
September 8, 1907

The office divinely committed to us of feeding the Lord's flock has especially this duty assigned to it by Christ, namely, to guard with the greatest vigilance the deposit of the faith delivered to the saints, rejecting the profane novelties of words and oppositions of knowledge falsely so called. There has never been a time when this watchfulness of the supreme pastor was not necessary to the Catholic body; for, owing to the efforts of the enemy of the human race, there have never been lacking "men speaking perverse things" (*Acts.* xx., 30), "vain talkers and seducers" (*Tit.* i., 10), "erring and driving into error" (*II. Tim.* iii., 13). Still, it must be confessed that the number of the enemies of the cross of Christ has in these last days increased exceedingly, who are striving, by arts entirely new and full of subtlety, to destroy the vital energy of the Church, and, if they can, to overthrow utterly Christ's kingdom itself. Wherefore we may no longer be silent, lest we should seem to fail in our most sacred duty, and lest the kindness that, in the hope of wiser counsels, we have hitherto shown them should be attributed to forgetfulness of our office.

97 That we may make no delay in this matter is rendered necessary especially by the fact that the partisans of error are to be sought not only among the Church's open enemies; they lie hid, a thing to be deeply deplored and feared, in her very bosom and heart, and are the more mischievous the less

conspicuously they appear. We allude, Venerable Brethren, to many who belong to the Catholic laity, nay, and this is far more lamentable, to the ranks of the priesthood itself, who, feigning a love for the Church, lacking the firm protection of philosophy and theology, nay, more, thoroughly imbued with the poisonous doctrines taught by the enemies of the Church, and lost to all sense of modesty, vaunt themselves as reformers is most sacred in the work of Christ, not sparing even the person of the Divine Redeemer, whom, with sacrilegious daring, they reduce to a simple, mere man.

98

Though they express astonishment themselves, no one can justly be surprised that we number such men among the enemies of the Church, if, leaving out of consideration the internal disposition of soul, of which God alone is the judge, he is acquainted with their tenets, their manner of speech, their conduct. Nor, indeed, will He err in accounting them the most pernicious of all the adversaries of the Church. For, as we have said, they put their designs for her ruin into operation not from without, but from within; hence the danger is present almost in the very veins and heart of the Church, whose injury is the more certain, the more intimate is their knowledge of her. Moreover, they lay the axe not to the branches and shoots, but to the very root: that is, to the faith and its deepest fibres. And having struck at this root of immortality, they proceed to disseminate poison through the whole tree, so that there is no part of Catholic truth from which they hold their hand, none that they do not strive to corrupt. Further, none is more skillful, none more astute than they in the employment of a thousand noxious arts; for they double the parts of rationalist and Catholic, and this so craftily that they easily lead the unwary into error; and since audacity is their chief characteristic, there is no conclusion of any kind from which they shrink or which they do not thrust forward with pertinacity and assurance. To this must be added the fact, which indeed is well calculated to deceive souls, that they lead a life of the greatest activity of assiduous and ardent application to every branch of learning, and that they possess, as a rule, a reputation for the strictest morality. Finally, and this almost destroys all hope of cure, their very doctrines have given such a bent to their minds that they disdain all authority and brook no restraint; and, relying upon a false conscience, they attempt to ascribe to a love of truth that which is in reality the result of pride and obstinacy.

99 Once, indeed, we had hopes of recalling them to a better sense, and to this end we first of all showed them kindness as our children, then we treated them with severity, and at last we have had recourse, though with great reluctance, to public reproof. But you know, Venerable Brethren, how fruitless has been our action. They bowed their head for a moment, but it was soon uplifted more arrogantly than ever. If it were a matter which concerned them alone, we might perhaps have overlooked it; but the security of the Catholic name is at stake. Wherefore, as to maintain it longer would be a crime, we must now break silence, in order to expose before the whole Church in their true colors those men who have assumed this bad disguise.

100 But since the modernists (as they are commonly and rightly called) employ a very clever artifice, namely, to present their doctrines without order and systematic arrangement into one whole, scattered and disjointed one from another, so as to appear to be in doubt and uncertainty, while they are in reality firm and steadfast, it will be of advantage, Venerable Brethren, to bring their teachings together here into one group, and to point out the connection between them, and thus to pass to an examination of the sources of the errors and to prescribe remedies for averting the evil.

101 To proceed in an orderly manner in this recondite subject, it must first of all be noted that every modernist sustains and comprises within himself many personalities; he is a philosopher, a believer, a theologian, an historian, a critic, an apologist, a reformer. These roles must be clearly distinguished from one another by all who would accurately know their system and thoroughly comprehend the principles and the consequences of their doctrines.

102 We begin, then, with the philosopher. Modernists place the foundation of religious philosophy in that doctrine which is usually called agnosticism. According to this teaching, human

reason is confined entirely within the field of phenomena; that is to say, to things that are perceptible to the senses, and in the manner in which they are perceptible. It has no right and no power to transgress these limits. Hence it is incapable of lifting itself up to God and of recognizing His existence, even by means of visible things. From this it is inferred that God can never be the direct object of science, and that, as regards history, He must not be considered as an historical subject. Given these premises, all will readily perceive what becomes of natural theology, of the motives of credibility, of external revelation. The modernists simply make away with them altogether; they include them in intellectualism, which they call a ridiculous and long ago defunct system. Nor does the fact that the Church has formally condemned these portentous errors exercise the slightest restraint upon them. Yet the Vatican Council has defined: "If any one says that the one true God, our Creator and Lord, cannot be known with certainty by the natural light of human reason by means of the things that are made, let him be anathema" (*De Revel.*, can. 1); and also: "If any one says that it is not possible or not expedient that man be taught, through the medium of divine revelation, about God and the worship to be paid Him, let him be anathema" (*Ibid.*, can. 2); and, finally: "If any one says that divine revelation cannot be made credible by external signs, and that therefore men should be drawn to the faith only by their personal internal experience or by private inspiration, let him be anathema" (*De Fide*, can. 3). But how the modernists make the transition from agnosticism, which is a state of pure nescience, to scientific and historic atheism, which is a doctrine of positive denial; and, consequently, by what legitimate process of reasoning, starting from ignorance as to whether God has in fact intervened in the history of the human race or not, they proceed, in their explanation of this history, to ignore God altogether, as if He really had not intervened, let him answer who can. Yet it is a fixed and established principle among them that both science and history must be atheistic: and within their boundaries there is room for nothing but phenomena; God and all that is divine are utterly excluded. We shall soon see clearly what, according to this most absurd teaching, must be held touching the most sacred person of Christ, what concerning the mysteries of His life and death, and of His resurrection and ascension into heaven.

103 However, this agnosticism is only the negative part of the system of the modernist: the positive side of it consists in what they call vital immanence. This is how they advance from one to the other. Religion, whether natural or supernatural, must like every other fact, admit of some explanation. But when natural theology has been destroyed, the road to revelation closed through the rejection of the arguments of credibility, and all external revelation absolutely denied, it is clear that this explanation will be sought in vain outside man himself. It must, therefore, be looked for in man; and since religion is a form of life, the explanation must certainly be found in the life of man. Hence the principle of religious immanence is formulated. Moreover, the first actuation, so to say, of every vital phenomenon, and religion, as has been said, belongs to this category, is due to a certain necessity or impulsion; but it has its origin, speaking more particularly of life, in a movement of the heart, which movement is called a sentiment. Therefore, since God is the object of religion, we must conclude that faith, which is the basis and the foundation of all religion, consists in a sentiment which originates from a need of the divine. This need of the divine, which is experienced only in special and favorable circumstances, cannot of itself appertain to the domain of consciousness; it is at first latent within the consciousness, or, to borrow a term from modern philosophy, in the subconsciousness, where also its roots lie hidden and undetected.

104 Should any one ask how it is that this need of the divine which man experiences within himself grows up into a religion, the modernists reply thus: Science and history, they say, are confined within two limits, the one external, namely, the visible world, the other internal, which is consciousness. When one or other of these boundaries has been reached, there can be no further progress, for beyond is the unknowable. In presence of this unknowable, whether it is outside man and beyond the visible world of nature or lies hidden

within the subconsciousness, the need of the divine, according to the principles of fideism, excites in a soul with a propensity towards religion a certain special sentiment, without any previous advertence of the mind: and this sentiment possesses, implied within itself both as its own object and as its intrinsic cause, the reality of the divine, and in a way unites man with God. It is this sentiment to which modernists give the name of faith, and this it is which they consider the beginning of religion.

105 But we have not yet come to the end of their philosophy, or, to speak more accurately, their folly. For modernism finds in this sentiment not faith only, but with and in faith, as they understand it, revelation, they say, abides. For what more can one require for revelation? Is not that religious sentiment which is perceptible in the consciousness revelation, or at least the beginning of revelation? Nay, is not God Himself, as He manifests Himself to the soul, indistinctly it is true, in this same religious sense, revelation? And they add: Since God is both the object and the cause of faith, this revelation is at the same time of God and from God; that is, God is both the revealer and the revealed.

106 Hence, Venerable Brethren, springs that ridiculous proposition of the modernists, that every religion, according to the different aspect under which it is viewed, must be considered as both natural and supernatural. Hence it is that they make consciousness and revelation synonymous. Hence the law, according to which religious consciousness is given as the universal rule, to be put on an equal footing with revelation, and to which all must submit, even the supreme authority of the Church, whether in its teaching capacity or in that of legislator in the province of sacred liturgy or discipline.

107 However, in all this process, from which, according to the modernists, faith and revelation spring, one point is to be particularly noted, for it is of capital importance on account of the historico-critical corollaries which are deduced from it.—For the unknowable they talk of does not present itself to faith as something solitary and isolated, but rather in close conjunction with some phenomenon, which, though it belongs to the realm of science and history, yet to some

extent oversteps their bounds. Such a phenomenon may be a fact of nature containing within itself something mysterious; or it may be a man, whose character, actions and words cannot, apparently, be reconciled with the ordinary laws of history. Then faith, attracted by the unknowable, which is united with the phenomenon, possesses itself of the whole phenomenon, and, as it were, permeates it with its own life. From this two things follow. The first is a sort of transfiguration of the phenomenon, by its elevation above its own true conditions, by which it becomes more adapted to that form of the divine which faith will infuse into it. The second is a kind of disfigurement, which springs from the fact that faith, which has made the phenomenon independent of the circumstances of place and time, attributes to it qualities which it has not; and this is true particularly of the phenomena of the past, and the older they are, the truer it is. From these two principles the modernists deduce two laws, which, when united with a third which they have already got from agnosticism, constitute the foundation of historical criticism. We will take an illustration from the person of Christ. In the person of Christ, they say, science and history encounter nothing that is not human. Therefore, in virtue of the first canon deduced from agnosticism, whatever there is in His history suggestive of the divine must be rejected. Then, according to the second canon, the historical person of Christ was transfigured by faith; therefore, everything that raises it above historical conditions must be removed. Lastly, the third canon, which lays down that the person of Christ has been disfigured by faith, requires that everything should be excluded deeds and words and all else that is not in keeping with His character, circumstances and education, and with the place and time in which He lived. A strange style of reasoning, truly; but it is modernist criticism.

108 Therefore, the religious sentiment, which through the agency of vital immanence emerges from the lurking-places of the subconsciousness, is the germ of all religion, and the explanation of everything that has been or ever will be in any religion. This sentiment, which was at first only rudimentary and almost formless, gradually matured, under the

influence of that mysterious principle from which it originated, with the progress of human life, of which as has been said, it is a form. This, then, is the origin of all religion, even supernatural religion; it is only a development of this religious sentiment. Nor is the Catholic religion an exception; it is quite on a level with the rest, for it was engendered, by the process of vital emmanence, in the consciousness of Christ, who was a man of the choicest nature, whose like has never been, nor will be.—Those who hear these audacious, these sacrilegious assertions are simply shocked. And yet, Venerable Brethren, these are not merely the foolish babblings of infidels. There are many Catholics, yea, and priests, too, who say these things openly; and they boast that they are going to reform the Church by these ravings! There is no question now of the old error, by which a sort of right to the supernatural order was claimed for the human nature. We have gone far beyond that: we have reached the point when it is affirmed that our most holy religion, in the man Christ as in us, emanated from nature spontaneously and entirely. Than this there is surely nothing more destructive of the whole supernatural order. Wherefore the Vatican Council most justly decreed: "If any one says that man cannot be raised by God to a knowledge and perfection which surpasses nature, but that he can and should, by his own efforts and by a constant development, attain finally to the possession of all truth and good, let him be anathema" (*De Revel.*, can. 3).

109

So far, Venerable Brethren, there has been no mention of the intellect. Still it also, according to the teaching of the modernists, has its part in the act of faith. And it is of importance to see how.—in the sentiment of which we have frequently spoken, since sentiment is not knowledge, God indeed presents Himself to man, but in a manner so confused and indistinct that He can hardly be perceived by the believer. It is therefore necessary that a ray of light should be cast upon this sentiment, so that God may be clearly distinguished and set apart from it. This is the task of the intellect, whose office it is to reflect and to analyze, and by means of which man first transforms into mental pictures the vital phenomena which arise within him, and then expresses them in words. Hence the common saying of modernists: that the religious man must ponder his faith.—The intellect, then, encountering this sentiment, directs itself upon it, and produces in it a work resembling that of a painter who restores and gives new life to a picture that has perished with age. The simile is that of one of the leaders of modernism. The operation of the intellect in this work is a double one: First, by a natural and spontaneous act it expresses its concept in a simple, ordinary statement; then, on reflection and deeper consideration, or, as they say, by elaborating its thought, it expresses the idea in secondary propositions, which are derived from the first, but are more perfect and distinct. These secondary propositions, if they finally receive the approval of the supreme magisterium of the Church, constitute dogma.

110 Thus we have reached one of the principal points in the modernists' system, namely, the origin and the nature of dogma. For they place the origin of dogma in those primitive and simple formulas, which, under a certain aspect, are necessary to faith; for revelation, to be truly such, requires the clear manifestation of God in the consciousness. But dogma itself, they apparently hold, is contained in the secondary formulas.

111 To ascertain the nature of dogma we must first find the relation which exists between the religious formulas and the religious sentiment. This will be readily perceived by him who realizes that these formulas have no other purpose than to furnish the believer with a means of giving an account of his faith to himself. These formulas therefore stand midway between the believer and his faith; in their relation to the faith they are the inadequate expression of its object, and are usually called symbols; in their relation to the believer they are mere instruments.

112 Hence it is quite impossible to maintain that they express absolute truth, for, in so far as they are symbols, they are the images of truth, and so must be adapted to the religious sentiment in its relation to man; and as instruments they are the vehicles of truth, and must therefore in their turn be adapted to man in his relation to the religious sentiment. But

the object of the religious sentiment, since it embraces the absolute, possesses an infinite variety of aspects, of which now one, now another, may present itself. In like manner, he who believes may pass through different phases. Consequently the formulas, too, which we call dogmas, must be subject to these vicissitudes, and are therefore liable to change. Thus the way is open to the intrinsic evolution of dogma. An immense collection of sophisms this, that ruins and destroys all religion. Dogma is not only able, but ought to evolve and to be changed. This is strongly affirmed by the modernists, and as clearly flows from their principles. For amongst the chief points of their teaching is this which they deduce from the principle of vital immanence: that religious formulas, to be really religious and not merely theological speculations, ought to be living and to live the life of the religious sentiment. This is not to be understood in the sense that these formulas, especially if merely imaginative, were to be made for the religious sentiment; it has no more to do with their origin than with number or quality; what is necessary is that the religious sentiment, when needful, introduced some modification, should vitally assimilate them. In other words, it is necessary that the primitive formula be accepted and sanctioned by the heart; and, similarly, the subsequent work from which spring the secondary formulas must proceed under the guidance of the heart. Hence it comes that these formulas, to be living, should be, and should remain, adapted to the faith and to him who believes. Wherefore, if for any reason this adaptation should cease to exist, they lose their first meaning, and accordingly must be changed. And since the character and lot of dogmatic formulas is so precarious, there is not room for surprise that modernists regard them so lightly and in such open disrespect. And so they audaciously charge the Church both with taking the wrong road from inability to distinguish the religious and moral sense of formulas from their surface meaning and with clinging tenaciously and vainly to meaningless formulas whilst religion is allowed to go to ruin. Blind that they are, and leaders of the blind, inflated with a boastful science, they have reached that pitch of folly where they pervert the eternal concept of truth and the true nature of the religious sentiment; with that new system of theirs they are seen to be under the sway of a blind and unchecked passion for novelty, thinking not at all of finding some solid foundation of truth, but despising the holy and apostolic traditions, they embrace other vain, futile, uncertain doctrines condemned by the Church, on which, in the height of their vanity, they think they can rest and maintain truth itself. (Gregory XVI., Encyl. "*Singulari Nos.*" 7 Kal., Jul., 1834.)

113 Thus far, Venerable Brethren, of the modernist considered as philosopher. Now if we proceed to consider him as believer, seeking to know how the believer, according to modernism, is differentiated from the philosopher, it must be observed that although the philosopher recognizes as the object of faith the divine reality, still this reality is not to be found but in the heart of the believer, as being an object of sentiment and affirmation: and therefore confined within the sphere of phenomena. But as to whether it exists outside that sentiment and affirmation is a matter which in no way concerns the philosopher. For the modernist believer, on the contrary, it is an established and certain fact that the divine reality does really exist in itself and quite independently of the person who believes in it. If you ask on what foundation this assertion of the believer rests, they answer: In the experience of the individual. On this head the modernists differ from the rationalists only to fall into the opinion of the Protestants and pseudomystics. This is their manner of putting the question: In the religious sentiment one must recognize a kind of intuition of the heart which puts man in immediate contact with the very reality of God, and infuses such a man in immediate contact with the very reality of God, and infuses such a persuasion of God's existence and His action both within and without man as to excel greatly any scientific conviction. They assert, therefore, the existence of a real experience, and one of a kind that surpasses all rational experience. If this experience is denied by some, like the rationalists, it arises from the fact that such persons are unwilling to put themselves in the moral state which is necessary to produce it. It is this experience which, when a

person acquires it, makes him properly and truly a believer.

114

How far off we are here from Catholic teaching we have already seen in the decree of the Vatican Council. We shall see later how, with such theories, added to the other errors already mentioned, the way is opened wide for atheism. Here it is well to note at once that, given this doctrine of experience, united with the other doctrine of symbolism, every religion, even that of paganism, must be held to be true. What is to prevent such experiences from being met with in every religion? In fact, that they are to be found is asserted by not a few. And with what right will modernists deny the truth of an experience affirmed by a follower of Islam? With what right can they claim true experiences for Catholics alone? Indeed, modernists do not deny, but actually admit, some confusedly, others in the most open manner, that all religions are true. That they cannot feel otherwise is clear. For on what ground, according to their theories, could falsity be predicated of any religion whatsoever? It must be certainly on one of these two: either on account of the falsity of the religious sentiment or on account of the falsity of the formula pronounced by the mind. Now, the religious sentiment, although it may be more perfect or is less perfect, is always one and the same; and the intellectual formula, in order to be true, has but to respond to the religious sentiment and to the believer, whatever be the intellectual capacity of the latter. In the conflict between different religions, the most that modernists can maintain is that the Catholic has more truth because it is more living, and that it deserves with more reason the name of Christian because it corresponds more fully with the origins of Christianity. That these consequences flow from the premises will not seem unnatural to anybody. But what is amazing is that there are Catholics and priests who, we would fain believe, abhor such enormities, yet act as if they fully approved of them. For they heap such praise and bestow such public honor on the teachers of these errors as to give rise to the belief that their admiration is not meant merely for the persons, who are perhaps not devoid of a certain merit, but rather for the errors which these persons openly profess, and which they do all in their power to propagate.

115 But this doctrine of experience is also under another aspect entirely contrary to Catholic truth. It is extended and applied to tradition, as hitherto understood by the Church, and destroys it. By the modernists tradition is understood as a communication to others, through preaching, by means of the intellectual formula, of an original experience. To this formula, in addition to its representative value, they attribute a species of suggestive efficacy which acts both in the person who believes to stimulate the religious sentiment should it happen to have grown sluggish and to renew the experience once acquired, and in those who do not yet believe to awake for the first time the religious sentiment in them and to produce the experience. In this way is religious experience propagated among the peoples; and not merely among contemporaries by preaching, but among future generations both by books and by oral transmission from one to another. Sometimes this communication of religious experience takes root and thrives, at other times it withers at once and dies. For the modernists to live is a proof of truth, since for them life and truth are one and the same thing. Hence again it is given to us to infer that all existing religions are equally true, for otherwise they would not live.

116 Having reached this point, Venerable Brethren, we have sufficient material in hand to enable us to see the relations which modernists establish between faith and science, including history and also under the name of science. And in the first place it is to be held that the object of the one is quite extraneous to and separate from the object of the other. For faith occupies itself solely with something which science declares to be unknowable for it. Hence each has a separate field assigned to it: science is entirely concerned with the reality of phenomena, into which faith does not enter at all; faith, on the contrary, concerns itself with the divine reality, which is entirely unknown to science. Thus the conclusion is reached that there can never be any dissension between faith and science, for if each keeps on its own ground they can never meet, and therefore never be in contradiction. And if it be objected that in the visible world there are some things which appertain to faith, such as the

human life of Christ, the modernists reply by denying this. For though such things come within the category of phenomena, still in as far as they are lived by faith and in the way already described have been by faith transfigured, and disfigured, they have been removed from the world of sense and translated to become material for the divine. Hence should it be further asked whether Christ was wrought real miracles, and made real prophecies, whether He rose truly from the dead and ascended into heaven, the answer of agnostic science will be in the negative and the answer of faith in the affirmative—yet there will not be on that account any conflict between them. For it will be denied by the philosopher as philosopher, speaking to philosophers and considering Christ only in His historical reality; and it will be affirmed by the believer, speaking to believers and considering the life of Christ as lived again by the faith and in the faith.

117 Yet it would be a great mistake to suppose that, given these theories, one is authorized to believe that faith and science are dependent of one another. On the side of science the independence is indeed complete, but it is quite different with regard to faith, which is subject to science not on one, but on three grounds. For in the first place it must be observed that in every religious fact, when you take away the divine reality and the experience of it which the believer possesses, everything else, and especially the religious formulas of it, belongs to the sphere of phenomena, and therefore falls under the control of science. Let the believer leave the world if he will, but so long as he remains in it he must continue, whether he like it or not, to be subject to the laws, the observation, the judgments of science and of history. Further, when it is said that God is the object of faith alone, the statement refers only to the divine reality, not to the idea of God. The latter also is subject to science, which while it philosophizes in what is called the logical order, soars also to the absolute and the ideal. It is therefore the right of philosophy and of science to form conclusions concerning the idea of God, to direct it in its evolution and to purify it of any extraneous elements which may become confused with it.

Finally, man does not suffer a dualism to exist in him, and the believer therefore feels within him an impelling need so to harmonize faith with science that it may never oppose the general conception which science sets forth concerning the universe.

118 Thus it is evident that science is to be entirely independent of faith, while, on the other hand, and notwithstanding that they are supposed to be strangers to each other, faith is made subject to science. All this, Venerable Brothers, is in formal opposition with the teachings of our predecessor, Pius IX., where he lays it down that: In matters of religion it is the duty of philosophy not to command, but to serve; not to prescribe what is to be believed, but to embrace what is to be believed with reasonable obedience; not to scrutinize the depths of the mysteries of God, but to venerate them devoutly and humbly. (Brev. ad Ep. Wratislaw, 15 Jun., 1857.)

119 The modernists completely invert the parts, and to them may be applied the words of another predecessor of ours, Gregory IX., addressed to some theologians of his time: "Some among you, inflated like bladders with the spirit of vanity, strive by profane novelties to cross the boundaries fixed by the fathers, twisting the sense of the heavenly pages. . . . to the philosophical teaching of the rationals, not for the profit of their hearers, but to make a show of science . . . these, seduced by strange and eccentric doctrines, make the head of the tail and force the queen to serve the servent." (Ep. ad. Magistros theol. Paris non, Jul., 1224.)

120 This becomes still clearer to anybody who studies the conduct of modernists, which is in perfect harmony with their teachings. In their writings and addresses they seem not unfrequently to advocate now one doctrine, now another, so that one would be disposed to regard them as vague and doubtful. But there is a reason for this, and it is to be found in their ideas as to the mutual separation of science and faith. Hence in their books you find some things which might well be expressed by a Catholic, but in the next page you find other things which might have been dictated by a rationalist. When they write history, they make no mention of the divinity of Christ, but when they are in the pulpit they pro-

fess it clearly. Again, when they write history they pay no heed to the fathers and the councils, but when they catechize the people, they cite them respectfully. In the same way they draw their distinctions between theological and pastoral exegesis and scientific and historical exegesis. So, too, acting on the principle that science in no way depends upon faith, when they treat of philosophy, history, criticism, feeling no horror at treading in the footsteps of Luther." (Prop. 29 damn. a Leone X. Bull, "*Exsurge Domine,*" 16 mail 1520. "*Via nobis facta est enervandi auctoritatem Conciliorum, et libere contradicendi eorum gestis, et iudicanti corum decreta, et confidenter confletendi quidquid verum videtur, sive probatum fuerit, sive reprobatum a quocumque Concilio.*") They are wont to display a certain contempt for Catholic doctrines, for the Holy Fathers, for the Ecumenical Councils, for the ecclesiastical magisterium; and should they be rebuked for this, they complain that they are being deprived of their liberty. Lastly, guided by the theory that faith must be subject to science, they continuously and openly criticize the Church because of her sheer obstinacy in refusing to submit and accommodate her dogmas to the opinions of philosophy; while they, on their side, after having blotted out the old theology, endeavor to introduce a new theology which shall follow the vagaries of their philosophers.

121 And thus, Venerable Brethren, the road is open for us to study the modernists in the theological arena—a difficult task, yet one that may be disposed of briefly. The end to be attained is the conciliation of faith with science, always, however, saving the primacy of science over faith. In this branch the modernist theologian avails himself of exactly the same principles which we have seen employed by the modernist philosopher, and applies them to the believer: the principles of immanence and symbolism. The process is an extremely simple one. the philosopher has declared: The principle of faith is immanent; the believer has added: This principle is God; and the theologian draws the conclusion: God is immanent in man. Thus we have theological immanence. So, too, the philosopher regards as certain that the representations of the object of faith are merely symbolical; the be-

liever has affirmed that the object of faith is God in Himself; and the theologian proceeds to affirm that the representations of the divine reality are symbolical. And thus we have theological symbolism. Truly enormous errors both, the pernicious character of which will be seen clearly from an examination of their consequences. For, to begin with symbolism, since symbols are but symbols in regard to their objects, and only instruments in regard to the believer, it is necessary, first of all, according to the teachings of the modernists, that the believer do not lay too much stress on the formula, but avail himself of it only with the scope of uniting himself to the absolute truth which the formula at once reveals and conceals; that is to say, endeavors to express, but without succeeding in doing so. They would also have the believer avail himself of the formulas only in as far as they are useful to him, for they are given to be a help and not a hindrance: with proper regard, however, for the social respect due to formulas which the public magisterium has deemed suitable for expressing the common consciousness until such time as the same magisterium provide otherwise. Concerning immanence, it is not easy to determine what modernists mean by it, for their own opinions on the subject vary. Some understand it in the sense that God working in man is more intimately present in him than man is in even himself, and this conception, if properly understood, is free from reproach. Others hold that the divine action is one with the action of nature, as the action of the first cause is one with the action of the secondary cause, and this would destroy the supernatural order. Others, finally, explain it in a way which savors of pantheism, and this, in truth, is the sense which tallies best with the rest of their doctrines.

122 With this principle of immanence is connected another, which may be called the principle of divine permanence. It differs from the first in much the same way as the private experience differs from the experience transmitted by tradition. An example will illustrate what is meant, and this example is offered by the Church and the sacraments. The Church and the sacraments, they say, are not to be regarded as having been instituted by Christ Himself. This is for-

bidden by agnosticism, which sees in Christ nothing more than a man whose religious consciousness has been like that of all men, formed by degrees; it is also forbidden by the law of immanence, which rejects what they call external application; it is further forbidden by the law of evolution, which requires for the development of the germs a certain time and a certain series of circumstances; it is, finally, forbidden by history, which shows that such, in fact, has been the course of things. Still, it is to be held that both Church and sacraments have been founded mediately by Christ. But how? In this way: All Christian consciences were, they affirm, in a manner virtually included in the conscience of Christ as the plant is included in the seed. But as the shoots live the life of the seed, so, too, all Christians are to be said to live the life of Christ. But the life of Christ is according to faith, and so, too, is the life of Christians. And since this life produced, in the course of ages, both the Church and the sacraments, it is quite right to say that their origin is from Christ and is divine. In the same way they prove that the Scriptures and the dogmas are divine. And thus the modernistic theology may be said to be complete. No great thing, in truth, but more than enough for the theologian who professes that the conclusions of science must always, and in all things, be respected. The application of these theories to the other points we shall proceed to expound anybody may easily make for himself.

123 Thus far we have spoken of the origin and nature of faith. But as faith has many shoots, and chief among them the Church dogma, worship, the books which we call "sacred," of these also we must know what is taught by the modernists. To begin with dogma, we have already indicated its origin and nature. Dogma is born of the species of impulse or necessity, by virtue of which the believer is constrained to elaborate his religious thought so as to render it clearer for himself and others. This elaboration consists entirely in the process of penetrating and refining the primative formula, not indeed in itself and according to logical development, but as required by circumstances, or vitally, as the modernists more abstrusely put it. Hence it happens that around the

primitive formula secondary formulas gradually continue to be formed, and these subsequently grouped into bodies of doctrine, or into doctrinal constructions, as they prefer to call them, and further sanctioned by the public magisterium as responding to the common consciousness, are called dogma. Dogma is to be carefully distinguished from the speculations of theologians, which, although not alive with the life of dogma, are not without their utility as serving to harmonize religion with science and remove opposition between the two in such a way as to throw light from without on religion, and it may be even to prepare the matter for future dogma. Concerning worship there would not be much to be said were it not that under this head are comprised the sacraments, concerning which the modernists fall into the gravest errors. For them the sacraments are the resultant of a double need—for, as we have seen, everything in their system is explained by inner impulses or necessities. In the present case the first need is that of giving some sensible manifestation to religion; the second is that of propagating it, which could not be done without some sensible form and consecrating acts, and these are called sacraments. But for the modernists the sacraments are mere symbols or signs, though not devoid of a certain efficacy—an efficacy, they tell us, like that of certain phrases vulgarly described as having "caught on," inasmuch as they have become the vehicle for the diffusion of certain great ideas which strike the public mind. What the phrases are to the ideas, that the sacraments are to the religious sentiment—that and nothing more. The modernists would be speaking more clearly were they to affirm that the sacraments are instituted solely to foster the faith—but this is condemned by the Council of Trent: "If any one say that these sacraments are instituted solely to foster the faith, let him be anathema." (Sess. VII. *de Sacramentis in genere*, can 5.)

124 We have already touched upon the nature and origin of the sacred books. According to the principles of the modernists, they may be rightly described as a collection of experiences; not indeed of the kind that may come to anybody, but those extraordinary and striking ones which have happened in any

religion. And this is precisely what they teach about our books of the Old and New Testament. But to suit their own theories they note with remarkable ingenuity that, although experience is something belonging to the present, still it may derive its material from the past and the future alike, inasmuch as the believer by memory lives the past over again after the manner of the present, and lives the future already by anticipation. This explains how it is that the historical and apocalyptical books are included among the sacred writings. God does indeed speak in these books—through the medium of the believer, but only, according to modernistic theology, by vital immanence and permanence. Do we inquire concerning inspiration? Inspiration, they reply, is distinguished only by its vehemence from that impulse which stimulates the believer to reveal the faith that is in him by words or writing. It is something like what happens in poetical inspiration, of which it has been said: "There is a God in us, and when He stirreth He sets us afire." And it is precisely in this sense that God is said to be the origin of the inspiration of the sacred books. The modernists affirm, too, that there is nothing in these books which is not inspired. In this respect some might be disposed to consider them as more orthodox than certain other moderns, who somewhat restrict inspiration, as, for instance, in what have been put forward as tacit citations. But it is all mere juggling of words. For if we take the Bible, according to the tenets of agnosticism, to be a human work, made by men for men, but allowing the theologian to proclaim that it is divine by immanence, what room is there left in it for inspiration? General inspiration in the modernist sense it is easy to find, but of inspiration in the Catholic sense there is not a trace.

125 A wider field for comment is opened when you come to treat of the vagaries devised by the modernist school concerning the Church. You must start with the supposition that the Church has its birth in a double need, the need of the individual believer, especially if he has had some original and special experience, to communicate his faith to others, and the need of the Mass when the faith has become common to many, to form itself into a society and to guard, increase and

propagate the common good. What, then, is the Church? It is the product of the collective conscience; that is to say, of the society of individual consciences which, by virtue of the principle of vital permanence, all depend on one first believer, who for Catholics is Christ. Now, every society needs a directing authority to guide its members towards the common end, to conserve prudently the elements of cohesion, which in a religious society are doctrine and worship. Hence the triple authority in the Catholic Church—disciplinary, dogmatic, liturgical. The nature of this authority is to be gathered from its origin, and its rights and duties from its nature. In past times it was a common error that authority came to the Church from without; that is to say, directly from God; and it was then rightly held to be autocratic. But this conception has now grown obsolete. For in the same way as the Church is a vital emanation of the collectivity of consciences, so, too, authority emanates vitally from the Church itself. Authority, therefore, like the Church, has its origin in the religious conscience, and, that being so, is subject to it. Should it disown this dependence, it becomes a tyranny. For we are living in an age when the sense of liberty has reached its fullest development, and when the public conscience has in the civil order introduced popular government. Now, there are not two consciences in man, any more than there are two lives. It is for the ecclesiastical authority, therefore, to shape itself to democratic forms, unless it wishes to provoke and foment an intentine conflict in the consciences of mankind. The penalty of refusal is disaster. For it is madness to think that the sentiment of liberty, as it is now spread abroad, can surrender. Were it forcibly confined and held in bonds, terrible would be its outburst, sweeping away at once both Church and religion. Such is the situation for the modernists, and their one great anxiety is, in consequence, to find a way of conciliation between the authority of the Church and the liberty of believers.

126 But it is not with its own members alone that the Church must come to an amicable arrangement—besides its relations with those within, it has others outside. The Church does not occupy the world all by itself; there are other societies in the

world, with which it must necessarily have contact and relations. The rights and duties of the Church towards civil societies must, therefore, be determined, and determined, of course, by its own nature, as it has been already described. The rules to be applied in this matter are those which have been laid down for science and faith, though in the latter case the question is one of objects, while here we have one of ends. In the same way, then, as faith and science are strangers to each other, by reason of the diversity of their objects, Church and State are strangers by reason of the diversity of their ends, that of the Church being spiritual, while that of the State is temporal. Formerly it was possible to subordinate the temporal to the spiritual, and to speak of some questions as mixed, allowing to the Church the position of queen and mistress in all such, because the Church was then regarded as having been instituted immediately by God as the author of the supernatural order. But this doctrine is to-day repudiated alike by philosophy and history. The State must, therefore, be separated from the Church, and the Catholic from the citizen. Every Catholic, from the fact that he is also a citizen, has the right and the duty to work for the common good in the way he thinks best, without troubling himself about the authority of the Church, without paying any heed to its wishes, its counsels, its orders—nay, even in spite of its reprimands. To trace out and prescribe for the citizen any line of conduct, on any pretext whatsoever, is to be guilty of an abuse of ecclesiastical authority, against which one is bound to act with all one's might. The principles from which these doctrines spring have been solemnly condemned by our predecessor, Pius VI., in his Constitution "*Austorem fidei.*" (Prop. 2. "*Proposito, quae statuit, potestatem a Deo datam Ecclesiae ut communicaretur Pastoribus, qui sunt eius ministri pro salute animarum; sic intellecta, ut a communitate fidelium in Pastores derivetur ecclesiastici ministerii ac regimminis potestas; haeretica.*"—Prop. 3. "*Insuper, quae statuit Romanum Pontificem esse caput ministeriale; sic explicata ut Romanus Pontifex non a Christo in persona beati Petri, sed ab Ecclesia potestatem ministerii accipiat, qua velut Petri successor, verus Christi vicarius ac totius Ecclesiae caput pollet in universa Ecclesia; haeretica.*")

127 But it is not enough for the modernist school that the State should be separated from the Church. For as faith is to be subordinated to science, as far as phenomenal elements are concerned, so, too, in temporal matters the Church must be subject to the State. They do not say this openly as yet, but they will say it when they wish to be logical on this head. For, given the principle that in temporal matters the State possesses absolute mastery, it will follow that when the believer, not fully satisfied with his merely internal acts of religion, proceeds to external acts, such, for instance, as the administration or reception of the sacraments, these will fall under the control of the State. What will then become of ecclesiastical authority, which can only be exercised by external acts? Obviously, it will be completely under the dominion of the State. It is this inevitable consequence which impels many among liberal Protestants to reject all external worship, nay, all external religious community, and makes them advocate what they call individual religion. If the modernists have not yet reached this point, they do ask the Church in the meanwhile to be good enough to follow spontaneously where they lead her and adapt herself to the civil forms in vogue. Such are their ideas about disciplinary authority. But far more advanced and far more pernicious are their teachings on doctrinal and dogmatic authority. This is their conception of the magisterium of the Church: No religious society, they say, can be a real unit unless the religious conscience of its members be one, and one also the formula which they adopt. But this double unity requires a kind of common mind, whose office is to find and determine the formula that corresponds best with the common conscience, and it must have, moreover, an authority sufficient to enable it to impose on the community the formula which has been decided upon. From the combination and, as it were, fusion of these two elements the common mind which draws up the formula and the authority which imposes it arises, according to the modernists, the notion of the ecclesiastical magisterium. And as this magisterium springs, in its last analysis, from the individual consciences and possesses its mandate of public utility for their benefit, it follows that the

ecclesiastical magisterium must be subordinate to them, and should therefore take democratic forms. To prevent individual consciences from revealing freely and openly the impulses they feel, to hinder criticism from impelling dogmas towards their necessary evolutions—this is not a legitimate use, but an abuse of a power given for the public utility. So, too, a due method and measure must be observed in the exercise of authority. To condemn and prescribe a work without the knowledge of the author, without hearing his explanations, without discussion assuredly savors of tyranny. And thus here again a way must be found to save the full rights of authority on the one hand and of liberty on the other. In the meanwhile the proper course for the Catholic will be to proclaim publicly his profound respect for authority—and continue to follow his own bent. Their general directions for the Church may be put in this way: Since the end of the Church is entirely spiritual, the religious authority should strip itself of all that external pomp which adorns it in the eyes of the public. And here they forget that while religion is essentially for the soul, it is not exclusively for the soul, and that the honor paid to authority is reflected back on Jesus Christ, who instituted it.

128 To finish with this whole question of faith and its shoots, it remains to be seen, Venerable Brethren, what the modernists have to say about their development. First of all, they lay down the general principle that in a living religion everything is subject to change, and must, in fact, change: and in this way they pass to what may be said to be among the chief of their doctrines, that of evolution. To the laws of evolution everything is subject—dogma, Church, worship, the books we revere as sacred, even faith itself—and the penalty of disobedience is death. The enunciation of this principle will not astonish anybody who bears in mind what the modernists have had to say about each of these subjects. Having laid down this law of evolution, the modernists themselves teach us how it works out. And first with regard to faith. The primitive form of faith, the tell us, was rudimentary and common to all men alike, for it had its origin in human nature and human life. Vital evoluation brought with it

progress, not by the accretion of new and purely adventitious forms from without, but by an increasing penetration of the religious sentiment in the conscience. This progress was of two kinds: negative, by the elimination of all foreign elements, such, for example, as the sentiment of family or nationality; and positive by that intellectual and moral refining of man, by means of which the idea was enlarged and enlightened, while the religious sentiment became more elevated and more intense. For the progress of faith no other causes are to be assigned than those which are adduced to explain its origin. But to them must be added those religious geniuses whom we call prophets, and of whom Christ was the greatest; both because in their lives and their words there was something mysterious which faith attributed to the divinity, and because it fell to their lot to have new and original experiences fully in harmony with the needs of their time. The progress of dogma is due chiefly to the obstacles which faith has to surmount, to the enemies it has to vanquish, to the contradictions it has to repel. Add to this a perpetual striving to penetrate ever more profoundly its own mysteries. Thus, to omit other examples, has it happened in the case of Christ: in Him that divine something which faith admitted in Him expanded in such a way that He was at last held to be God. The chief stimulus of evolution in the domain of worship consists in the need of adapting itself to the uses and customs of peoples, as well as the need of availing itself of the value which certain acts have acquired by long usage. Finally, evolution in the Church itself is fed by the need of accommodating itself to historical conditions and of harmonizing itself with existing forms of society. Such is religious evolution in detail. And here, before proceeding further, we would have you note well this whole theory of necessities and needs, for it is at the root of the entire system of the modernists, and it is upon it that they will erect that famous method of theirs called the historical.

129 Still continuing the consideration of the evolution of doctrine, it is to be noted that evolution is due no doubt to those stimulants styled needs, but if left to their action alone it would run a great risk of bursting the bounds of tradition,

and thus, turned aside from its primitive vital principle, would lead to ruin instead of progress. Hence, studying more closely the ideas of the modernists, evolution is described as resulting from the conflict of two forces, one of them tending towards progress, the other towards conservation. The conserving force in the Church is tradition, and tradition is represented by religious authority, and this both by right and in fact: for by right it is the very nature of authority to protect tradition, and, in fact, for authority, raised as it is above the contingencies of life, feels hardly or not at all the spurs of progress. The progressive force, on the contrary, which responds to the inner needs, lies in the individual conscience and ferments there—especially in such of them as are in most intimate contact with life. Note here, Venerable Brethren, the appearance already of that most pernicious doctrine which would make of the laity a factor of progress in the Church. Now, it is by a species of compromise between the forces of conservation and of progress—that is to say, between authority and individual consciences—that changes and advances take place. The individual consciences of some of them act on the collective conscience, which brings pressure to bear on the depositaries of authority until the latter consent to a compromise, and, the pact being made, authority sees to its maintenance.

130 With all this in mind, one understands how it is that the modernists express astonishment when they are reprimanded or punished. What is imputed to them as a fault they regard as a sacred duty. Being in intimate contact with consciences, they know better than anybody else, and certainly better than the ecclesiastical authority, what needs exist—nay, they embody them, so to speak, in themselves. Having a voice and a pen, they use both publicly, for this is their duty. Let authority rebuke them as much as it pleases, they have their own conscience on their side and an intimate experience which tells them with certainty that what they deserve is not blame, but praise. Then they reflect that, after all, there is no progress without a battle, and no battle without its victim; and victims they are willing to be, like the prophets and Christ Himself. They have no bitterness in their hearts against

the authority which uses them roughly, for, after all, it is only doing its duty as authority. Their sole grief is that it remains deaf to their warnings, because delay multiplies the obstacles which impede the progress of souls, but the hour will most surely come when there will be no further chance for tergiversation, for if the laws of evoluation may be checked for awhile, they cannot be ultimately destroyed. And so they go their way, reprimands and condemnations notwithstanding, masking an incredible audacity under a mock semblance of humility. While they make a show of bowing their heads, their hands and minds are more intent than ever on carrying out their purposes. And this policy they follow willingly and wittingly, both because it is part of their system that authority is to be stimulated, but not dethroned, and because it is necessary for them to remain within the ranks of the Church in order that they may gradually transform the collective conscience—thus unconsciously avowing that the common conscience is not with them, and that they have no right to claim to be its interpreters.

131 Thus, then, Venerable Brethren, for the modernists, both as authors and propagandists, there is to be nothing stable, nothing immutable in the Church. Nor, indeed, are they without precursors in their doctrines, for it was of these that our predecessor, Pius IX., wrote: "These enemies of divine revelation extol human progress to the skies, and with rash and sacrilegious daring would have it introduced into the Catholic religion, as if this religion were not the work of God, but of man, or some kind of philosophical discovery susceptible of perfection by human efforts." (Encycl. "*Qui pluribus,*" 9 Nov., 1846.) On the subject of revelation and dogma in particular, the doctrine of the modernists offers nothing new. We find it condemned in the syllabus of Pius IX., where it is enunciated in these terms: "Divine revelation is imperfect, and therefore subject to continual and indefinite progress, corresponding with the progress of human reason." (Syll. Prop. 5.) And condemned still more solemnly in the Vatican Council: "The doctrine of the faith which God has revealed has not been proposed to human

intelligences to be perfected by them as if it were a philosophical system, but as a divine deposit entrusted to the Spouse of Christ to be faithfully guarded and infallibly interpreted. Hence the sense, too, of the sacred dogmas is that which our Holy Mother the Church has once declared, nor is this sense ever to be abandoned on plea or pretext of a more profound comprehension of the truth." (Const. "*Dei Filius,*" cap. iv.) Nor is the development of our knowledge, even concerning the faith, impeded by this pronouncement; on the contrary, it is aided and promoted. For the same council continues: "Let intelligence and science and wisdom, therefore, increase and progress abundantly and vigorously in individuals and in the mass, in the believer and in the whole Church, throughout the ages and the centuries—but only in its own kind; that is, according to the same dogma, the same sense, the same acceptation." (Loc. cit.)

132 After having studied the modernist as philosopher, believer and theologian, it now remains for us to consider him as historian, critic, apologist, reformer.

133 Some modernists, devoted to historical studies, seem to be greatly afraid of being taken for philosophers. About philosophy, they tell you, they know nothing whatever—and in this they display remarkable astuteness, for they are particularly anxious not to be suspected of being prejudiced in favor of philosophical theories, which would lay them open to the charge of not being objective, to use the word in vogue. And yet the truth is that their history and their criticism are saturated with their philosophy, and that their historico-critical conclusions are the natural fruit of their philosophical principles. This will be patent to anybody who reflects. Their three first laws are contained in those three principles of their philosophy already dealt with: the principle of agnosticism, the principle of the transfiguration of things by faith, and the principle which we have called disfiguration. Let us see what consequences flow from each of them. Agnosticism tells us that history, like every other science, deals entirely with phenomena, and the consequence is that God, and every intervention of God in human affairs, is to be relegated to the domain of faith as belonging to it

alone. In things where a double element, the divine and the human, mingles—in Christ, for example, or the Church, or the sacraments, or the many other objects of the same kind, a division must be made and the human element assigned to history, while the divine will go to faith. Hence we have that distinction, so current among the modernists, between the Christ of history and the Christ of faith, between the Church of history and the Church of faith, between the sacraments of history and the sacraments of faith, and so on. Next we find that the human element itself, which the historian has to work on as it appears in the documents, has been by faith transfigured; that is to say, raised above its historical conditions. It becomes necessary, therefore, to eliminate also the accretions which faith has added, to assign them to faith itself and to the history of faith. Thus, when treating of Christ the historian must set aside all that surpasses man in his natural condition, either according to the psychological conception of him or according to the place and period of his existence. Finally, by virtue of the third principle even those things which are not outside the sphere of history they pass through the crucible, excluding from history and relegating to faith everything which, in their judgment, is not in harmony with what they call the logic of facts and in character with the persons of whom they are predicted. Thus, they will not allow that Christ ever uttered those things which do not seem to be within the capacity of the multitudes that listened to Him. Hence they delete from His real history and transfer to faith all the allegories found in His discourses. Do you inquire as to the criterion they adopt to enable them to make these divisions? The reply is that they argue from the character of the man, from his condition of life, from his education, from the circumstances under which the facts took place—in fact, from criteria which, when one considers them all, are purely subjective. Their method is to put themselves into the position and person of Christ, and then to attribute to Him what they would have done under like circumstances. In this way, absolutely a priori and acting on philosophical principles, which they admit they hold, but which they affect to ignore, they proclaim that Christ, according to what they call

His real history, was not God and never did anything divine, and that as man He did and said only what they, judging from the time in which He lived, can admit Him to have said or done.

134 And as history receives its conclusions ready-made from philosophy, so, too, criticism takes its own from history. The critic, on the data furnished him by the historian, makes two parts of all his documents. Those that remain after the triple elimination above described go to form the real history; the rest is attributed to the history of the faith, or, as it is styled, to internal history. For the modernists distinguish very carefully between these two kinds of history, and it is to be noted that they oppose the history of the faith to real history precisely as real. Thus we have a double Christ: a real Christ and a Christ, the one of faith, who never really existed; a Christ who has lived at a given time and in a given place and a Christ who has never lived outside the pious meditations of the believer—the Christ, for instance, whom we find in the Gospel of St. John, which is pure contemplation from beginning to end.

135 But the dominion of philosophy over history does not end here. Given that division, of which we have spoken, of the documents into two parts, the philosopher steps in again with his principle of vital immanence, and shows how everything in the history of the Church is to be explained by vital emanation. And since the cause or condition of every vital emanation whatsoever is to be found in some need, it follows that no fact can antedate the need which produced it—historically, the fact must be posterior to the need. See how the historian works on this principle. He goes over his documents again, whether they be found in the sacred books or elsewhere, draws up from them his list of the successive needs of the Church, whether relating to dogma or liturgy or other matters, and then he hands his list over to the critic. The critic takes in hand the documents dealing with the history of faith and distributes them, period by period, so that they correspond with the lists of needs, always guided by the principle that the narration must follow the facts, as the facts follow the needs. It may at times happen that some part of

the Sacred Scriptures, such as the Epistles, themselves constitute the fact created by the need. Even so, the rule holds that the age of any document can only be determined by the age in which each need has manifested itself in the Church. Further, a distinction must be made between the beginning of a fact and its development, for what is born one day requires time for growth. Hence the critic must once more go over his documents, ranged as they are through the different ages, and divide them again into two parts, and divide them into two lots, separating those that regard the first stage of the facts from those that deal with their development, and these he must again range according to their periods.

136 Then the philosopher must come in again to impose on the historian the obligation of following in all his studies the precepts and laws of evolution. It is next for the historian to scrutinize his documents and conditions affecting the Church during the different periods, the conserving force she has put forth, the needs, both internal and external, that have stimulated her to progress, the obstacles she has had to encounter; in a word, everything that helps to determine the manner in which the laws of evolution have been fulfilled in her. This done, he finishes his work by drawing up in its broad lines a history of the development of the facts. The critic follows and fits in the rest of the documents with this sketch; he takes up his pen and soon the history is made complete. Now we ask here: Who is the author of this history? The historian? The critic? Assuredly, neither of these, but the philosopher. From beginning to end everything in it is "a priori," and "a priori" in a way that reeks of heresy. These men are certainly to be pitied, and of them the apostle might well say: "They became vain in their thoughts . . . professing themselves to be wise, they became fools." (*Rom.* i., 21, 22.) But at the same time they excite just indignation when they accuse the Church of torturing the texts, arranging and confusing them after its own fashion, and for the needs of its cause. In this they are accusing the Church of something for which their own conscience plainly reproaches them.

137 The result of this dismembering of the sacred books and this partition of them throughout the centuries is naturally

that the Scriptures can no longer be attributed to the authors whose names they bear. The modernists have no hesitation in affirming commonly that these books, and especially the Pentateuch and the first three Gospels, have been gradually formed by additions to a primitive brief narration—by interpolations of theological or allegorical interpretation, by transitions, by joining different passages together. This means, briefly, that in the sacred books we must admit a vital evolution, springing from and corresponding with the evolution of faith. The traces of this evolution, they tell us, are so visible in the books that one might almost write a history of them. Indeed, this history they do actually write, and with such an easy security that one might believe them to have with their own eyes seen the writers at work through the ages amplifying the sacred books. To aid them in this they call to their assistance that branch of criticism which they call textual, and labor to show that such a fact or such a phrase is not in its right place, and adducing other arguments of the same kind. They seem, in fact, to have constructed for themselves certain types of narration and discourses, upon which they base their decision as to whether a thing is out of place or not. Judge if you can how men with such a system are fitted for practicing this kind of criticism. To hear them talk about their works on the sacred books, in which they have been able to discover so much that is defective, one would imagine that before them nobody ever even glanced through the pages of Scripture, whereas the truth is that a whole multitude of doctors, infinitely superior to them in genius, in erudition, in sanctity, have sifted the sacred books in every way, and so far from finding imperfections in them, have thanked God more and more the deeper they have gone into them for His divine bounty in having vouchsafed to speak thus to men. Unfortunately, these great doctors did not enjoy the same aids to study that are possessed by the modernists for their guide and rule—a philosophy borrowed from the negation of God, and a criterion which consists of themselves.

138 We believe, then, that we have set forth with sufficient clearness the historical method of the modernists. The

philosopher leads the way, the historian follows, and then in due order come internal and textual criticism. And since it is characteristic of the first cause to communicate its virtue to secondary causes, it is quite clear that the criticism we are concerned with is an agnostic, immanentist and evolutionist criticism. Hence anybody who embraces it and employs it makes profession thereby of the errors contained in it, and places himself in opposition to Catholic faith. This being so, one cannot but be greatly surprised by the consideration which is attached to it by certain Catholics. Two causes may be assigned for this: First, the close alliance, independent of all differences of nationality and religion, which the historians and critics of this school have formed among themselves; second, the boundless effrontery of these men. Let one of them but open his mouth and the others applaud him in chorus, proclaiming that science has made another step forward. Let an outsider but hint at a desire to inspect the new discovery with his own eyes, and they are on him in a body. Deny it, and you are an ignoramus; embrace it and defend it, and there is no praise too warm for you. In this way they win over many who, did they but realize what they are doing, would shrink back with horror. The impudence and the domineering of some, and the thoughtlessness and imprudence of others have combined to generate a pestilence in the air which penetrates everywhere and spreads the contagion. But let us pass to the apologist.

139 The modernist apologist depends in two ways on the philosopher. First, indirectly, inasmuch as his theme is history—history dictated, as we have seen, by the philosopher; and, secondly, directly, inasmuch as he takes both his laws and his principles from the philosopher. Hence that common precept of the modernist school that the new apologetics must be fed from psychological and historical sources. The modernist apologists, then, enter the arena by proclaiming to the rationalists that though they are defending religion, they have no intention of employing the data of the sacred books or the histories in current use in the Church, and composed according to old methods, but real history, written on modern principles and according to rigorously

modern methods. In all this they are not using an "argumentum ad hominem," but are stating the simple fact that they hold that the truth is to be found only in this kind of history. They feel that it is not necessary for them to dwell on their own sincerity in their writings—they are already known to and praised by the rationalists as fighting under the same banner, and they not only plume themselves on these encomiums, which are a kind of salary to them, but would only provoke nausea in a real Catholic, but use them as an offset to the reprimands of the Church.

140 But let us see how the modernist conducts his apologetics. The aim he sets before himself is to make the non-believer attain that experience of the Catholic religion which, according to the system, is the basis of faith. There are two ways open to him, the objective and the subjective. The first of them proceeds from agnosticism. It tends to show that religion, and especially the Catholic religion, is endowed with such vitality as to compel every psychologist and historian of good faith to recognize that its history hides some unknown element. To this end it is necessary to prove that this religion, as it exists to-day, is that which was founded by Jesus Christ; that is to say, that it is the product of the progressive development of the germ which He brought into the world. Hence it is imperative first of all to establish what this germ was, and this the modernist claims to be able to do by the following formula: Christ announced the coming of the kingdom of God, which was to be realized within a brief lapse of time, and of which He was to become the Messiah, the divinely-given agent and ordainer. Then it must be shown how this germ, always immanent and permanent in the bosom of the Church, has gone on slowly developing in the course of history, adapting itself successively to the different mediums through which it has passed, borrowing from them by vital assimilation all the dogmatic, cultutal, ecclesiastical forms that served its purpose; whilst, on the other hand, it surmounted all obstacles, vanquished all enemies and survived all assaults and all combats. Anybody who well and duly considers this mass of obstacles, adversaries, attacks, combats and the vitality and fecundity which the Church has shown

throughout them all must admit that if the laws of evolution are visible in her life, they fail to explain the whole of her history—the unknown rises forth from it and presents itself before us. Thus do they argue, never suspecting that their determination of the primitive germ is an "a priori" of agnostic and evolutionist philosophy, and that the formula of it has been gratuitously invented for the sake of buttressing their position.

141 But while they endeavor by this line of reasoning to secure access for the Catholic religion into souls, these new apologists are quite ready to admit that there are many distasteful things in it. Nay, they admit openly, and with ill-concealed satisfaction, that they have found that even its dogma is not exempt from errors and contradictions. They add also that this is not only excusable, but, curiously enough, even right and proper. In the sacred books there are many passages referring to science or history where manifest errors are to be found. But the subject of these books is not science or history, but religion and morals. In them history and science serve only as a species of covering to enable the religious and moral experiences wrapped up in them to penetrate more readily among the masses. The masses understood science and history as they are expressed in these books, and it is clear that had science and history been expressed in a more perfect form this would have proved rather a hindrance than a help. Then, again, the sacred books being essentially religious, are consequently necessarily living. Now, life has its own truth and its own logic—quite different from rational truth and rational logic, belonging as they do to a different order, viz., truth of adaptation and of proportion both with the medium in which it exists and with the end towards which it tends. Finally, the modernists, losing all sense of control, go so far as to proclaim as true and legitimate everything that is explained by life.

142 We, Venerable Brethren, for whom there is but one and only truth, and who hold that the sacred books, written under the inspiration of the Holy Ghost, have God for their author (Conc. Vat., *De Revel.*, c. 2), declare that this is equivalent to attributing to God Himself the lie of utility or

officious lie, and we say with St. Augustine: "In an authority so high, admit but one officious lie, and there will not remain a single passage of those apparently difficult to practice or to believe, which on the same most pernicious rule may not be explained as a lie uttered by the author willfully and to serve a purpose." (*Epist.* 28.) And thus it will come about, the holy doctor continues, that everybody will believe and refuse to believe what he likes or dislikes. But the modernists pursue their way gaily. They grant also that certain arguments adduced in the sacred books, like those, for example, which are based on the prophecies, have no rational foundation to rest on. But they will defend even these as artifices of preaching, which are justified by life. Do they stop here? No, indeed; for they are ready to admit, nay, to proclaim, that Christ Himself manifestly erred in determining the time when the coming of the kingdom of God was to take place, and they tell us that we must not be surprised at this, since even Christ was subject to the laws of life! After this, what is to become of the dogmas of the Church? The dogmas brim over with flagrant contradictions, but what matter that, since, apart from the fact that vital logic accepts them, they are not repugnant to symbolical truth. Are we not dealing with the infinite, and has not the infinite an infinite variety of aspects? In short, to maintain and defend these theories they do not hesitate to declare that the noblest homage that can be paid to the Infinite is to make it the object of contradictory propositions! But when they justify even contradictions, what is it that they will refuse to justify?

143 But it is not solely by objective arguments that the non-believer may be disposed to faith. There are also subjective ones at the disposal of the modernists, and for those they return to their doctrine of immanence. They endeavor, in fact, to persuade their non-believer that down in the very deeps of his nature and his life lie the need and the desire for religion, and this not a religion of any kind, but the specific religion known as Catholicism, which, they say, is absolutely postulated by the perfect development of life. And here we cannot but deplore once more, and grievously, that there are Catholics who, while rejecting immanence as a doctrine,

employ it as a method of apologetics, and who do this so imprudently that they seem to admit that there is in human nature a true and rigorous necessity with regard to the supernatural order—and not merely a capacity and a suitability for the supernatural, such as has at all times been emphasized by Catholic apologists. Truth to tell, it is only the moderate modernists who make this appeal to an exigency for the Catholic religion. As for the others, who might be called integralists, they would show to the non-believer, hidden away in the very depths of his being, the very germ which Christ Himself bore in His conscience, and which He bequeathed to the world. Such, Venerable Brethren, is a summary description of the apologetic method of the modernists, in perfect harmony, as you may see, with their doctrines—methods and doctrines brimming over with errors, made not for edification, but for destruction; not for the formulation of Catholics, but for the plunging of Catholics into heresy; methods and doctrines that would be fatal to any religion.

144 It remains for us now to say a few words about the modernist as reformer. From all that has preceded, some idea may be gained of the reforming mania which possesses them: in all Catholicism there is absolutely nothing on which it does not fasten. Reform of philosophy, especially in the seminaries: the scholastic philosophy is to be relegated to the history of philosophy among obsolete systems, and the young men are to be taught modern philosophy, which alone is true and suited to the times in which we live. Reform of theology: rational theology is to have modern philosophy for its foundation, and positive theology is to be founded on the history of dogma. As for history, it must be for the future written and taught only according to their modern methods and principles. Dogmas and their evolution are to be harmonized with science and history. In the catechism no dogmas are to be inserted except those that have been duly reformed and are within the capacity of the people. Regarding worship, the number of external devotions is to be reduced, or at least steps must be taken to prevent their further increase, though, indeed, some of the admirers of symbolism are disposed to be more indulgent on this head. Ecclesiastical government re-

quires to be reformed in all its branches, but especially in its disciplinary and dogmatic parts. Its spirit and its external manifestations must be put in harmony with the public conscience, which is now wholly for democracy; a share in ecclesiastical government should therefore be given to the lower ranks of the clergy, and even to the laity, and authority should be decentralized. The Roman congregations, and especially the Index and the Holy Office, are to be reformed. The ecclesiastical authority must change its line of conduct in the social and political world; while keeping outside political and social organization, it must adapt itself to those which exist in order to penetrate them with its spirit. With regard to morals, they adopt the principle of the Americanists, that the active virtues are more important than the passive, both in the estimation in which they must be held and in the exercise of them. The clergy are asked to return to their ancient lowliness and poverty, and in their ideas and action to be guided by the principles of modernism; and there are some who, echoing the teaching of their Protestant masters, would like the suppression of ecclesiastical celibacy. What is there left in the Church which is not to be reformed according to their principles?

145 It may be, Venerable Brethren, that some may think we have dwelt too long on this exposition of the doctrines of the modernists. But it was necessary, both in order to refute their customary charge that we do not understand their ideas and to show that their system does not consist in scattered and unconnected theories, but in a perfectly organized body, all the parts of which are solidly joined, so that it is not possible to admit one without admitting all. For this reason, too, we have had to give this exposition a somewhat didactic form and not to shrink from employing certain uncouth terms in use among the modernists. And now can anybody who takes a survey of the whole system be surprised that we should define it as the synthesis of all heresies? Were one to attempt the task of collecting together all the errors that have been broached against the faith and to concentrate the sap and substance of them all into one, he could not better succeed than the modernists have done. Nay, they have done more

than this, for, as we have already intimated, their system means the destruction not of the Catholic religion alone, but of all religion. With good reason do the rationalists applaud them, for the most sincere and the frankest among the rationalists warmly welcome the modernists as their most valuable allies.

146 For let us return for a moment, Venerable Brethren, to that most disastrous doctrine of agnosticism. By it every avenue that leads the intellect to God is barred, but the modernists would seek to open others available for sentiment and action. Vain efforts! For, after all, what is sentiment but the reaction of the soul on the action of the intelligence or the senses? Take away the intelligence, and man, already inclined to follow the senses, becomes their slave. Vain, too, from another point of view, for all these fantasias on the religious sentiment will never be able to destroy common sense, and common sense tells us that emotion and everything that leads the heart captive proves a hindrance instead of a help to the discovery of truth. We speak, of course, of truth in itself—as for that other purely subjective truth, the fruit of sentiment and action, if it serves its purpose for the jugglery of words, it is of no use to the man who wants to know above all things whether outside himself there is a God into whose hands he is one day to fall. True, the modernists do call in experience to eke out their system, but what does this experience add to sentiment? Absolutely nothing beyond a certain intensity and a proportionate deepening of the conviction of the reality of the object. But these two will never make sentiment into anything but sentiment, nor deprive it of its characteristic, which is to cause deception when the intelligence is not there to guide it; on the contrary, they but confirm and aggravate this characteristic, for the more intense sentiment is, the more it is sentimental. In matters of religious sentiment and religious experience, you know, Venerable Brethren, how necessary is prudence, and how necessary, too, the science which directs prudence. You know it from your own dealings with souls, and especially with souls in whom sentiment predominates; you know it also from your reading of ascetical books—books for which

the modernists have but little esteem, but which testify to a science and a solidity very different from theirs, and to a refinement and subtlety of observation of which the modernists give no evidence. Is it not really folly, or at least sovereign imprudence, to trust one's self without control to modernists' experiences? Let us for a moment put the question: If experiences have so much value in their eyes, why do they not attach equal weight to the experience that thousands upon thousands of Catholics have that the modernists are on the wrong road? Is it, perchance, that all experiences except those felt by the modernists are false and deceptive? The vast majority of mankind holds, and always will hold firmly, that sentiment and experience alone, when not enlightened and guided by reason, do not lead to the knowledge of God. What remains, then, but the annihilation of all religion—atheism? Certainly it is not the doctrine of symbolism that will save us from this. For if all the intellectual elements, as they call them, of religion are pure symbols, will not the very name of God or of divine personality be also a symbol? And if this be admitted, will not the personality of God become a matter of doubt and the way opened to pantheism? And to pantheism that other doctrine of the divine immanence leads directly. For does it, we ask, leave God distinct from man or not? If yes, in what does it differ from Catholic doctrine, and why reject external revelation? If no, we are at once in pantheism. Now, the doctrine of immanence in the modernist acceptation holds and professes that every phenomenon of conscience proceeds from man as man. The rigorous conclusion of this is the identity of man with God, which means pantheism. The same conclusion follows from the distinction modernists make between science and faith. The object of science, they say, is the reality of the knowable. Now, what makes the unknowable unknowable is its disproportion with the intelligible—a disproportion which nothing whatever, even in the doctrine of the modernists, can suppress. Hence the unknowable remains, and will eternally remain, unknowable to the believer as well as to the man of science. Therefore, if any religion at all is possible, it can only be the religion of an unknowable reality.

And why this religion might not be that universal soul of the universe, of which a rationalist speaks, is something we do not see. Certainly, this suffices to show superabundantly by how many roads modernism leads to the annihilation of all religion. The first step in this direction was taken by Protestism; the second is made by modernism; the next will plunge headlong into atheism.

147 To penetrate still deeper into modernism, and to find a suitable remedy for such a deep sore, it behooves us, Venerable Brethren, to investigate the causes which have engendered it and which foster its growth. That the proximate and immediate cause consists in a perversion of the mind cannot be open to doubt. The remote causes seem to us to be reduced to two: curiosity and pride. Curiosity by itself, if not prudently regulated, suffices to explain all errors. Such is the opinion of our predecessor, Gregory XVI., who wrote: "A lamentable spectacle is that presented by the aberrations of human reason when it yields to the spirit of novelty, when, against the warnings of the apostle, it seeks to know beyond what it is meant to know; and when relying too much on itself it thinks it can find the truth outside the Church, wherein truth is found without the slightest shadow of error." (Ep. Encycl. *Singulari* nos, 7 Kal., July, 1834.)

148 But it is pride which exercises an incomparably greater sway over the soul to blind it and plunge into error; and pride sits in modernism as in its own house, finding sustenance everywhere in its doctrines and an occasion to flaunt itself in all its aspects. It is pride which fills modernists with that confidence in themselves and leads them to hold themselves up as the rule for all, pride which puffs them up with that vainglory which allows them to regard themselves as the sole possessors of knowledge and makes them say, inflated with presumption, "We are not as the rest of men," and which, to make them really not as other men, leads them to embrace all kinds of the most absurd novelties. It is pride which rouses in them the spirit of disobedience, and causes them to demand a compromise between authority and liberty; it is pride that makes of them the reformers of others, while they forget to reform themselves, and which begets their absolute want of

respect for authority, not excepting the supreme authority. No, truly, there is no road which leads so directly and so quickly to modernism as pride. When a Catholic layman or a priest forgets that precept of the Christian life which obliges us to renounce ourselves if we would follow Jesus Christ, and neglects to tear pride from his heart, ah! but he is a fully ripe subject for the errors of modernism. Hence, Venerable Brethren, it will be your first duty to thwart such proud men, to employ them only in the lowest and obscurest offices; the higher they try to rise, the lower let them be placed, so that their lowly position may deprive them of the power of causing damage. Sound your young clerics, too, most carefully, by yourselves and by the directors of your seminaries, and when you find the spirit of pride among any of them, reject them without compunction from the priesthood. Would to God that this had always been done with the proper vigilance and constancy.

149 If we pass from the moral to the intellectual causes of modernism, the first which presents itself, and the chief one, is ignorance. Yes, these very modernists who pose as doctors of the Church, who puff out their cheeks when they speak of modern philosophy, and show such contempt for scholasticism, have embraced the one with all its false glamor because their ignorance of the other has left them without the means of being able to recognize confusion of thought, and to refute sophistry. Their whole system, with all its errors, has been born of the alliance between faith and false philosophy.

150 If only they had displayed less zeal and energy in propagating it! But such is their activity and such their unwearying capacity for work on behalf of their cause that one cannot but be pained to see them waste such labor in endeavoring to ruin the Church when they might have been of such service to her had their efforts been better employed. Their artifices to delude men's minds are of two kinds, the first to remove obstacles from their path, the second to devise and apply actively and patiently every instrument that can serve their purpose. They recognize that the three chief difficulties for them are scholastic philosophy, the authority of the fathers

and tradition, and the magisterium of the Church, and on these they wage unrelenting war. For scholastic philosophy and theology they have only ridicule and contempt. Whether it is ignorance or fear, or both, that inspires this conduct in them, certain it is that the passion for novelty is always united in them with hatred of scholasticism, and there is no surer sign that a man is on the way to modernism than when he begins to show his dislike for this system. Modernists and their admirers should remember the proposition condemned by Pius IX.: "The method and principles which have served the doctors of scholasticism when treating of theology no longer correspond with the exigencies of our time or the progress of science." (Syll. Prop. 13.) They exercise all their ingenuity in diminishing the force and falsifying the character of tradition, so as to rob it of all its weight. But for Catholics the second Council of Nicea will always have the force of law, where it condemns those "who dare, after the impious fashion of heretics, to deride the ecclesiastical traditions, to invent novelties of some kind . . . or endeavor by malice or craft to overthrow any of the legitimate traditions of the Catholic Church." And Catholics will hold for law also the profession of the fourth Council of Constantinople: "We therefore profess to conserve and guard the rules bequeathed to the Holy Catholic and Apostolic Church by the holy and most illustrious apostles, by the orthodox councils, both general and local, and by every one of those divine interpreters, the fathers and doctors of the Church." Wherefore, the Roman Pontiffs, Pius IV. and Pius IX., ordered the insertion in the profession of faith of the following declaration: "I most firmly admit and embrace the apostolic and ecclesiastical traditions and other observations and constitutions of the Church." The modernists pass the same judgment on the most holy fathers of the Church as they pass on tradition, decreeing, with amazing effrontery, that, while personally most worthy of all veneration, they were entirely ignorant of history and criticism, for which they are only excusable on account of the time in which they lived. Finally, the modernists try in every way to diminish and weaken the authority of the ecclesiastical magisterium itself by sacrilegiously falsifying its origin, character and rights, and by freely repeating the calumnies of its adversaries. To all the band of modernists may be applied those words which our predecessor wrote with such pain: "To bring contempt and odium on the mystic Spouse of Christ, who is the true light, the children of darkness have been wont to cast in her face before the world a stupid calumny, and perverting the meaning and force of things and words, to depict her as the friend of darkness and ignorance and the enemy of light, science and progress" (*Motu-proprio, Ut mysticum*, 14 March, 1891). This being so, Venereble Brethren, no wonder the modernists vent all their gall and hatred on Catholics who sturdily fight the battles of the Church. But of all the insults they heap on them, those of ignorance and obstinacy are the favorites. When an adversary rises up against them with an erudition and force that render him redoubtable, they try to make a conspiracy of silence around him to nullify the effects of his attack, while, in flagrant contrast with this policy towards Catholics, they load with constant praise the writers who range themselves on their side, hailing their works, exuding novelty in every page, with choruses of applause; for them the scholarship of a writer is in direct proportion to the recklessness of his attacks on antiquity, and of his efforts to undermine tradition and the ecclesiastical magisterium. When one of their number falls under the condemnations of the Church, the rest of them, to the horror of good Catholics, gather around him, heap public praise upon him, venerate him almost as a martyr of truth. The young, excited and confused by all this clamor of praise and abuse, some of them afraid of being branded as ignorant, others ambitious to be considered learned, and both classes, goaded internally by curiosity and pride, often surrender and give themselves up to modernism.

151 And here we have already some of the artifices employed by modernists to exploit their wares. What efforts they make to win new recruits! They seize upon chairs in the seminaries and universities, and gradually make of them chairs of pestilence. From these sacred chairs they scatter, though not always openly, the seeds of their doctrines; they proclaim their teachings without disguise in congresses; they introduce

them and make them the vogue in social institutions. Under their own names and under pseudonyms they publish numbers of books, newspapers, reviews, and sometimes one and the same writer adopts a variety of pseudonyms to trap the incautious reader into believing in a whole multitude of modernist writers—in short, they leave nothing untried, in action, discourses, writings, as though there was a frenzy of propaganda upon them. And the results of all this? We have to lament at the sight of many young men, once full of promise and capable of rendering great services to the Church, now gone astray. And there is another sight that saddens us, too—that of so many other Catholics who, while they certainly do not go so far as the former, have yet grown into the habit, as though they had been breathing a poisoned atmosphere, of thinking and speaking and writing with a liberty that ill becomes Catholics. They are to be found among the laity and in the ranks of the clergy, and they are not wanting even in the last place where one might expect to meet them—in religious institutes. If they treat of Biblical questions, it is upon modernist principles; if they write history, it is to search out with curiosity and to publish openly, on the pretext of telling the whole truth and with a species of ill-concealed satisfaction, everything that looks to them like a stain in the history of the Church. Under the sway of certain a priori rules, they destroy as far as they can the pious traditions of the people, and bring ridicule on certain relics highly venerable from their antiquity. They are possessed by the empty desire of being talked about, and they know they would never succeed in this were they to say only what has been always said. It may be that they have persuaded themselves that in all this they are really serving God and the Church—in reality they only offend both, less perhaps by their works themselves than by the spirit in which they write and by the encouragement they are giving to the extravagances of the modernists.

152 Against this host of grave errors, and its secret and open advance, our predecessor, Leo XIII., of happy memory, worked strenuously, especially as regards the Bible, both in his words and his acts. But, as we have seen, the modernists

are not easily deterred by such weapons; with an affectation of submission and respect they proceeded to twist the words of the Pontiff to their own sense, and his acts they described as directed against others than themselves. And the evil has gone on increasing from day to day. We therefore, Venerable Brethren, have determined to adopt at once the most efficacious measure in our power, and we beg and conjure you to see to it that in this most grave matter nobody will ever be able to say that you have been in the slightest degree wanting in vigilance, zeal or firmness. And what we ask of you and expect of you we ask and expect also of all other pastors of souls, of all educators and professors of clerics, and in a very special way of the superiors of religious institutions.

153 In the first place, with regard to studies, we will and ordain that scholastic philosophy be made the basis of the sacred sciences. It goes without saying that if anything is met with among the scholastic doctors which may be regarded as an excess of subtlety, or which is altogether destitute of probability, we have no desire whatever to propose it for the imitation of present generations. (Leo XIII. Enc. "*Aeterni patris*.") And let it be clearly understood above all things that the scholastic philosophy we prescribe is that which the Angelic Doctor has bequeathed to us, and we, therefore, declare that all the ordinances of our predecessor on this subject continue fully in force, and, as far as may be necessary, we do decree anew and confirm and ordain that they be by all strictly observed. In seminaries where they may have been neglected let the Bishops impose them and require their observance, and let this apply also to the superiors of religious institutions. Further, let professors remember that they cannot set St. Thomas aside, especially in metaphysical questions, without grave detriment.

154 On this philosophical foundation the theological edifice is to be solidly raised. Promote the study of theology, Venerable Brethren, by all means in your power, so that your clerics on leaving the seminaries may admire and love it, and always find their delight in it. For in the vast and varied abundance of studies opening before the mind desirous of truth everybody knows how the old maxim describes the-

ology as so far in front of all others that every science and art should serve it and be to it as handmaidens. (Leo XIII., Lett. ap. "In Magna," Dec. 10, 1889.) We will add that we deem worthy of praise those who, with full respect for tradition, the Holy Fathers and the ecclesiastical magisterium, undertake, with well-balanced judgment, and guided by Catholic principles (which is not always the case), seek to illustrate positive theology by throwing the light of true history upon it. Certainly, more attention must be paid to positive theology than in the past, but this must be done without detriment to scholastic theology, and those are to be disapproved as of modernist tendencies who exalt positive theology in such a way as to seem to despise the scholastic.

155 With regard to profane studies, suffice it to recall here what our predecessor has admirably said: "Apply yourselves energetically to the study of natural sciences: the brilliant discoveries and the bold and useful applications of them made in our times, which have won such applause by our contemporaries, will be an object of perpetual praise for those that come after us." (Leo XIII. Alloc., March 7, 1880.) But this do without interfering with sacred studies, as our predecessor in these most grave words prescribed: "If you carefully search for the cause of those errors, you will find that it lies in the fact that in these days, when the natural sciences absorb so much study, the more severe and lofty studies have been proportionately neglected; some of them have almost passed into oblivion, some of them are pursued in a half-hearted or superficial way, and, sad to say, now that they are fallen from their old estate, they have been disfigured by perverse doctrines and monstrous errors (*loco cit*). We ordain, therefore, that the study of natural science in the seminaries be carried on under this law."

156 All these prescriptions and those of our predecessor are to be borne in mind whenever there is question of choosing directors and professors for seminaries and Catholic universities. Anybody who in any way is found to be imbued with modernism is to be excluded without compunction from these offices, and those who already occupy them are to be withdrawn. The same policy is to be adopted towards those

who favor modernism either by extolling the modernists or excusing their culpable conduct, by criticizing scholasticism, the Holy Father, or by refusing obedience to ecclesiastical authority in any of its depositories: and towards those who show a love of novelty in history, archaeology, Biblical exegesis, and finally towards those who neglect the sacred sciences or appear to prefer them to the profane. In all this question of studies, Venerable Brethren, you cannot be too watchful or too constant, but most of all in the choice of professors, for as a rule the students are modeled after the pattern of their masters. Strong in the consciousness of your duty, act always prudently, but vigorously.

157 Equal diligence and severity are to be used in examining and selecting candidates for holy orders. Far, far from the clergy be the love of novelty: God hates the proud and the obstinate. For the future the doctorate of theology and canon law must never be conferred on anybody who has not made the regular course of scholastic philosophy; if conferred, it shall be held as null and void. The rules laid down in 1896 by the Sacred Congregation of Bishops and Regulars for the clerics, both secular and regular, of Italy, concerning the frequenting of the universities, we now decree to be extended to all nations. Clerics and priests inscribed in a Catholic institute or university must not in the future follow in civil universities those courses for which there are chairs in the Catholic institutes to which they belong. If this has been permitted anywhere in the past, we ordain that it be not allowed for the future. Let the Bishops who form the governing board of such Catholic institutes or universities watch with all care that these our commands be constantly observed.

158 It is also the duty of the Bishops to prevent writings infected with modernism or favorable to it from being read when they have been published, and to hinder their publication when they have not. No book or paper or periodical of this kind must ever be permitted to seminarists or university students. The injury to them would be equal to that caused by immoral reading—nay, it would be greater, for such writings poison Christian life at its very fount. The same decision is to be taken concerning the writings of some

Catholics, who, though not badly disposed themselves, but ill instructed in theological studies and imbued with modern philosophy, strive to make this harmonize with the faith, and, as they say, to turn it to the account of the faith. The name and reputation of these authors cause them to be read without suspicion, and they are, therefore, all the more dangerous in preparing the way for modernism.

159 To give you some more general directions, Venerable Brethren, in a matter of such moment, we bid you do everything in your power to drive out of your dioceses, even by solemn interdict, any pernicious books that may be in circulation there. The Holy See neglects no means to put down writings of this kind, but the number of them has now grown to such an extent that it is impossible to censure them all. Hence it happens that the medicine sometimes arrives too late, for the disease has taken root during the delay. We will, therefore, that the Bishops, putting aside all fear and the prudence of the flesh, despising the outcries of the wicked, gently, by all means, but constantly, do each his own share of this work, remembering the injunctions of Leo XIII. in the Apostolic Constitution "*Officiorum*:" "Let the ordinaries, acting in this also as delegates of the Apostolic See, exert themselves to proscribe and to put out of reach of the faithful injurious books or other writings printed or circulated in their dioceses." In this passage the Bishops, it is true, receive a right, but they have also a duty imposed on them. Let no Bishop think that he fulfills this duty by denouncing to us one or two books while a great many others of the same kind are being published and circulated. Nor are you to be deterred by the fact that a book has obtained the "imprimatur" elsewhere, both because this may be merely simulated and because it may have been granted through carelessness or easiness or excessive confidence in the author, as may sometimes happen in religious orders. Besides, just as the same food does not agree equally with everybody, it may happen that a book harmless in one may, on account of the different circumstances, be hurtful in another. Should a Bishop, therefore, after having taken the advice of prudent persons, deem it right to condemn any of such books in his diocese, we not

only give him ample faculty to do so, but we impose it upon him as a duty to do so. Of course, it is our wish that in such action proper regard be used, and sometimes it will suffice to restrict the prohibition to the clergy; but even in such cases it will be obligatory on Catholic booksellers not to put on sale books condemned by the Bishop. And while we are on this subject of booksellers we wish the Bishops to see to it that they do not, through desire for gain, put on sale unsound books. It is certain that in the catalogues of some of them the books of the modernists are not infrequently announced with no small praise. If they refuse obedience, let the Bishops have no hesitation in depriving them of the title of Catholic booksellers; so, too, and with more reason, if they have the title of episcopal booksellers, and if they have that of pontifical let them be denounced to the Apostolic See. Finally, we remind all of the twenty-sixth article of the above-mentioned Constitution "*Officiorum*:" "All those who have obtained an apostolic faculty to read and keep forbidden books are not thereby authorized to read books and periodicals forbidden by the local ordinaries, unless the apostolic faculty expressly concedes permission to read and keep books condemned by anybody."

160 But it is not enough to hinder the reading and the sale of bad books: it is also necessary to prevent them from being printed. Hence, let the Bishops use the utmost severity in granting permission to print. Under the rules of the Constitution "*Officiorum*," many publications require the authorization of the ordinary, and in some dioceses it has been made the custom to have a suitable number of official censors for the examination of writings. We have the highest praise for this institution, and we not only exhort, but we order that it be extended to all dioceses. In all episcopal curias, therefore, let censors be appointed for the revision of works intended for publication, and let the censors be chosen from both ranks of the clergy, secular and regular, men of age, knowledge and prudence, who will know how to follow the golden mean in their judgments. It shall be their office to examine everything which requires permission for publication according to Articles XLI. and XLII. of the above-

mentioned constitution. The censor shall give his verdict in writing. If it be favorable, the Bishop will give the permission for publication by the word "Imprimatur," which must always be preceded by the "Nihil obstat" and the name of the censor. In the Curia of Rome official censors shall be appointed just as elsewhere, and the appointment of them shall appertain to the master of the sacred palaces, after they have been proposed to the Cardinal Vicar and accepted by the Sovereign Pontiff. It will also be the office of the master of the sacred palaces to select the censor for each writing. Permission for publication will be granted by him as well as by the Cardinal Vicar or his vicegerent; and this permission, as above prescribed, must always be preceded by the "Nihil obstat" and the name of the censor. Only on very rare and exceptional occasions, and on the prudent decision of the Bishop, shall it be possible to omit mention of the censor. The name of the censor shall never be made known to the authors until he shall have given a favorable decision, so that he may not have to suffer annoyance either while he is engaged in the examination of a writing or in case he should deny his approval. Censors shall never be chosen from the religious orders until the opinion of the provincial, or, in Rome, of the general, has been privately obtained; and the provincial or the general must give a conscientious account of the character, knowledge and orthodoxy of the candidate. We admonish religious superiors of their solemn duty never to allow anything to be published by any of their subjects without permission from themselves and from the ordinary. Finally, we affirm and declare that the title of censor has no value, and can never be adduced to give credit to the private opinions of the person who holds it.

161 Having said this much in general, we now ordain in particular a more careful observance of Article XLII. of the above-mentioned Constitution "*Officiorum*." It is forbidden to secular priests, without the previous consent of the ordinary, to undertake the direction of papers or periodicals. This permission shall be withdrawn from any priest who makes a wrong use of it after having been admonished. With regard to priests who are correspondents or collaborators of periodicals,

as it happens not unfrequently that they write matter infected with modernism for their papers or periodicals, let the Bishops see to it that this is not permitted to happen, and should it happen, let them warn the writers or prevent them from writing. The superiors of religious orders, too, we admonish with all authority to do the same; and should they fail in this duty, let the Bishops make due provision with authority delegated by the Supreme Pontiff. Let there be, as far as this is possible, a special censor for newspapers and periodicals written by Catholics. It shall be his office to read in due time each number after it has been published, and if he find anything dangerous in it, let him order that it be corrected. The Bishop shall have the same right even when the censor has seen nothing objectionable in a publication.

162 We have already mentioned congresses and public gatherings as among the means used by the modernists to propagate and defend their opinions. In the future Bishops shall not permit congresses of priests except on very rare occasions. When they do permit them, it shall only be on condition that matters appertaining to the Bishops or the Apostolic See be not treated in them, and that no motions or postulates be allowed that would imply a usurpation of sacred authority; and that no mention be made in them of modernism, presbyterianism or laicism. At congresses of this kind, which can only be held after permission in writing has been obtained in due time and for each case, it shall not be lawful for priests of other dioceses to take part without the written permission of their ordinary. Further, no priest must lose sight of the solemn recommendation of Leo XIII.: "Let priests hold as sacred the authority of their pastors; let them take it for certain that the sacerdotal ministry, if not exercised under the guidance of the Bishops, can never be either holy or very fruitful or respectable." (Lett. Encyc. "*Nobilissima Gallorum*," 10 Feb., 1884.)

163 But of what avail, Venerable Brethren, will be all our commands and prescriptions if they be not dutifully and firmly carried out? And in order that this may be done it has seemed expedient to us to extend to all dioceses the regulations laid down with great wisdom many years ago by the Bishops of Umbria for theirs.

164 "In order," they say, "to extirpate the errors already propagated, and to prevent their further diffusion, and to remove those teachers of impiety through whom the pernicious effects of such diffusion are being perpetuated, this sacred assembly, following the example of St. Charles Borromeo, has decided to establish in each of the dioceses a council consisting of approved members of both branches of the clergy, which shall be charged with the task of noting the existence of errors and the devices by which new ones are introduced and propagated, and to inform the Bishop of the whole, so that he may take counsel with them as to the best means for nipping the evil in the bud and preventing it spreading for the ruin of souls, or, worse still, gaining strength and growth." (Acts of the Congress of the Bishops of Umbria, Nov., 1948, tit. 2, art. 6.) We decree, therefore, that in every diocese a council of this kind, which we are pleased to name "the Council of Vigilance," be instituted without delay. The priests called to form part in it shall be chosen somewhat after the manner above prescribed for the censors, and they shall meet every two months on an appointed day under the presidency of the Bishop. They shall be bound to secrecy as to their deliberations and decisions, and their function shall be as follows: They shall watch most carefully for every trace and sign of modernism, both in publications and in teaching, and, to preserve from it the clergy and the young, they shall take all prudent, prompt and efficacious measures. Let them combat novelties of words, remembering the admonitions of Leo XIII. (Instruct. S. C. NN. EE. EE., 27 Jan., 1902): "It is impossible to approve in Catholic publications of a style inspired by unsound novelty, which seems to deride the piety of the faithful and dwells on the introduction of a new order of Christian life, on new directions of the Church, on new aspirations of the modern soul, on a new vocation of the clergy, on a new Christian civilization." Language of this kind is not to be tolerated either in books or from chairs of learning. The councils must not neglect the books treating of the pious traditions of different places or of sacred relics. Let them not permit such questions to be discussed in periodicals destined to stimulate piety, neither with expressions savoring

of mockery or contempt, nor by dogmatic pronouncements, especially when, as is often the case, what is stated as a certainty either does not pass the limits of probability or is merely based on prejudiced opinion. Concerning sacred relics, let this be the rule: When Bishops, who alone are judges in such matters, know for certain that a relic is not genuine, let them remove it at once from the veneration of the faithful; if the authentications of a relic happen to have been lost through civil disturbances, or in any other way, let it not be exposed for public veneration until the Bishop has verified it. The argument of prescription or well-founded presumption is to have weight only when devotion to a relic is commendable by reason of its antiquity, according to the sense of the decree issued in 1896 by the Congregation of Indulgences and Sacred Relics: "Ancient relics are to retain the veneration they have always enjoyed, except when in individual instances there are clear arguments that they are false or suppositious." In passing judgment on pious traditions, be it always borne in mind that in this matter the Church uses the greatest prudence, and that she does not allow traditions of this kind to be narrated in books except with the utmost caution and with the insertion of the declaration imposed by Urban VIII., and even then she does not guarantee the truth of the fact narrated; she simply does not forbid belief in things for which human arguments are not wanting. On this matter the Sacred Congregation of Rites, thirty years ago, decreed as follows: "These apparitions and revelations have neither been approved nor condemned by the Holy See, which has simply allowed that they be believed on purely human faith, on the tradition which they relate, corroborated by testimonies and documents worthy of credence." (Decree, May 2, 1877.) Anybody who follows this rule has no cause for fear. For the devotion based on any apparition, in as far as it regards the fact itself—that is to say, in as far as it is relative—always implies the hypothesis of the truth of the fact; while in as far as it is absolute, it must always be based on the truth, seeing that its object is the persons of the saints who are honored. The same is true of relics. Finally, we entrust to the Councils of Vigilance the duty of overseeing assiduously and diligently social institutions, as well as writings on social questions, so that they may harbor no trace of modernism, but obey the prescriptions of the Roman Pontiffs.

165 Lest what we have laid down thus far should fall into oblivion, we will and ordain that the Bishops of all dioceses, a year after the publication of these letters, and every three years thenceforward, furnish the Holy See with a diligent and sworn report on all the prescriptions contained in them, and on the doctrines that find currency among the clergy, and especially in the seminaries and other Catholic institutions, we impose the like obligation on the generals of religious orders with regard to those under them.

166 This, Venerable Brethren, is what we have thought it our duty to write to you for the salvation of all who believe. The adversaries of the Church will doubtless abuse what we have said to refurbish the old calumny by which we are traduced as the enemy of science and of the progress of humanity. In order to oppose a new answer to such accusations, which the history of the Christian religion refutes by never-failing arguments, it is our intention to establish and develop by every means in our power a special institute in which, through the cooperation of those Catholics who are most eminent for their learning, the progress of science and other realms of knowledge may be promoted under the guidance and teaching of Catholic truth. God grant that we may happily realize our design with the ready assistance of all those who bear a sincere love for the Church of Christ. But of this we will speak on another occasion.

167 Meanwhile, Venerable Brethren, fully confident in your zeal and work, we beseech for you with our whole heart and soul the abundance of heavenly light, so that in the midst of this great perturbation of men's minds from the insidious invasions of error from every side, you may see clearly what you ought to do and may perform the task with all your strength and courage. May Jesus Christ, the author and finisher of our faith, be with you by His power; and may the Immaculate Virgin, the destroyer of all heresies, be with you by her prayers and aid. And we, as a pledge of our affection and of divine assistance in adversity, grant most affec-

tionately and with all our heart to you, your clergy and people the apostolic benediction.

Given at St. Peter's, Rome, on the 8th day of September, 1907, the fifth year of our pontificate. 168

QUAS PRIMAS

Encyclical Letter of Pope Pius XI
on the Feast of Christ the King
December 11, 1925

In the first Encyclical Letter We addressed, at the beginning of Our Pontificate, to the Bishops of the Universal Church, when reviewing the chief causes of the disasters that We saw mankind oppressed and harassed by, We stated clearly that this deluge of misfortune over the world was due to the attitude of the majority of men who had banished Jesus Christ and His holy law, not only from their personal lives and conduct, but from family and public life. And We added that no hope of lasting peace among nations could be reasonably entertained while individuals and States denied and rejected the sovereign rule of Our Saviour. We claimed that the *Peace of Christ* was to be sought in the *Kingdom of Christ*, and We stated that We would make good this claim in so far as would be granted to Us. Yes, in the Kingdom of Christ; for it seemed to Us that no more efficacious means for establishing peace on a lasting basis could be found than by restoring the sovereign rule of Our Lord.

170 In the interval signs of better times to come have not been wanting. We have noticed a spirit of zeal towards Christ and His Church, the sole medium of salvation, a spirit of zeal now for the first time manifested by some, in others characterized by marked intensity. And so it appears that many who held the kingship of Christ in contempt, and who had exiled themselves from His kingdom, are making for a speedy and auspicious return to their duties of obedience.

171 The many notable and memorable events that have occurred during this Holy Year have given great honour and glory to Our Lord and High King, the Founder of the Church. Take for instance the Missionary Exhibition. How wonderful the impression it made on the minds and hearts of men. Whether they regarded the unceasing zeal of the Church to extend daily the kingdom of the Spouse unto all continents and islands, even to the farthest limits of the ocean; whether they considered the great number of lands that have been won over to the Catholic name, at the cost indeed of toil and blood, by missionaries of supreme courage and indomitable spirit; or whether, lastly, they considered the vast extent of territory that yet remains to be brought under the sweet and saving yoke of our King—wonderful indeed was the impression on men's minds and hearts. And the vast numbers that visited the city from all quarters, led by their prelates or priests, during the holy time, were impelled by no other motive than the desire to become duly cleansed from the guilt of sin, and at the tombs of the Apostles and in Our presence, to make profession of their loyalty to the sovereign rule of Christ and of their determination so to abide.

172 And when We ourselves raised by decree to the honour of the altar six confessors and virgins, after due proof of their heroic virtue, a new ray of splendour seemed to be shed on the kingdom of Our Saviour. What joy was Ours, what consolation, when in the august surroundings of the Basilica of St. Peter Our decree was acclaimed by an immense multitude with the hymn of thanksgiving, '*Tu rex gloriae Christe*'—*Thou, O Christ, art King of Glory*. For while men and States who have turned away from God are driven along paths of raging hatred, discord and revolution to courses of destruction and ruin, the Church of God, ever breaking to mankind the bread of spiritual life, is ever raising up for Christ, in ceaseless succession, holy generations of men and women; while He, in reward for their fidelity and obedience during the period of subjection in the earthly kingdom, is ever summoning His faithful ones to the reward of everlasting happiness in celestial bliss.

173 Moreover, since this Jubilee Year marks the sixteenth centenary of the Council of Nice, We commanded that event to be celebrated, and We have done so in the Vatican Basilica. There is a special reason for this, in that the Nicene Synod defined and proposed for Catholic belief the dogma of the consubstantiality of the Only-begotten with the Father, and affirmed the kingly dignity of Christ by inserting in its symbol or formula of faith the words: *cuius regni non erit finis—of whose kingdom there shall be no end.*

174 Seeing, therefore, the many opportunities this Holy Year has offered for shedding lustre on the Kingdom of Christ, We feel We shall be acting in thorough accordance with the spirit of Our Apostolic office, if in concession to the requests of many Cardinals, Bishops, and faithful—requests individually and collectively presented—We mark the close of this year by introducing into ecclesiastical liturgy a special Feast of the Kingship of Our Lord Jesus Christ. And so dear to Us is this matter that We desire to address you, Venerable Brethren, at some length concerning it, for the duty will be yours to explain afterwards to the faithful, in language they can feel and understand, the substance of Our words concerning devotion to Christ as King, so that manifold advantages may attend upon, and result from, the annual celebration of the Feast that is to be instituted.

175 It has long been a common custom to give to Christ the metaphorical title of King, because of His supreme excellence, His surpassing preeminence among all created things. So He is said to reign *in the minds of men*, both by reason of His great mental vision and His abounding knowledge, and also because he is Truth, and from Him as source men must needs draw off and obediently accept truth. *In the wills of men*, too, He is said to reign, not only because His human will is in entire and perfect consonance with, and in submission to, the Holy Divine Will, but also because from Him comes the moving force and inspiration whereby our free wills are ever incited to the noblest endeavour. Finally, Christ is recognized as ruler of our hearts, because of his love that surpasseth knowledge,[1] and His meekness and kindness that draw souls to Him. For never has it been granted to anyone, and never shall

it be granted, to be loved so much and so universally as Jesus Christ has been loved and shall be loved.

176 But if we examine this matter more closely, we cannot fail to see that the name King, in its literal sense, and kingly power must needs be prerogatives of Christ as man. For it is only as man that He can be said to have received from the Father *power and glory and a kingdom*,[2] since the Divine Lord, being consubstantial with the Father, must have all things in common with the Father, and so must have supreme and absolute sovereignty over all creatures. And, indeed, we find it broadcast in the pages of Sacred Scripture that Christ is King. He is spoken of as the ruler that shall arise from Jacob,[3] who has been set by the Father as King over Sion, His holy mount, and shall have the Gentiles for His inheritance, and the utmost parts of the earth for His possession.[4] In the nuptial hymn, where the true King of Israel, who was to come, is hailed as a rich and powerful monarch, we find the words: *Thy throne, O God, is for ever and ever; the sceptre of thy kingdom is a sceptre of righteousness.*[5] Passing by many references of this kind, we find in another passage, whose purport is to outline more definitely, as it were, the characteristic features of Christ, presage made of His kingdom which is to know no bounds, and where justice and peace will function in fulness: *In His days shall justice spring up, and abundance of peace . . . And He shall rule from sea to sea, and from the river unto the ends of the earth.*[6]

177 More abundant still is the testimony of the Prophets. That of Isaias is well known: *For a Child is born to us and a Son is given to us and the government is upon His shoulder, and His Name shall be called Wonderful, Counsellor, God the mighty, the Father of the world to come, the Prince of Peace. His empire shall be multiplied, and there shall be no end of peace. He shall sit upon the throne of David and upon his kingdom; to establish it and to strengthen it with judgment and with justice, from henceforth and for ever.*[7] And the utterances of the other prophets are in exact accord with Isaias. Jeremiah foretells of the *just seed* that shall arise from the house of David, the Son of David, that shall reign as king, *and shall be wise, and shall execute judgment and justice in*

the earth.[8] Daniel prophesies a kingdom to be founded by the God of Heaven, a kingdom *that shall never be destroyed . . . and shall stand for ever.* And he adds almost immediately: *I beheld therefore in the vision of the night, and lo! one like the Son of man came with the clouds of heaven. And He came even to the Ancient of days: and they presented Him before him. And he gave Him power and glory and a kingdom, and all peoples, tribes and tongues shall serve Him. His power is an everlasting power and shall not be taken away, and His kingdom shall not be destroyed.*[9] And the holy Evangelists themselves recognized and bore testimony to the fulfilment of Zachary's prophecy concerning the gentle King, who, *riding upon an ass and the colt of an ass*, was to enter Jerusalem as the *just one and Saviour* amid the acclamations of multitudes.[10]

178 Now this same doctrine of the Kingship of Christ, to which We have made passing reference, as contained in the books of the Old Testament, is found also in the New Testament, laid down in language unequivocal and sublime. Just to mention the message of the Archangel. He announces to the Virgin that she shall give birth to a Son, *to whom the Lord God shall give the throne of David His father, and He shall reign in the house of Jacob for ever, and of His kingdom there shall be no end.*[11] Christ, Himself, bears testimony to His sovereign power on numerous occasions: in His last discourse to the people, when He spoke about the rewards or punishments that were to be the eternal meed of the just or damned; in His reply to the Roman governor, who asked Him publicly if He was king; after His resurrection, when He gave to His Apostles the commission of teaching and baptizing all nations—whenever the occasion offered. He took the name of King[12] and openly declared He was King,[13] and solemnly proclaimed that all power in heaven and on earth was given to Him.[14] These words can be taken to mean nothing but the greatness of His power and the infinite extent of His kingdom. Is it any wonder, then, that He who is called by St. John, 'prince of the kings of the earth'[15] hath on His garments and on His thigh written *King of Kings and Lord of Lords,*[16] as He appeared in the Apostle's vision of the future.

Christ it is whom the Father *hath appointed heir of all things,*[17] and so He must reign until at the end of the world He puts all enemies *beneath the feet of God and the Father.*[18]

179 This, then, being the common teaching of the Sacred Books, it ought surely to follow that the Catholic Church, which is the Kingdom of Christ on earth, to be extended to all men and to all lands, should in profuse and dutiful spirit of veneration salute in the annual round of her sacred liturgy, her Author and Founder, as King and Lord and King of Kings. These titles of honour, indeed—whose meaning is one and the same, beautiful and varied as are the expressions—the Church applied in the old psalmody and in the ancient sacramentaries; and she applies them to-day in the daily prayers publicly offered to the Divine Majesty, and in the immolation of the Immaculate Victim. There is, in fact, an admirable and manifest harmony between the Eastern liturgies and ours in the perpetual praise of Christ as King, illustrating, in this connexion also, the truth of the axiom: *Legem, credendi lex statuit supplicandi—the rule followed in prayer indicates the rule of faith.*

180 The basis of this dignity and power of Our Lord has been well observed by Cyril of Alexandria: *In a word,* he says, *Christ has dominion over all creatures, a dominion not seized by violence, nor got from any other source than that of His own nature and essence.*[19] That is to say: His Kingship is founded on the ineffable hypostatic union. Hence it follows that Christ is to be adored by angels and men, not only as God, but that angels and men must obey and be subject to His sovereignty as man; that by sole virtue of the hypostatic union, Christ has power over all creatures. But what reflection can give us more pleasure and joy than the reflection that Christ is our King, not only by natural but by acquired right by virtue of His Redemption?

181 Would that men who forget what price we have cost Our Saviour would all reflect upon these words: *You were not redeemed by corruptible things such as gold and silver, but with the precious blood of Christ as of a lamb unspotted and undefiled.*[20] We are no longer our own property, since Christ

has purchased us *with a great price*[21] our very bodies are *the members of Christ.*[22]

182 Now to explain briefly the meaning and nature of this sovereign power: it consists, We need scarcely say, of a threefold power, and if this is lacking, the idea of sovereignty is scarcely intelligible. This is abundantly clear from the Scriptural testimony already adduced concerning the universal sovereignty of Our Redeemer. And it is a dogma of Catholic faith that Christ Jesus was given to men as a Redeemer, in whom they are to place their trust, and at the same time as a legislator whom they are to obey.[23] Not only do the Gospels tell us that He made laws, they represent Him in the act of making them. And the Divine Master says on different occasions and in different words that those who keep these laws will give proof of their love for Him, and that they will abide in His love.[24] Judicial power Jesus Himself claims as assigned Him by the Father, when the Jews accused Him of violating the Sabbath rest by the miraculous cure of a sick man: *For neither doth the Father judge any man, but hath given all judgment to the Son.*[25] In this power is included the privilege of rewarding and punishing, of His own right, all living men, for such privilege is inseparable from the power of judging. Executive power also must belong to Christ, for all must needs obey His sovereign rule, and against those who refuse to yield obedience, He has issued a penalty of punishment which none may escape.

183 That this kingdom, indeed, is in a special manner spiritual and concerned with things spiritual, is quite plain from the extracts from Scripture above quoted: and Christ's own line of action confirms this view. For on many occasions, when the Jews, and even the Apostles themselves, wrongly supposed that the Messiah would emancipate the people and restore the kingdom of Israel, He effectively rejected that idle hope and fancy. When the admiring throng surrounded Him and would have proclaimed Him king, He refused the title and honour by taking flight and lying in concealment. In presence of the Roman governor He declared His kingdom was not 'of this world.' In the Gospels this kingdom is represented as one such as men prepare to enter by way of

penance, but cannot actually enter except by faith and baptism; and baptism, although an external rite, signifies and produces an interior regeneration. This kingdom is opposed only to the kingdom of Satan and the power of darkness; it demands from its subjects, not only a spirit of detachment from riches and earthly things, not only that they show gentleness in their lives and hunger and thirst after justice, but also that they deny themselves and take up their Cross. Since Christ, as Redeemer, purchased the Church by His own Blood, and as Priest offered Himself as a victim for our sins, and continues to offer Himself is it not plain that His kingly office assumes, and shares in, the nature of both these offices?

184

He, however, would be guilty of shameful error who would deny to Christ as man authority over civil affairs, no matter what their nature, since by virtue of the absolute dominion over all creatures He holds from the Father, all things are in His power. Nevertheless, during His life on earth He refrained altogether from exercising such dominion, and despising then the possession and administration of earthly goods, He left them to their possessors then, and he does so to-day. As it is well put: '*Non eripit mortalia qui regna dat caelestina*[26]*—He does not seize earthly kingdoms Who gives heavenly kingdoms.*' And so, the empire of Our Redeemer embraces all men. To quote the words of Our immortal predecessor, Pope Leo XIII: 'His empire manifestly includes not only Catholic nations, not only those who were baptised, and of right belong to the Church, though error of doctrine leads them astray or schism severs them from her fold; but it includes also all those who are outside the Christian faith, so that truly the human race in its entirety is subject to the power of Jesus Christ.'[27] Nor, in this connexion, is there any difference between individuals and communities, whether family or State, for community aggregates are just as much under the dominion of Christ as individuals. The same Christ assuredly is the source of the individual's salvation and of the community's salvation: *Neither is there salvation in any other, for there is no other name under heaven given to men whereby we must be saved.*[28] He is the author of prosperity and of genuine happiness for every citizen and for the nation. *For the happiness of the State comes from exactly the same source as the happiness of the individual, the State being nothing else than a number of individuals living in harmony.*[29] If rulers, therefore, of nations wish to preserve their own authority, and to promote and increase their country's prosperity, let them not refuse, themselves and their people, to give public observance of reverence and obedience to the rule of Christ. What we said at the beginning of Our Pontificate concerning the decline of public authority and want of respect for those in power, is equally true at the present day. *With God and Jesus Christ,* We complained, *excluded from the Constitution and from the administration of the State, with authority derived not from God but from man, the very foundations of that authority are torn asunder, because the chief reason of the distinction between ruler and subject has been eliminated. With the result that human society must collapse because it has no secure support to rest upon.*[30]

185 Whenever men recognize both in public and in private life, Christ's royal power, wonderful blessings would be immediately vouchsafed to all society, such as true liberty, discipline, tranquillity, concord and peace. For Our Lord's royal dignity, just as it invests the human authority of princes and rulers with a religious significance, ennobles the citizen's duty of obedience. Wherefore St. Paul, although he ordered wives to revere Christ in their husbands, and slaves to revere Christ in their masters, warned them to give them obedience, not as men, but only as taking the place of Christ, since it is not becoming that men redeemed by Christ should serve their fellow-men: *You are bought with a price; be not made the bondslaves of men.*[31] If princes and magistrates duly elected be convinced that they rule not by their own right, but by the mandate and in the place of the divine King, assuredly they will exercise their authority in a holy manner and wisely, and in making laws and administering them they will take into consideration the common good, and also the human dignity of their subjects. The result will be order and stable tranquillity, for there will be no cause of discontent remaining. Men may see in their king or in other rulers of the

State, beings like themselves, unworthy perhaps and open to blame, but they will not for that reason deny their right to command, if they see reflected in these rulers the authority of Christ, God and Man.

186

In the interests of peace and harmony, too, it is clear that with the spread and universal extent of the Kingdom of Christ, men will become the more conscious of the link that binds them together, and so many conflicts will be altogether prevented, or at least their bitterness assuaged. Nor, if the Kingdom of Christ embraced all peoples in reality, as it does by right, would there be any reason to despair of that peace which the King of Peace brought to earth, the King who came to *reconcile all things,* who *came not to be ministered unto, but to minister,* and though *Lord of all* gave Himself *a model of humility,* and made humility His chief law, joining with it the precept of charity. Who said, moreover, *My yoke is sweet and My burden light.* Oh, what happiness would be ours if individuals and families and States allowed themselves to be governed by Christ. To quote the words which Our predecessor, Pope Leo XIII, addressed twenty-five years ago to the Bishops of the Universal Church: *It is only then,* said he, *that so many wounds may be healed, then will the old time respect for law revive, and peace in its beauty will be restored, and the sword will fall from men's hands and arms will be cast aside, when all men freely acknowledge Christ's sovereignty and obey it, and every tongue confesses that the Lord Jesus Christ is in the glory of God the Father.*[32]

187

Now to secure an abundant and permanent harvest of those blessings in Christian society it is necessary that Our Saviour's royal dignity should be as widely as possible recognized and understood, and nothing can better serve this end than the institution of a special feast in honour of Christ as King. For people are better instructed in the truths of faith and brought to appreciate the interior joys of religion far more effectively by the annual celebration of our sacred mysteries than by even the weightiest pronouncements of the teaching of the Church. For such pronouncements reach only the few, and these generally the more learned, whereas all the faithful are stirred and taught by the celebration of feasts; pronouncements speak once; celebrations speak annually and for ever; pronouncements affect the mind primarily, celebrations have a salutary influence on the mind and heart, on the whole man. Man, being composed of body and soul, is so moved and stimulated by the external solemnities of festivals, and such is the variety and beauty of the sacred rites, that he drinks more deeply of divine doctrine, assimilates it into his very system, and makes it a source of strength for progress in his spiritual life.

188 Besides, we know from the pages of history that such festivals were instituted in the course of the ages, one after another, as the needs or utility of the people of Christ seemed to demand; as, for instance, when men needed to be strengthened in face of a comon danger, or to be guarded from insidious heresies, or to be urged to the pious consideration of some mystery of faith or of some divine blessing. Thus, in the earlier ages of the Christian era, when Christians were being cruelly persecuted, the cult of the martyrs was begun, in order, says St. Augustine, that *the feasts of the martyrs might incite men to martyrdom.*[30] The liturgical honours that were afterwards paid to confessors, virgins and widows had wonderful results in an increased zest for virtue amongst the faithful, necessary even in times of peace. But especially fruitful were the feasts instituted in honour of the Blessed Virgin. As a result of them the Christian people grew, not only in their devotion to the Mother of God, as an ever present advocate, but also in their love for her as a Mother bequeathed them by their Redeemer. Nor least among the benefits that have resulted from the public and legitimate devotion to the Mother of God and the saints, is the constant victory of the Church at all times over heresy and error. And in this matter we may well admire the Providence of God, Who brings good even out of evil, and has from time to time allowed the faith and piety of men to slacken, and Catholic truth to be assailed by false doctrine, with the result, however, that truth shone forth resplendent with a new light, and men's faith, aroused from its lethargy, made greater efforts to higher grades of sanctity.

189 The festivals that have been introduced into the liturgy in more recent times have had a similar origin, and have been attended with similar results. When reverence and devotion to the Blessed Sacrament had grown cold the Feast of Corpus Christi was instituted, and the solemn procession and prayers for eight days' duration had the effect of bringing men once more to render public homage to the Lord. The Feast of the Sacred Heart of Jesus was introduced when men had become dispirited and despondent, as the result of the sad and gloomy severity of Jansenism, when their hearts had grown cold, being deterred from the love of God and trust in salvation.

190 If We ordain that the whole Catholic world shall worship Christ as King, We shall minister to the needs of the present day, and at the same time provide an excellent remedy for the plague which now infests society. We refer to the plague of secularism, its errors and impious activities. This evil thing you know, Venerable Brethren, has not come to the surface in one day. Its seeds have been long developing within the vitals of nations. First, Christ's authority to rule over all nations was denied. The Church's right, which follows on that of Christ, to teach the human race, to make laws, to rule over peoples unto their eternal salvation, was denied. Then, by degrees, the religion of Christ was put on a footing with false religions, and placed ignominiously in the same category with them. It was next put under civil authority, and tolerated more or less at the whim of princes and rulers. Some went further, and desired to have a natural religion, mere natural instinct, set up in place of divine religion. There were not wanting States that thought they could dispense with God, and make their religion consist in impiety and neglect of God. Bitter, indeed, are the fruits that this revolt of individuals and of nations against Christ has borne so frequently and for such long periods. The disastrous consequences of this revolt We lamented in the Encyclical *Ubi Arcano*, and today We iterate the lament: the seeds of discord have been sown on every side; enmities and rivalries between nations have been enkindled, and are a great hindrance to the cause of peace; a spirit of insatiable greed is abroad that often

wears the mask of public spirit and patriotism; and following on it are discord and division between citizens, and a blind unrestrained self-love which makes private advantage and private gain its one aim and universal standard. We see, too, that peace in the home has been utterly ruined, because men forget or neglect their duties; that the stability of family life has been undermined; society, in a word, shaken to its foundations and on the road to ruin. We earnestly hope that the Feast of the Kingship of Christ, which in future will be yearly observed, may hasten the return of society to our loving Saviour.

191 It would be the duty of Catholics to do all they can to bring about this happy result. Many of them, however, do not seem to enjoy the social status or to wield the influence befitting those who bear the torch of truth. This drawback may, perhaps, be due to slowness and timidity on the part of good people, who shrink from contest or offer but a weak resistance; with the result that the enemies of the Church become more and more reckless and more daring in their attacks. But if the faithful would generally understand that it is their duty to fight bravely and continually under the banner of Christ their King, then, fired with apostolic zeal, they would endeavour to win over to Our Lord those who are estranged from Him or know Him not, and would valiantly defend His rights.

192 Moreover, the annual and universal celebration of the Feast of the Kingship of Christ is very much calculated to fix men's attention on, and remedy in some way, this public revolt from Christ that may be traced to secularism, to the great ruin of sociaty. While nations insult the sweet name of Our Redeemer by suppressing all mention of it in their conferences and parliaments, we ought all the more loudly proclaim it, and all the more universally affirm the privileges of His royal dignity and power.

193 We find, too, that ever since the end of the last century the way has been well and happily prepared for the institution of this festival: It is well known that this devotion has been the subject of much sound and learned discussion, books dealing with it in many languages having been published throughout

the whole world. That pious custom, too, practised by innumerable families, of dedicating and surrendering themselves to the Sacred Heart of Jesus, is an acknowledgment of the kingship and sovereign rule of Christ. And not only families have observed this practice, but nations and kingdoms as well. In fact, the whole human race was, at the instance of Pope Leo XIII, in the year 1900, consecrated to the Divine Heart. It should be remarked also that the frequent Eucharistic Congresses, which are held in our age, have had a wonderful influence toward solemnly sanctioning Christ's kingly power over human society. For thus the people of each diocese, district, or nation, people from the whole world, are summoned together to venerate and worship Christ the King, hidden under the veil of the Eucharistic Species. And thus, by means of sermons preached at meetings and in the churches, by public adoration of the Blessed Sacrament and by solemn processions, they have an opportunity of cordially saluting Christ as the King given them by the Father. It may, indeed, with justice, be said that it is divine inspiration that prompts the people of Christ to bring forth Jesus from His silent hiding-place in the sacred edifice, and escort in triumph through the streets of the cities Him whom impious men refused to receive when He came unto His own, and thus restore to Him in full His kingly rights.

194 The Holy Year now coming to its close affords the best possible opportunity of fulfilling the intention We have mentioned, for now God, in His great kindness, has showered on the minds and hearts of the faithful heavenly blessings that surpass all understanding; He has either enriched them once more with His grace; or, stimulating them anew to strive for higher gifts, He has strengthened their purpose on the way of virtue. Whether, therefore, We consider the many petitions that have been addressed to Us, or whether We consider the events of this great year of Jubilee, We have every reason for thinking that the desired moment is at length at hand for proclaiming that Christ is to be worshipped by a special and proper Feast as King of the whole human race. For in this year, as We have said in the beginning of this letter, the Divine King, *truly wonderful in His saints, has been glorious-*

ly magnified, for a new company of His soldiers have been elevated to the honours of saints. In this year, too, men have seen strange sights—one might say, works—so that all were in a position to admire the victories won for Christ by the heralds of the Gospel, in the extension of His kingdom. In this year, finally, by celebrating the centenary of the Council of Nice, We have commemorated the defence of the doctrine that the Incarnate Word is consubstantial with the Father; and hereon is based Christ's sovereign power over all men.

195 Therefore by Our Apostolic Authority We institute the Feast of the Kingship of Our Lord Jesus Christ to be observed yearly throughout the whole world, on the last Sunday of the month of October—the Sunday, that is, that immediately precedes the Feast of All Saints. We prescribe also that the dedication of mankind to the Sacred Heart of Jesus, which Our predecessor of holy memory, Pope Pius X, commanded to be renewed yearly, be made annually on that day. This year, however, We wish that this dedication be observed on the thirty-first day of the present month, on which day We Ourselves shall celebrate pontifically in honour of the Kingship of Christ, and shall command that this same dedication be performed in Our presence. We think We cannot better or in more fitting manner bring the Holy Year to its close, or better signify Our own gratitude and, We may add, the gratitude of the whole Catholic world to Christ, the immortal King of the ages, for the blessings showered on Us, on the Church, and on the whole Catholic world during this holy time.

196 It is unnecessary to explain to you at any great length, Venerable Brethren, Our reason for commanding a special Feast of Christ's Kingship to be celebrated, as distinct from those other Feasts that signify, in a manner, and celebrate His kingly dignity. We need only remark that, whereas in all the Feasts of Our Lord the material object of worship is Christ, the formal object, however, is something entirely distinct from His royal power and title. We have commanded its observance on a Sunday in order that not only the clergy may perform their duties to the Divine King by celebration of Mass and by reciting their Office, but that the laity, too,

free from their daily occupations, may, in a spirit of holy joy, give ample testimony of their obedience and subjection to Christ. The last Sunday of October seemed the most convenient for the celebration of this Feast, because it approximately marks the end of the liturgical year, and so the solemn festival of Christ's Kingship will be a fitting completion and consummation of the mysteries of the life of Jesus already commemorated during the year; and before we celebrate the glory of all the saints, His glory will be proclaimed and extolled, Who triumphs in all the Saints and Elect. Accordingly, Venerable Brethren, let it be your duty and your task to have sermons preached on fixed dates before the annual celebration of this Feast to the people of every parish, so that they may be thoroughly instructed in the nature of this Feast, its meaning and importance, and that they may be warned so to direct and regulate their lives as becomes faithful and loyal subjects of the Divine King.

In conclusion, Venerable Brethren, We wish to state briefly the blessings We confidently hope will accrue to the Church and society, and to the faithful individually, from this public veneration of Christ as King. 197

By the honours thus offered to the Sovereign Kingship men must needs be reminded that the Church, founded by Christ as a perfect society, has a natural and inalienable right to full freedom and immunity from the power of the State; and that in fulfilling the task committed to her by God, of teaching, ruling and guiding to eternal happiness all who belong to the Kingdom of Christ, she cannot be dependent on any external power. Furthermore, the State is bound to give similar liberty to the Orders and Communities of religious of either sex, who give most valuable help to the Pastors of the Church, and labour most strenuously for the extension and establishment of the Kingdom of Christ. By their sacred vows they fight against the threefold concupiscence of the world and by their very profession of a more perfect life they make that holiness, which the Divine Founder ordained as a distinguishing mark of the Church, shine forth in brilliancy before the eyes of all with everlasting and daily-increased splendour. 198

199 The very celebration of the Feast, too, by its annual recurrence, will serve to remind nations that not only private individuals, but State officials and rulers, are bound by the obligation of worshipping Christ publicly and rendering Him obedience. They will be thus led to reflect on that last judgment, in which Christ, Who has been cast out of public life, despised, neglected and ignored, will severely revenge such insults; for His kingly dignity demands that the constitution of the whole State should conform to the Divine Commandments and Christian principles, whether in the making of laws, the administration of justice, or in the moulding of the minds of the young on sound doctrine and upright morals.

200 The faithful, moreover, by diligently meditating on these matters, will gain much strength and courage, enabling them to fashion their own lives on the true Christian ideal. For if to Christ Our Lord is given all power in heaven and on earth; if mankind, through being purchased by His most precious Blood, are, by a new title, so to speak, subjected to His jurisdiction; and if this power that Christ wields is exercised over human nature in its entirety, it is abundantly clear that not one of our faculties is exempt from His all-embracing sovereign sway. He must reign in the mind of man, which ought to assent with perfect submission and firm unwavering belief to the revealed truths and doctrines of Christ. He must reign in man's will, which ought to obey the laws and precepts of God. He must reign in the body and in its members, which ought to serve as instruments towards the interior sanctification of our souls, or as the Apostle Paul says *of instruments of justice to God.*[33]

201 If all these considerations are presented to the faithful for their thorough inquiry and meditation, they will prove great aids to perfection. It is Our earnest prayer, Venerable Brethren, that those without the fold may seek after and accept unto their salvation the sweet yoke of Christ; and that we, who by the mercy of God are of the household of the faith, may bear that yoke, not with complaint, but with joy, with love and with devotion; that having regulated our lives in accordance with the laws of the Divine Kingdom, we may reap the good fruits in rich abundance, and, counted by

Christ as good and faithful servants, we be made partakers of eternal bliss and glory with Him in His heavenly kingdom.

Accept, Venerable Brethren, this devout wish as token of Our paternal love, now that the Feast of the Nativity of Our Lord Jesus Christ is drawing near, and receive the Apostolic Benediction as a pledge of divine blessings, which with loving heart we impart to you, Venerable Brethren, to your clergy and people. 202

Given at St. Peter's, Rome, on the eleventh day of the month of December, in the Holy Year nineteen hundred and twenty-five, the fourth year of Our Pontificate. 203

MISERENTISSIMUS REDEMPTOR

Encyclical Letter of Pope Pius XI
on the Reparation Due to the Sacred Heart
May 9, 1928

Our most merciful Redeemer, having assured the salvation of the human race by His death on the Cross, before He ascended to His Heavenly Father, said these consoling words to His sorrowing Apostles and disciples: "Behold I am with you all days, even to the consummation of the world" (*Matt.* xxviii, 20). These happy words are also Our own source of hope and salvation, words which, Venerable Brothers, come readily to mind every time when, from this high watchtower, as it were, We look down upon the human family afflicted by so many grievous ills, and upon the Church, assailed without respite by attacks and plots. As a matter of fact, this promise of Our Divine Lord, as it once upon a time raised high the fallen spirits of the Apostles and urged them on to spread most zealously the seed of the Gospel through all the earth, so also it has guided the Church to victory over the powers of Hell. Assuredly, Our Lord Jesus Christ has always assisted His Church; and most powerfully and effectively on those very occasions when she was encompassed by the greatest dangers and calamities. Christ then bestowed on her precisely those helps most necessary to meet the conditions of the times, by His wisdom which "reacheth from end to end mightily and ordereth all things sweetly" (*Wisdom* viii, 1). Nor in our own times has "the hand of the Lord been shortened" (*Isaias* lix, 1), especially on such occasions when an erroneous doctrine is being taught and spread about throughout the world, and by reason of which we fear that the sources of the Christian life may be dried up, for by such errors men are led to forsake the Christian life and the love of God.

205 Since some Christians, perhaps, are ignorant of, and others are indifferent to, the sorrows which the most loving Jesus revealed to St. Margaret Mary Alacoque in His apparitions to her, as well as His wishes and desires which He manifested to mankind, all of which in the last analysis work to man's advantage, it is Our pleasure, Venerable Brothers, to write you at some length of the obligation which rests upon all to make those amends which we owe to the Most Sacred Heart of Jesus. We feel certain that each of you will zealously teach to your own flocks what We herein write and that you will exhort them to do all that We wish to be done.

206 From among all the proofs of the infinite goodness of Our Saviour none stands out more prominently than the fact that, as the love of the Faithful grew cold, He, Divine Love Itself, gave Himself to us to be honored by a very special devotion and that the rich treasury of the Church was thrown wide open in the interests of that devotion by which we honor the Most Sacred Heart of Jesus "in whom are hid all the treasures of wisdom and knowledge" (*Col.* ii, 3). As formerly Divine Goodness wished to exhibit to the human race, as it came from the Ark of Noe, a sign of the renewed covenant between them, "my bow which appears in the clouds" (*Gen.* ix, 14), so in our own so troubled times, while that heresy held sway which is known as Jansenism, the most insidious of all heresies, enemy of the love of God and of filial affection for Him—for this heresy preached that God was not so much to be loved by us as a Father as to be feared as an unrelenting Judge—the most kind Jesus manifested to the nations His Sacred Heart, unfolding our banner of peace and love to the breeze, an augury of certain victory in the battle before us. Wherefore Our Predecessor, Leo XIII, admiring as he did the great possibilities which devotion to the Most Sacred Heart of Jesus contains, with reason wrote in his Encyclical *Annum Sacrum*: "Just as when the newly born Church lay helpless under the yoke of the Cæsars, there appeared in the heavens a

cross, at once the sign and cause of the marvelous victory which was soon to follow," so today behold before our very eyes there appears another most happy and holy sign, the Most Sacred Heart of Jesus, crowned by a brilliant cross set among raging flames. In this Sacred Heart we should place all our hopes, from it, too, we ask and await salvation.

207 Are, we not to see, Venerable Brothers, in that blessed sign and in the devotion which flows from it, the very substance of our holy religion, as well as the rules to guide us toward a more perfect form of life, since the Sacred Heart is the road which will most surely lead us to know intimately Jesus Christ and will cause our hearts to love more tenderly and to imitate Him more generously than we have heretofore done? Since this is so, it is no wonder then that Our Predecessors have always defended this most praiseworthy devotion to the Sacred Heart from the objections launched by those who will not accept it, that they have praised it most highly and have always promoted it with the greatest possible zeal in so far as the conditions of time and place seemed to demand such action. Certainly, it is due to nothing short of the inspiration of God that the childlike love of the Faithful for the Sacred Heart increases day by day; that pious associations to promote devotion to the Sacred Heart have come into being everywhere, and that the custom has become quite common of receiving Holy Communion on the First Friday of the month, a custom which had its origin in the wish of Jesus Christ Himself.

208 Among the different practices which directly accompany devotion to the Most Sacred Heart assuredly the foremost is the act of consecration by which we offer to the Hearts of Jesus both ourselves and all that belongs to us, recognizing that all we have comes to us from the infinite charity of God. Our Lord, having revealed to that most pure lover of His Sacred Heart, St. Margaret Mary how much more He insisted on the immense love which He has borne toward us than on His rights over us, asked that mankind pay Him this tribute of devotion. Therefore the Saint herself, together with her Spiritual Director, Claude de la Colombiere, first of all offered Him an act of consecration. In the course of

time individuals began paying Him the same tribute, then whole families and certain associations, and last of all, public officials, the inhabitants of cities, and whole nations. Due to the machinations of wicked persons, both in the century just ended and in this century, things had come to such a pass that men despised the rule of Christ and publicly declared war upon His Church by means of laws and popular enactments contrary to both the Divine and natural law even going so far as to cry out publicly: "We will not have this man to reign over us" (*Luke* xix, 14). But by this act of consecration there burst forth, in startling contrast to these cries, the unanimous voice of the lovers of the Sacred Heart, rising to vindicate the glory and defend the rights of the same Sacred Heart, "for he must reign" (*1 Cor.* xv, 25) "may Thy Kingdom come." Finally, at the beginning of the century as a happy consequence of all this, the whole human race which belongs by inherent right to Christ, "in whom all things are reestablished" (*Eph.* i, 10), was consecrated to His Most Sacred Heart by Our Predecessor then happily reigning, Leo XIII, amid the applause of the whole Christian world.

209 These auspicious and happy beginnings We Ourselves, through the great goodness of God, brought to completion, as was pointed out in Our Encyclical *Quas Primas,* on the occasion when, acceding to the desires and wishes expressed by numerous bishops and the Faithful, We instituted at the close of the Jubilee Year the Feast of Christ the King of all men, which feast We ordered to be celebrated solemnly all over the Christian world. By that act We not only brought forth clearly into the light of day the fact of the supreme dominion of Christ over all things, over civil society and the home, as well as over individuals; We also experienced beforehand the joy of that most happy day when the whole world will submit joyfully and willingly to the sweet yoke of Christ the King. Wherefore We commanded that, together with the celebration of this feast, there should be renewed annually the act of consecration, and this We did in order to obtain more surely and in greater quantities the fruits of such a consecration and to bind with Christian love in

the communion of peace all peoples to the heart of the King of Kings and Sovereign of Sovereigns.

210 Moreover, to all these expressions of veneration, and especially to that most fruitful one, the act of consecration, which by means of the institution of the Feast of Christ the King has been, as it were, again confirmed, it is expedient that another be added, and of this last, Venerable Brothers, We wish to speak now somewhat at length. We refer to the act of expiation or of reparation, as it is called, to be made to the Sacred Heart of Jesus.

211 If in the act of consecration the intention to exchange, as it were, for the love of the Creator the love of us creatures stands out most prominently, there follows almost naturally from this another fact, namely, that if this same Uncreated Love has either been passed over through forgetfulness or saddened by reason of our sins, then we should repair such outrages, no matter in what manner they have occurred. Ordinarily, we call this duty, reparation. If we are held to both these duties for the same reasons, we are held to the duty of making reparation by the most powerful motives of justice and of love of justice, in order to expiate the injury done God by our sins and to reestablish, by means of penance, the Divine order which has been violated; and of love, in order to suffer together with Christ, patient and covered with opprobrium, so that we may bring to Him, in so far as our human weakness permits, some comfort in His sufferings. Since we are all sinners, burdened with many offenses, we should honor God. This should take place not only by means of that cult by which we adore, in the veneration due Him from us, His Infinite Majesty, or by means of prayer when recognize His supreme dominion over us, or by acts of thanksgiving when we praise His infinite generosity toward us: it is necessary to do more than all this. We must also satisfy the just anger of God because of "the numberless sins, offenses, and negligences" which we have committed. Therefore, we must add to the act of consecration, by virtue of which we offer ourselves to God and become thereby, as it were, sacred to Him by reason of the sanctity which necessarily flows from an act of consecration, as the Angelic Doctor

teaches (*Summa Theol.* IIa-IIae, q. 81. a. 8, c.), an act of expiation, by means of which all our faults are blotted out, lest perchance the sanctity of infinite Justice spurn our arrogant unworthiness and look upon our gift as something to be rejected rather than to be accepted.

212 All men are obliged to make reparation since, according to the teachings of our holy Faith, our souls have been disfigured, as a result of the pitiable fall of Adam, by original sin; we are subject also to our passions and corrupted in a truly sad way, and have thus made ourselves worthy of eternal damnation. It is true that the proud philosophers of this world deny the above truth, resurrecting in its place the ancient heresy of Pelagius which conceded to human nature a certain inborn goodness which, by our own powers, raises us up to ever higher levels of perfection. These false theories, born of human pride, have been condemned by the Apostle who admonishes us that "we were by nature children of wrath" (*Eph.* ii, 3). As a matter of fact, from the very creation of the world mankind has recognized, in one way or another, the obligation of making reparation, and impelled, as it were, by a natural instinct, has tried to placate the Deity by offering Him public sacrifices.

213 But no effort on our part would have been great enough to expiate the faults of men if the Son of God had not assumed human nature in order to redeem us. The Saviour of mankind announced this truth speaking through the Psalmist: "Sacrifice and oblation Thou wouldst not; but a body Thou hast fitted to Me. Holocausts for sin did not please Thee. Then said I: Behold I come" (*Heb.* xi, 5-7). In truth "He hath borne our infirmities and carried our sorrows: He was wounded for our iniquities" (*Isaias,* liii, 4, 5), "who His own self bore our sins in His body on the tree" (*I Peter* ii, 24), "blotting out the handwriting of the decree that was against us, which was contrary to us, and He hath taken the same out of the way, fastening it to the cross" (*Col.* ii, 14), so "that we, being dead to sins, should live to justice" (*I Peter* ii, 24).

214 Though the ample redemption of Christ more than abundantly satisfied for all our offenses (cf. *Col.* ii, 13), nevertheless, by reason of that marvelous disposition of

Divine Wisdom by which we may complete those "things that are wanting of the sufferings of Christ in our own flesh, for His body, which is the Church" (*Col.* i, 24), we are able, in fact, we should add to the acts of praise and satisfaction which "Christ in the name of sinners has presented to God," our own acts of praise and satisfaction. However, we must always remember that the expiatory value of our acts depends solely on the bloody sacrifice of Christ, which is renewed without interruption on our altars in an unbloody manner, since in both cases "the victim is the same, the one who offers himself by means of the ministry of the priesthood is the same, the very same one who offered Himself on the Cross, the only difference being in the manner in which the sacrifice is made" (Conc. Trid. Sess. xxii, c. 2). For this reason we must bring together, in the august sacrifice of the Blessed Eucharist, the act of immolation made by the priest with that of the Faithful, so that they, too, may offer themselves up as "a living sacrifice, holy, pleasing unto God" (*Rom.* xii, 1). Therefore, St. Cyprian dared to affirm that "the sacrifice of Our Lord is not complete as far as our sanctification is concerned unless our offerings and sacrifices correspond to His passion" (*Ep.* 63, n. 381).

215 The Apostle admonished us that "bearing about in our body the mortification of Jesus" (*II Cor.* iv, 10) and "buried together with him by Baptism unto death" (*Rom.* vi. 4), not only should we "crucify our flesh with the vices and concupiscences" (*Gal.* v. 24) "flying the corruption of that concupiscence which is in the world" (*II Peter* i, 4), but also that the "Life of Jesus be made manifest in our bodies" (*II Cor.* iv, 10), and, having become partakers in His holy and eternal priesthood, we should offer up "gifts and sacrifices for sins" (*Heb.* v, 1). For not only are they partakers in the mysteries of this priesthood and in the duty of offering sacrifices and satisfaction to God, who have been appointed by Jesus Christ the High Priest as the ministers of such sacrifices, to offer God "a clean oblation in every place from the rising of the sun even to the going down" (*Malach.* i, 10), but also those Christians called, and rightly so, by the Prince of the Apostles, "a chosen generation, a kingly priesthood" (*I Peter* ii, 9),

who are to offer "sacrifices for sin" (*Heb.* v, 1) not only for themselves but for all mankind, and this in much the same way as every priest and "High priest taken from among men is ordained for men in the things that appertain to God" (*Heb.* v, 1).

216 In the degree to which our oblation and sacrifice will the more perfectly correspond to the sacrifice of Our Lord, that is to say, to the extent to which we have immolated love of self and our passions and crucified our flesh in that mystical crucifixion of which the Apostle writes, so much the more plentiful fruits of propitiation and of expiation will we garner for ourselves and for others. A wondrous bond joins all the Faithful to Christ, the same bond which unites the head with the other members of the body, namely, the communion of saints, a bond full of mystery which we believe in as Catholics and by virtue of which individuals and nations are not only united to one another but likewise with the head itself, "who is Christ: from whom the whole body, being compacted and fiftly joined together, by what every joint supplieth, according to the operation in the measure of every part, maketh increase of the body, unto the edifying of itself in charity" (*Eph.* v. 15, 16). This, too, was the prayer which Jesus Christ Himself, the Mediator between God and men, at the hour of His death made to His Father, "I in them and Thou in Me: that they may be made perfect in one" (*John* xvii, 23).

217 As the act of consecration proclaims and confirms our union with Christ, so the act of expiation, by purifying us from sins, is the beginning of such union; our participation in the sufferings of Christ perfects it, the offering we make to Him of our sacrifices for the welfare of our brethren brings such union to its final consummation. This was precisely the design of the mercy of Jesus when He unveiled to our gaze His Sacred Heart, surrounded by the emblems of His Passion, and aflame with the fire of love that we on the one hand, perceiving the infinite malice of sin, and on the other, filled with a knowledge of the infinite love of Our Redeemer, might detest more cordially sin and substitute for it an ardent love of Him.

218 The spirit of expiation or of reparation has always played one of the chief roles in the devotion to the Sacred Heart of Jesus. Certainly, reparation is most consonant, with the origin, nature, efficacy, and particular practices of this special devotion, a fact confirmed by history and the customs of the Faithful, by the sacred liturgy, and by the official documents of Roman Pontiffs. As a matter of fact, on the occasion when Jesus revealed Himself to St. Margaret Mary, though He then insisted on the immensity of His love, at the same time, with sorrowful mien, He grieved over the great number of horrible outrages heaped upon Him by the ingratitude of mankind. He used then these words which should be graven on the hearts of all pious souls so as never to be forgotten by them: "Behold this Heart which has loved men so much, which has heaped upon them so many benefits. In exchange for this infinite love It finds ingratitude; instead It meets with forgetfulness, indifference, outrages, and all this at times even from souls bound closely to It in the bonds of a very special love."

219 In order to make reparation for such faults. He, among other requests, made this special request as one which would be most acceptable to Him, namely, that the Faithful, inspired by the intention of making reparation, should receive Holy Communion—and for this reason it is called the "Communion of Reparation"—and for an hour should practice acts and prayers of reparation before the Blessed Sacrament—which devotion is rightly called the "Holy Hour." The Church has not only approved these devotions but has enriched them with very special spiritual favors.

220 But how can we one may ask, believe that Christ reigns happily in Heaven if it is possible to console Him by such acts as those of reparation? We answer in the language of St. Augustine, words quite apposite to our subject: "The soul which truly loves will comprehend what I say" (In Ioan. Evang. Tract. xxvi, 4).

221 Every soul which burns with true love of God, if it but turns its thoughts to the past, sees in meditation and can contemplate Jesus suffering for mankind, afflicted by grief in the midst of sorrows suffered "for us men and for our sal-

vation," weighed down by agony and reproaches, "bruised for our sins" (*Isaias* liii, 5), in the very act of healing us by His bruises. With so much the more understanding can pious souls meditate upon these mysteries if they appreciate that the sins and crimes of men, no matter when committed, were the real reason why the Son of God was condemned to death and that even sins committed now would be able of themselves to cause Christ to die a death accompanied by the same sufferings and agonies as His death on the cross, since every sin must be said to renew in a certain way the Passion of Our Lord, "crucifying again to themselves the of God and making Him a mockery" (*Heb*. vi, 6). And if, in view of our own future sins, foreseen by Him, the soul of Jesus became sad even unto death, there can be no doubt that by His prevision at the same time of our acts of reparation He was in some way comforted when "there appeared an angel from heaven" (*Luke* xxii, 43) to console that Heart of His bowed down with sorrow and anguish.

222 At the present time, we too, in a marvelous but no less true manner, may and ought to console that Sacred Heart which is being wounded continually by the sins of thoughtless men, since—and we read this also in the sacred liturgy—Christ Himself grieved over the fact that He was abandoned by His friends. For He said, in the words of the Psalmist, "My heart hath expected reproach and misery. And I looked for one that would grieve together with Me, but there was none: and for one that would comfort Me, and I found none" (*Psalm* lxviii, 21).

223 To the above we may add that the expiatory passion of Jesus Christ is renewed and in a certain manner continued in His mystic body, the Church. To use again the words of St. Augustine, "Christ suffered all that He had to suffer: nothing at all is lacking to the number of His sufferings. Therefore His sufferings are complete, but in Him as in the head; there remain even now the sufferings of Christ to be endured in the body" (*On Psalm* lxxxvi). In fact, Christ Himself made the same statement, for to Saul "breathing out threatenings and slaughter against the disciples of the Lord" (*Acts* ix, 1), He said, "I am Jesus whom thou persecutest" (*Acts* ix, 5). By

this He plainly affirmed that persecutions visited on the Church are in reality directed against the Head of the Church. Therefore, Christ, suffering in His mystical body, with reason desires to have us as companions in His own acts of expiation. He asks to be united with us for since we "are the body of Christ and members of member" (*I Cor.* xii, 27), in so far as the Head suffers so also should the members suffer with it (Cf. *I Cor.* xii, 26).

224 Now, anyone who uses his eye and mind, if he but think of this world "seated in wickedness" (*I John* v, 19), can see, as We stated above, how urgent, especially in our own times, is the need of expiation or of reparation. There come to Our ears from every side the cries of nations, whose rulers or governments have actually risen up and have conspired together against the Lord and against His Church (Cf. *Psalm* ii, 2). We have seen both human and Divine rights overthrown in these countries, churches destroyed to their very foundations, religious and consecrated virgins driven from their homes, thrown into prison, made to go hungry, treated with unspeakable savagery. We have seen troops of boys and girls, torn from the bosom of Holy Mother Church, made to deny and blaspheme Christ, and urged to commit the worst sins against purity. We have seen a whole Christian people menaced, oppressed, in constant peril of apostasy from the Faith or of a most barbarous death. These happenings, sorrowful as they are, seem to have been foreseen in such calamities as are now occurring, and to anticipate "the beginning of those sorrows" which will be revealed by "the man of sin who is lifted above all that is called God or that is worshipped" (*II Thes.* ii, 4).

225 Nor is that other spectacle, Venerable Brothers, less sad that even among the Faithful, washed as they have been by Baptism in the Blood of the Innocent Lamb and enriched by His grace, we encounter so many of every station in life who, ignorant of things Divine, are poisoned by false doctrines and live a sinful life far from their Father's house, without the light of the true Faith, without the joy of hope in a future life, deprived of the strength and comfort which come with the spirit of love. Of them one may

say quite truthfully that they are immersed in darkness and in the shadow of death. Moreover, disrespect for the discipline of the Church is on the increase among the Faithful as also disrespect for ancient traditions, upon which the Christian life has been built, by which domestic society is governed, by which the sanctity of marriage is protected. The process of educating youth has been weakened or spoiled by too much effeminacy, and even the right to educate children in their religion has been taken away from the Church. Christian modesty is forgotten, sad to say, both in our manner of life and of dress, especially by women. There has come into existence, too, an uncontrollable desire to possess the base things of this world, an unreasonable regard for civil interests, an intemperate searching after popular applause, a despisal of legitimate authority and of the Word of God, by all of which the Faith itself is shaken to its foundations or placed in jeopardy.

226 There must be added to this accumulation of evils the sloth and laziness of those who, like the Apostles asleep or like those disciples who had fled away, since they are not firmly rooted in the Faith, have shamefully abandoned Christ, burdened with sorrows and attacked by the satellites of Satan, as well as the perfidy of those others who, following in the footsteps of Judas the traitor, either with sacrilegious temerity approach Holy Communion or go over to the camp of the enemy. There thus comes to mind, almost involuntarily, the thought that we have arrived at the hour prophesied by Our Lord when He said: "And because iniquity has abounded, the charity of many shall grow cold" (*Matt.* xxiv, 12).

227 If the Faithful, burning with love for the suffering Christ, should meditate on all these considerations, it would be unthinkable that they should not expiate with greater zeal both their own and the faults of others, that they should not repair the honor of Christ, be filled with zeal for the eternal salvation of souls. Assuredly, We may adapt to our own age to describe it what the Apostle wrote: "When sin abounded, grace did more abound" (*Rom.* v, 20), for even though the sinfulness of man has greatly increased,

by the grace of the Holy Ghost, there has also increased the number of the Faithful who most gladly try to make satisfaction to the Divine Heart of Jesus for the numerous injuries heaped on Him. What is more, they joyfully offer themselves to Christ as victims for sin.

228 Anyone who has been considering in a spirit of love all that has been recalled to his mind up to this, if he has impressed these thoughts, as it were, upon the fleshy tablets of his heart, such a one assuredly cannot but abhor and flee all sin as the greatest of evils. He will also offer himself whole and entire to the will of God and will strive to repair the injured majesty of God by constant prayer, by voluntary penances, by patient suffering of all those ills which shall befall him; in a word, he will so organize his life that in all things it will be inspired by the spirit of reparation.

229 From this spirit of reparation there have been born many families of religious men and women, who, day and night, in tireless manner, have set before themselves the task of taking, in as far as that is possible, the place of the Angel who comforted Jesus in the garden. Likewise, certain pious associations, approved by the Holy See and enriched with indulgences, have as their ideal to make reparation for sin by means of certain practices of piety and of the virtues. And not to speak of all these holy works, We select out one for mention, namely, the frequent practice of making solemn reparation not only by individuals but often by whole parishes, dioceses, and even nations.

230 Venerable Brothers, just as the act of consecration, which began in a small way and afterwards came into general use, achieved, by reason of Our approval, the splendid purposes and ends desire, so We wish ardently that this devotion of reparation, which has already been introduced and is the pious custom of certain places, posses the seal of highest approval of Our apostolic authority, so that it likewise may come to be practiced universally and in a most solemn manner by all Christian peoples. We establish, therefore, and We order that annually, on the Feast of the Sacred Heart, in all the churches of the world, there take place a

solemn act of reparation (the same formula must be used by all and is the one attached to the Encyclical) to our most loving Redeemer, in order that we may, by this act, make reparation for our own sins and may repair the rights which have been violated of Christ, the King of Kings and our most loving Master.

231 Nor can We doubt, Venerable Brothers, that from this holy practice now reestablished and extended to the whole Church We may expect many signal blessings, not only for individuals but for society itself, domestic and civil, since Christ Himself promised to St. Margaret Mary that "He would shower abundantly His graces upon those who rendered this honor to His Sacred Heart." Assuredly sinners "looking on Him whom they pierced" (*John* xix, 37), stricken by the sorrow of the Church, detesting the injuries offered to the King of Kings "will return to themselves." (*Isaias* xlvi, 8), for they cannot become obstinate in sin in the presence of Him whom they have wounded "coming in the clouds of heaven" (*Matt.* xxvi, 64), for then too late and without hope, shall they "bewail themselves of him" (*Apoc.* i, 7).

232 But the just will "be justified still and the holy will be justified still" (*Apoc.* xxii, 11). They will consecrate themselves with renewed ardor to the service of their King. Seeing Him so despised and so often attacked, seeing too that so many injuries are inflicted on Him, certainly their zeal for the salvation of souls will be increased when they hear the lament of the Divine Victim, "What profit is there in My Blood?" (*Psalm* xxix, 10) and, at the same time, meditate upon the joy of the Sacred Heart "over the sinner who doth penance" (*Luke* xv, 7).

233 We, before all other things, hope and greatly desire that the justice of God, which would have pardoned Sodom if only ten just had been found therein, shall be exercised with more mercy towards all mankind. The Faithful, in union with Christ, the Mediator and our Head, will pray for and ask from God such mercy. May the most gracious Mother of God be propitious to these Our wishes and to these Our commands; she who gave us Christ the Redeemer, who watched over Him, and, at the foot of the Cross, offered Him a victim for

our sins. She, too, by reason of her wondrous union with Him and of a most singular grace of God, became and is piously known as the Mother of Reparation. Confiding in her intercession with Jesus, "the one mediator of God and man" (*I Tim.* ii, 5), who wished to associate his own Mother with Himself as the advocate of sinners, as the dispenser and mediatrix of grace, We impart from Our heart, as an augury of Divine favors and a proof of our fatherly love, to you, Venerable Brothers, and to all the flock confided to your care, the Apostolic Blessing.

234 Given at Rome, at St. Peter's, the ninth of May, 1928, the seventh year of Our Pontificate.

Ephesinam Synodum
Letter to Cardinal Sincero
December 25, 1930

We are all aware that after the Council of Nicea the Council of Ephesus was the most celebrated of the Ecumenical Councils. The first defined and solemnly decreed against Arius the Divinity of Jesus Christ; the second defined and decreed against Nestorius the dogma of the Hypostatic Union and the divine Maternity of Mary. The universal Church, therefore, which five years ago commemorated the Council of Nicea, will shortly, as is fitting, celebrate in the most suitable way possible the fifteenth centenary of the Council of Ephesus.

236 Ancient historians narrate that Our Predecessor of holy memory, Celestine I, in the case against the Nestorian heresy, not only chose as his Vicar Cyril, the irresistible Patriarch of Alexandria, but that he also sent in 431, in the office of legates to the Council which was to be held at Ephesus, in the presence of Emperor Theodosius II, the bishops Arcadius and Projectus and with them the priest Philip, giving them the following instructions: "The authority of the Apostolic See must be protected. We command it. . .If questions for debate arise, you should be judges of the opinions put forth, but do not allow yours to be discussed."

237 From this it follows that the Roman Pontiff had already taken up arms against the Nestorian heresy even before the Council pronounced sentence against it. Indeed, in the first session over which Cyril of Alexandria, as Vicar of Pope

Celestine presided, when they decreed that "Mary was the true Mother of God," the Fathers of the Council declared that they had passed sentence against Nestorius according to the Canons and the letter of their most holy Father and protector Celestine. Thus, in this text the primacy of the Roman Pontiff is at the same time clearly demonstrated.

238 We are told that while the bishops ardently defended the dignity of the Mother of God against Nestorius, the people of Ephesus crowded before the hall where the Council was held. When, towards evening, after a long and lively discussion the doors opened and it was solemnly decreed that "Mary was true Mother of God" the devotion of the people was so great that on hearing it they acclaimed the Fathers with an outpouring of joy, and, organizing a procession with blazing torches as signs of faith, they accompanied the bishops to their dwellings. Today, after many centuries all the Christian people manifest the liveliest devotion towards Mary. Thus is fully verified the prophecy of the Virgin Mary herself: "Behold from now on all the generations shall call me blessed."[1]

239 Therefore as it is Our desire that the whole Catholic world which so much enjoys the motherly aid of the Virgin should commemorate the Council of Ephesus, We ordain by this letter, Venerable Brethren, that inasmuch as under Our authority you direct the affairs of the Oriental Church, and exercise your zeal in promoting them, do all in your power to make known in the East this Council and all that relates to it. To that end you will convoke a Council made up of men of ability, who, under your presidency, shall decide on the most suitable means to commemorate worthily this anniversary; and also choose talented persons who in their learned writings and by means of their discourses shall pay tribute to this happy event.

240 We trust that Marian devotion will receive new vigor from this, and that at the same time the Orientals, through the triumph of Mary, the thoughtful Mother of all, will finally return to the bosom of the Roman Church, whose preeminence the Council of Ephesus among others of history's examples so clearly attests.

LUX VERITATIS

Encyclical Letter of Pope Pius XI
on the Light of Truth
December 25, 1931

History as the light of truth and witness of the ages, if properly investigated and diligently explored, shows that the divine promise made by Jesus Christ: "I am with you all days, even to the consummation of the world"[1] has never failed His spouse, the Church, and will certainly never fail in future. Nay, more the fiercer the waves on which the divine bark of Peter is tossed, in the course of the centuries, the closer at hand and stronger is the aid of divine grace. This is what happened in the early days of the Church, not only when the Christian name was a hated stigma to be punished by death, but also when the True Faith of Christ, owing to the treachery of the sowers of heresies, especially in Eastern countries, was greatly confused and in imminent peril. As the persecutors of Catholicity one after another perished miserably, and the Roman Empire itself fell in ruins, so the heretics all, as withered branches[2] severed from the divine vine, could not drink in the sap of life, nor produce fruit.

242 The Church of God, however, amid so many storms and changes in perishable institutions, relying solely on God has at all times proceeded on her way with sure and stately step, and has never ceased to guard devotedly the sacred deposit of evangelical truth confided to her by her Founder.

243 These things occur to Our mind, Venerable Brethren, as We begin to address you by this letter on the most happy

event, the celebration of the fifteenth centenary of the Ecumenical Council of Ephesus, in which the cunning impudence of the erring was exposed, and, supported by heavenly aid, the unshaken faith of the Church shone brightly.

244 We know how at Our request two excellent men[3] formed a committee to commemorate as worthily as possible this centenary, not only here in the chief city of the Catholic world, but among the nations everywhere. We know also how those to whom this charge was given by Us spared neither study nor labor, each to the best of his ability, that this salutary undertaking might be carried forward. On this alacrity of minds—with which nearly everywhere and with an altogether admirable cooperation bishops and distinguished members of the laity freely responded to their utmost—We express Our hearty congratulations. By it We are confident the Catholic cause will reap in the future no slight advantage.

245 Considering this event and all the facts and circumstances connected with it, as the celebration draws to a close, and the sacred season when the Blessed Virgin Mary brought forth for us the Saviour comes round again, We, by the apostolical office which We hold from on high, deem it proper to communicate with you by this Encyclical Letter on this most important matter. We cherish the good hope that not only will Our words be pleasing and useful to you and yours, but also, that if the many who are separated from the Apostolic See, brothers and sons most dear to us, being moved by the quest of truth, reflect and ponder on them, they cannot help being led by history as teacher of life, and affected by the desire at least of one fold and one Shepherd, and of embracing the true faith which is ever kept sound and entire in the Roman Church. In the process which the Fathers of the Council of Ephesus followed, in opposing the Nestorian heresy and conducting the Council, three dogmas of the Catholic Religion, which We shall treat principally, shine forth with brilliancy in the eyes of all: namely, that the person of Jesus Christ is one and divine; that the Blessed Virgin Mary should be acknowledged and venerated by everyone as really and truly the Mother of God;

and that when matters of faith or morals are concerned the Roman Pontiff has from on high an authority which is supreme above all others and subject to none.

246 To proceed with order, as a beginning, We make Our own the sentiment and warning of the Apostle of the Gentiles to the Ephesians: "Until we all meet into the unity of faith, and of the knowledge of the Son of God, unto a perfect man, unto the measure of the age of the fulness of Christ; That henceforth we be no more children tossed to and fro, and carried about with every wind of doctrine by the wickedness of men, by cunning craftiness, by which men lie in wait to deceive. But doing the truth in charity, we may in all things grow up in Him Who is the Head, even Christ: From Whom the whole body, being compacted and fitly joined together, by what every joint supplieth, according to the operation in the measure of every part, maketh increase of the body, unto the edifying of itself in charity."[4]

247 Just as the Fathers of the Council followed this apostolical exhortation with wonderful unanimity, so We wish that everyone without discrimination or prejudice should take it as addressed to himself and turn it to good account.

248 As all know, Nestorius was the author of the whole controversy. He did not originate new doctrine by his own talent and study, but borrowed it from Theodore, Bishop of Mopsuestia, and undertook to popularize it zealously, after developing it and clothing it with the appearance of novelty with great array of language and sentiment, excelling as he did in the gift of expression.

249 Born in Germanicia, a town of Syria, he went as a youth to Antioch there to be instructed in sacred and profane learning. In that city, so famous at the time, he first embraced the monastic life and next, owing to instability of character, left it and became a priest, taking wholly to preaching in the quest of human applause more than the glory of God. The fame of his eloquence inflamed the multitude and spread so far and wide that he was invited to Constantinople, then widowed of its Shepherd, and not long after, with the hearty approbation of all, he was raised to the episcopal dignity. In this truly distinguished See,

instead of ceasing to spread his perverse doctrines, he continued to teach and popularize them with still greater authority and boastfulness.

250 To appreciate the matter properly, it will help to touch briefly on the principal points of the Nestorian heresy. This highly elated man, claiming that there were two hypostases, the human of Jesus, and the divine of the Word, meeting in one common "prosopo" as he termed it, denied the marvellous and substantial union of the two natures, which we call hypostatic, and asserted that the only begotten Word of God was not made man, but was in human flesh only by indwelling, by good pleasure and by virtue of operating in it: that therefore He should be called not God but "Theophoron," or god-bearer, in much the same manner as prophets and other holy men, owing to the divine grace imparted to them, might be called god-bearing.

251 From these perverse fabrications of Nestorius it was easy to recognize in Christ two persons, one divine, the other human. It followed necessarily that the Blessed Virgin Mary is not truly the Mother of God, *Theotocos,* but Mother rather of the man Christ *Christotocos*, or at most *Theodochos*, that is, the recipient of God.[5]

252 Wicked dogmas of this kind, proclaimed not covertly nor obscurely by a private individual, but openly and plainly by the very Bishop of the See of Constantinople, created the greatest mental disturbance, especially in the Eastern Church. Among the opponents of the Nestorian heresy, who were numerous in the Eastern Empire's capital city itself, was that most holy man and champion of Catholic integrity, Cyril, Patriarch of Alexandria, who holds without question the principal place. As soon as he heard of the perverse opinions of the Bishop of Constantinople, he earnestly defended the orthodox faith, as he was most zealous not only for his own sons, but also for the erring brethren, and endeavored by letters to Nestorius written in a fraternal spirit to bring him back to the norm of Catholic truty.

253 When, however, the obdurate pertinacity of Nestorius made useless this earnest effort of charity, Cyril, dutifully aware, and fearless champion, of the authority of the Roman

Church, would not urge the matter by himself nor in so grave a case pass sentence without previously petitioning and obtaining the judgment of the Apostolic See. To the "Most Blessed" therefore "and most dear to God Father Celestine" he wrote a most respectful letter in which, in filial spirit, he says, among other sings: "The longstanding custom of the Church requires that such matters be made known to Your Holiness."[6] . . . "We are not breaking off communion with him openly and plainly until we shall have made these things known to your loving kindness. Deign therefore to declare your opinion so that it may be clearly known to us whether we should have anything in common with him, or tell him plainly that no one can have anything in common with one who fosters and preaches such erroneous doctrine. Furthermore, your entire opinion and your decision in this matter should be clearly made known to the most pious and godfearing bishops of Macedonia and to every bishop in the East."[7]

254 Nestorius was not ignorant of the supreme authority of the Bishop of Rome over the universal Church. More than once, in fact, by letters written to Celestine, he attempted to prove the correctness of his teaching, and to preoccupy and win over the mind of the Pontiff to himself, but in vain. Since therefore the ill-coined words of the heresiarch expressed serious errors, no sooner had the Bishop of the Apostolic See perceived these than, applying the remedy, lest the plague of heresy might become more dangerous by delay, he solemnly condemned the errors found by a synodal examination, and decreed that they should be condemned by all.

255 Now here We request you, Venerable Brethren, to observe closely how greatly the procedure of the Roman Pontiff in this case differed from that which was followed by the Bishop of Alexandria. Although the latter occupied the See which ranked as primatial in the Eastern Church, he was unwilling, as We have said, to adjudge this most grave controversy about Catholic faith until he could learn the sacred decision of the Apostolic See. Celestine, on the other hand, convoking a synod in Rome, and weighing the matter

carefully, by virtue of his supreme and absolute authority over the universal flock of Christ, solemnly decreed and sanctioned what follows about the teaching of the Bishop of Constantinople. He wrote to Nestorius: "Know plainly therefore that this is Our sentence: Unless you preach what the Roman, the Alexandrian, and the Universal Catholic Church holds, and what the sacred and holy Church of Constantinople held so well up to your time, and unless within ten days from the time this covenant becomes known to you, you shall have in open and written confession condemned this perfidious innovation; which aims at separating what the venerable Scripture has joined together, you are cast out from communion with the universal Catholic Church. This formula of Our judgment, with all the documents, We have forwarded by Our esteemed deacon Possidonius to my saintly fellow priest, the Bishop of the renowned city of Alexandria, who has fully reported to Us on this subject, so that as Our vicegerent he may make known Our decision to you and to all the brethren, as they should all know what is done, since the matter treated concerns them all."[8]

256 The Roman Pontiff enjoined on the Patriarch of Alexandria the execution of this sentence in these grave words: "Armed with the authority of Our See, and acting in Our stead, you will execute this sentence with strict vigor so that within the ten days as numbered in this covenant, he shall condemn his perverse preachings by written profession, and affirm that he holds concerning the birth of Christ as God the faith which the Roman Church, the Church of your holiness, and the faithful hold universally. Unless he shall do this, let your holiness provide for that Church, and let him know that he is in every way removed from our body."[9]

257 Some writers, however, both of earlier and more recent date, as if attempting to make light of the indisputable authority of the documents We have quoted, have put forth this opinion of the whole affair often in a proud and boastful spirit. Grant, they say thoughtlessly, that the Roman Bishop did issue a peremptory and absolute judgment which the Alexandrian Bishop, through enmity with Nestorius,

had provoked and gladly made his own: nevertheless, the Council of Ephesus, convened afterwards, again passed judgment on the whole matter, that had been already judged and wholly reprobated by the Holy See, and decided by its own supreme authority what all should think of it. Whence, as they conclude, it follows that an Ecumenical Council has rights more powerful and valid than the authority of the Bishop of Rome.

258 However, all who look diligently into facts and written documents for honest history, with minds wholly free of prejudices, can see how these men strive vainly to invest a counterfeit with semblance of truth. First of all, be it observed that when the Emperor Theodosius, and his colleague Valentinian in his name, convoked an Ecumenical Council, the sentence of Celestine had not yet reached Constantinople, and was in no way known there. Besides, when Celestine learned that the Council of Ephesus had been convoked, he did not object to the proposed deliberation; nay he even wrote to Theodosius[10] and the Alexandrian Archbishop[11] praising this proposal, and delegated and sent as his legates to preside over the Council, the Patriarch Cyril, the Bishops Arcadius and Projectus, and the priest Philip.

259 Now in doing this the Roman Pontiff did not leave to the arbitration of the Council the case as if undecided, but firmly adhering to "what has already been decided by Us,"[12] he ordered the Fathers of the Council to execute the sentence imposed by him so that, conferring among themselves and offering prayers to God, they might endeavor to bring back the erring Bishop of the Constantinopolitan See to the unity of the Faith. Cyril inquired from the Pontiff how he should act in the business, "whether the Sacred Council should admit a man who condemned what it held; or whether, as the time for indulgence had passed, the sentence already imposed should take effect."

260 Celestine wrote: "Let this be the part of your holiness and of the venerable brethren in the Council, that the strife arisen in the Church be suppressed, and let Us learn that, God helping, the affair is closed with the avowed correction. We do not say We are not of the Council, because

We cannot be absent from those, wherever they may be, with whom one faith still unites Us . . . We are there because what is done there for all is in Our thoughts; We are acting spiritually, because We do not appear to act corporally. I am eager for Catholic peace, and I am eager for the salvation of one perishing if only he be willing to admit his ailment. This We say lest perhaps We might seem to be wanting to one who may be willing to correct himself. Let this show that Our feet are not swift to shed blood, since he knows that the remedy is offered to him."[13]

261 These words of Celestine reveal his paternal spirit, and prove most convincingly that before everything else he sought to have the true light of faith shine upon blinded minds and that he would rejoice at the return of the erring to the Church. Moreover, what he prescribed to his legates as they set out for Ephesus makes clear the concern and solicitude with which he ordered that the divinely bestowed rights of the Roman See should be kept safe and secure: "We command that the authority of the Apostolic See be protected, as the instructions which have been given you state. You are to be present at the Council since, should disputes arise, you are to judge of the various opinions, not to take part in the contest."[14]

262 The legates did as instructed, with the Fathers of the sacred Council in full agreement. Indeed, in firm and faithful accordance with the most absolute commands of the Pontiff as stated above, when they arrived at Ephesus after the conclusion of the first session, they insisted that all the decrees enacted at the previous session should be submitted to them, to be confirmed and approved in the name of the Apostolic See: "We request you to direct that we be shown all the acts of this sacred Council so that in accordance with the decision of our blessed Pope and of this sacred gathering, we also may confirm . . . "[15]

263 Before the entire Council the priest Philip uttered that remarkable opinion on the primacy of the Roman Church which the dogmatic Constitution of the Vatican Council itself quotes (*Pastor Aeternus*)[16]: "No one doubts, nay for centuries it has been known that the holy and most blessed

Peter, prince and head of the Aspostles, column of faith, and foundation of the Catholic Church, received from Our Lord Jesus Christ, Saviour and Redeemer of the human race, the keys of the Kingdom, that the power of binding and loosing sins was given to him; that up till now and forever he lives in his successors and exercises judgment."[17]

264

What more? Did the Fathers of the Ecumenical Council object to the way the legates acted, or were they in any way opposed to it? On the contrary. Written documents have come down which establish most clearly their obediental respect and reverence. In the second section of the Council when the pontifical legates, reading Celestine's letters, said among other things: "In Our solicitude We have directed Our holy brothers and fellow priests, one in mind with Us, the Bishops Arcadius and Projectus and Our fellow priest Philip, to be present at what is done and to perform what We have before decreed, not doubting that the assent of your holiness will be given to this . . . "[18] So far from resenting this ruling of the supreme judge, the Fathers of the Council, praising it, with one voice acclaimed the Supreme Pontiff with these utterances: "A just judgment! To the new Paul Celestine, to the new Paul Cyril, to Celestine, guardian of the faith, to Celestine one in heart with the Council, to Celestine the whole Council gives thanks; one Celestine, one Cyril, one faith in the Council, one faith the world over!"[19]

265

When it came to condemning and reprobating Nestorius, the Fathers of the Council did not think that the matter was for them to judge freely and all over again, but plainly professed themselves anticipated and bound by the oracle of the Roman Pontiff. "Overtaking him (Nestorius) as thinking and preaching impiously, and obliged by the sacred canons and the letter of our most holy father and fellow in the ministry, Celestine, Bishop of the Church of Rome, in a flood of tears we have to arrive at this sad sentence against him. Wherefore Our Lord Jesus Christ, outraged by his blasphemous utterances, by this most sacred Council has defined that the same Nestorius is deprived of the episcopal dignity and cut off from all sacerdotal association and gathering."[20]

266 Firmus, Bishop of Caesarea, proclaimed the very same thing in the second session of the Council: "The Apostolic and Holy See by letters of the most holy Bishop Celestine, which he has sent to most devoted Bishops, . . . even before he prescribed the decision and rule concerning this affair, which we also have followed . . . since Nestorius, when cited by us, has not appeared, we command that the formula be executed pronouncing on him canonical and apostolic judgment."[21]

267 Now therefore the documents quoted by Us establish so expressly and significantly that the belief in the authority of the Roman Pontiff over the entire flock of Christ, subject to none and infallible, flourished in those days in the universal Church, as to recall to Our mind that clear and brilliant statement of Augustine a few years before the judgment brought by Pope Zosimus in his Tractorial Letter against the Pelagians: "In these words of the Holy See Catholic Belief is so venerable and well founded, so certain and clear, that no Christian may doubt it."[22]

268 Would that the most holy Bishop of Hippo could have been present at the Council of Ephesus; grasping with his keen intellect the point at issue between the disputants, how able he would have shed light on the dogmas of Catholic truth and defended them with his courage! However, when the legates of the Emperors reached Hippo, to hand him the letters of invitation, there was nothing to be done, except to mourn over the extinction of that surpassing splendor of Christian wisdom and his See ravaged by the Vandals.

269 You are aware, Venerable Brethren, that some who are engaged in historical investigation specialize not only in clearing Nestorius from the stain of heresy, but also in accusing the most holy Alexandrian bishop Cyril of a wicked rivalry, of calumniating Nestorius as an enemy and of contending with all his might to bring about his condemnation for things he did not teach. Indeed, the defenders of the Bishop of Constantinople do not hesitate to brand with this grave incrimination Our most blessed predecessor Celestine himself and even the sacrosanct Council of Ephesus.

However, the universal Church answers by reprobating this vain and rash venture. At all times she has recognized that the condemnation of Nestorius was justly pronounced, that Cyril's doctrine was orthodox, and she has ever regarded with veneration the Council of Ephesus as one of the Ecumenical Councils celebrated under the inspiration of the Holy Spirit. 270

Indeed, passing by many of the most convincing written documents, everyone surely knows that very many of the disciples of Nestorius—who had before their eyes the course of events, and who had no tie of relationship with Cyril—although they had been drawn to the other side out of friendship with Nestorius and on account of the strong attraction of his writings and the very exciting ardor of his controversies, after the Council of Ephesus, as if they had been stricken by the light of truth, they gradually deserted the heretical Constantinopolitan Bishop as one to be shunned by the law of the Church. Of these there were certainly many survivors when Our predecessor of happy memory, Leo the Great, wrote as follows to Paschasinus, Bishop of Lilybaeum, his legate to the Council of Chalcedon: "You know that the whole Church of Constantinople with all its monasteries and many bishops agreed in subscribing to anathematize Nestorius and Eutyches and their dogmas.[23] In a dogmatic letter to the Emperor Leo he proclaimed Nestorius in the plainest terms as a heretic and teacher of heresy with no one to gainsay it. "Anathema therefore," he says, "to Nestorius, who believed the Blessed Virgin Mary was Mother not of God but of man only; who did not believe that there was one Christ in the Word and in the flesh, but one person in the flesh and another of the Deity, and preached as separate and apart one son of God, another son of man."[24] As all should know, the Council of Chalcedon sanctioned this by reprobating Nestorius again and praising the doctrine of Cyril. Our most holy predecessor, Gregory the Great, had scarcely been raised to the Chair of Peter when in his synodical letter to the Eastern Bishops, after mentioning the four Ecumenical Councils—of Nice, Constantinople, Ephesus and Chalcedon—he makes this most noble and most 271 important statement: "On these as on a foursquare stone rises and stands the structure of faith and of each one's life and action. Whosoever does not cling to their solidity, even though he be a stone, lies outside the structure."[25]

272 It should be clear to all therefore that Nestorius really preached heretical tenets, that the Patriarch of Alexandria was a strenuous defender of Catholic faith, and that the Pontiff Celestine, with the Council of Ephesus, guarded the ancient doctrine and the supreme authority of the Apostolic See.

273 Let us now, Venerable Brethren, proceed to investigate further those points of doctrine which the Ecumenical Council of Ephesus openly professed and sanctioned with its authority by the condemnation of Nestorius. Besides condemning Pelagius and his followers—one of whom Nestorius surely was—the principal matter in question, and one on which the Fathers solemnly and almost unanimously agreed, was that the opinion of the heresiarch was impious and opposed to Holy Writ, and that what he rejected is therefore certain, namely, that there is one person in Christ, and that divine. Since Nestorius, as We have said, stubbornly contended that the Divine Word is not substantially and hypostatically united with human nature, but by a certain accidental and moral bond, the Fathers at Ephesus, in condemning the Bishop of Constantinople, clearly professed the right doctrine of the Incarnation to be held firmly by all. In letters and capitularies sent previously to Nestorius, and inserted in the Acts of this Ecumenical Council, Cyril, in wonderful agreement with the Roman Church, maintained this in these learned and insistent words . . . "On no account is it lawful to divide our one Lord Jesus Christ into two sons . . . For Scripture does not say that the Word associated with Himself the person of man, but was made flesh. That the Word was made flesh means It communicated like us with flesh and blood. It made our body its own and came forth as man from a woman not losing divinity nor origin from the Father, but, in assuming flesh, It remained what It was."[26]

274 We are taught by Sacred Scripture and by divine tradition that the Word of God united Itself not to any individ-

ual man, already in existence, but that the one and the same Christ is the Word of God dwelling in the bosom of God before all ages, and made man in time. Divinity and humanity in Jesus Christ, Redeemer of the human race, are bound together in the wonderful union which is justly styled hypostatic, and this is proved most clearly in Holy Writ wherein the one Christ is called not only God and Man, but distinctly held also as God and likewise as man, and, finally, as man to die, and as God to rise from the dead.

275 In other words, He Who is conceived in the womb of the Virgin by the action of the Holy Spirit, born, laid in the crib, calling Himself son of man, suffers, dies nailed to the Cross, is altogether the same, called by the Eternal Father in a wonderful and solemn manner: "My Beloved Son,"[27] with divine power grants pardon for sin,[28] restores by His own power the sick to health[29] and recalls the dead to life.[30] All this is clear evidence of two natures in Christ, from which proceed works that are divine and human, and shows also very clearly that Christ is one, God and man alike, through the unity of the Divine Person by which he is called "Theantropos."

276 It is clear to all that this doctrine handed down by the Church has been approved and confirmed by the dogma of human Redemption. For how could Christ, said to be "First born of many brethren,"[31] wounded on account of our iniquities,[32] redeem us from the servitude of sin unless, like ourselves, he possessed human nature? In like manner, by what right could He be said to satisfy the justice of the Heavenly Father, outraged by the human race, unless by His Divine Person He was able to do so by His immense and infinite dignity?

277 This principle of Catholic truth cannot be contradicted for the reason that our Redeemer, not having a human person, should seem to lack some perfection of His human nature and therefore as man be inferior to ourselves. As Aquinas shrewdly and wisely reminds us: "Personality belongs to the dignity and perfection of any being in so far as the dignity and perfection of any being require that it should have its own existence as is understood, by the term person.

It is, however, a greater dignity for anyone to exist in someone of greater dignity than to have one's own existence. Therefore human nature is more dignified in Christ than in us, because in us with our own existence it has its own personality, whereas in Christ it exists in the person of the Word. As it pertains to the dignity of the form to be the completion of the species, so the sensitive nature in man is more noble because of its conjunction with the more noble completing form than it is in the brute animal in which it is the completing form."[33]

278 Moreover it is worth while observing that as Arius, that most nefarious subverter of Catholic unity, opposed the divine nature of the Word consubstantial with the Eternal Father, so Nestorius, arguing in a wholly different manner, by denying the hypostatic union of the Redeemer, denied to Christ divinity full and entire as not being the Word. If, as he rashly divined, the divine and human nature in Christ were united only by a moral connection—which, as We have said, the prophets and others of heroic Christian holiness had obtained on account of their union with God—the Saviour of the human race would differ little or not at all from those whom He redeemed by His grace and blood. With the abandonment therefore of the doctrine of the hypostatic union, on which the dogma of the Incarnation and human Redemption rests and depends, the whole foundation of the Catholic religion falls away in ruin. We do not wonder therefore that the entire Catholic world trembled before the periolous advance of the Nestorian heresy; nor do we wonder that the Council of Ephesus zealously resisted its rash and very crafty attack on the Roman Pontiff, overthrew it with dire anathema.

279 We therefore, responding with minds in concord with every age of the Christian era, venerate as Redeemer of the human race not "Elias . . . nor one of the Prophets" in whom the God of heaven dwells by His grace, but with the Prince of the Apostles, acknowledging like him this heavenly mystery, with one voice proclaim: "Thou art Christ, Son of the living God."[34]

280 With this dogma of truth safely established, it is easy to conclude that the entire fabric of mundane things has by the mystery of the Incarnation been invested with a dignity greater than can be imagined, far greater than that to which the work of creation was raised. Among the offspring of Adam there is One, namely Christ, Who attained everlasting and infinite divinity, and Who is united with it in a mysterious and most intimate manner; Christ, We repeat, our brother, possessed of human nature, but God with us, or Emmanuel. Who by His grace and merits has brought us back to the divine Author and recovered for us that heavenly blessedness from which by original sin we had fallen away. Let us therefore be of grateful mind, follow our precepts, imitate our examples. In this way we shall be partakers of the Divinity, "Who deigned to partake of our human nature."[35]

281 At all times, as We have said, through the course of ages the true Church of Jesus Christ has diligently safeguarded this genuine and incorrupt doctrine on the personal unity and divinity of its Founder, but unfortunately it is otherwise among those who wander most pitiably outside the one fold of Christ. We regret that, whenever anyone separates himself obstinately from the infallible teaching of the Church, he loses gradually the certain and true doctrine about Jesus Christ. If we should ask the many different sects, those especially dating from the XVI and XVII centuries and still bearing the honored name Christian, all of which at the time they broke away professed firm belief in Christ as God and man, what they now think of Him, we would receive various and often conflicting answers. Indeed, few of them have kept the right doctrine and full faith concerning the person of our Redeemer; the others, even when they affirm something like it, seem to be like evaporated perfumes bereft of their essence. They present Jesus Christ as man, endowed with divine gifts, united more than others in some hidden way with divinity, very close to God; but they are removed from a full and sincere profession of Catholic faith. Others still admit nothing divine in Christ, believe He is merely man favored, it is true, with unusual gifts of body and soul, but

liable to error and to human frailties. Hence it appears clearly that all these, like Nestorius, wish by rash endeavor "to dissolve Christ," and therefore, according to the Apostle John, are not of God.[36]

282 From the exalted summit of this Apostolic See We therefore, with fatherly spirit, call upon all who glory in being disciples of Christ, and who place in Him their hope of salvation, of each one in particular and of human society, to cling always fast to the Roman Church in which Christ is believed with one faith, whole and perfect, worshipped with sincere adoration, and loved with undying flame of burning charity. Let those who preside over flocks separated from us remember how their forerunners solemnly professed the faith of Ephesus, and how in the past as in the present it has been kept and earnestly defended by this supreme Chair of Truth. Let them remember that this genuine unity of the faith rests and stands only on the one rock set by Christ, and further that it has been preserved safe and secure by the supreme authority of the successors of Blessed Peter.

283 On this unity of the Catholic religion We discoursed a few years ago in the Encyclical Letter *Mortalium Animos*, but it will help to recall this briefly to mind, since the hypostatic union of Christ, solemnly affirmed in the Council of Ephesus, brings back and puts before us the image of that unity by which our Redeemer wishes His mystical Body, the Church, to be distinguished as one body[37] "fully compacted and joined together."[38] If the personal unity of Christ exists as the mysterious exemplar with which He wishes the structure of Christian society to conform, everyone can see that this certainly cannot result from a feigned combination of discordances, but only from one hierarchy, one teaching body, one rule of belief, one Christian faith.[39] To this unity of the Church which is kept by communion with the Apostolic See Philip, the legate of the Bishop of Rome, witnessed when, reading the letters of Celestine with the unanimous applause of the Fathers of the Council, he uttered these memorable words: "We give thanks to this sacred and venerable Council, for as the letters of our holy and blessed Father were read to you, your holy members

have followed them with your holy salute to the holy head, and with your holy acclamations. Your holiness is aware that the blessed Apostle Peter is the source of all faith and chief of the Apostles."[40]

284 Now if ever, Venerable Brethren, all good men should be bound together in professing one and the same sincere faith in Jesus Christ and His mystical Spouse the Church, when everywhere so many men strive to throw off the yoke of Christ, spurn the light of His doctrine, shut off the channels of His grace, repudiate the divine authority of Him Who has become a "sign of contradiction."[41] Since innumerable evils result from this deplorable desertion of Christ and increase daily, it is time that all should seek a remedy from Him Who is the One "under heaven given unto men, whereby we must be saved."[42]

285 In this way alone, with the Sacred Heart of Jesus inspiring the souls of mortals, can happier times come to the individual, the family and to civil society, so bitterly disturbed in these days.

286 From this principle of Catholic doctrine, which We have treated thus far, there necessarily follows the dogma of the divine motherhood which we predicate of the Blessed Virgin Mary, as Cyril reminds us, "not that the nature or divinity of the Word took its origin or beginning from the holy Virgin, but that He derived from her His sacred body perfected by an intelligent soul to which the Word of God hypostatically united is said to be born according to the flesh."[43]

287 If the Son of the Blessed Virgin Mary is God, she certainly who bore Him should rightly and deservingly be called Mother of God. If the person of Jesus Christ is one and divine, surely Mary is not only Mother of Christ but she should be called *Deipara, Theotocos*. She who was saluted by Elizabeth, her relative, "Mother of my Lord,"[44] who is said by the Martyr Ignatius to have brought forth God,[45] she from whom Tertullian says God was born,[46] we can all venerate as the benign parent of God, whom the eternal Godhead favored with fulness of grace and honored with so much dignity.

288 Moreover, no one can reject this truth handed down from the first ages of the Church, because the Blessed Virgin Mary gave to Jesus Christ a body but did not generate the Word of the heavenly Father, for Cyril in his day rightly and luminously answers that as all in whose womb our earthly fabric is procreated, but not a human soul, are truly mothers and are styled so, so in like manner through the unity of person of the Son she acquired divine maternity.[47] Rightly therefore the impious opinion of Nestorius which the Bishop of Rome, led by the divine spirit, had condemned the year before, was again solemnly reprobated by the Council of Ephesus.

289 So great was the piety of the people of Ephesus to the Virgin as *Deipara,* and so intense their love that on hearing the judgment of the Fathers of the Council they acclaimed them with an outpouring of joy, and forming ranks with blazing torches they accompanied them to their homes. Surely she, the great *Parens Dei*, smiling sweetly from heaven on that remarkable spectacle, took care of her children of Ephesus and all the faithful of Christ in the Catholic world who were disturbed by the treachery of the Nestorian heresy, with maternal heart and ever ready assistance.

290 From this dogma of the divine maternity, as from a hidden spring of gushing water, flows the singular grace of Mary and, after God, her great dignity. Indeed, as Aquinas "The Blessed Virgin is Mother of God, and therefore by far certain infinite dignity from the infinite good God is."[48] This Cornelius a Lapide develops and explains more fully: "The Blessed Virgin Mother of God, and therefore by far excels all the angels, even the seraphim and cherubim. She is Mother of God, therefore most pure and holy, so much so that under God no greater purity can be imagined. She is Mother of God, and therefore whatever privilege has been granted to any of the saints (in the way of grace ingratiating, *gratum faciens*), that she has above all."[49]

291 Why therefore should so many innovators and non-Catholics bitterly condemn our piety toward the Virgin as *Deipara* as if we took away a worship due to God alone? Do they not know or consider attentively that nothing can be more

pleasing to Christ Jesus, Who certainly loves His mother with a boundless love, than that we should venerate her, love her ardently, and, by imitating her most holy example, endeavor to obtain her powerful patronage?

292 Here We cannot pass over in silence what is of great comfort to Us, the fact that in our days some of the innovators know better the dignity of the Virgin as *Deipara* and are drawn and disposed to reverence and honor her diligently. Provided this proceeds from a serious and sincere conscience, and not with the motive of winning the favor as Catholics, as we have found in some places, We trust that, through the works and prayers of all good people, and the intercession of the Blessed Virgin, these may be at length brought back to the fold of Jesus Christ, and in this way to Us, who, though unworthy, act in His place on earth and exercise His authority.

293 We feel that We should mention another function of the Motherhood of Mary, Venerable Brethren, which is still more pleasant and delightful. Since she brought forth the Redeemer of the human race and of all of us, whom the Lord Christ has willed to regard as brothers, she is in a certain manner the most benign mother.[50]

294 Our predecessor of happy memory, Leo XIII, wrote: "Such a one God gave us in whom, as He chose her for Mother of His Only Begotten, He implanted a maternal heart, capable of nothing but love and forgiveness; such by His own acts Jesus Christ manifested her, since He was subject and of His own accord obedient to her as a son to a mother; such He proclaimed her from the Cross when He committed the whole human race, through the disciple John, to be cared for and cherished by her, such finally she dedicated herself when, assuming, with great courage, the vast responsibility of the heritage left by her divine Son, she began at once to discharge maternal duties to all."[51]

295 Wherefore let us be drawn to her by a certain very powerful impulse and let us trust to her confidently all that is ours—joys, if we rejoice; woes, if we are in trial; hopes, if we endeavor to rise to better things. If the Church falls on difficult times, if faith wanes and charity grows cold, if morals, private and public, grow worse, if any danger threaten

the Catholic cause or civil society, let us have recourse to her begging help from heaven; in the supreme trial of death, when all hope, all help, is gone, let us lift up our eyes in tears and trembling, imploring through her pardon from her Son and eternal joy in heaven.

296 With more ardent effort therefore in the present needs under which we labor, let all go to her, and with supplication beg earnestly "that, by interceding with her Son, the preerring nations may return to Christian principles and precepts, on which the foundation of public welfare rests, and through which desirable peace and true happiness flourish in abundance. From her also let them more earnestly pray for what all should have most a heart, that Mother Church may have liberty and the fruit of it in tranquility, a liberty which it will use for the sole purpose of procuring the highest interests of mankind, and from which harm has never come to individuals or states, but always many very great benefits."[52]

297 Under the auspices of the heavenly Queen, We desire all to beg for a very special favor of the greatest importance, that she who is loved and venerated with such ardent piety by the people of the East, may not permit that they should be unhappily wandering and still kept apart from the unity of the Church and thus from her Son, Whose Vicar on earth We are. May they return to the common Father whose judgment the Fathers of the Council of Ephesus accepted so reverently, and whom they all saluted as "guardian of the faith." May all return to Us, who feel for all a paternal kindness, and who repeat as Our own those most loving words with which Cyril appealed to Nestorius: "May the peace of the Church be preserved and may the bond of love and concord remain unbroken among the priests of God!"[53]

298 Would, moreover, that very soon the happiest of days might dawn when the Virgin Mother of God, looking out through her image so exquisitely worked in mosaic under Our predecessor Sixtus III in the Liberian Basilica, and restored by Us to its original beauty, would see the separated children returning to venerate her with Us with one mind and one faith! That certainly would be Our greatest possible joy.

We deem it auspicious that We are celebrating Our tenth anniversary; We, who have defended the dignity and sanctity of the chastity of marriage against the assault of all manner of fallacy,[54] and who have solemnly championed the sacred rights of the Catholic Church in the instruction of youth, and set forth and explained the manner in which it is to be imparted and the principles to which it should conform.[55] The directions We have given on both subjects are in accordance with the exalted exemplar of the divine maternity and of the family of Nazareth. As Our predecessor of happy memory, Leo XIII, says: "In Joseph fathers of families have the most beautiful model of fatherly attention and providence; in the most holy Virgin Mother of God the most extraordinary pattern of love, modesty, perfect submission and fidelity; in Jesus, Who as son of the household was subject to them, a Divine Exemplar of obedience to admire, cultivate and imitate."[56] 299

In a special manner is it opportune that those mothers of our day who, wearied of child-bearing or of the matrimonial bond, have neglected or violated the obligation they assumed, should look and meditate intently upon Mary, who ennobled the responsible charge of motherhood to the highest degree. This inspires the hope that with the grace received through the Queen of Heaven, they may become ashamed of the dishonor branded on the great sacrament of matrimony and be happily moved, as far as possible, to attain to her wonderfully laudable virtues. 300

If all these things should result as We counsel, if domestic society—the principle and foundation of all human intercourse—should revert to the most exalted standard of this holiness, we could in time provide a remedy for our dangerous evil conditions. 301

May it so happen that "the peace of God which surpasseth all understanding keep the minds and hearts of all and, with all our minds and forces united, may the longed-for Kingdom of Christ be established!"[57] 302

We shall not conclude this Letter without announcing something that will surely please you greatly. We desire that this centenary shall have a liturgical memorial, which will 303 help to revive piety toward the great Mother of God among clergy and people. Wherefore We have directed the supreme Congregation of Sacred Rites to issue a Mass and Office of the Divine Maternity to be celebrated by the universal Church.

304 Meantime, as presage of heavenly gifts and a mark of Our paternal will, We bestow affectionately in Our Lord on you, each and all, Venerable Brethren, and on your clergy and people, the Apostolical Benediction.

305 Given at Rome, in Saint Peter's, 25 December, on the Feast of the Birth of Our Lord Jesus Christ, in the year 1931, the tenth of Our Pontificate.

MYSTICI CORPORIS

Encyclical Letter of Pope Pius XII
on the Mystical Body of Christ
and Our Union in It with Christ
June 29, 1943

The doctrine of the Mystical Body of Christ, which is the church,[1] was first taught us by the Redeemer Himself. Illustrating as it does the great and inestimable privilege of our intimate union with so exalted a Head, this doctrine by its sublime dignity invites all those who are drawn by the Holy Spirit to study it, and gives them, in the truths of which it proposes to the mind, a strong inceptive to the performance of such good works as are conformable to its teaching. For this reason, We deem it fitting to speak to you on this subject through this Encyclical Letter, developing and explaining above all, those points which concern the Church Militant. To this We are urged not only by the surpassing grandeur of the subject but also by the circumstances of the present time.

2. For We intend to speak of the riches stored up in this Church which Christ purchased with His own Blood,[2] and whose members glory in a thorn-crowned Head. The fact that they thus glory is a striking proof that the greatest joy and exaltation are born only of suffering, and hence that we should rejoice if we partake of the sufferings of Christ, that when His glory shall be revealed we may also be glad with exceeding joy.[3] 307

3. From the outset it should be noted that the society established by the Redeemer of the human race resembles its divine Founder who was persecuted, calumniated and 308

tortured by those very men whom He had undertaken to save. We do not deny, rather from a heart filled with gratitude to God We admit, that even in our turbulent times there are many who, though outside the fold of Jesus Christ, look to the Church as the only haven of salvation; but We are also aware that the Church of God not only is despised and hated maliciously by those who shut their eyes to the light of Christian wisdom and miserably return to the teachings, customs and practices of ancient paganism, but is ignored, neglected, and even at times looked upon as irksome by many Christians who are allured by specious error or caught in the meshes of the world's corruption. In obedience, therefore, Venerable Brethren, to the voice of Our conscience and in compliance with the wishes of many, We will set forth be fore the eyes of all and extol the beauty, the praises, and the glory of Mother Church to whom, after God, we owe everything.

309 4. And it is to be hoped that Our instructions and exhortations will bring forth abundant fruit in the souls of the faithful in the present circumstances. For We know that if all the sorrows and calamities of these stormy times, by which countless multitudes are being sorely tried, are accepted from God's hands with calm submission, they naturally lift souls above the passing things of earth to those of heaven that abide forever, and arouse a certain secret thirst and intense desire for spiritual things. Thus, urged by the Holy Spirit, men are moved, and, as it were, impelled to seek the Kingdom of God with greater diligence; for the more they are detached from the vanities of this world and from inordinate love of temporal things, the more apt they will be to perceive the light of heavenly mysteries. But the vanity and emptiness of earthly things are more manifest today than perhaps at any other period, when Kingdoms and States are crumbling, when enormous quantities of goods and all kinds of wealth are being sunk in the depths of the sea, and cities, towns and fertile fields are strewn with massive ruins and defiled with the blood of brothers.

310 5. Moreover, We trust that Our exposition of the doctrine of the Mystical Body of Christ will be acceptable and useful

to those also who are without the fold of the Church, not only because their good will towards the Church seems to grow from day to day, but also because, while before their eyes nation rises up against nation, kingdom against kingdom and discord is sown everywhere together with the seeds of envy and hatred, if they turn their gaze to the Church, if they contemplate her divinely-given unity—by which all men of every race are united to Christ in the bond of brotherhood—they will be forced to admire this fellowship in charity, and with the guidance and assistance of divine grace will long to share in the same union and charity.

311

6. There is a special reason too, and one most dear to Us, which recalls this doctrine to Our mind and with it a deep sense of joy. During the year that has passed since the twenty-five anniversary of Our Episcopal consecration, We have had the great consolation of witnessing something that has made the image of the Mystical Body of Jesus Christ stand out most clearly before the whole world. Though a long and deadly war has pitilessly broken the bond of brotherly union between nations, We have seen Our children in Christ, in whatever part of the world they happened to be, one in will and affection, lift up their hearts to the common Father, who, carrying in His own heart the cares and anxieties of all, is guiding the barque of the Catholic Church in the teeth of a raging tempest. This is a testimony to the wonderful union existing among Christians, but it also proves that, as Our paternal love embraces all peoples, whatever their nationality and race, so Catholics the world over, though their countries may have drawn the sword against each other, look to the Vicar of Jesus Christ as to the loving Father of them all, who, with absolute impartiality and incorruptible judgment, rising above the conflicting gales of human passions, takes upon himself with all his strength the defense of truth, justice and charity.

312

7. We have been no less consoled to know that with spontaneous generosity a fund has been created for the erection of a Church in Rome to be dedicated to Our saintly predecessor and patron Eugene I. As this temple, to be built by the wish and through the liberality of all the faithful, will be

a lasting memorial of this happy event, so We desire to offer this Encyclical Letter in testimony of Our gratitude. It tells of those living stones which rest upon the living corner-stone, which is Christ, and are built together into a holy temple, far surpassing any temple built by hands, into a habitation of God in the Spirit.[4]

313 8. But the chief reason for Our present exposition of this sublime doctrine is Our solicitude for the souls entrusted to Us. Much indeed has been written on this subject; and We know that many today are turning with greater zest to a study which delights and nourishes Christian piety. This, it would seem, is chiefly because a revived interest in the sacred liturgy, the more widely spread custom of frequent Communion, and the more fervent devotion to the Sacred Heart of Jesus practised today, have brought many souls to a deeper consideration of the unsearchable riches of Christ which are preserved in the Church. Moreover recent pronouncements on Catholic Action by drawing closer the bonds of union between Christians and between them and the ecclesiastical hierarchy and especially the Roman Pontiff, have undoubtedly helped not a little to place this truth in its proper light. Nevertheless, while We can derive legitimate joy from these considerations, We must confess that grave errors with regard to this doctrine are being spread among those outside the true Church, and that among the faithful, also, inaccurate or thoroughly false ideas are being disseminated which turn minds aside from the straight path of truth.

314 9. For while there still survives a false rationalism, which ridicules anything that transcends and defies the power of human genius, and which is accompanied by a cognate error, the so-called *popular naturalism*, which sees and wills to see in the Church nothing but a juridical and social union, there is on the other hand a false *mysticism* creeping in, which, in its attempt to eliminate the immovable frontier that separates creatures from their Creator, falsifies the Sacred Scriptures.

315 10. As a result of these conflicting and mutually antagonistic schools of thought, some through vain fear, look upon so profound a doctrine as something dangerous, and so they

shrink from it as from the beautiful but forbidden fruit of paradise. But this is not so. Mysteries revealed by God cannot be harmful to men, nor should they remain as treasures hiddin in a field, useless. They have been given from on high precisely to help the spiritual progress of those who study them in a spirit of piety. For, as the Vatican Council teaches, "reason illumined by faith, if it seeks earnestly, piously and wisely, does attain under God, to a certain and most helpful knowledge of mysteries, by considering their analogy with what it knows naturally, and their mutual relations, and their common relations with man's last end," although, as the same holy Synod observes, reason, even thus illumined, "is never capable of understanding those mysteries as it does those truths which form its proper object."[5]

11. After pondering all this long and seriously before God We consider it part of Our pastoral duty to explain to the entire flock of Christ through this Encyclical Letter the doctrine of the Mystical Body of Christ and of the union in this Body of the faithful with the divine Redeemer; and then, from this consoling doctrine, to draw certain lessons that will make a deeper study of this mystery bear yet richer fruits of perfection and holiness. Our purpose is to throw an added ray of glory on the supreme beauty of the Church; to bring out into fuller light the exalted supernatural nobility of the faithful who in the Body of Christ are united with their Head; and finally, to exclude definitively the many errors current with regard to this matter. 316

12. When one reflects on the origin of this doctrine, there comes to mind at once the words of the Apostle: "Where sin abounded, grace did more abound."[6] All know that the father of the whole human race was constituted by God in so exalted a state that he was to hand on to his posterity, together with earthly existence, the heavenly life of divine grace. But after the unhappy fall of Adam, the whole human race, infected by the hereditary stain, lost their participation in the divine nature,[7] and we were all "children of wrath."[8] But the all-merciful God, "so loved the world as to give his only-begotten Son",[9] and the Word of the Eternal Father with the same divine love assumed human nature from the 317

race of Adam—but an innocent and spotless nature—so that He, as the new Adam, might be the source whence the grace of the Holy Spirit should flow unto all the children of the first parent. Through the sin of the first man they had been excluded from adoption as children of God; through the Word incarnate, made brothers according to the flesh of the only-begotten Son of God, they receive also the power to become the sons of God.[10] As He hung upon the Cross, Christ Jesus not only appeased the justice of the Eternal Father which had been violated, but He also won for us, His brethren, an ineffable flow of graces. It was possible for Him of Himself to impart these graces to mankind directly; but He willed to do so only through a visible Church made up of men, so that through her all might cooperate with Him in dispensing the graces of Redemption. As the Word of God willed to make use of our nature, when in excruciating agony He would redeem mankind, so in the same way throughout the centuries He makes use of the Church that the work begun might endure.[11]

318 13. If we would define and describe this true Church of Jesus Christ—which is the One, Holy, Catholic, Apostolic Roman Church[12]—we shall find nothing more noble, more sublime, or more divine than the expression "the Mystical Body of Jesus Christ"—an expression which springs from and is, as it were, the fair flowering of the repeated teaching of the Sacred Scriptures and the holy Fathers.

319 14. That the Church is a body is frequently asserted in the Sacred Scriptures. "Christ," says the Apostle, "is the Head of the Body of the Church."[13] But it is not enough that the Body of the Church should be an unbroken unity; it must be an unbroken unity, according to those words of Paul: "Though many we are as one body in Christ."[14] But it is not enough that the Body of the Church should be an unbroken unity; it must also be something definite and perceptible to the senses as Our predecessor of happy memory, Leo XIII, in his Encyclical *Satis Cognitum* asserts: "the Church is visible because she is a body."[15] Hence they err in a matter of divine truth, who imagine the Church to be invisible, intangible, a something merely "pneumato-

logical" as they say, by which many Christian communities, though they differ from each other in their profession of faith, are united by an invisible bond.

15. But a body calls also for a multiplicity of members, which are linked together in such a way as to help one another. And as in the body when one member suffers, all the other members share its pain, and the healthy members come to the assistance of the ailing, so in the Church the individual members do not live for themselves alone, but also help their fellows, and all work in mutual collaboration for the common comfort and for the more perfect building up of the whole Body. 320

16. Again, as in nature a body is not formed by any haphazard grouping of members but must be constituted of organs, that is of members, that have not the same function and are arranged in due order; so for this reason above all the Church is called a body, that it is constituted by the coalescence of structurally united parts, and that it has a variety of members reciprocally dependent. It is thus the Apostle describes the Church when he writes: "As in one body we have many members, but all the members have not the same office: so we being many are one body in Christ, and every one members one of another."[16] 321

17. One must not think, however, that this ordered or "organic" structure of the body of the Church contains only hierarchical elements and with them is complete; or, as an opposite opinion holds, that it is composed only of those who enjoy chrismatic gifts—though members gifted with miraculous powers will never be lacking in the Church. That those who exercise sacred power in this Body are its first and chief members, must be maintained uncompromisingly. It is through them, by commission of the Divine Redeemer Himself, that Christ's apostolate as Teacher, King and Priest is to endure. At the same time, when the Fathers of the Church sing the praises of this Mystical Body of Christ, with its ministries, its variety of ranks, its officers, its conditions, its orders, its duties, they are thinking not only of those who have received Holy Orders, but of all those too, who, following the evangelical counsels, pass their lives 322

either actively among men, or hidden in the silence of the cloister, or who aim at combining the active and contemplative life according to their Institute; as also of those who, though living in the world, consecrate themselves wholeheartedly to spiritual or corporal works of mercy, and of those who live in the state of holy matrimony. Indeed, let this be clearly understood, especially in these our days; fathers and mothers of families, those who are godparents through Baptism, and in particular those members of the laity who collaborate with the ecclesiastical hierarchy in spreading the Kingdom of the Divine Redeemer occupy an honourable, if often a lowly, place in the Christian community, and even they under the impulse of God and with His help, can reach the heights of supreme holiness, which, Jesus Christ has promised, will never be wanting to the Church.

323 18. Now we see that the human body is given the proper means to provide for its own life, health and growth, and for that all of its members. Similarly the Saviour of mankind out of His infinite goodness has provided in a wonderful way for His Mystical Body, endowing it with the Sacraments, so that, as though by an uninterrupted series of graces, its members should be sustained from birth to death, and that generous provision might be made for the social needs of the Church. Through the waters of Baptism those who are born into this world dead in sin are not only born again and made members of the Church, but being stamped with a spiritual seal they become able and fit to receive the other Sacraments. By the chrism of Confirmation, the faithful are given added strength to protect and defend the Church, their Mother, and the faith she has given them. In the Sacrament of Penance a saving medicine is offered for the members of the Church who have fallen into sin, not only to provide for their own health, but to remove from other members of the Mystical Body all danger of contagion, or rather to afford them an incentive to virtue, and the example of a virtuous act.

324 19. Nor is that all; for in the Holy Eucharist the faithful are nourished and strengthened at the same banquet and by

a divine, ineffable bond are united with each other and with the Divine Head of the whole Body. Finally, like a devoted mother, the Church is at the bedside of those who are sick unto death; and if it be not always God's will that by the holy anointing she restore health to the mortal body, nevertheless she administers spiritual medicine to the wounded soul and sends new citizens to heaven—to be her new advocates—who will enjoy forever the happiness of God.

20. For the social needs of the Church Christ has provided in a particular way by the institution of two other Sacraments. Through Matrimony, in which the contracting parties are ministers of grace to each other, provision is made for the external and duly regulated increase of Christian society, and what is of greater importance, for the correct religious education of the children, without which this Mystical Body would be in grave danger. Through Holy Orders men are set aside and consecrated to God, to offer the Sacrifice of the Eucharistic Victim, to nourish the flock of the faithful with the Bread of Angels and the food of doctrine, to guide them in the way of God's commandments and counsels and to strengthen them with all other supernatural helps. 325

21. In this connection it must be borne in mind that, as God at the beginning of time endowed man's body with most ample power to subject all creatures to himself, and to increase and multiply and fill the earth, so at the beginning of the Christian era, He supplied the Church with the means necessary to overcome countless dangers and to fill not only the whole world but the realm of heaven as well. 326

22. Actually only those are to be included as members of the Church who have been baptized and profess the true faith, and who have not been so unfortunate as to separate themselves from the unity of the Body, or been excluded by legitimate authority for grave faults committed. "For in one spirit" says the Apostle, "were we all baptized into one Body, whether Jews or Gentiles, whether bond or free."[17] As therefore in the true Christian community there is only one Body, one Spirit, one Lord, and one Baptism, so there can be only one faith.[18] And therefore if a man refuse to hear the Church let him be considered—so the Lord com- 327

mands—as a heathen and a publican.[19] It follows that those who are divided in faith or government cannot be living in the unity of such a Body, nor can they be living the life of its one Divine Spirit.

328 23. Nor must one imagine that the Body of the Church, just because it bears the name of Christ, is made up during the days of its earthly pilgrimage only of members conspicuous for their holiness, or that it consists only of those whom God has predestined to eternal happiness. It is owing to the Saviour's infinite mercy that place is allowed in His Mystical Body here below for those whom, of old, He did not exclude from the banquet.[20] For not every sin, however grave it may be, is such as of its own nature to sever a man from the Body of the Church, as does schism or heresy or apostasy. Men may lose charity and divine grace through sin, thus becoming incapable of supernatural merit, and yet not be deprived of all life if they hold fast to faith and Christian hope, and if, illumined from above, they are spurred on by the interior promptings of the Holy Spirit to salutary fear and are moved to prayer and penance for their sins.

329 24. Let everyone then abhor sin, which defiles the mystical members of our Redeemer; but if anyone unhappily falls and his obstinacy has not made him unworthy of communion with the faithful, let him be received with great love, and let eager charity see in him a weak member of Jesus Christ. For, as the Bishop of Hippo remarks, it is better "to be cured within the Church's community than to be cut off from its body as incurable members."[21] "As long as a member still forms part of the body there is no reason to dispair of its cure, once it has been cut off, it can be neither cured nor healed."[22]

330 25. In the course of the present study, Venerable Brethren, we have thus far seen that the Church is so constituted that it may be likened to a body. We must now explain clearly and precisely why it is to be called not merely a body, but the Body of Jesus Christ. This follows from the fact that our Lord is the Founder, the Head, the Support and the Saviour of this Mystical Body.

26. As We set out briefly to expound in what sense Christ founded His social Body, the following though of Our predecessor of happy memory, Leo XIII, occurs to Us at once: "The Church which, already conceived, came forth from the side of the second Adam in His sleep on the Cross, first showed Herself before the eyes of men on the great day of Pentecost."[23] For the Divine Redeemer began the building of the mystical temple of the Church when by His preaching He made known His precepts; He completed it when He hung glorified on the Cross; and He manifested and proclaimed it when He sent the Holy Ghost as Paraclete in visible form on His disciples. 331

27. For while fulfilling His office as preacher He chose Apostles, sending them as He had been sent by the Father[24] —namely, as teachers, rulers, instruments of holiness in the assembly of the believers; He appointed their Chief and His Vicar on earth;[25] He made known to them all things whatsoever He had heard from His Father;[26] He also determined that through Baptism[27] those who should believe would be incorporated in the Body of the Church; and finally, when He came to the close of His life, He instituted at the Last Supper the wonderful Sacrifice and Sacrament of the Eucharist. 332

28. That He completed His work on the gibbet of the Cross is the unanimous teaching of the holy Fathers who assert that the Church was born from the side of our Saviour and on the Cross like a new Eve, mother of all the living.[28] "And it is now," says the great St. Ambrose, speaking of the pierced side of Christ, "that it is built, it is now that it is formed, it is now that it is . . . moulded, it is now that it is created . . . Now it is that arises a spiritual house, a holy priesthood."[29] One who reverently examines this venerable teaching will easily discover the reasons on which it is based. 333

29. And first of all, by the death of our Redeemer, the New Testament took the place of the Old Law which had been abolished; then the Law of Christ together with its mysteries, enactments, institutions, and sacred rites was ratified for the whole world in the blood of Jesus Christ. For, while our Divine Saviour was preaching in a restricted 334

area—He was not sent but to the sheep that were lost of the house of Israel[30]—the Law and the Gospel were together in force;[31] but on the gibbet of His death Jesus made void the Law with its decrees,[32] fastened the handwriting of the Old Testament to the Cross,[33] establishing the New Testament in His blood shed for the whole human race.[34] "To such an extent, then" says St. Leo the Great, speaking of the Cross of our Lord, "was there effected a transfer from the Law to the Gospel, from the Synagogue to the Church, from many sacrifices to one Victim, that, as our Lord expired, that mystical veil which shut off the innermost part of the temple and its sacred secret was rent violently from top to bottom."[35]

335 30. On the Cross then the Old Law died, soon to be buried and to be a bearer of death,[36] in order to give way to the New Testament of which Christ had chosen the Apostles as qualified ministers,[37] and although He had been constituted the Head of the whole human family in the womb of the Blessed Virgin, it is by the power of the Cross that our Saviour exercises fully the office itself of Head in His Church. "For it was through His triumph on the Cross," according to the teaching of the Angelic and Common Doctor, "that He won power and dominion over the gentiles",[38] by that same victory He increased the immense treasure of graces, which, as He reigns in glory in heaven, He lavishes continually on His mortal members, it was by His blood shed on the Cross that God's anger was averted and that all the heavenly gifts, especially the spiritual graces of the New and Eternal Testament, could then flow from the fountains of our Saviour for the salvation of men, of the faithful above all; it was on the tree of the Cross, finally, that He entered into possession of His Church, that is, of all the members of His Mystical Body; for they would not have been united to this Mystical Body through the waters of Baptism except by the salutary virtue of the Cross, by which they had been already brought under the complete sway of Christ.

336 31. But if our Saviour, by His death, became, in the full and complete sense of the word, the Head of the Church, it was likewise through His blood that the Church was enriched

with the fullest communication of the Holy Spirit, through which, from the time when the Son of man was lifted up and glorified on the Cross by His sufferings, she is divinely illumined. For then, as Augustine notes,[39] with the rending of the veil of the temple it happened that the dew of the Paraclete's gifts, which heretofore had descended only on the fleece, that is on the people of Israel, fell copiously and abundantly (while the fleece remained dry and deserted) on the whole earth, that is on the Catholic Church, which is confined by no boundaries of race or territory. Just as at the first moment of the Incarnation the Son of the Eternal Father adorned with the fullness of the Holy Spirit the human nature which was substantially united to Him, that it might be a fitting instrument of the Divinity in the sanguinary work of the Redemption, so at the hour of His precious death He willed that His Church should be enriched with the abundant gifts of the Paraclete in order that in dispensing the divine fruits of the Redemption she might be, for the Incarnate Word, a powerful instrument that would never fail. For both the juridical mission of the Church, and the power to teach, govern and administer the Sacraments, derive their supernatural efficacy and force for the building up of the Body of Christ from the fact that Jesus Christ, hanging on the Cross, opened up to His Church the fountain of those divine gifts, which prevent her from ever teaching false doctrine and enable her to rule them for the salvation of their souls through divinely enlightened pastors and to bestow on them an abundance of heavenly graces.

32. If we consider closely all these mysteries of the Cross, those words of the Apostle are no longer obscure, in which he teaches the Ephesians that Christ by His blood made the Jews and Gentiles one "breaking down the middle wall of partition . . . in his flesh" by which the two peoples were divided; and that He made the Old Law void "that he might make the two in himself into one new man," that is, the Church, and might reconcile both to God in one Body by the Cross.[40] 337

33. The Church which He founded by His Blood, He strengthened on the day of Pentecost by a special power, 338

given from heaven. For, having solemnly installed in his exalted office him whom He had already nominated as His Vicar, He had ascended into heaven; and sitting now at the right hand of the Father He wished to make known and proclaim His Spouse through the visible coming of the Holy Spirit with the sound of a mighty wind and tongues of fire.[41] For just as He Himself when He began to preach was made known by His Eternal Father through the Holy Spirit descending and remaining on Him in the form of a dove,[42] so likewise, as the Apostles were about to enter upon their ministry of preaching, Christ our Lord sent the Holy Spirit down from Heaven, to touch them with tongues of fire and to point out, as by the finger of God, the supernatural mission and office of the Church.

339 34. That this Mystical Body which is the Church should be called Christ's is proven in the second place from the fact that He must be universally acknowledged as its actual Head. "He," as St. Paul says, "is the Head of the Body, the Church."[43] He is the Head from whom the whole body perfectly organized, "groweth and maketh increase unto the edifying of itself."[44]

340 35. You are familiar, Venerable Brethren, with the admirable and luminous language used by the masters of Scholastic Theology, and chiefly by the Angelic and Common Doctor, when treating this question; and you know that the reasons advanced by Aquinas are a faithful reflection of the mind and the writings of the holy Fathers, who moreover merely repeated and commented on the inspired word of Sacred Scripture.

341 36. However for the good of all We wish to touch on this point briefly. And first of all it is clear that the Son of God and of the Blessed Virgin is to be called the Head of the Church by reason of His singular pre-eminence. For the Head is in the highest place. But who is in a higher place than Christ God, who as the Word of the Eternal Father must be acknowledged to be the "firstborn of every creature?"[45] Who has reached more lofty heights than Christ Man, who, though born of the Immaculate Virgin, is the true and natural Son of God, and in virtue of His miraculous and

glorious resurrection, a resurrection triumphant over death, has become the "firstborn of the dead?"[46] Who finally has been so exalted as He, who as "the one mediator of God and men"[47] has in a most wonderful manner linked earth to heaven, who, raised on the Cross as on a throne of mercy, has drawn all things to Himself,[48] who, as the Son of Man chosen from among thousands, is beloved of God beyond all men, all angels and all created things?[49]

37. Because Christ is so exalted, He alone by every right rules and governs the Church; and herein is yet another reason why He must be likened to a head. As the head is the "royal citadel" of the body[50]—to use the words of Ambrose—and all the members over whom it is placed for their good[51] are naturally guided by it as being endowed with superior powers, so the Divine Redeemer holds the helm of the universal Christian community and directs its course. And as to govern human society signifies to lead men to the end proposed by means that are expedient, just and helpful,[52] it is easy to see how our Saviour, model and ideal of good Shepherds,[53] performs all these functions in a most striking way. 342

38. While still on earth, He instructed us by precept, counsel and warning in words that shall never pass away, and will be spirit and life[54] to all men of all times. Moreover He conferred a triple power on His Apostles and their successors, to teach, to govern, to lead men to holiness, making this power, defined by special ordinances, rights and obligations, the fundamental law of the whole Church. 343

39. But our Divine Saviour governs and guides the Society which He founded directly and personally also. For it is He who reigns within the minds and hearts of men, and bends and subjects their wills to His good pleasure, even when rebellious. "The heart of the King is in the hand of the Lord; whithersoever he will, he shall turn it."[55] By this interior guidance He, the "Shepherd and Bishop of our souls,"[56] not only watches over individuals but exercises His providence over the universal Church, whether by enlightening and giving courage to the Church's rulers for the loyal and effective performance of their respective duties, or by sing- 344

ling out from the body of the Church—especially when times are grave—men and women of conspicuous holiness, who may point the way for the rest of Christendom to the perfecting of His Mystical Body. Moreover from heaven Christ never ceases to look down with especial love on His spotless Spouse so sorely tried in her earthly exile; and when He sees her in danger, saves her from the tempestuous sea either Himself or through the ministry of His angels,[57] or through her whom we invoke as the Help of Christians, or through other heavenly advocates, and in calm and tranquil waters comforts her with the peace "which surpasseth all understanding."[58]

345 40. But we must not think that He rules only in a hidden[59] or extraordinary manner. On the contrary, our Divine Redeemer also governs His Mystical Body in a visible and normal way through His Vicar on earth. You know, Venerable Brethren, that after He had ruled the "little flock"[60] Himself during His mortal pilgrimage, Christ our Lord, when about to leave this world and return to the Father, entrusted to the Chief of the Apostles the visible government of the entire community He had founded. Since He was all wise He could not leave the body of the Church He had founded as a human society without a visible head. Nor against this may one argue that the primacy of jurisdiction established in the Church gives such a Mystical Body two heads. For Peter in virtue of his primacy is only Christ's Vicar; so that there is only one chief Head of this Body, namely Christ, who never ceases Himself to guide the Church invisibly, though at the same time He rules it visibly, through him who is His representative on earth. After His glorious Ascension into heaven this Church rested not on Him alone, but on Peter too, its visible foundation stone. That Christ and His Vicar constitute one only Head is the solemn teaching of Our predecessor of immortal memory Boniface VIII in the Apostolic Letter *Unam Sanctam*;[61] and his successors have never ceased to repeat the same.

346 41. They, therefore, walk in the path of dangerous error who believe that they can accept Christ as the Head of the Church, while not adhering loyally to His Vicar on earth.

They have taken away the visible head, broken the visible bonds of unity and left the Mystical Body of the Redeemer so obscured and so maimed, that those who are seeking the haven of eternal salvation can neither see it nor find it.

42. What We have thus far said of the Universal Church must be understood also of the individual Christian communities, whether Oriental or Latin, which go to make up the one Catholic Church. For they, too, are ruled by Jesus Christ through the voice of their respective Bishops. Consequently, Bishops must be considered as the more illustrious members of the Universal Church, for they are united by a very special bond to the divine Head of the whole Body and so are rightly called "principal parts of the members of the Lord",[62] moreover, as far as his own diocese is concerned, each one as a true Shepherd feeds the flock entrusted to him and rules it in the name of Christ.[63] Yet in exercising this office they are not altogether independent, but are subordinate to the lawful authority of the Roman Pontiff, although enjoying the ordinary power of jurisdiction which they receive directly from the same Supreme Pontiff. Therefore, Bishops should be revered by the faithful as divinely appointed successors of the Apostles,[64] and to them, even more than to the highest civil authorities should be applied the words: "Touch not my anointed ones."[65] For Bishops have been anointed with the chrism of the Holy Spirit. 347

43. That is why We are deeply pained when We hear that not a few of Our Brother Bishops are being attacked and persecuted not only in their own persons, but—what is more cruel and heartrending for them—in the faithful committed to their care, in those who share their apostolic labours, even in the virgins consecrated to God, and all this, merely because they are a pattern of the flock from the heart[66] and guard with energy and loyalty, as they should the sacred "deposit of faith"[67] confided to them; merely because they insist on the sacred laws that have been engraved by God on the souls of men, and after the example of the Supreme Shepherd defend their flock against ravenous wolves. Such an offence We consider as committed against Our own person and We repeat the noble words of Our predecessor of immor- 348

tal memory Gregory the Great: "Our honour is the honour of the Universal Church; Our honour is the united strength of Our Brethren; and We are truly honoured when honour is given to each and every one."[68]

349 44. Because Christ the Head holds such an eminent position, one must not think that he does not require the help of the Body. What Paul said of the human organism is to be applied likewise to the Mystical Body: "The head cannot say to the feet. I have no need of you."[69] It is manifestly clear that the faithful need the help of the Divine Redeemer, for He has said: "Without me you can do nothing,"[70] and according to the teaching of the Apostle every advance of this Mystical Body towards its perfection derives from Christ the Head.[71] Yet this, also, must be held, marvellous though it may seem: Christ has need of His members. First, because the person of Jesus Christ is represented by the Supreme Pontiff, who in turn must call on others to share much of his solicitude lest he be overwhelmed by the burden of his pastoral office, and must be helped daily by the prayers of the Church. Moreover as our Saviour does not rule the Church directly in a visible manner, He wills to be helped by the members of His Body in carrying out the work of redemption. This is not because He is indigent and weak, but rather because He has so willed it for the greater glory of His spotless Spouse. Dying on the Cross He left to His Church the immense treasury of the Redemption, towards which she contributed nothing. But when those graces come to be distributed, not only does He share this work of sanctification with His Church, but He wills that in some way it be due to her action. This is a deep mystery, and an inexhaustible subject of mediation, that the salvation of many depends on the prayers and voluntary penances which the members of the Mystical Body of Jesus Christ offer for this intention and on the cooperation of pastors of souls and of the faithful, especially of fathers and mothers of families, a cooperation which they must offer to our Divine Saviour as though they were His associates.

350 45. To the reasons thus far adduced to show that Christ our Lord should be called the Head of the Society which is

His Body there may be added three others which are closely related to one another.

46. We begin with the similarity which we see existing between Head and body, in that they have the same nature, although inferior to that of the angels, nevertheless through God's goodness has risen above it: "For Christ," as Aquinas says, "is Head of the angels; for even in His humanity He is superior to angels. . . .Even as man He illumines the angelic intellect and influences the angelic will. But in respect to similarity of nature Christ is not Head of the angels, because He did not take hold of the angels–to quote the Apostle–but of the seed of Abraham."[72] And Christ not only took our nature; He became one of our flesh and blood with a frail body that could suffer and die. But "if the Word emptied himself taking the form of a slave,"[73] it was that He might make His brothers according to the flesh partakers of the divine nature,[74] through sanctifying grace in this earthly exile, in heaven through the joys of eternal bliss. For the reason why the only-begotten Son of the Eternal Father willed to be a son of man was that we might be made conformed to the image of the Son of God[75] and be renewed according to the image of Him who created us.[76] Let all those, then, who glory in the name of Christian, look to our Divine Saviour as the most exalted and the most perfect exemplar of all virtues; but let them also, by careful avoidance of sin and assiduous practice of virtue, bear witness by their conduct to His teaching and life, so that when the Lord shall appear they may be like unto Him and see Him as He is.[77] 351

47. It is the will of Jesus Christ that the whole body of the Church, no less than the individual members, should resemble Him. And we see this realized when, following in the footsteps of her Founder, the Church teaches, governs, and offers the divine Sacrifice. When she embraces the evangelical counsels she reflects the Redeemer's poverty, obedience, and virginal purity. Adorned with institutes of many different kinds as with so many precious jewels, she represents Christ deep in prayer on the mountain, or preaching to the people, or healing the sick and wounded and 352

bringing sinners back to the path of virtue—in a word, doing good to all. What wonder then, if, while on this earth she, like Christ, suffer persecutions, insults and sorrows.

353 48. Christ must be acknowledged Head of the Church for this reason too, that, as supernatural gifts have their fulness and perfection in Him, it is of this fulness that His Mystical Body receives. It is pointed out by many of the Fathers, that as the Head of our mortal body is the seat of all the senses, while the other parts of our organism have only the sense of touch, so all the powers that are found in Christian society, all the gifts, all the extraordinary graces, attain their utmost perfection in the Head, Christ. "In him it hath well pleased *the father* that all fulness should dwell."[78] He is gifted with those supernatural powers that accompany the hypostatic union, since the Holy Spirit dwells in Him with a fulness of grace than which no greater can be imagined. To Him has been given "power over all flesh";[79] "all the treasures of wisdom and knowledge are in Him"[80] abundantly. The knowledge which is called "vision" He possesses with such clarity and comprehensiveness that it surpasses similar celestial knowledge found in all the saints of heaven. So full of grace and truth is He that of His inexhaustible fulness we have all received.[81]

354 49. These words of the disciple whom Jesus loved lead us to the last reason why Christ our Lord should be declared in a very particular way Head of His Mystical Body. As the nerves extend from the head to all parts of the human body and give them power to feel and move, in like manner our Saviour communicates strength and power to His Church so that the things of God are understood more clearly and are more eagerly desired by the faithful. From Him streams into the body of the Church all the light with which those who believe are divinely illumined, and all the grace by which they are made holy as He is holy.

355 50. Christ enlightens His whole Church, as numberless passages from the Sacred Scriptures and the holy Fathers prove. "No man hath seen God at any time, the only-begotten Son who is in the bosom of the Father, he hath declared him."[82] Coming as a teacher from God[83] to give testimony

to the truth,[84] He shed such light upon the nascent apostolic Church that the Prince of the Apostles exclaimed: "Lord, to whom shall we go? thou hast the words of eternal life";[85] from heaven He assisted the evangelists in such a way that as members of Christ they wrote what they had learnt, as it were, at the dictation of the Head.[86] And for us today, who linger on in this earthly exile, He is still the author of faith as in our heavenly home He will be its finisher.[87] It is He who imparts the light of faith to believers; it is He who enriches pastors and teachers and above all His Vicar on earth with the supernatural gifts of knowledge, understanding and wisdom, so that they may loyally preserve the treasury of faith, defend it vigorously, and explain and confirm it with reverence and devotion. Finally it is He who, though unseen, presides at the Councils of the Church and guides them.[88]

51. Holiness begins from Christ; and Christ is its cause. For no act conducive to salvation can be performed unless it proceeds from Him as from its supernatural source. "Without me," He says, "you can do nothing."[89] If we grieve and do penance for our sins, if, with filial fear and hope, we turn again to God, it is because He is leading us. Grace and glory flow from His inexhaustible fulness. Our Saviour is continually pouring out His gifts of counsel, fortitude, fear and piety, especially on the leading members of His Body, so that the whole Body may grow ever more and more in holiness and in integrity of life. When the Sacraments of the Church are administered by external rite, it is He who produces their effect in souls.[90] He nourishes the redeemed with His own flesh and blood and thus calms the turbulent passions of the soul; He gives increase of grace and prepares future glory for souls and bodies. All these treasures of His divine goodness He is said to bestow on the members of His Mystical Body, not merely because He, as the Eucharistic Victim on earth and the glorified Victim in heaven, through His wounds and His prayers pleads our cause before the Eternal Father, but because He selects, He determines, He distributes every single grace to every single person "according to the measure of the giving of Christ."[91] Hence it follows that from our Divine Redeemer as from a fountainhead "the whole body, being

356

compacted and fitly joined together, by what every joint supplieth according to the operation in the measure of every part, maketh increase of the body, unto the edifying of itself in charity."[92]

357 52. These truths which We have expounded, Venerable Brethren, briefly and succinctly tracing the manner in which Christ our Lord wills that His abundant graces should flow from His fulness into the Church, in order that she should resemble Him as closely as possible, help not a little to explain the third reason why the social Body of the Church should be honoured by the name of Christ—namely, that our Saviour Himself sustains in a divine manner the society which He founded.

358 53. As Bellarmine notes with acumen and accuracy,[93] this appellation of the Body of Christ is not to be explained solely by the fact that Christ must be called the Head of His Mystical Body, but also by the fact that He so sustains the Church, and so in a certain sense lives in the Church, that she is, as it were, another Christ. The Doctor of the Gentiles, in his letter to the Corinthians, affirms this when without further qualification, he calls the Church "Christ,"[94] following no doubt the example of his Master who called out to him from on high when he was attacking the Church: "Saul, Saul, why persecutest thou me?"[95] Indeed, if we are to believe Gregory of Nyssa, the Church is often called simply "Christ" by the Apostle;[96] and you are familiar, Venerable Brethren, with that phrase of St. Augustine: "Christ preaches Christ."[97]

359 54. Nevertheless this most notable title of the Church must not be so understood as if that ineffable bond by which the Son of God assumed a definite human nature belongs to the universal Church; but it consists in this, that our Saviour shares prerogatives peculiarly His own with the Church in such a way that she may portray, in her whole life, both exterior and interior, a most faithful image of Christ. For in virtue of the juridical mission by which our Divine Redeemer sent His Apostles into the world, as He had been sent by the Father,[98] it is He who through the Church baptizes, teaches, rules, looses, binds, offers, sacrifices.

55. But in virtue of that higher, interior, and wholly sublime communication, with which We dealt when We described the manner in which the Head invluences the members, Christ our Lord wills the Church to live His own supernatural life, and by His divine power permeates His whole Body and nourishes and sustains each of the members according to the place which they occupy in the Body, in the same way as the vine nourishes and makes fruitful the branches which are jointed to it.[99] 360

56. If we examine closely this divine principle of life and power given by Christ, in so far as it constitutes the very source of every gift and created grace, we easily perceive that it is nothing else than the Holy Spirit, the Paraclete, who proceeds from the Father and the Son, and who is called in a special way the "Spirit of Christ" or the "Spirit of the Son."[100] For it was by this Breath of grace and truth that the Son of God anointed His soul in the immaculate womb of the Blessed Virgin; this Spirit delights to dwell in the beloved soul of our Redeemer as in His most cherished shrine; this Spirit Christ merited for us on the Cross by shedding His own blood; this Spirit He bestowed on the Church for the remission of sins, when He breathed on the Apostles;[101] and while Christ alone received this Spirit without measure,[102] to the members of the Mystical Body He is imparted only according to the measure of the giving of Christ from Christ's own fulness.[103] But after Christ's glorification on the Cross, His Spirit is communicated to the Church in an abundant outpouring, so that she, and her individual members, may become daily more and more like to our Saviour. It is the Spirit of Christ that has made us adopted sons of God[104] in order that one day "we all beholding the glory of the Lord with open face may be transformed into the same image from glory to glory."[105] 361

57. To this Spirit of Christ, also, as to an invisible principle is to be ascribed the fact that all the parts of the Body are joined one with the other and with their exalted Head; for He is entire in the Head, entire in the Body, and entire in each of the members. To the members He is present and assists them in proportion to their various duties and offices, 362

and the greater or less degree of spiritual health which they enjoy. It is He who through His heavenly grace is the principle of every supernatural act in all parts of the Body. It is He who while He is personally present and divinely active in all the members, nevertheless in the inferior members acts also through the ministry of the higher members. Finally, while by His grace He provides for the continual growth of the Church, He yet refuses to dwell through sanctifying grace in those members that are wholly severed from the Body. This presence and activity of the Spirit of Jesus Christ is tersely and vigorously described by Our predecessor of immortal memory Leo XIII in his Encyclical Letter *Divinum Illud* in these words: "Let it suffice to say that, as Christ is the Head of the Church, so is the Holy Spirit her soul."[106]

363 58. If that vital principle, by which the whole community of Christians is sustained by its Founder, be considered not now in itself, but in the created effects which proceed from it, it consists in those heavenly gifts which our Redeemer, together with His Spirit, bestows on the Church, and which He and His Spirit, from whom come supernatural light and holiness, make operative in the Church. The Church, then, no less than each of her holy members can make this great saying of the Apostle her own: "And I live, now not I, but Christ liveth in me."[107]

364 59. What We have said concerning the "mystical Head"[108] would indeed be incomplete if We were not at least briefly to touch on this saying of the same Apostle: "Christ is the Head of the Church: he is the Saviour of his Body."[109] For in these words we have the final reason why the Body of the Church is given the name of Christ, namely, that Christ is the Divine Saviour of this Body. The Samaritans were right in proclaiming Him "Saviour of the world";[110] for indeed He most certainly is to be called the "Saviour of all men," even though we must add with Paul: "especially of the faithful,"[111] since, before all others, He has purchased with His Blood His members who constitute the Church.[112] But as We have already treated this subject fully and clearly when speaking of the birth of the Church on the Cross, of Christ as the source of life and the principle of sanctity, and of

Christ as the support of His Mystical Body, there is no reason why We should explain it further; but rather let us all, while giving perpetual thanks to God, meditate on it with a humble and attentive mind. For that which our Lord began when hanging on the Cross, He continues unceasingly amid the joys of heaven: "Our Head" says St. Augustine "intercedes for us. some members He is receiving, others He is chastising, others cleansing, others consoling, others creating, others calling, others recalling, others correcting, others renewing."[113] But it is for us to cooperate with Christ in this work of salvation, "from one and through one saved and saviours."[114]

60. And now, Venerable Brethren, We come to that part of Our explanation in which We desire to make clear why the Body of Christ, which is the Church, should be called mystical. This name, which is used by many early writers, has the sanction of numerous Pontifical documents. There are several reasons why it should be used; for by it we may distinguish the Body of the Church, which is a Society whose Head and Ruler is Christ, from His physical Body, which, born of the Virgin Mother of God, now sits at the right hand of the Father and is hidden under the Eucharistic veils; and, that which is of greater importance in view of modern errors, this name enables us to distinguish it from any other body, whether in the physical or the moral order. 365

61. In a natural body the principle of unity unites the parts in such a manner that each lacks its own individual subsistence; on the contrary, in the mystical Body the mutual union, though intrinsic, links the members by a bond which leaves to each the complete enjoyment of his own personality. Moreover, if we examine the relations existing between the several members and the whole body, in every physical, living body, all the different members are ultimately destined to the good of the whole alone; while if we look to its ultimate usefulness, every moral association of men is in the end directed to the advancement of all in general and of each single member in particular; for they are persons. And thus—to return to Our theme—as the Son of the Eternal Father came down from heaven for the salvation of us all, He like- 366

wise established the body of the Church and enriched it with the divine Spirit to ensure that immortal souls should attain eternal happiness according to the words of the Apostle: "All things are yours; and you are Christ's; and Christ is God's."[115] For the Church exists both for the good of the faithful and for the glory of God and of Jesus Christ whom He sent.

367 62. But if we compare a mystical body with a moral body, it is to be noted that the difference between them is not slight, rather it is very considerable and very important. In the moral body the principle of union is nothing else than the common end, and the common cooperation of all under the authority of society for the attainment of that end; whereas in the Mystical Body of which We are speaking, this collaboration is supplemented by another internal principle, which exists effectively in the whole and in each of its parts, and whose excellence is such that of itself it is vastly superior to whatever bonds of union may be found in a physical or moral body. As We said above, this is something not of the natural but of the supernatural order; rather it is something in itself infinite, uncreated: the Spirit of God, who, as the Angelic Doctor says, "numerically one and the same, fills and unifies the whole Church."[116]

368 63. Hence, this word in its correct signification gives us to understand that the Church, a perfect society of its kind, is not made up of merely moral and juridical elements and principles. It is far superior to all other human societies;[117] it surpasses them as grace surpasses nature, as things immortal are above all those that perish.[118] Such human societies, and in the first place civil Society, are by no means to be despised or belittled; but the Church in its entirety is not found within this natural order, any more than the whole of man is encompassed within the organism of our mortal body.[119] Although the juridical principles, on which the Church rests and is established, derive from the divine constitution given to it by Christ and contribute to the attaining of its supernatural end, nevertheless that which lifts the Society of Christians far above the whole natural order is the Spirit of our Redeemer who penetrates and fills every part of the

Church's being and is active within it until the end of time as the source of every grace and every gift and every miraculous power. Just as our composite mortal body, although it is a marvelous work of the Creator, falls far short of the eminent dignity of our soul, so the social structure of the Christian community, though it proclaims the wisdom of its divine Architect, still remains something inferior when compared to the spiritual gifts which give it beauty and life, and to the divine source whence they flow.

64. From what We have thus far written and explained, Venerable Brethren, it is clear, We think, how grievously they err who arbitrarily claim that the Church is something hidden and invisible, as they also do who look upon her as a mere human institution possessing a certain disciplinary code and external ritual, but lacking power to communicate supernatural life.[120] On the contrary, as Christ, Head and Exemplar of the Church "is not complete, if only His visible human nature is considered . . . , or if only His divine, invisible nature . . . , but He is one through the union of both and one in both . . . so is it with His Mystical Body."[121] since the Word of God took unto Himself a human nature liable to sufferings, so that He might consecrate in His blood the visible Society founded by Him and "lead man back to things invisible under a visible rule."[122] 369

65. For this reason We deplore and condemn the pernicious error of those who dream of an imaginary Church, a kind of society that finds its origin and growth in charity, to which, somewhat contemptuously, they oppose another, which they call juridical. But this distinction which they introduce is false: for they fail to understand that the reason which led our Divine Redeemer to give to the community of man He founded the constitution of a Society, perfect of its kind and containing all the juridical and social elements—namely, that He might perpetuate on earth the saving work of Redemption[123]—was also the reason why He willed it to be enriched with the heavenly gifts of the Paraclete. The Eternal Father indeed willed it to be the "kingdom of the Son of his predilection;"[124] but it was to be a real kingdom, in which all believers should make Him the entire offering 370

of their intellect and will,[125] and humbly and obediently model themselves on Him, Who for our sake "was made obedient unto death."[126] There can, then, be no real opposition or conflict between the invisible mission of the Holy Spirit and the juridical commission of Ruler and Teacher received from Christ, since they mutually complement and perfect each other—as do the body and soul in man—and proceed from our one Redeemer who not only said as He breathed on the Apostles "Receive ye the Holy Spirit,"[127] but also clearly commanded: "As the Father hath sent me, I also send you";[128] and again: "He that heareth you heareth me."[129]

371 66. And if at times there appears in the Church something that indicates the weakness of our human nature, it should not be attributed to her juridical constitution, but rather to that regrettable inclination to evil found in each individual, which its Divine Founder permits even at times in the most exalted members of His Mystical Body, for the purpose of testing the virtue of the Shepherds no less than of the flocks, and that all may increase the merit of their Christian faith. For, as We said above, Christ did not wish to exclude sinners from His Church; hence if some of her members are suffering from spiritual maladies, that is no reason why we should lessen our love for the Church, but rather a reason why we should increase our devotion to her members. Certainly the loving Mother is spotless in the Sacraments, by which she gives birth to and nourishes her children; in the faith which she has always preserved inviolate; in her sacred laws imposed on all, in the evangelical counsels which she recommends; in those heavenly gifts and extraordinary graces through which, with inexhaustible fecundity,[130] she generates hosts of martyrs, virgins and confessors. But it cannot be laid to her charge if some members fall, weak or wounded. In their name she prays to God daily: "Forgive us our trespasses"; and with the brave heart of a mother she applies herself at once to the work of nursing them back to spiritual health. When therefore we call the Body of Jesus Christ "mystical," the very meaning of the word conveys a solemn warning. It is a warning that echoes in these words of St. Leo: "Recognize, O

Christian, your dignity, and being made a sharer of the divine nature go not back to your former worthlessness along the way of unseemly conduct. Keep in mind of what Head and of what Body you are a member."[131]

67. Here, Venerable Brethren, We wish to speak in a very special way of our union with Christ in the Body of the Church, a thing which is, as Augustine justly remarks, sublime, mysterious and divine;[132] but for that very reason it often happens that many misunderstand it and explain it incorrectly. It is at once evident that this union is very close. In the Sacred Scriptures it is compared to the chaste union of man and wife, to the vital union of branch and vine, and to the cohesion found in our body.[133] Even more, it is represented as being so close that the Apostle says: "He (Christ) is Head of the Body of the Church,"[134] and the unbroken tradition of the Fathers from the earliest times teaches that the Divine Redeemer and the Society which is His Body form but one mystical person, that is to say, to quote Augustine, the whole Christ.[135] Our Saviour Himself in His sacerdotal prayer did not hesitate to liken this union to that wonderful unity by which the Son is in the Father, and the Father in the Son.[136] 372

68. Our union in and with Christ is first evident from the fact that, since Christ wills His Christian community to be a Body which is a perfect Society, its members must be united because they all work together towards a single end. The nobler the end towards which they strive, and the more divine the motive which actuates this collaboration, the higher, no doubt, will be the union. Now the end in question is supremely exalted; the continual sanctifying of the members of the Body for the glory of God and of the Lamb that was slain.[137] The motive is altogether divine: not only the good pleasure of the Eternal Father, and the most earnest wish of our Saviour, but the interior inspiration and impulse of the Holy Spirit in our minds and hearts. For if not even the smallest act conducive to salvation can be performed except in the Holy Spirit, how can countless multitudes of every people and every race work together harmoniously for the supreme glory of the Triune God, except in the power 373

of Him who proceeds from the Father and the Son in one eternal act of love?

374 69. Now since its Founder willed this social body of Christ to be visible, the cooperation of all its members must also be externally manifest through their profession of the same faith and their sharing the same sacred rites, through participation in the same Sacrifice, and the practical observance of the same laws. Above all, it is absolutely necessary that the Supreme Head, that is, the Vicar of Jesus Christ on earth, be visible to the eyes of all, since it is He who gives effective direction to the work which all do in common in a mutually helpful way towards the attainment of the proposed end. As the Divine Redeemer sent the Paraclete, the Spirit of Truth, who in His name[138] should govern the Church in an invisible way, so, in the same manner, He commissioned Peter and his successors to be His personal representatives on earth and to assume the visible government of the Christian community.

375 70. These juridical bonds in themselves far surpass those of any other human society, however exalted; and yet another principle of union must be added to them in those three virtues, Christian faith, hope and charity, which link us so closely to each other and to God.

376 71. "One Lord, one faith,"[139] writes the Apostle: the faith, that is, by which we hold fast to God, and to Jesus Christ whom He has sent.[140] The beloved disciple teaches us how closely this faith binds us to God: "Whosoever shall confess that Jesus is the Son of God, God abideth in him, and he in God."[141] This Christian faith binds us no less closely to each other and to our divine Head. For all we who believe, "having the same spirit of faith,"[142] are illumined by the same light of Christ, nourished by the same food of Christ, and live under the teaching authority of Christ. If the same spirit of faith breathes in all, we are all living the same life "in the faith of the Son of God who loved us and delivered himself for us."[143] And once we have received Christ, our Head, through an ardent faith so that He dwells within our hearts,[144] as He is the author so He will be the finisher of our faith.[145]

72. As by faith on this earth we hold fast to God as the Author of truth, so by Christian hope we long for Him as the fount of blessedness, "looking for the blessed hope and coming of the glory of the great God."[146] It is because of this universal longing for the heavenly Kingdom, that we do not desire a permanent home here below but seek for one above,[147] and because of our yearning for the glory on high, that the Apostle of the Gentiles did not hesitate to say: "One Body and one Spirit, as you are called in one hope of your calling";[148] nay rather that Christ in us is our hope of glory.[149] 377

73. But if the bonds of faith and hope, which bind us to our Redeemer in His Mystical Body are weighty and important, those of charity are certainly no less so. If even in the natural order the love of friendship is something supremely noble, what shall we say of that supernatural love, which God infuses into our hearts? "God is charity and he that abideth in charity abideth in God and God in him."[150] The effect of this charity–such would seem to be God's law–is to compel Him to enter into our loving hearts to return love for love, as He said: "If anyone love me . . . , my Father will love him and we will come to him and will make our abode with him."[151] Charity then, more than any other virtue binds us closely to Christ. How many children of the Church, on fire with this heavenly flame, have rejoiced to suffer insults for Him, and to face and overcome the hardest trials, even at the cost of their lives and the shedding of their blood. For this reason our Divine Saviour earnestly exhorts us in these words: "Abide in my love." And as charity, if it does not issue effectively in good works, is something altogether empty and unprofitable, He added immediately: "If you keep my commandments you shall abide in my love; as I also have kept my Father's commandments and do abide in his love."[152] 378

74. But, corresponding to this love of God and of Christ, there must be love of the neighbour. How can we claim to love the Divine Redeemer, if we hate those whom He has redeemed with His precious blood, so that He might make 379

them members of His Mystical Body? For that reason the beloved disciple warns us: "If any man say: I love God, and hateth his brother, he is a liar. For he that loveth not his brother whom he seeth, how can he love God whom he seeth not. And this commandment we have from God, that he who loveth God love also his brother."[153] Rather it should be said that the more we become "members one of another."[154] "mutually careful one for another"[155] the closer we shall be united with God and with Christ; as on the other hand, the more ardent the love that binds us to God and to our divine Head, the closer we shall be united to each other in the bonds of charity.

380 75. Now the only-begotten Son of God embraced us in His infinite knowledge and undying love before the world began. And that He might give a visible and exceedingly beautiful expression to this love, He assumed our nature in hypostatic union: hence—as Maximus of Turin with a certain unaffected simplicity remarks—"in Christ our own flesh loves us."[156] But the knowledge and love of our Divine Redeemer, of which we were the object from the first moment of His Incarnation, exceed all that the human intellect can hope to grasp. For hardly was He conceived in the womb of the Mother of God, when He began to enjoy the beatific vision, and in that vision all the members of His Mystical Body were continually and unceasingly present to Him, and He embraced them with His redeeming love. O marvelous condescension of divine love for us! O inestimable dispensation of boundless charity! In the crib, on the Cross, in the unending glory of the Father, Christ has all the members of the Church present before Him and united to Him in a much clearer and more loving manner than that of a mother who clasps her child to her breast, or than that with which a man knows and loves himself.

381 76. From all that We have hitherto said, you will readily understand, Venerable Brethren, why Paul the Apostle so often writes that Christ is in us and we in Christ. In proof of which, there is this other more subtle reason. Christ is in us through His Spirit, whom He gives to us and through whom He acts within us in such a way that all divine activity of the

Holy Spirit within our souls must also be attributed to Christ.[157] "If a man hath not the Spirit of Christ, he is none of his," says the Apostle, "but if Christ be in you . . . , the spirit liveth because of justification."[158]

77. This communication of the Spirit of Christ is the channel through which all the gifts, powers, and extraordinary graces found superabundantly in the Head as in their source flow into all the members of the Church, and are perfected daily in them according to the place they hold in the Mystical Body of Jesus Christ. Thus the Church becomes, as it were, the filling out and the complement of the Redeemer, while Christ in a sense attains through the Church a fulness in all things.[159] Herein we find the reason why, according to the opinion of Augustine already referred to, the mystical Head, which is Christ, and the Church, which here below as another Christ shows forth His person, constitute one new man, in whom heaven and earth are joined together in perpetuating the saving work of the Cross: Christ We mean, the Head and the Body, the whole Christ. 382

78. For indeed We are not ignorant of the fact that this profound truth—of our union with the Divine Redeemer and in particular of the indwelling of the Holy Spirit in our souls—is shrouded in darkness by many a veil that impedes our power to understand and explain it, both because of the hidden nature of the doctrine itself, and of the limitations of our human intellect. But We know, too, that from well-directed and earnest study of this doctrine, and from the clash of diverse opinions and the discussion thereof, provided that these are regulated by the love of truth and by due submission to the Church, much light will be gained, which, in its turn will help to progress in kindred sacred sciences. Hence We do not censure those who in various ways, and with diverse reasonings make every effort to understand and to clarify the mystery of this our wonderful union with Christ. But let all agree uncompromisingly on this, if they would not err from truth and from the orthodox teaching of the Church: to reject every kind of mystic union by which the faithful of Christ should in any way pass beyond the sphere of creatures and wrongly enter the divine, were it 383

only to the extend of appropriating to themselves as their own but one single attribute of the eternal Godhead. And, moreover, let all hold this as certain truth, that all these activities are common to the most Blessed Trinity, in so far as they have God as supreme efficient cause.

384 79. It must also be borne in mind that there is question here of a hidden mystery, which during this earthly exile can only be dimly seen through a veil, and which no human words can express. The Divine Persons are said to indwell inasmuch as they are present to beings endowed with intelligence in a way that lies beyond human comprehension, and in a unique and very intimate manner, which transcends all created nature, these creatures enter into relationship with Them through knowledge and love.[160] If we would attain, in some measure, to a clearer perception of this truth, let us not neglect the method strongly recommended by the Vatican Council[161] in similar cases, by which these mysteries are compared one with another and with the end to which they are directed, so that in the light which this comparison throws upon them we are able to discern, at least partially, the hidden things of God.

385 80. Therefore, Our most learned predecessor Leo XIII of happy memory, speaking of our union with Christ and with the Divine Paraclete who dwells within us, and fixing his gaze on that blessed vision through which this mystical union will attain its confirmation and perfection in heaven says: "This wonderful union, or indwelling properly so-called, differs from that by which God embraces and gives joy to the elect only by reason of our earthly state."[162] In that celestial vision it will be granted to the eyes of the human mind strengthened by the light of glory, to contemplate the Father, the Son, and the Holy Spirit in an utterly ineffable manner, to assist throughout eternity at the processions of the Divine Persons, and to rejoice with a happiness like to that with which the holy and undivided Trinity is happy.

386 81. It seems to Us that something would be lacking to what We have thus far proposed concerning the close union of the Mystical Body of Jesus Christ with its Head, were We

not to add here a few words on the Holy Eucharist, by which this union during this mortal life reaches, as it were, a culmination.

82. By means of the Eucharistic Sacrifice Christ our Lord willed to give to the faithful a striking manifestation of our union among ourselves and with our divine Head, wonderful as it is and beyond all praise. For in this Sacrifice the sacred minister acts as the vicegerent not only of our Saviour but of the whole Mystical Body and of each one of the faithful. In this act of Sacrifice through the hands of the priest, by whose word alone the Immaculate Lamb is present on the altar, the faithful themselves, united with him in prayer and desire, offer to the Eternal Father a most acceptable victim of praise and propitiation for the needs of the whole Church. And as the Divine Redeemer, when dying on the Cross, offered Himself to the Eternal Father as Head of the whole human race, so "in this clean oblation"[163] He offers to the heavenly Father not only Himself as Head of the Church, but in Himself His mystical members also, since He holds them all, even those who are weak and ailing, in His most loving Heart. 387

83. The Sacrament of the Eucharist is itself a striking and wonderful figure of the unity of the Church, if we consider how in the bread to be consecrated many grains go to form one whole,[164] and that in it the very Author of supernatural grace is given to us, so that through Him we may receive the spirit of charity in which we are bidden to live now no longer our own life but the life of Christ, and to love the Redeemer Himself in all the members of His social Body. 388

84. As then in the sad and anxious times through which we are passing there are many who cling so firmly to Christ the Lord hidden beneath the Eucharistic veils that neither tribulation, nor distress, nor famine, nor nakedness, nor danger, nor persecution, nor the sword can separate them from His love,[165] surely no doubt can remain that Holy Communion which once again in God's providence is much more frequented even from early childhood, may become a source of that fortitude which not infrequently makes Christians into heroes. 389

390 85. If the faithful, Venerable Brethren, in a spirit of sincere piety understand these things accurately and hold to them steadfastly, they will the more easily avoid those errors which arise from an irresponsible investigation of this difficult matter, such as some have made not without seriously endangering Catholic faith and disturbing the peace of souls.

391 86. For some there are who neglect the fact that the Apostle Paul has used metaphorical language in speaking of this doctrine, and failing to distinguish as they should the precise and proper meaning of the terms the physical body, the social body, and the mystical Body, arrive at a distorted idea of unity. They make the Divine Redeemer and the members of the Church coalesce in one physical person, and while they bestow divine attributes on man, they make Christ our Lord subject to error and to human inclination to evil. But Catholic faith and the writings of the holy Fathers reject such false teaching as impious and sacrilegious; and to the mind of the Apostle of the Gentiles it is equally abhorrent, for although he brings Christ and His Mystical Body into a wonderfully intimate union, he nevertheless distinguishes one from the other as Bridegroom from Bride.[166]

392 87. No less far from the truth is the dangerous error of those who endeavor to deduce from the mysterious union of us all with Christ a certain unhealthy *quietism*. They would attribute the whole spiritual life of Christians and their progress in virtue exclusively to the action of the divine Spirit, setting aside and neglecting the collaboration which is due from us. No one of course can deny that the Holy Spirit of Jesus Christ as the one source of whatever supernatural powers enters into the Church and its members. For "the Lord will give grace and glory" as the Psalmist says.[167] But that men should persevere constantly in their good works, that they should advance eagerly in grace and virtue, that they should strive earnestly to reach the heights of Christian perfection and at the same time to the best of their power should stimulate others to attain the same goal,—all this the heavenly Spirit does not will to effect unless they contribute their daily share of zealous activity. "For divine favours are

conferred not on those who sleep, but on those who watch" as St. Ambrose says.[168] For if in our mortal body the members are strengthened and grow through continued exercise, much more truly can this be said of the social Body of Jesus Christ in which each individual member retains his own personal freedom, responsibility, and principles of conduct. For that reason he who said: "I live, now not I, but Christ liveth in me"[169] did not at the same time hesitate to assert: "His (God's) grace in me has not been void, but I have laboured more abundantly than all they: yet not I, but the grace of God with me."[170] It is perfectly clear, therefore, that in these false doctrines the mystery which we are considering is not directed to the spiritual advancement of the faithful but is turned to their deplorable ruin.

88. The same result follows from the opinions of those who assert that little importance should be given to the frequent confession of venial sins. Far more important, they say, is that general confession which the Spouse of Christ, surrounded by her children in the Lord, makes each day by the mouth of the priest as he approaches the altar of God. As you well know, Venerable Brethren, it is true that venial sins may be expiated in many ways which are to be highly commended. But to ensure more rapid progress day by day in the path of virtue, We will that the pious practice of frequent confession, which was introduced into the Church by the inspiration of the Holy Spirit, should be earnestly advocated. By it genuine self-knowledge is increased, Christian humility grows, bad habits are corrected, spiritual neglect and tepidity are resisted, the conscience is purified, the will strengthened, a salutary self-control is attained, and grace is increased in virtue of the Sacrament itself. Let those, therefore, among the younger clergy who make light of or lessen esteem for frequent confession realize that what they are doing is alien to the Spirit of Christ and disastrous for the Mystical Body of our Saviour. 393

89. There are others who deny any impetratory power to our prayers, or who endeavor to insinuate into men's minds the idea that prayers offered to God in private should be considered of little worth, whereas public prayers which are 394

made in the name of the Church are those which really matter, since they proceed from the Mystical Body of Jesus Christ. This opinion is false; for the divine Redeemer is most closely united not only with His Church, which is His beloved Spouse, but also with each and every one of the faithful, and He ardently desires to speak with them heart to heart, especially after Holy Communion. It is true that public prayer, inasmuch as it is offered by Mother Church, excels any other kind of prayer by reason of her dignity as Spouse of Christ; but no prayer, even the most private, is lacking in dignity or power, and all prayer is of the greatest help to the Mystical Body in which, through the Communion of Saints, no good can be done, no virtue practised by individual members, which does not redound also to the salvation of all. Neither is a man forbidden to ask for himself particular favours even for this life merely because he is a member of this Body, provided he is always resigned to the divine will; for the members retain their own personality and remain subject to their own individual needs.[171] Moreover, how highly all should esteem mental prayer is proved not only by ecclesiastical documents but also by the custom and practice of the saints.

395 90. Finally there are those who assert that our prayers should be directed not to the person of Jesus Christ but rather to God, or to the Eternal Father through Christ, since our Saviour as Head of His Mystical Body is only "Mediator of God and men."[172] But this certainly is opposed not only to the mind of the Church and to Christian usage but to truth. For, to speak exactly, Christ is Head of the universal Church as He exists at once in both His natures;[173] moreover He Himself has solemnly declared: "If you shall ask me anything in my name, that I will do."[174] For although prayers are very often directed to the Eternal Father through the only-begotten Son, especially in the Eucharistic Sacrifice—in which Christ, at once Priest and Victim, exercises in a special manner the office of Mediator—nevertheless not infrequently even in this Sacrifice prayers are addressed to the Divine Redeemer also; for all Christians must clearly know and understand that the man Jesus Christ is also the Son of

God and God Himself. And thus when the Church militant offers her adoration and prayers to the Immaculate Lamb, the Sacred Victim, her voice seems to re-echo the never-ending chorus of the Church triumphant: "To him that sitteth on the throne and to the Lamb benediction and honour and glory and power for ever and ever."[175]

91. Venerable Brethren, in Our exposition of this mystery which embraces the hidden union of us all with Christ, We have thus far, as Teacher of the Universal Church, illumined the mind with the light of truth, and Our pastoral office now requires that We provide an incentive for the heart to love this Mystical Body with that ardour of charity which is not confined to thoughts and words but which issues in deeds. If those who lived under the Old Law could sing of their earthly city: "If I forget thee O Jerusalem let my right hand be forgotten; let my tongue cleave to my jaws if I do not remember thee, if I make not Jerusalem the beginning of my joy,"[176] how much greater then should be the joy and exultation that should fill our hearts who dwell in a City built on the holy mountain of living and chosen stones, "Jesus Christ himself being the chief corner-stone."[177] For nothing more glorious, nothing nobler, nothing surely more honourable can be imagined than to belong to the Holy, Catholic, Apostolic and Roman Church, in which we become members of one Body as venerable as it is unique; are guided by one supreme Head; are filled with one divine Spirit; are nourished during our earthly exile by one doctrine and one heavenly Bread, until at last we enter into the one, unending blessedness of heaven. 396

92. But lest we be deceived by the angel of darkness who transforms himself into an angel of light,[178] let this be the supreme law of our love: to love the Spouse of Christ as Christ willed her to be, and as He purchased her with His blood. Hence not only should we cherish exceedingly the Sacraments with which holy Mother Church sustains our life, the solemn ceremonies which she celebrates for our solace and our joy, the sacred chant and the liturgical rites by which she lifts our minds up to heaven, but also the sacramentals and all those exercises of piety by which she consoles the hearts of the faithful and sweetly imbues them with the 397

Spirit of Christ. As her children, it is our duty, not only to make a return to her for her maternal goodness to us, but also to respect the authority which she has received from Christ in virtue of which she brings into captivity our understanding unto the obedience of Christ.[179] Thus we are commanded to obey her laws and her moral precepts, even if at times they are difficult to our fallen nature; to bring our rebellious body into subjection through voluntary mortification; and at times we are warned to abstain even from harmless pleasures. Nor does it suffice to love this Mystical Body for the glory of its divine Head and for its heavenly gifts; we must love it with an effective love as it appears in this our mortal flesh—made up, that is, of weak human elements, even though at times they are little fitted to the place which they occupy in this venerable Body.

398 93. In order that such a solid and undivided love may abide and increase in our souls day by day, we must accustom ourselves to see Christ Himself in the Church. For it is Christ who lives in His Church, and through her teaches, governs and sanctifies; it is Christ also who manifests Himself differently in different members of His society. If the faithful strive to live in a spirit of lively faith, they will not only pay due honour and reverence to the more exalted members of this Mystical Body, especially those who according to Christ's mandate will have to render an account of our souls,[180] but they will take to their hearts those members who are the object of our Saviour's special love: the weak, We mean, the wounded, and the sick who are in need of material or spiritual assistance; children whose innocence is so easily exposed to danger in these days, and whose young hearts can be moulded as wax; and finally the poor, in helping whom we recognize, as it were, through His supreme mercy, the very person of Jesus Christ.

399 94. For as the Apostle with good reason admonishes us: "Those that seem the more feeble members of the Body are more necessary; and those that we think the less honourable members of the Body, we surround with more abundant honour."[181] Conscious of the obligations of Our high office We deem it necessary to reiterate this grave statement today,

when to Our profound grief We see at times the deformed, the insane, and those suffering from hereditary disease deprived of their lives, as though they were a uselss burden to Society; and this procedure is hailed by some as a manifestation of human progress, and as something that is entirely in accordance with the common good. Yet who that is possessed of sound judgment does not recognize that this not only violates the natural and the divine law[182] written in the heart of every man, but that it outrages the noblest instincts of humanity? The blood of these unfortunate victims who are all the dearer to our Redeemer because they are deserving of greater pity "cries to God from the earth."[183]

95. In order to guard against the gradual weakening of that sincere love which requires us to see our Saviour in the Church and in its members, it is most fitting that we should look to Jesus Himself as the perfect model of love for the Church. 400

96. And first of all let us imitate the breath of His love. For the Church, the Bride of Christ, is one; and yet so vast is the love of the divine Spouse that it embraces in His Bride the whole human race without exception. Our Saviour shed His blood precisely in order that He might reconcile men to God through the Cross, and might constrain them to unite in one Body, however widely they may differ in nationality and race. True love of the Church, therefore, requires not only that we should be mutually solicitous one for another[184] as members of the same Body, rejoicing in the glory of the other members and sharing in their suffering,[185] but likewise that we should recognize in other men, although they are not yet joined to us in the Body of the Church, our brothers in Christ according to the flesh, called, together with us, to the same eternal salvation. It is true, unfortunately, especially today, that there are some who extol enmity, hatred, and spite as if they enhanced the dignity and the worth of man. Let us, however, while we look with sorrow on the disastrous consequences of this teaching, follow our peaceful King who taught us to love not only those who are of a different nation or race,[186] but even our enemies.[187] While Our heart overflows with the sweetness of the teaching of the Apostle of the Gentiles, We extol with him the length, 401

and the breadth, and the height, and the depth of the charity of Christ,[188] which neither diversity of race or customs can diminish, nor the trackless wastes of the ocean weaken, nor wars, whether just or unjust, destroy.

402 97. In this gravest of hours, Venerable Brethren, when bodies are racked with pain and souls are oppressed with grief, every individual must be aroused to this supernatural charity so that by the combined efforts of all good men, striving to outdo each other in pity and mercy—We have in mind especially, those who are engaged in any kind of relief work—the immense needs of mankind, both spiritual and corporal, may be alleviated, and the devoted generosity, the inexhaustible fruitfulness of the Mystical Body of Jesus Christ, may shine resplendently throughout the whole world.

403 98. As the vastness of the charity with which Christ loved His Church is equalled by its constant activity, we all, with the same assiduous and zealous charity must love the Mystical Body of Christ. Now from the moment of His Incarnation, when he laid the first foundations of the Church, even to His last mortal breath, our Redeemer never ceased for an instant, though He was the Son of God, to labour unto weariness in order to establish and strengthen the Church, whether by giving us the shining example of His holiness, or by preaching, or conversing, or gathering and instructing disciples. And so We desire that all who claim the Church as their mother, should seriously consider that not only the clergy and those who have consecrated themselves to God in the religious life, but the other members of the mystical Body of Jesus Christ as well have, each in his degree, the obligation of working hard and constantly for the building up and increase of this Body. We wish this to be borne in mind especially by members of Catholic Action who assist the Bishops and the priests in their apostolic labours—and to their praise be it said, they do realize it—and also by those members of pious associations who work for the same end. There is no one who does not realize that their energetic zeal is of the highest importance and of the greatest weight especially in the present circumstances.

99. In this connection We cannot pass over in silence the fathers and mothers of families to whom our Saviour has entrusted the youngest members of His Mystical Body. We plead with them most earnestly, for the love of Christ and the Church, to take the greatest possible care of the children confided to them, and to protect them from the snares of every kind into which they can be lured so easily today. 404

100. Our Redeemer showed His burning love for the Church especially by praying for her to His heavenly father. To recall but a few examples: everyone knows, Venerable Brethren, that just before the crucifixion He prayed repeatedly for Peter,[189] for the other Apostles,[190] for all who, through the preaching of the holy Gospel, would believe in Him.[191] 405

101. After the example of Christ we too should pray daily to the Lord of the harvest to send labourers into His harvest.[192] Our united prayer should rise daily to heaven for all the members of the Mystical Body of Jesus Christ; first for Bishops who are responsible in a special way for their respective dioceses; then for priests and religious, both men and women, who have been called to the service of God, and who, at home and in the foreign missions, are protecting, increasing, and advancing the Kingdom of the Divine Redeemer. No member of this venerated Body must be forgotten in this common prayer; and let there be a special remembrance of those who are weighed down with the sorrows and afflictions of this earthly exile, as also for the suffering souls in Purgatory. Neither must those be neglected who are being instructed in Christian doctrine, so that they may be able to receive baptism without delay. 406

102. Likewise, We must earnestly desire that this united prayer may embrace in the same ardent charity both those who, not yet enlightened by the truth of the Gospel, are still without the fold of the Church, and those who, on account of regrettable schism, are separated from Us, who though unworthy, represent the person of Jesus Christ on earth. Let us then re-echo that divine prayer of our Saviour to the heavenly Father: "That they all may be one, as thou Father in me, and I in thee, that they also may be one in us; that the world may believe that thou hast sent me."[193] 407

408 103. As you know, Venerable Brethren, from the very beginning of Our Pontificate, We have committed to the protection and guidance of heaven those who do not belong to the visible Body of the Catholic Church, solemnly declaring that after the example of the Good Shepherd We desire nothing more ardently than that they may have life and have it more abundantly.[194] Imploring the prayers of the whole Church We wish to repeat this solemn declaration in this Encyclical Letter in which We have proclaimed the praises of the "great and glorious Body of Christ,"[195] and from a heart overflowing with love We ask each and every one of them to correspond to the interior movements of grace, and to seek to withdraw from that state in which they cannot be sure of their salvation.[196] For even though by an unconscious desire and longing they have a certain relationship with the Mystical Body of the Redeemer, they still remain deprived of those many heavenly gifts and helps which can only be enjoyed in the Catholic Church. Therefore may they enter into Catholic unity and, joined with Us in the one, organic Body of Jesus Christ, may they together with us run on to the one Head in the Society of glorious love.[197] Persevering in prayer to the Spirit of love and truth, We wait for them with open and outstretched arms to come not to a stranger's house, but to their own, their father's home.

409 104. Though We desire this unceasing prayer to rise to God from the whole Mystical Body in common, that all the straying sheep may hasten to enter the one fold of Jesus Christ, yet We recognize that this must be done of their own free will; for no one believes unless he wills to believe.[198] Hence they are most certainly not genuine Christians[199] who against their belief are forced to go into a church, to approach the altar and to receive the Sacraments; for the "faith without which it is impossible to please God"[200] is an entirely free "submission of intellect and will."[201] Therefore whenever it happens, despite the constant teaching of this Apostolic See,[202] that anyone is compelled to embrace the Catholic faith against his will, Our sense of duty demands that We condemn the act. For men must be effectively drawn to the truth by the Father of light through the Spirit of His

beloved Son, because, endowed as they are with free will, they can misuse their freedom under the impulse of mental agitation and base desires. Unfortunately many are still wandering far from Catholic truth, being unwilling to follow the inspirations of divine grace, because neither they[203] nor the faithful pray to God with sufficient fervour for this intention. Again and again We beg all who ardently love the Church to follow the example of the Divine Redeemer and to give themselves constantly to such prayer.

105. And likewise, above all in the present crisis, it seems to Us not only opportune but necessary that earnest supplications should be offered for kings, princes, and for all those who govern nations and are thus in a position to assist the Church by their protecting power, so that, the conflict ended, "peace the work of justice"[204] under the impulse of divine charity may emerge from out this raging tempest and be restored to wearied man, and that holy Mother Church "may lead a quiet and peaceable life in all piety and chastity."[205] We must plead with God to grant that the rulers of nations may love wisdom,[206] so that the severe judgment of the Holy Spirit may never fall on them: "Because being ministers of his kingdom you have not judged rightly, nor kept the law of justice, nor walked according to the will of God; horribly and speedily will he appear to you; for a most severe judgement shall be for them that bear rule. For to him that is little, mercy is granted, but the mighty shall be mightily tormented. For God will not except any man's person, neither will he stand in awe of any man's greatness; for he made the little and the great, and he hath equally care of all. But a greater punishment is ready for the more mighty. To you, therefore, O Kings, are these my words, that you may learn wisdom and not fall from it."[207] 410

106. Moreover, Christ proved His love for His spotless Bride not only at the cost of immense labour and constant prayer, but by His sorrows and His sufferings which He willingly and lovingly endured for her sake. "Having loved his own . . . he loved them unto the end."[208] Indeed it was only at the price of His blood that He purchased the Church.[209] Let us then follow gladly in the bloodstained footsteps of 411

our King, for this is necessary to ensure our salvation. "For if we have been planted together in the likeness of his death, we shall be also in the likeness of his resurrection,"[210] and "if we be dead with him we shall live also with him."[211] Also our zealous love for the Church demands it, and our brotherly love for the souls she brings forth to Christ. For although our Saviour's cruel passion and death merited for His Church an infinite treasure of graces, God's inscrutable providence has decreed that these graces should not be granted to us all at once; but their greater or lesser abundance will depend in no small part on our good works, which draw down on the souls of men a rain of heavenly gifts freely bestowed by God. These heavenly gifts will surely flow more abundantly if we not only pray fervently to God, especially by participating every day if possible in the Eucharistic Sacrifice; if we not only try to relieve the distress of the needy and of the sick by works of Christian charity, but if we also set our hearts on the good things of eternity rather than on the passing things of this world, if we restrain this mortal body by voluntary mortification, denying it what is forbidden, and forcing it to do what is hard and distasteful; and finally, if we humbly accept as from God's hands the burdens and sorrows of this present life. Thus, according to the Apostle, "we shall fill up those things that are wanting of the sufferings of Christ in our flesh for his Body, which is the Church."[212]

412 107. As We write these words there passes before Our eyes, alas, an almost endless throng of unfortunate beings for whom We shed tears of sorrow; sick, poor, disabled, widows, orphans and many not infrequently languishing even unto death on account of their own painful trials or those of their families. With the heart of a father We exhort all those who from whatever cause are plunged in grief and anguish to lift their eyes trustfully to heaven and to offer their sorrows to Him who will one day reward them abundantly. Let them all remember that their sufferings are not in vain, but that they will turn to their own immense gain and that of the Church, if to this end they bear them with patience. The daily use of the offering made by the members of the Apostleship of

Prayer will contribute very much to make this intention more efficacious and We welcome this opportunity of recommending this Association highly, as one which is most pleasing to God.

108. There never was a time, Venerable Brethren, when the salvation of souls did not impose on all the duty of associating their sufferings with the torments of our Divine Redeemer. But today that duty is clearer than ever, when a gigantic conflict has set almost the whole world on fire and leaves in its wake so much death, so much misery, so much hardship; in the same way today, in a special manner, it is the duty of all to fly from vice, the attraction of the world, the unrestrained pleasures of the body, and also from worldly frivolity and vanity which contribute nothing to the Christian training of the soul nor to the gaining of Heaven. Rather let those weighty words of Our immortal predecessor Leo the Great be deeply engraven up our minds, that by Baptism we are made flesh of the Crucified;[213] and that beautiful prayer of St. Ambrose; "Carry me, Christ, on the Cross, which is salvation to the wanderers, sole rest for the wearied, wherein alone is life for those who die."[214] 413

109. Before concluding, We cannot refrain from again and again exhorting all to love holy Mother Church with a devoted and active love. If we have really at heart the salvation of the whole human family, purchased by the precious Blood, we must offer every day to the Eternal Father our prayers, works and sufferings, for her safety and for her continued and ever more fruitful increase. And while the skies are heavy with storm clouds, and exceeding great dangers threaten the whole of human Society and the Church herself, let us commit ourselves and all that we have to the Father of mercies, crying out: "Look down, we beseech Thee Lord, on this Thy family, for which our Lord Jesus Christ did not hesitate to be betrayed into the hands of evil men and to undergo the torment of the Cross."[213] 414

110. Venerable Brethren, may the Virgin Mother of God hear the prayers of Our paternal heart—which are yours also—and obtain for all a true love of the Church—she whose sinless soul was filled with the divine Spirit of Jesus Christ 415

above all other created souls, and who "in the name of the whole human race" gave her consent "for a spiritual marriage between the Son of God and human nature."[216] Within her virginal womb Christ our Lord already bore the exalted title of Head of the Church; in a marvellous birth she brought Him forth as the source of all supernatural life, and presented Him newly born, as Prophet, King, and Priest to those who, from among Jews and Gentiles, were the first to come to adore Him. Furthermore, her only Son, condescending to His mother's prayer in "Cana of Galilee," performed the miracle by which "his disciples believed in him."[217] It was she, the second Eve who, free from all sin, original or personal, and always most intimately united with her Son, offered Him on Golgotha to the Eternal Father for all the children of Adam, sin-stained by his unhappy fall, and her mother's rights and mother's love were included in the holocaust. Thus she who, according to the flesh, was the mother of our Head, through the added title of pain and glory became, according to the Spirit, the mother of all His members. She it was who through her powerful prayers obtained that the Spirit of our Divine Redeemer, already given on the Cross, should be bestowed, accompanied by miraculous gifts, on the newly founded Church at Pentecost; and finally, bearing with courage and confidence the tremendous burden of her sorrows and desolation, she, truly the Queen of Martyrs, more than all the faithful "filled up those things that are wanting of the sufferings of Christ . . . for His Body, which is the Church";[218] and she continues to have for the Mystical Body of Christ, born of the pierced Heart of the Saviour,[219] the same motherly care and ardent love with which she cherished and fed the Infant Jesus in the crib.

416 111. May she, then, the most holy Mother of all the members of Christ,[220] to whose Immaculate Heart We have trustfully consecrated all mankind, and who now reigns in heaven with her Son, her body and soul refulgent with heavenly glory—may she never cease to beg from Him that copious streams of grace may flow from its exalted Head into all the members of the Mystical Body. May she throw about the Church today, as in times gone by, the mantle of her protec-

tion and obtain from God that now at last the Church and all mankind may enjoy more peaceful days.

112. Confiding in this sublime hope, from an overflowing heart We impart to you, one and all, Venerable Brethren, and to the flocks entrusted to your care, as a pledge of heavenly graces and a token of Our special affection, the Apostolic Benediction. 417

113. Given at Rome, at St. Peter's, on the twenty-ninth day of June, the Feast of the Holy Apostles Peter and Paul, in the year 1943, the fifth of Our Pontificate. 418

ORIENTALIS ECCLESIÆ DECUS

Encyclical Letter of Pope Pius XII
on St. Cyril, Patriarch of Alexandria
April 9, 1944

St. Cyril, Patriarch of Alexandria, glory of the Eastern Church and celebrated champion of the Virgin Mother of God, has always been held by the Church in the highest esteem, and We welcome the opportunity of recalling his merits in this brief Letter, now that fifteen centuries have passed since he happily exchanged this earthly exile for his heavenly home.

420 2. Our Predecessor St. Celestine I hailed him as 'good defender of the Catholic faith,'[1], as 'excellent priest,'[2] as 'apostolic man.'[3] The œcumenical Council of Chalcedon not only used his doctrine for the detecting and refuting of the latest errors, but went so far as to compare it with the learning of St. Leo the Great[4]; and in fact the latter praised and commended the writings of this great Doctor because of their perfect agreement with the faith of the holy Fathers.[5] The fifth œcumenical Council, held at Constantinople, treated St. Cyril's authority with similar reverence[6]; and many years later, during the controversy about the two wills in Christ, his teaching was rightly and triumphantly vindicated, both in the first Lateran Council[7] and in the sixth œcumenical Council, against the false charge of being tainted with the error of Monothelitism. He was, as Our saintly Predecessor Agatho proclaimed, 'a defender of the truth'[8] and 'a consistent teacher of the orthodox faith.'[9]

3. We therefore think it proper in this Letter to give some account of his spotless life, faith, and virtue; and this for the benefit of all, but especially of those who belong to the Eastern Church and therefore have good reason to be proud of this luminary of Christian wisdom, this valiant hero of the apostolate. 421

4. Born of distinguished family, he was raised to the See of Alexandria—so tradition tells us—in the year 412. His first conflict was with the Novatians and others who attacked the integrity and purity of the faith, and against these he preached, wrote, and issued decrees, ever alert, ever fearless. Later, when the blasphemous heresy of Nestorius began to spread gradually through the East the watchful Pastor was quick to perceive the growth of these new errors and zealous in protecting his flock against them. Throughout this stormy period, and especially at the Council of Ephesus, he showed himself the invincible champion and learned teacher of the divine maternity of the Virgin Mary, of the hypostatic union in Christ, and of the Primacy of the Roman Pontiff. But the leading part which St. Cyril played in these important events has already been admirably described and explained by Our immediate Predecessor of happy memory Pius XI, in the Encyclical *Lux veritatis*[10] with which in the year 1931 he celebrated the fifteenth centenary of the œcumenical Council, and therefore it would be superfluous to enter into the details of it here. 422

5. For Cyril, however, it was not enough to fight vigorously against heresies as they arose, not enough to guard the integrity of Catholic doctrine with energy and solicitude and throw the fullest possible light upon it; he was also untiring in his labours to recall his erring brethren to the straight path of the truth. For when the Bishops of the Province of Antioch were still refusing to recognize the authority of the holy Council of Ephesus, it was due to his efforts that they were at length, after long vicissitudes, brought to complete agreement. And it was only after he had succeeded with God's help in accomplishing this happy reunion and in guarding and securing it against misconceptions that, being now ripe for 423

the reward of everlasting glory, he was taken up to heaven in the year 444, mourned by all men of good will.

424 6. The faithful of the Eastern rite not only count St. Cyril amoung the 'Œcumenical Fathers,' but also honour him with the deepest veneration in their liturgical prayers. Thus the Greeks chant in the *Menaia* of the 9th June:

> Enlightened in mind by the flames of the Holy Spirit, thou hast uttered oracles even as the sun sends forth its rays. To the ends of the earth and to all the faithful thy teaching has gone forth, O most blessed Saint, illuminating all sorts and conditions of men, and dispelling the darkness of heresy by the power and strength of that Light who was born of the Virgin.

425 7. And the sons of the Eastern Church have every right to rejoice and take pride in this holy Father as one who is peculiarly and especially their own. For he is above all preeminent in those three qualities which have so greatly distinguished the other Fathers of the East: an outstanding sanctity of life, marked by a specially ardent devotion to the august Mother of God; exceptional learning, such that the Sacred Congregation of Rites, by a decree of the 28th July, 1882, declared him a Doctor of the Universal Church; and finally an energetic zeal in fearlessly repelling the attacks of heretics, in asserting the Catholic faith; and in defending and spreading the Gospel to the full extent of his power.

426 8. But our great joy in the deep veneration which all the Christian peoples of the East have for St. Cyril is mingled with an equal regret that not all of them have come together into that desired unity of which he was the ardent lover and promoter. And especially do We deplore that this should be so at the present time, when it is above all necessary that all Christ's faithful ones should labour together in heart and endeavour for union in the one Church of Jesus Christ, so that they may present a common, serried, united, and unyielding front to the daily growing attacks of the enemies of religion.

427 9. For this to be brought about it is absolutely necessary that all should take St. Cyril as their model in striving for a true harmony of souls, a harmony established by that triple bond which Christ Jesus, the Founder of the Church, willed

to be the supernatural and unbreakable link provided by Him for binding and holding together: the bond of one faith, of one charity towards God and all men, and of one obedience and rightful submission to the hierarchy established by the Divine Redeemer Himself. As you know full well, Venerable Brethren, these three bonds are so necessary that, if any one of them be lacking, true unity and harmony in the Church of Christ is unthinkable.

10. Throughout the troubled times of his life on earth the Patriarch of Alexandria taught all men, both by word and by conspicuous example, how this true harmony is to be achieved and steadfastly maintained—and We would have him do this also to-day. 428

11. At first, as regards the unity of the Christian faith, St. Cyril's untiring energy and unyielding tenacity in guarding it are well known. 429

> We (he writes), to whom the truth and the doctrines of truth are most dear, refuse to follow these (heretics); we, taking the faith of the holy Fathers as our guide, will guard against all errors the divine revelation committed to our trust.[11]

12. In this cause he was prepared to fight even to death and at the cost of the greatest sufferings: 430

> For the faith that is in Christ (he says) it is my greatest wish to toil, to live, and to die.[12] Only let the faith be kept safe and untarnished . . . and no insults, no injuries, no reproaches can move me.[13]

13. And he expressed his valiant and noble desire for the palm of martyrdom in these generous words: 431

> I have made up my mind that for the faith of Christ I will undergo any labour, suffer any torments, even those tortures which are counted most grievous, until I am granted the joy of dying for this cause.[14] . . . For if we are deterred by the fear of suffering some misfortune from preaching God's truth for His glory, with what countenance can we preach to the people in praise of the sufferings and triumphs of the holy martyrs?[15]

14. Animated discussions about the new Nestorian heresy were going on in the monasteries of Egypt, and the watchful 432

Bishop writes to warn the monks of the fallacies and dangers of this doctrine, not, however, in order to foment dissensions and controversies,

> but (he says) so that if any should chance to attack you, you may be able to oppose their vanities with the truth, and so not only yourselves be saved from the disaster of error but also be able fraternally to convince others with suitable arguments, and thus help them to preserve for ever in their hearts the pearl of that faith which was delivered through the holy Apostles to the Churches.[16]

433 15. Moreover, he plainly saw—as may be gathered easily from a reading of his letters on the subject of the Antiochene Bishops—that this Christian faith, which we must at all costs preserve and protect, has been delivered to us through the Sacred Scriptures and through the teaching of the Holy Fathers,[17] and is clearly and authentically set forth by the living and infallible teaching authority of the Church. Thus, when the Bishops of the Province of Antioch claimed that for the restoration and maintenance of peace it was enough if they kept the faith of the Council of Nicaea, St. Cyril, while himself firmly adhering to the Nicene Creed, also required of his brethren in the Episcopate, as a condition of reunion, that they should reject and condemn the Nestorian heresy. For he quite well understood that it is not enough to accept willingly the ancient pronouncements of the teaching office of the Church, but that it is also necessary to believe humbly and loyally all that is subsequently enjoined upon our faith by the Church in virtue of her supreme authority.

434 16. Even on the plea of promoting unity it is not allowed to dissemble one single dogma; for, as the Patriarch of Alexandria warns us, 'although the desire of peace is a noble and excellent thing, yet we must not for its sake neglect the virtue of loyalty in Christ.'[18] Consequently, the much desired return of erring sons to true and genuine unity in Christ will not be furthered by exclusive concentration on those doctrines which all, or most, communities glorying in the Christian name accept in common. The only successful method will be that which bases harmony and agreement

among Christ's faithful ones upon all the truths, and the whole of the truths, which God has revealed.

17. Let St. Cyril of Alexandria be a model to all in the energy and fortitude with which he defended the faith and kept it inviolate. No sooner did he discover the error of Nestorius than he wrote letters and other works in refutation of it, appealed to the Roman Pontiff and, acting in his name at the Council of Ephesus, crushed and condemned the growing heresy with admirable learning and unflinching courage. The result was that, when Cyril's 'dogmatic' letter had been publicly read, all the Fathers of the Council acclaimed it by solemn verdict as being in complete accordance with the true faith. 435

18. His apostolic energy led to his being unjustly deposed from his episcopal see, insulted by his brethren, condemned by an illegitimate council, and subjected to prison, and many hardships; but he bore all with unruffled and invincible courage. And not only did he oppose the Bishops who had gone astray from the path of truth and unity; he did not hesitate, in the conscientious discharge of his holy duty, openly to resist even the Emperor himself. In addition to all this, as everybody knows, he wrote countless works in support and defence of the Christian faith, works which bear striking testimony to his extraordinary learning, his intrepid courage, and his pastoral zeal. 436

19. But faith must be accompanied by charity, charity which unites us all with one another and with Christ; charity which, under the inspiration and motion of the Divine Spirit, welds the members of the mystical Body of the Redeemer together by an unbreakable bond. 437

20. This charity, however, must not refuse to embrace also those who have gone astray from the path of truth; and of this we may see an example in St. Cyril's remarkable conduct. Vigorously though he fought against the heresy of Nestorius, yet such was the ardent charity which animated him that, as he openly declared, he yielded to none in his love for Nestorius himself.[19] And in this he was right. Those who wander from the straight path are to be considered as 438

ailing brethren, and treated with gentle and loving care. The Patriarch of Alexandria's prudent advice on this point is worth quoting:

> This is a matter calling for the greatest moderation[20] . . . In many cases a violent clash only drives people to insolence; and it is better to treat your opponents with kindness than to make them suffer by applying the rigour of the law. If they were physically ill you would handle their bodies gently; so in like manner prudence is the best medicine to use in the treatment of ailing souls. Gradually they too will be brought to a proper state of mind.[21]

439 21. And elsewhere he adds:

> We followed the example of skilful doctors, who do not immediately apply the drastic remedies of fire and steel as soon as disease or hurt have appeared in the human body; first they soothe the wound with milder liniments, and only when the proper time has come do they use cautery and the knife.[22]

440 22. Filled with this spirit of compassion and loving-kindness towards erring souls, he professes that he is 'the friend of peace and altogether averse to controversy and quarrels; a man, in short, who desires to love everybody and to be loved by everybody in return.'[23]

441 23. The Holy Doctor's ready inclination for peace was shown especially when he mitigated his earlier severity and devoted his energies to bringing about reunion with the Bishops of the Province of Antioch. Referring to their ambassador he writes:

> He was probably expecting great difficulty in persuading us that it was needful to unite the Churches in peace and harmony, to deprive the heterodox of the excuse for mockery, and to repel the forces of diabolical malice. He found us, on the contrary, so much disposed to this course that he met with no difficulty whatsoever. For we are mindful of our Saviour's words: 'My peace I give to you, my peace I leave unto you.'[24]

442 24. Among the obstacles to this reunion were the twelve 'Chapters' which St. Cyril had drawn up at the Synod of

Alexandria, and which were rejected by the Antiochene Bishops as unorthodox because they spoke of a 'physical union' in Christ. With the utmost readiness the Patriarch, while not withdrawing or repudiating these writings—for the doctrine they contained was orthodox—nevertheless wrote several letters to explain his meaning and remove any possibility of misunderstanding, and so clear the way to peace and harmony. These explanations he gave to the Bishops, treating them 'as brethren, and not as adversaries.'[25] 'For the sake of the peace of the Churches,' he says elsewhere, 'and to prevent them from being divided by difference of opinion, it is worth while to waive one's dignity.'[26] In this way St. Cyril's charity bore in abundance the desired fruits of peace; and when at last it was granted him to see the dawn of that reconciliation, when the Bishops of the Province of Antioch had condemned the Nestorian heresy and he was able to embrace them as brothers, he exclaimed with holy joy:

> 'Let the heavens rejoice and let the earth be glad.' For the middle wall of partition has been broken down; that which had caused us grief is now at peace; every matter of contention has now been removed; Christ, the Saviour of us all, has granted peace to His churches.[27]

25. As it was in those times long past, Venerable Brethren, so will it be also to-day. More effective than anything else for promoting that reunion of all our separated sons with the one Church of Christ for which all good men are striving, will be a sincere and practical goodwill, with the help and inspiration of God. The fruit of such goodwill is mutual understanding, an understanding which Our Predecessors have sought so earnestly to foster and increase by various means, in particular by founding in Rome the Pontifical Institute of higher Oriental Studies. 443

26. This goodwill implies also a proper respect for those traditions which are the special heritage of the peoples of the East, whether these be concerned with the sacred liturgy and the hierarchical Orders or with other observances of the Christian life, so long as they are in keeping with the true faith and with the moral law. Each and every nation of Oriental rite must have its rightful freedom in all that is 444

bound up with its own history and its own genius and character, saving always the truth and integrity of the doctrine of Jesus Christ.

445 27. We would have this to be known and appreciated by all, both by those who were born within the bosom of the Catholic Church, and by those who are wafted towards her, as it were, on the wings of yearning and desire. The latter especially should have full assurance that they will never be forced to abandon their own legitimate rites or to exchange their own venerable and traditional customs for Latin rites and customs. All these are to be held in equal esteem and equal honour, for they adorn the common Mother Church with a royal garment of many colours. Indeed this variety of rites and customs, preserving inviolate what is most ancient and most valuable in each, presents no obstacle to a true and genuine unity. It is especially in these times of ours, when the strife and discord of war have estranged men's hearts from one another nearly all the world over, that all must be impelled by the stimulus of Christian charity to promote union in Christ and through Christ by every means in their power.

446 28. But the work of faith and charity would remain incomplete and powerless to establish unity firmly in Christ Jesus, unless it rested upon that unshaken rock upon which the Church is divinely founded, that is, upon the supreme authority of Peter and his Successors.

447 29. And this fact is proved clearly by the Patriarch of Alexandria's conduct in this important matter. Both in his work of repressing the Nestorian heresy and in that of reconciling the Bishops of the Province of Antioch, he remained constantly in close union with this Apostolic See.

448 30. As soon as the watchful Prelate perceived that the errors of Nestorius were spreading and growing, with increasing danger to the orthodox faith, he wrote to Our Predecessor St. Celestine I in the following terms:

> Since God requires us to be vigilant in these matters, and since the ancient custom of the Church persuades us that questions of this kind should be communicated to Your Holiness, I write, driven by necessity.[28]

31. In reply the Roman Pontiff writes that 'he had embraced Cyril as though present in his letter,' since it was clear that 'they were of one mind concerning the Lord.'[29] So orthodox was the faith of this Doctor that the Sovereign Pontiff delegated to him the authority of the Apostolic See, in virtue of which he was to give effect to the decrees which had already been issued against Nestorius in the Synod of Rome. And it is evident, Venerable Brethren, that at the Council of Ephesus the Patriarch of Alexandria acted as the legal representative of the Roman Pontiff; for, although the latter also sent his own Legates, the chief instruction he gave them was that they should support the action and the authority of St. Cyril. It was therefore in the name of the Sovereign Pontiff that he presided at this holy Council, and he was the first to sign its proceedings. Indeed, so manifest was the agreement between the Apostolic See and that of Alexandria that, after the public reading of St. Celestine's letter in the second session of the Council, the Fathers exclaimed: 449

> This judgement is just. To Celestine, a new Paul; to Cyril, a new Paul; to Celestine, guardian of the faith; to Celestine, who is of one mind with the Synod, the whole of this Synod gives thanks. One Celestine, one Cyril, one faith of the Synod, one faith of the whole world.[30]

32. No wonder, then, that Cyril could write shortly afterwards: 450

> To my orthodox faith the Roman Church has borne witness, and so too has a holy Synod gathered together, so to speak, from the whole of the earth that is under heaven.[31]

33. The same constant union of St. Cyril with the Apostolic See is clearly apparent in all that he did to effect and consolidate reunion with the Bishops of the Province of Antioch. Although Our Predecessor St. Celestine approved and ratified all that the Patriarch of Alexandria had done at the Council of Ephesus, he made an exception for the sentence of excommunication which the President of the Council, together with the other Fathers, had passed upon the Antiochenes. The Sovereign Pontiff wrote: 451

> With regard to those who appear to have been of one mind and one impiety with Nestorius . . . , We have read the sentence you have passed upon them. Nevertheless, We also decree what seems to Us opportune. In these cases many circumstances have to be considered which the Apostolic See has always borne in mind. . . Should the Bishop of Antioch offer hope of being corrected, We would have Your Fraternity come to some agreement with him by letter. . . . We must trust that by the divine mercy all may return to the way of truth.[32]

And it was in obedience to this instruction of the Roman See that St. Cyril began to take measures for bringing about reunion with the Bishops of the Province of Antioch.

452 34. Meanwhile, after St. Celestine's holy death, a report having been spread that his Successor St. Xystus III had objected to the deposition of Nestorius from his episcopal see, the Patriarch of Alexandria refuted these rumours: '(Xystus) has written in terms agreeing with the holy Synod,' he said; 'he has ratified all its proceedings and is of one mind with us.'[33]

453 35. All this shows plainly enough that St. Cyril was in perfect accord with this Apostolic See and that Our Predecessors regarded his measures as their own, and gave them their complete approval. Thus St. Celestine, after other numerous proofs of his confidence in St. Cyril and his gratitude towards him writes as follows:

> We rejoice in the vigilance shown by Your Holiness, wherein you surpass even the example set by your predecessors, themselves always defenders of the orthodox faith. . . . You have laid bare all the wiles of crafty teachers. . . . This is indeed a great triumph that you have won for our faith, in asserting our truth so valiantly and thus overcoming opposition to it by the testimony of Holy Writ.[34]

454 36. And when St. Xystus III, his successor in the Papacy, had received news from the Patriarch of Alexandria that peace and reconciliation had been established, he wrote to him joyfully as follows:

> Behold while We were suffering great anxiety—for We would have none to perish—Your Holiness' letter brought Us news that the Body of the Church has been made whole again. Now that the structure of its members has been fitted together again, We see none outside or gone astray, for their one faith testifies that all are at their places within. . . . The whole brotherhood has now come to agreement with the blessed Apostle Peter; behold here an auditorium befitting the hearers, befitting the things heard therein. . . . Our brethren are come back to us, to us whose common aim had been to attack the disease that we might bring health to souls. . . . Rejoice, beloved Brother, rejoice in triumph over the return of our brethren to us. The Church had been seeking those whom she has now received back again. If we would not have any even of the little ones to perish, how much more must we rejoice now that their rulers are safe.[35]

37. It was with the consolation which he derived from these words of Our Predecessor that the Prelate of Alexandria, this invincible champion of the orthodox faith, this most earnest promoter of Christian unity, passed to his rest in the peace of Christ. 455

38. And We, Venerable Brethren, as We celebrate the fifteenth centenary of this heavenly birthday, have no more earnest desire than to see all who can be called Christians take St. Cyril as their model, and work ever more and more zealously for the happy return of our separated brethren in the East to Us and to the one Church of Jesus Christ. Let there be in all one faith inviolate; in all one charity, uniting all together in the mystical Body of Jesus Christ; in all one earnest and practical loyalty to the See of Blessed Peter. 456

39. The furtherance of this worthy and meritorious work must be the special endeavour of those who live in the East and who, by mutual esteem, by friendly intercourse, and by the example of their spotless life, can more easily induce our separated brethren, and especially their clergy, to become reunited with the Church. But all the faithful, besides, can contribute by their prayers and supplications that God may 457

establish throughout the world the one Kingdom of the divine Redeemer and His one fold for all.

458 40. Indeed, to all alike We recommend in a particular way that most effective aid, which in any work for the saving of souls must take the first place both in order of time and efficacy: fervent, humble, and confident prayer to God. And We would have them invoke the most powerful patronage of the Virgin Mother of God, that, through the gracious intercession of this most loving Mother of us all, the Divine Spirit may enlighten the minds of Eastern peoples with His heavenly light, and that all of us may be one in the one Church which Jesus Christ founded, and which that same Spirit, the Paraclete, nourishes with an unceasing rain of graces and stirs to sanctity.

459 41. To seminarists and to pupils of other colleges We specially commend the observance of the 'Day for the East'; on that day let prayers more than usually fervent be made to the Divine Shepherd of the whole Church, and let the hearts of the young be stimulated to a burning zeal for the achievement of this holy unity. Finally, let all, alike those who are in Sacred Orders and those who, as members of Catholic Action and other associations, are co-operating with the hierarchy of the Church, perseveringly direct their prayers, their writings, their discourses, to promoting this desired union of all Easterns with the common Father.

460 42. And God grant that this Our fatherly and urgent appeal may be given a friendly hearing by those separated Bishops and their flocks who, though divided from Us, yet admire and venerate the Patriarch of Alexandria as a hero of their own land. Let this great Doctor's teaching and example move them to restore peace by means of that triple bond which he himself so strongly urged as indispensable, and by which the divine Founder of the Church willed all His sons to be united together. Let them remember that We, by the Providence of God, to-day occupy that same Apostolic See to which the Patriarch of Alexandria felt bound in conscience to appeal, when he wanted to provide a sure defence of the orthodox faith against the errors of Nestorius, and to set a divine seal, so to speak, upon the reconciliation achieved with

his separated brethren. And let them be assured that the same charity which inspired Our Predecessors inspires Us too; and that the chief object of Our constant desires and prayers is that the age-old obstacles between us may be happily removed, and the day dawn at last when there shall be one flock in one fold, all obedient with one mind to Jesus Christ and to His Vicar on earth.

43. We address a particular appeal to those of Our separated sons in the East who, though they hold St. Cyril in great veneration, yet refuse to acknowledge the authority of the Council of Chalcedon, because it solemnly defined that there are two natures in Jesus Christ. Let these bear in mind that the decrees which were later issued by the Council of Chalcedon as new errors arose are in no way contrary to the teaching of the Patriarch of Alexandria. As he himself clearly says, 461

> Not everything that heretics say is to be denied and rejected out of hand, for they profess much of what we also assert. . . . So it is also with Nestorius. He is not wrong in saying that there are two natures in Christ, so far as he means that the flesh is distinct from the Word of God; for the nature of the Word is indeed distinct from the nature of flesh. But he does not profess the union of the natures as we do.[36]

44. Moreover, there is reason to hope that the modern followers of Nestorius also, if they examine St. Cyril's writings with unprejudiced mind and study them carefully, may see the path of truth lying open before them and, through the inspiration and help of God, feel themselves called back to the bosom of the Catholic Church. 462

45. It only remains for Us now, Venerable Brethren, on the occasion of this fifteenth centenary of St. Cyril, to implore the most powerful patronage of this Holy Doctor for the whole Church, and especially for all those in the East who glory in the Christian name, imploring for our separated brethren and children that blessing which he himself once so joyfully described: 463

> Behold the sundered members of the Body of the Church are reunited once again, and no further discord

remains to divide the ministers of the Gospel of Christ.[37]

464 46. Sustained by this happy hope, We grant most lovingly in the Lord to each and every one of you, Venerable Brethren, and to the flocks committed to your care, as a pledge of heavenly blessings and in token of Our fatherly goodwill, Our Apostolic Benediction.

465 Given at St. Peter's, Rome, on the 9th day of April, Easter Sunday, in the year 1944, the sixth of Our Pontificate.

SEMPITERNUS REX CHRISTUS

Encyclical Letter of Pope Pius XII
on the Ecumenical Council of Chalcedon
on the Occasion of its Fifteen Hundredth Anniversary
September 8, 1951

Christ, the Eternal King, before he promised the headship of the Church to Peter, the son of John, called together his disciples, and asking them what they and other men believed about himself, praised the faith which would conquer all the storms and attacks of the evil powers, and which Peter, enlightened by the Eternal Father, had declared in these words: 'Thou art Christ, the Son of the Living God' (*Matt.* xvi, 16). It is this faith which is 'the strength of God for the salvation of every believer' (*Rom.* i, 16), and which brings forth the apostle's crown, the martyr's palm and the virgin's lily. This faith has been defended and lucidly clarified especially by three œcumenical councils, those of Nicea, Ephesus and Chalcedon. It is now fifteen hundred years since the last of these was concluded. It is fitting, therefore, that both at Rome and in the whole Catholic world, this most happy event should be celebrated with due solemnity; and so giving thanks to God the inspirer of all holy counsels, with deeply moved hearts, we institute those solemnities.

467 As our predecessor Pope Pius XI of happy memory solemnly commemorated the Nicene council in 1925 in the sacred city, and by his encyclical letter *Lux Veritatis* recalled the sacred council of Ephesus in 1931, so we by the present letter pay a tribute of equal honour to the council of Chalcedon. For inasmuch as both councils, Ephesus and Chalcedon,

were concerned with the hypostatic union of the Incarnate Word, they are intimately connected with one another. From the earliest times both councils have enjoyed the highest honour, equally in the East, where they are celebrated in the liturgy, and in the West. St. Gregory the Great bears witness in the West to this fact when he praises both councils together with two of the preceding century, namely, those of Nicea and Constantinople, in the memorable sentence:—'On them, as on a four-cornered stone, the building of the holy faith stands erect, and whoever does not hold their firm doctrine, whatever may be his life or activity, even if he seems to be a rock, nevertheless lies outside the building' (*Regist. Epist.* i, 25 [24]. PL. lxxvii, 478, ed. Ewald i, 36).

468 From the consideration of this event and its attendant circumstances, two points arise and stand out, and these we wish, as far as possible, to make yet more clear. They are: the primacy of the Roman pontiff which shone forth clearly in this very grave christological controversy and, secondly, the great importance and weight of the dogmatic definition of Chalcedon. Let those who, through the evils of the time, are separated from the bosom and unity of the Church, especially those who dwell in Eastern lands, not delay to follow the example and the customs of their ancestors in paying due respect to the Roman primacy. And let those who are involved in the errors of Nestorius or Eutyches penetrate with clearer insight into the mystery of Christ and at last accept this definition in its completeness. Those, also, who are led by an excessive desire for new things and, in their investigation of the mystery of our redemption boldly dare to go beyond the sacred and inviolable limits [of true doctrine], should ponder this definition more truly and more deeply. Finally, let all those who bear the Catholic name draw from it strong encouragement; let them hold fast this evangelical pearl of great price; let them profess and hold it with unadulterated faith; let them render it due honour inwardly and outwardly; and—what is still more important—let them pay it the tribute of lives in which, through God's mercy, they shun whatever is unworthy, incongruous or blameable, and in which they shine with the beauty of virtue, so that they

may become sharers of his divinity, who deigned to be a partaker of our humanity.

Now, to treat of things in due order, let us recall from the beginning the events which we commemorate. The originator of the whole controversy under discussion at Chalcedon was Eutyches, a priest and archimandrite in a famous monastery of Constantinople. This man, in refuting the Nestorian heresy which maintained that there were two persons in Christ, fell into the opposite error. 469

'A rash man and quite unskilled' (St. Leo the Great to Flavian, *Ep.* xxviii, I. PL. liv, 775 s.), with an extremely obstinate disposition, Eutyches asserted that two moments of time should be distinguished: thus before the Incarnation there were two natures in Christ, the human and the divine; after their union, however, only one existed, since the Word had absorbed the human nature *(Hominen);* the body of the Lord came from the Virgin Mary, but was not of our substance and matter; if, indeed, it was human, it was not consubstantial with us, nor with her who gave birth to Christ according to the flesh (cf. Flavian to St. Leo, *Ep.* xxvi; PL. liv, 745). Therefore, it was not in true human nature that Christ was born, suffered, was fastened to the cross and rose from the tomb. 470

Eutyches did not grasp that before the union the human nature of Christ did not exist at all, for it only began at the time of his conception; and it is absurd to suppose that after the union one nature resulted from the coalescence of two; for there is no way in which two true and distinct natures can be reduced to one, and the more so [in this case] since the divine nature is infinite and unchangeable. 471

Whoever judges wisely of these opinions will quickly conclude that by them the mystery of the divine dispensation is dissipated into shadowy absurdities and riddles. It was quite clear to those who were of sound piety and theology that this absurd novelty, so repugnant to the teachines of the prophets, to the words of the Gospel and to the dogma contained in the Apostles' Creed and the Nicene profession of faith, had been taken from the vaults of Apollinaris and Valentine. 472

473 A special synod was called at Constantinople; St. Flavian, bishop of that city, presided; Eutyches, who had been vigorously spreading his errors throughout the monasteries, was accused of heresy by Bishop Eusebius of Dorylaeum, and condemned. He considered that an injury had been done to him who had withstood the growth of the Nestorian heresy, and appealed to the judgement of some of the bishops placed in higher authority. And so St. Leo the Great, bishop of the Apostolic See, also received letters of appeal of this kind. No one could have been more suitable and capable for the refutation of Eutyches's error. His solid and shining virtues, his zealous watch equally over peace and religion, his strenuous defence of the dignity of the Roman see, his skill in the spoken word and equally in the management of affairs, have won for him the admiration of all succeeding ages. Moreover, he was accustomed in his allocutions and letters to maintain with great piety and pious greatness that the mystery of the one person and the two natures in Christ could never be preached sufficiently. 'The Catholic Church lives by this faith, and is nourished by it, that in Jesus Christ, neither is the humanity believed without the true Divinity, nor the divinity without true humanity' (St. Leo the Great, *Ep*. xxviii, 5. PL. liv, 777).

474 The Archimandrite Eutyches, however, was not confident of the patronage of the Roman pontiff. So he craftily made use of his friend Chrysaphius, who was a favourite of the emperor, to persuade Theodosius II to take his part and to summon another council at Ephesus under the presidency of Dioscorus, bishop of Alexandria. This man, who was both a friend to himself and an enemy to Flavian, bishop of Constantinople, deceived by a similarity of terms, gave it out that, like his predecessor Cyril, he was determined to defend with all his power that, as there was one person in Christ, so after the 'unification', there was also one nature in Christ. For the sake of peace St. Leo the Great sent delegates to the council. Among other letters, they brought to the council two epistles, one addressed to the synod, and the other containing a perfect and full developed doctrine in which the errors of Eutyches were refuted, addressed to Flavian.

But at this synod of Ephesus, which St. Leo rightly called a 'Robbers' council', Dioscorus and Eutyches carried off everything with a high hand. The first places in the council were denied to the apostolic delegates; the letters of the pope were not allowed to be read, the votes of the bishops were extorted by threats and stratagems; among others Flavian was accused of heresy, deprived of his pastoral ministry and thrown into prison, where he died. The rash fury of Dioscorus even went to the length of criminally hurling an excommunication at the Apostolic See itself. As soon as St. Leo learnt from the deacon Hilary of the evil deeds of this council, he condemned and annulled all the decrees and decisions made by it. His grief at these crimes was greatly increased by the frequent appeals to his authority made by the numerous bishops who had been deposed. 475

Worthy of mention are the lines written by Flavian and by Theodoret of Cyrus to the chief pastor of the Church. These are Flavian's words: 'After the unjust sentence which it pleased Dioscorus to pronounce against me, everything, as if by some prearranged pact, turned against me; when I appealed to the throne of the prince of the apostles, the Apostolic See, and to the holy synod which is under the authority of your Holiness, a large number of soldiers surrounded me, prevented my taking refuge at the altar, and tried to drag me from the church' (Schwartz. Acta Concil. Ecum. II Vol. II, pars prior, p. 78). Theodoret wrote as follows: 'If Paul, the preacher of truth . . . betook himself to the great Peter, much more do we who are weak and lowly turn to the Apostolic See, that we may obtain from you a remedy for the ulcers of the Church. For it is your part to direct us in all things. I await the decision of the Apostolic See . . . above all that I may learn whether I ought to accept this unjust decision or not: for it is your decision that I await' (Theodoret to Leo the Great, *Ep.* lii, I, 5, 7. PL. liv, 847 and 851, cf. PG. lxxxiii, 1311s and 1315s). 476

Leo then urged Theodosius and Pulcheria in many letters to wipe out this stain. He proposed that they should remedy this sad state of affairs by summoning a council in Italy to reverse the decrees made at Ephesus. When the Emperor 477

Valentine III, his mother Galla and his wife Eudoxia were entering St. Peter's Basilica, he received them accompanied by an assembly of bishops, and besought them with sighs and tears to do all they could to remedy the evil condition of the Church. The emperor wrote to his brother emperor [in the East], and the royal ladies joined their entreaties to his. But it was all to no purpose. Theodosius was in the hands of evil counsellors and did nothing to amend the evil. However, he died suddenly; his sister Pulcheria succeeded him and took as her consort on the throne and in marriage one Marcian. Both of these persons were distinguished by their renown for wisdom and true religion. Then Anatolius, who had been illegally raised by Dioscorus to the see of Constantinople, accepted the letter which St. Leo wrote to Flavian on the Incarnation of our Lord. The remains of Flavian were brought back to Constantinople with great solemnity. The exiled bishops were restored to their sees, and the general hostility to the heresy of Eutyches grew so strong that there scarcely seemed to be any further need for a council. To this result the invasions of the barbarians, which were jeopardizing the safety of the Roman empire, also contributed.

478 Nevertheless, at the emperor's wish and with the pope's approval, a council was held. Chalcedon was a city of Bithynia near the Thracian Bosphorus, within sight of Constantinople, which was situated on the opposite bank. Here, in the vast suburban basilica of St. Euphemia, virgin and martyr, on the 8th October, assembled the fathers, who had previously met for this purpose in the city of Nicea. They were about 600 in number, all of the East, except for two exiles from Africa.

479 The book of the gospels was placed in the middle; nineteen representatives of the emperor and the senate took their places before the altar rails. The role of apostolic delegates had been entrusted to the devout Bishops Paschasinus of Lilybaeum in Sicily and Lucentius of Ascoli, and to the priests Boniface and Basil. To these was added Julian bishop of Cos, to aid them by his diligent labours. The delegates of the Roman pontiff took the first places among the bishops; they were named first, they spoke first, they signed the Acts first, and by virtue of their delegated authority, they con-

firmed or rejected the decisions of the others. For example, in the case of the condemnation of Dioscorus, the delegates ratified it in these words: 'The holy and blessed archbishop of great and ancient Rome, Leo, through us and through this holy synod, together with the blessed and praiseworthy Apostle Peter who is the rock and foundation of the Orthodox Faith, has deprived him (Dioscorus) of all episcopal dignity and removed him from every priestly office' (Mansi. *Conc. Ampl. Coll.* VI, 1047. [Act III]; Schwartz II, Vol. I, pars. altera p. 29 [225] [Act II]).

480 Furthermore, the papal delegates not only exercised the authority of presidents, but their right to this honour of presiding was recognized by all the fathers of the council, as was shown clearly by the letter sent by the synod to St. Leo 'For you', they wrote, 'showed us benevolence in presiding over us in the persons of those who held your place, as the head over the members' (synod of Chalcedon to St. Leo. Ep. xcviii, PL. liv, 951. Mansi vi, 147).

481 It is not necessary for us to relate the whole history of the synod, but we will touch only on the principal points which served to place the truth in full light and to foster the cause of religion. Therefore, since it concerns the dignity of the Apostolic See, we must mention canon XXVIII of this council, by which the next place of honour after the Roman see was granted to Constantinople, as the imperial city. Although there was nothing in this against the divine primacy of jurisdiction of the see of Peter, which indeed was taken for granted, nevertheless, this canon was passed in the absence of the papal legates, and they subsequently objected to it. It was therefore clandestine, surreptitious and lacking in all force of law and, as such, condemned by St. Leo in many letters. Marcian and Pulcheria accepted this rescissory sentence, and even Anatolius wrote to St. Leo excusing his blameworthy boldness: 'With regard to the decree laid down by the recent synod of Chalcedon on behalf of the see of Constantinople, let your Beatitude rest assured that this was not my fault. But it was the desire of the reverend clergy of Constantinople . . . the validity and confirmation of this action being reserved to the authority of your Beatitude' (Anatolius to St. Leo the Great. *Ep.* cxxxii, 4. PL. liv, 1084. Mansi vi, 278s).

482 Let us come now to the central point of the whole question, i.e. to the solemn definition of the Catholic faith, by which the pernicious error of Eutyches was rejected and condemned. In the fourth session of the sacred synod the representatives of the emperor asked that a new formula of the faith should be composed. But the papal legate, Paschasinus, expressed the feeling of all when he replied that it was not necessary; the ground, he said, was sufficiently covered by the creeds already in use, and the canonical documents approved by the Church; among these the letter of St. Leo to Flavian was the most important. 'Thirdly (i.e., after the creeds of Nicea and Constantinople and their explanations by St. Cyril at the council of Ephesus) the writings composed by the holy and apostolic Leo, pope of the Universal Church, against the heresies of Nestorius and Eutyches, have already shown what the true faith is. This holy synod likewise holds and follows this same faith' (Mansi, vii, 10 [Act. IV]).

483 It is useful to note here that this very important letter of St. Leo to Flavian concerning the Incarnation of the Word was read in the third session of the council, and hardly had the voice of the reader ceased, when there went up a unanimous cry: 'This is the faith of the Fathers, this is the faith of the Apostles. So we all believe, and so believe all orthodox Christians. Let him be anathema who does not believe this. Peter has spoken through Leo' (Schwartz, II, Vol. I, pars altera, p. 81 [277] [Act. III]; Mansi vi, 871. [Act. II]).

484 After this all unanimously agreed that the document of the bishop of Rome fully and perfectly concorded with the creeds of Nicea and Constantinople. Nevertheless, in the fifth session at the repeated requests of the representatives of the Emperor Marcian and the senate, a new definition of the faith was worked out by a select committee of the bishops congregated from diverse lands in the basilica of St. Euphemia. It was made up of a prologue, of the creeds of Nicea and Constantinople (which was promulgated for the first time) and of a condemnation of the doctrine of Eutyches. This rule of faith was approved by the unanimous consent of the council.

485 We think it of importance, Venerable Brethren, to delay a little in elucidating this document of the Roman pontiff,

which was such an outstanding vindication of the Catholic faith. Firstly, against the assertion of Eutyches: 'I confess that our Lord was of two natures before their union; after their union I confess that he had only one nature' (St. Leo, *Ep.* xxviii, 6. PL. liv, 777), the holy bishop, not without a certain indignation, opposed the following clear statement of the luminous truth: 'I am surprised that this absurd and perverse statement should have escaped the severe reprimand of those who gave judgement . . . the Only Begotten Son of God is impiously described as being of two natures before the Incarnation and, equally wickedly to the Word made Flesh is attributed only one nature' (Ibid.). He attached with equal force and directness the opposite errors of Nestorius. 'It is because there was only one person in both natures, that the Son of God took flesh from the Virgin from whom he was born. And again the Son of God is said to have been crucified and been buried, because he suffered these things in the weakness of his human nature, not in the divinity itself, for through the divinity the only Begotten is co-eternal and consubstantial with the Father. Wherefore in the Creed we all confess "the only Begotten Son of God to have been crucified and buried" ' (*Ep.* xxviii, 5. PL. liv, 771; cf. Augustinus, Contra Serm. Arianorum, c, 8. PL. xlii, 688).

486 In addition to the distinction of natures in Christ, there is clearly shown here the distinction of the properties and activities, which arise from his double nature, 'Since the properties of each nature remain intact, and they are joined together in one person, majesty accepts lowliness, strength accepts weakness and the Eternal becomes mortal' (*Ep.* xxviii, 3. PL. liv, 763. cf. St. Leo, Serm. xxi, 2. PL. liv, 192). And again: 'Each nature possesses its properties without defect' (*Ep.* xxviii, 3. PL. liv, 768. cf. Serm. xxiii, 2. PL. liv, 201).

487 But both sets of properties and activities are attributed to the One Person of the Word, because 'One and the same [Person] is . . . truly the Son of God and truly the Son of Man' (*Ep.* xxviii, 4. PL. liv, 767). Whence 'In his actions either nature with the co-operation of the other performs what is proper to it; thus the Word performs the part of the Word, and the humanity the part of the humanity' (Ibid). In

these expressions appears the use of what is called the Common Application of Terms (*Communicatio Idiomatum*), which Cyril vindicated against Nestorius. It depends on the firm foundation that both natures subsist by the One Person of the Word begotten before all ages of the Father and born of Mary according to the flesh in the course of time.

488 This sublime doctrine, which is drawn from the gospels and differs in no way from that of the council of Ephesus refutes Eutyches as well as Nestorius. The dogmatic definition of the council of Chalcedon concords with it absolutely and perfectly, for this definition likewise defines two distinct natures and one person in Christ in the following clear and precise words: 'This great and holy œcumenical council condemns those who pretend that there were two natures in the Lord before the union, and imagine that there was only one after the union. Following, therefore, in the traditions of the holy Fathers we teach that all with one voice confess that the Son [of God] and our Lord Jesus Christ are one and the same, and that he is perfect in his divinity, perfect in his humanity, true God and true man, made of a rational soul and a body, consubstantial with the Father in his divinity, consubstantial with us in his humanity, like to us in all things except sin, begotten before all ages of the Father in his divinity, and the same also in his humanity received from the Virgin Mary in recent times for our sake and for our salvation, one and the same Christ, the Son, the Lord, the Only Begotten, having two natures without confusion, change, division or separation; the distinction between the natures was not removed by the union, but the properties of each remain inviolate and are joined together in one person. He is not sundered or divided into two persons, but is one and the same Son and only Begotten God the Word, the Lord, Jesus Christ' (Mansi. vii, 114 and 115).

489 If anyone asks how it is that the statements of the council of Chalcedon are of such outstanding excellence in their clarity and their efficiency in the refutation of error, we reply that this arises from the fact that ambiguities have been removed and a most exact terminology was used. For in the Chalcedonian definition of the faith the same concept

underlies the terms 'Person' (ροσωπον) and 'hypostasis' (ὑπόστασις), the term 'Nature' has a totally different sense, and its meaning is never given to the other words. So that the Nestorians and Eutychians of old and certain modern writers err when they maintain that the council of Chalcedon corrected the decision of the council of Ephesus. Rather the one perfected the other, so that a synthesis or composition of the main Christological doctrine was available in fuller form for the second and third œcumenical of Constantinople.

490 It is indeed sad that the ancient adversaries of the council of Chalcedon (also called Monophysites) should have rejected this doctrine, so lucid, so coherent and so complete, on the strength of certain badly understood expressions of ancient writers. While they rejected the absurd teaching of Eutyches about the mixture of natures in Christ, they obstinately clung to the well-known expression: 'One Incarnate nature of the Word God'. This expression had been used by Cyril of Alexandria (who took it from St. Athanasius) with a perfectly correct meaning, since he used the term 'nature' to signify 'person'. The Fathers of Chalcedon, therefore, totally removed what was ambiguous or liable to cause error in these expressions. For they applied the same terms as are used in the theology of the Trinity, to the exposition of our Lord's Incarnation. Thus they made 'nature' and 'essence' (essentia, οὐσία) the same, and likewise 'Person' and 'Hypostasis', and they treated the latter two names as totally different in meaning, from the former two. Their approach, on the other hand, had made 'nature' the equivalent of 'person' not of 'essence' (*essentia*).

491 For the reason just given there are to-day some separated bodies in Egypt, Ethiopia, Syria, Armenia and elsewhere, who go wrong mainly in their use of words in defining the doctrine of the Incarnation. This may be demonstrated from their liturgical and theological books.

492 Moreover, in the twelfth century, a writer of the highest repute, among the Armenians, clearly expounded his views of this matter in these words: 'We speak of Christ as one nature, not to imply confusion as does Eutyches, nor diminution, as does Apollinaris, but in the sense of Cyril of Alexandria, who,

in his book *Scholiorum Adversus Nestorium* says, "There is one nature of the Incarnate Word as the Fathers taught". And we also teach this according to the tradition of the saints, but not according to the opinion of heretics. For they introduce confusion and change and alterations into the union in Christ. We say there is one nature referring to the hypostasis, which you also speak of in Christ; and this is correct and granted by us, and equally valid is our own expression: "One Nature". Nor do we refuse to say "two Natures", provided there is no implication of the division maintained by Nestorius, but the expression is used against the confusion introduced by Eutyches and Apollinaris' (Nerses iv, 1173 in his *Libellum Confessionis Fidei* to the Emperor Manuel Comnenus (cf. I. Capelletti *S. Narsetis Claiensis Armenorum Catholici, Opera.* I, Venice 1836, pp. 182-83).

493 If then it is the climax of gladness and the consummation of holy joy, when that comes to pass which the Psalmist said: 'Behold how good and how pleasant it is for brethren to live together in unity' (*Ps.* 132, 1); if then the glory of God combined with the greatest profit for all is apparent when the sheep of Christ are joined together in the fullness of truth and the fullness of charity, let those whom with sorrow and love we have mentioned above, consider whether it is right and expedient that, principally on account of the original ambiguity of certain words, they should still hold apart from the one Holy Church, founded on sapphires (cf. *Is.* liv, 11), that is to say, on the prophets and Apostles, on the supreme corner stone itself, Christ Jesus (cf. *Eph.* ii, 20).

494 There is another enemy of the faith of Chalcedon, widely diffused outside the fold of the Catholic religion. This is an opinion for which a rashly and falsely understood sentence of St. Paul's Epistle to the Philippians (ii, 7), supplies a basis and a shape. This is called the kenotic doctrine, and according to it, they imagine that the divinity was taken away from the Word in Christ. It is a wicked invention, equally to be condemned with the Docetism opposed to it. It reduces the whole mystery of the Incarnation and Redemption to empty and bloodless imaginations. 'With the entire and perfect

nature of man'—thus grandly St. Leo the Great—'He Who was true God was born, complete in his own nature, complete in ours' (*Ep.* xxviii, 3. PL. liv, 763. Cf. Serm. xxiii, 2. PL. lvi, 201).

495 While there is no reason why the humanity of Christ should not be studied more deeply also from a psychological point of view, there are, nevertheless, some who, in their arduous pursuit, desert the ancient teachings more than is right, and make an erroneous use of the authority of the definition of Chalcedon to support their new ideas.

496 These emphasize the state and condition of Christ's human nature to such an extent as to make it seem, at least psychologically, something existing in its own right (*subjectum quoddam sui juris*), and not as subsisting in the Word itself. But the council of Chalcedon in full accord with that of Ephesus, clearly asserts that both natures are united in 'One Person and subsistence', and rules out the placing of two individuals in Christ, as if some one man, completely autonomous in himself, had been taken up and placed by the side of the Word. St. Leo not only adheres to this opinion (i.e. that of Chalcedon), but he also indicates the source whence he derives his sound doctrine. 'Whatever', he says, 'we have written has manifestly clearly been taken from the doctrine of the Apostles and of the Gospels' (*Ep.* clii, PL. liv, 1123).

497 It is indeed the truth that from the earliest times and in the most ancient writings, sermons and liturgical prayers, the Church openly and without qualification professes that our Lord Jesus Christ, the only Begotten Son of the Eternal Father, was born on earth, suffered, was nailed to the cross, rose from the sepulchre and ascended into heaven. And, further, the words of sacred Scripture give to the one Christ, the Son of God, human attributes, and to the same [Christ] the Son of Man, divine attributes.

498 Thus St. John the Evangelist declares: 'The Word was made flesh' (*John* i, 14). St. Paul writes of him: 'When he was in the form of God . . . he humbled himself and became obedient even unto death' (*Phil* ii, 6-8); or again: 'But when the fullness of time was come, God sent his Son, made from a woman' (*Gal.* iv, 4), and our Divine Redeemer himself puts

the matter beyond doubt when he says: 'I and the Father are One' (*John* x, 30); and again, 'I went out from the Father and I came into the world' (*John* xvi, 28). The divine origin of our Redeemer is also manifest from this passage of the Gospel: 'I came down from heaven, not that I should do my own will, but the will of him that sent me' (*John* vi, 38). And again: 'He who descended, this is he who ascended above all the heavens' (*Eph.* iv, 10). St. Thomas Aquinas explains this last sentence thus: 'He who descended, this is the same as he who ascended. By these words is signified the unity of the person of God and man. For the Son of God came down by taking human nature, but the Son of Man ascended according to his human nature to the sublimity of eternal life. And so he is the same Son of God who came down and Son of Man who went up' (St. Thomas, Comm. in Ep. ad Eph. c iv. lect. iii *circa finem*).

499 This same doctrine was set forth by our predecessor Leo the Great in these words: 'What principally contributed to the justification of mankind was that the only Begotten Son of God deigned to become the Son of Man, so that being God ὁμοούσιος to the Father, that is of the same substance, the same [person] should exist as true man consubstantial with his mother in the flesh; we rejoice over both these things, since only by both are we saved; we admit no division of the visible from the invisible, the corporeal from the incorporeal, the passible from the impassible, the palpable from the impalpable, the form of the servant from the form of God. For although he remains the one from eternity, he began to be the other in time; these two have met in unity and can have neither separation nor end' (St. Leo. Serm. 30, 6. PL. liv, 233s).

500 Only, therefore, if we adhere to the holy inviolate faith, that there is one Person in Christ, that of the Word, in which two natures entirely distinct from each other, the divine and the human, distinct also in their properties and activities, converge—only if we adhere to this doctrine does the magnificence and the fatherly mercy of our ineffable redemption shine forth.

501 O height of the mercy and justice of God, who came to the rescue of guilty creatures and made them sons unto Himself! How the heavens bent down towards us, the wintry frosts vanished, the flowers appeared in our land, and we became new men, a new creation, a new structure, a holy people, a heavenly offspring. Truly the Word suffered in his flesh and shed his blood on the cross and paid for us sinners to the Eternal Father the superabounding price of our satisfaction. Hence it is that the certain hope of salvation sheds its light on those who in genuine faith and ardent charity adhere to him, and with the help of the graces that flow from him, produce the fruits of justice.

502 The very recalling of the memory of these distinguished and glorious events in the history of the Church naturally leads us to turn our thoughts to the Orientals with a yet more loving warmth of paternal affection. For the œcumenical council of Chalcedon is a monument of their outstanding glory, and one which, without doubt, will live throughout the ages. For in this council under the leadership of the Apostolic See, an assembly of 600 Oriental bishops vigilantly defended and wonderfully expounded against the rashness of the innovator, the doctrine of the unity of Christ, in whose person meet without confusion two distinct natures, the divine and the human. But alas! for long centuries many of those who dwell in the East have unhappily fallen away from the unity of the Mystical Body of Christ, of which the hypostatic union is the most luminous prototype. Would it not be holy, salutary and in accordance with the will of God that at last all these should return to the one sheepfold of Christ?

503 For our part we desire that they should always bear in mind that Our thoughts are thoughts of peace and not of affliction (cf. *Jer.* xxix, 11). It is well known, moreover, that we have demonstrated this by our actions. If, under the pressure we boast of this, then we boast in the Lord, who is the giver of every goodwill. For we have followed in the path of our predecessors and worked diligently to facilitate the return of the Oriental peoples to the Catholic Church. We have guarded their legitimate rites. We have promoted the

study of their affairs. We have promulgated beneficent laws for them. We have shown deep solicitude in our dealings with the sacred council of the Roman curia for oriental affairs. We have bestowed the Roman purple on the patriarch of the Armenians.

504 When the recent war was waging and producing its fruits of famine, want and disease, we made no distinction between them and those who are accustomed to call us Father, but sought everywhere to relieve the increasing misery; we strove to help widows, children, old people and the sick. We would have been happier truly had our means been equal to our desires! Let those then who, through the calamities of time, have been cut off, not be slow to pay due respect to this divinely erected and unbroken rock, this Apostolic See for whom to rule is to serve. Let them bear in mind and imitate Flavian, that second John Chrysostom, in his sufferings for justice; and the fathers of Chalcedon, those most worthy members of the Mystical Body of Christ; and Marcian, that strong, gentle and wise ruler; and Pulcheria, that resplendent lily of inviolate royal beauty. From such a return to the unity of the Church we foresee that there would flow a rich fountain of blessings unto the common good of the whole Christian world.

505 Truly we are aware of the accumulation of prejudice that tenaciously prevents the happy fulfilment of the prayer offered by Christ at the Last Supper to his Eternal Father for the followers of the Gospel: 'That they may be one' (*John* xvii, 21). But we know also that such is the strength of prayer, when those who pray are joined together in a common fervour, a strong faith, and a clear conscience, that it can lift up a mountain and cast it headlong into the sea (cf. *Mark* ii, 23). We desire then and we wish that all those who have at heart an earnest invitaton to Christian unity—and surely no one who belongs to Christ would belittle the importance of this matter—should pour forth their united prayers and supplications to God, from whom comes all unity, order and beauty, that the praiseworthy desires of every right-thinking person may soon be brought to fulfilment. Let research be made without jealousy or anger to

straighten out the path by which this good may be reached; let us bear in mind that to-day we are accustomed to retrace and weigh the events of bygone ages more calmly than in the past.

506 Furthermore, there is another reason which demands the immediate coalition of all ranks under the single sign of the cross in order to oppose the turbulent attacks of the infernal enemy. Who is not horror struck at the ferocity and hatred with which the enemies of God, in many parts of the world, threaten to eradicate and wipe out everything divine and Christian? All those who are signed with the sacred character of baptism and are deputed by their state to fight the good fight of Christ, cannot remain disunited and dispersed against the confederated ranks of their enemies.

507 The chains, the agonies, the tortures, the groans, the blood of the unnumerable multitude of persons, known and unknown, who recently and even to-day, have suffered and still suffer on account of their courage and constancy in the profession of their faith, cry out to all with louder and louder voice as the days go by, to embrace the unity of the Church.

508 Our hope for the return of these brothers and sons separated from the Apostolic See is made stronger by this harsh crucifixion and these bloody martyrdoms of so many other brothers and sons. Let no one neglect or impede the saving work of God. To the blessings and joys of this return we exhort and urge all those who follow the erroneous doctrines of the Nestorians and the Monophysites. Let them be sure that we should think it the brightest gem in the crown of our apostolate if the opportunity were given us of treating with honour and charity those who are the more dear to us because the long period of their withdrawal has excited us in the greater desire [for their return].

509 This is our final wish, Venerable Brethren, that when through your diligence the memory of the sacred council of Chalcedon is celebrated, all should be urged to adhere with a most firm faith to Christ our Redeemer and our King. Let no one be deceived by the fallacies of human philosophy or led astray by the quibbles of human speech; let no one corrupt by perverse innovation or weaken by doubt the dogma con-

firmed at Chalcedon, namely, that there are in Christ two true and perfect natures, the divine and the human, not confused one with another, but joined together and subsisting in the one person of the Word. Let all then be joined in a close bond with the author of our salvation, who is 'the way of holy life, the truth of divine doctrine, and the life of eternal happiness' (St. Leo Serm. lxxii, 1. PL. liv, 390). Let all love our restored nature in him, let them cultivate the liberty bought by him; let them cast out the folly of the aged world; let them turn with joy to the wisdom that is ignorant of old age, the wisdom of spiritual infancy.

510 May God Who is One in Three, whose nature is goodness, whose will is power, receive these burning desires, through the intercession of the Blessed Virgin Mary, Mother of God, the Holy Apostles Peter and Paul, and Euphemia the Virgin Martyr, who triumphed at Chalcedon. Do you, Venerable Brethren, add your prayers to ours for this cause, and see that what we have written to you is made known as widely as possible. Giving you now our thanks for this, to you and to all priests and to all Christ's faithful, whose spiritual advancement lies in your care, lovingly we bestow the apostolic blessing. May it enable you to take with greater readiness Christ's yoke upon you, a yoke that is neither heavy nor harsh, and may you become more and more like to him in humility, of whose glory you hope to be sharers.

511 Given at St. Peter's Basilica, Rome, on the 8th September, the feast of the birthday of the Virgin Mary, in the year 1951, the thirteenth of our pontificate.

The Christmas Message of Pope Pius XII to the Whole World December 24, 1955

With a heart open to receive the tender joy which the Birth of the Redeemer will once again bring to the hearts of the faithful, We desire to express good wishes to you, beloved sons and daughters of Christendom, and to all men without distinction. We shall draw the theme of our discourse, as in past years, from the inexhaustible mystery of light and grace which shone forth from the cradle of the Divine Infant on the Holy Night in Bethlehem. The brilliance of that light will never be extinguished so long as there are heard on this earth the sorrowing footfalls of those who seek amid thorns the path of true life.

513 How We wish that all men scattered over the various continents, in cities and towns, in valleys, deserts, steppes and the vast reaches of glacier wastes, on the seas and over the whole earth, could hear again, as coming to each of them singly, the voice of the angel announcing the mystery of divine grandeur and of infinite love which closed a past of murk and condemnation and ushered in the reign of salvation and truth. "Do not be afraid; behold, I bring you good news of great joy which shall be to all the people; for today in the town of David a Savior has been born to you who is Christ the Lord." (*Luke* 2:10, 11).

514 How We wish that, like the simple shepherds who were among the first to hear in silent adoration the saving message, men of today might be overcome by that same sense

of wonder which surpasses human words and which turns the mind to meditative adoration when a sublime majesty is revealed to its gaze, that of God Incarnate.

515 There is reason, indeed, to ask with a certain anxious hesitancy if modern man is still disposed to allow himself to yield to a super-natural truth so sublime, to be penetrated by the joy it has to offer: this man so convinced of his own increasing power, inclined to measure his stature according to the capability of his instruments, his organizations, his weapons, the precision of his calculations, the vastness of his production, the distance his words can span, his gaze, his influence; man who has come to speak with pride of an age of easy prosperity as if one just had to reach out a hand for it; who is so sure of himself and his future that he dares all, urged by an insatiable desire to know nature's deepest secrets. He wants to bend its forces to his own will and is eager to penetrate in his own person interplanetary space.

516 The truth is that modern man, precisely because he is in possession of all that the mind and labor of man have produced, ought to recognize so much the more the infinite distance between his immediate potentiality and what proceeds from the limitless power of God.

517 But the reality is quite different because the false or limited concepts of the world and of life accepted by men not only hinder them from deriving a sense of admiration and joy from the works of God—especially the Incarnation of the Word—but make it impossible for them to recognize the indispensable basis which gives constancy and harmony to human accomplishment. Many permit themselves to be dazzled by the limited splendor deriving from these achievements, stubbornly resisting the inner stimulus to seek their source and end outside of even above, the world of science and technology.

518 Like the constructors of the Tower of Babel they are dreaming a false dream, "the divinization of man", supposedly suitable and sufficient for every need of physical and spiritual life. In them the Incarnation of God and "His dwelling among us" (*John* 1: 14) do not arouse either profound interest or fruitful emotion.

519 The Nativity has for them no other content or message than those expressed by a cradle. They are sentiments vital enough but never more than human, even when they have not been stifled by worldly and noisy customs which profane the simple aesthetic and familiar values which the Nativity diffuses through the greatness of its mystery, as might some distant reflection.

520 Still others, taking an opposite position, contemn the works of God and thus exclude themselves from access to the hidden joys of the Nativity. Schooled by the hard experience of the last twenty years which have shown (they would have it) modern society's brutality clothed in human form, they denounce bitterly the outward glitter of its appearance and deny all credit to man and his works; nor do they hide the deep disgust which man's excessive exaltation provokes in their souls. At the same time, they hope that man may renounce all this feverish external, and above all, technological expenditure of force, that he may enter within himself to find the richness of an interior life that is all his, exclusively human, one which will satisfy every possible need.

521 And yet, this wholly human interior life is incapable of fulfilling the promise attributed to it of measuring up to all of human need. It is rather a withdrawing from life prompted by disdain, almost despair, by a fear and incapacity of giving oneself to the external order. It has nothing in common with a genuine interior life which is complete, dynamic, and fruitful.

522 In the true interior life man is not alone but lives with Christ, sharing in His thoughts and actions, associating with Him as a friend, a disciple, and almost a collaborator—in turn being assisted and sustained by Him in facing the world according to the divine precepts because "He is the Shepherd and Guardian of our souls" (cf. 1 *Pet.* 2, 25).

523 Between this first and second type, whom an erroneous conception of man has drawn away from the guiding and salutary influence of God Incarnate, stands the vast throng of those who neither feel pride at the external splendor of modern society nor intend to withdraw into a solitary life of the spirit. They are those who say they are satisfied to

live for the moment, interested and desirious of nothing other than to be sure of enjoying the goods of the world in abundance and to be free from any fear lest tomorrow bring a lowering of their standard of life. Neither the greatness of God nor the dignity of man, both marvelously and visibly exalted in the mystery of the Nativity, make an impression on these impoverished spirits who have become insensible and incapable of providing their lives with meaning.

524 The presence of God incarnate having thus been ignored or cast aside, modern man has constructed a world in which marvels run side by side with wretched distress, a world filled with incongruities like a road without an exit or a house furnished with everything except that for a lack of a roof, it can give no security to the dwellers within. In some nations, notwithstanding enormous external progress, and despite the fact that every class of people is assured material sustenance, there is spreading and increasing an indefinable sense of forboding, an anxious awaiting of something which is bound to transpire. The expectancy of the simple shepherds of the countryside of Bethlehem comes to mind. They by their sensitive and prompt response can teach proud men of the twentieth century where that which is needed is to be sought after. "Let us go over to Bethlehem," they say, "and see this thing that has come to pass, which the Lord has made known to us." (*Luke* 2: 15). The event took place 2,000 years ago but its truth and influence must continue to take possession of men's consciences, namely the coming of God unto his own (cfr. *John* 1: 11).

525 Now mankind can not, without guilt, reject and put out of mind the coming and the stay of God on earth because it is in the economy of Providence, essential for the establishment of order and harmony between man and what he possesses, and between these possessions and God. The Apostle St. Paul has described the totality of this order in an admirable syntheses: "All is yours, and you are Christ's, and Christ is God's." (*1 Cor.* 3:22,23). Those who would have God and Christ fall out of this indestructible order,

retaining from these words of the Apostle only the right of man over other creatures, would effect an essential breach in the design of the Creator. St. Paul himself presses home the warning: "Therefore let no one take pride in men." (*1 Cor.* 3:21). Who does not see how much this admonition applies to the men of our time so proud of their inventors and discoverers? No longer are the latter made to suffer the hardships of isolation as was once the case; on the contrary, they have seized the fancy of the crowd and even the watchful attention of statesmen.

526 However, it is one thing to attribute to them due honor and still another to await from them and their discoveries the solution to the fundamental problem of life. The wealth and labor, the projects and inventions, the boasts and torments of our modern age must be considered in relation to man, the image of God.

527 If, therefore, what is called progress is not reconcilable with the divine laws of world order, it most certainly is not progress but marks the way to ruin. Neither the most perfected art of organization nor highly developed methods in the field of planning will put off the inevitable result. They have no power to create man's essential steadfastness, much less substitute for it.

528 Jesus Christ alone gives to man that interior steadfastness. "When the fullness of time was come" (*Gal.*, 4:4), the Word of God entered upon this earthly life taking a true human nature, and in that form entered into the historical and social life of the human race—here, too, "being made like unto men" (*Phil.* 2:7) though God from all eternity. His coming therefore indicates that Christ intended to set Himself as a guide for men and as their support in history and in society. The fact that man has won in the present technical and industrial era a marvelous power over both organic and inorganic substances in the world does not establish a right to be free from the duty of submission to Christ, the Lord of history, nor does it diminish the need that man has of being upheld by Him. Indeed, the uncertainty over well-being become ever more pressing.

529 Present day experience clearly shows that forgetfulness or negligence of Christ's presence in the world has brought on that sense of bewilderment, and absence of security and stability peculiar to the technical era. Forgetfulness of Christ has also led to an obscuration of the reality of human nature, established by God as normative for social life in the context of time.

530 How, then, must the search be made for security and inner stability in the social order, if not by drawing minds back towards preserving and bringing into life again the principles of true human nature willed by God? There is, in fact, a natural order, even if its outward appearance changes with historical and social developments, but the essential lines have been and ever remain the same: family and property as the basis of providing for individuals; then as complementary factors of security local and professional groups; and finally the state.

531 In accordance with these principles and directives, men strengthened by Christianity were, up until this era moved to bring about in theory and practice, and insofar as they were able, that order which guarantees security. But, different from the moderns, our forebears knew—by the errors from which their concrete attempts had been marked, as much as anything—that in the establishment of security human forces are of their nature limited. Therefore they had recourse to prayer to bring it about that a much higher power might make good their own inadequacy. The abandonment of the use of prayer in the so-called industrial era is the most revealing symptom of the pretensions to self-sufficiency which modern man boasts. There are too many today who no longer pray for security thinking that the petition "Give us this day our daily bread" (*Matt.* 6:11), which Our Lord put on men's lips, has been superseded by technical achievement; or, alternatively they pay it lip service without an interior conviction of its enduring necessity.

532 But can it be truly asserted that man has attained, or is on the way to attaining, full self-sufficiency? Modern achievements in scientific and technical development, unquestionably remarkable, will, it is true, be able to give man an

extensive mastery over the forces of nature, over sickness, and even over the beginning and the end of human life; but it is also certain that such mastery will not be able to transform the earth into a paradise of unassailable delight. How will each one of man's powers be reasonably attended to if in fact new false developments and new weaknesses, betray the one-sided character of an idea which would control life exclusively on the basis of quantitative analysis and synthesis? Its application to social life is not only false but also a simplification of many complex processes, in practice most hazardous business. Conditions being what they are, modern man needs also to pray, and, if he is wise, he is ready to pray for security.

533 Yet this does not mean that man must abandon new ways, that is to say, give up adapting to present conditions the order just referred to with its regard for true human nature, for the sake of security. There is no objection to stabilizing the security achieved by making use of developments in technology and industry. Yet it is necessary to resist the temptation to gain support for order and security in the above-mentioned purely quantative method which takes no account of the order of nature, as those who entrust man's destiny to the tremendous industrial power of the age would have it.

534 They think they are establishing complete security on an ever-increasing productivity and on the uninterrupted flow of a continually greater production in the national economy. This, they say—on the basis of a full and increasingly perfected automatic system of production, and supported by better methods of organization and accountancy—will guarantee to all workers a continuous and progressive return for their labor. In a subsequent phase, this return will become so great that, by means of social measures, it will be able to take care of the security of those who are not yet able or are no longer able to work—the young, the old, the sick. To achieve security, they conclude, there will no longer be any necessity to have recourse to property, whether in nature or in capital goods.

535 Now, this way of ordering the means of security is not one of those forms of adaptation of natural principles to new developments, but almost a frontal attack on the essence of man's natural relationships with his fellow men, with work, with society. In this excessively artificial system, man's security with regard to his life is dangerously divorced from the arrangements and the forces for the ordering of society inherent in human nature itself, which alone render possible the association of men in solidarity. In one way or other, although necessary adjustment must be made to the times, family and property have to remain among the fundamentals in a free systematization of persons. Somehow the lesser social units and the state must be able to come together as complementary agents of security.

536 It therefore appears true once again that a quantitative method, however perfected, neither can nor ought to dominate the social and historical reality of human existence. The ever-quickening pulse of life and constantly increased technical productivity are not criteria which of themselves provide authority for declaring that there is a genuine improvement in the economic life of a nation. Only a one-sided view of the present, or perhaps of the immediate future and no more, can be satisfied with such a test. From this view of things there results, it may be over a long period, rash consumption of reserves and of the resources of nature, even further, of the available human power to work; then gradually there results a greater and greater disproportion between the need to maintain dwellers on a country's land in reasonable adaptation to all its productive possibilities and an excessive crowding together of workers. In addition there is the break-down of society and especially the family; to each and every worker and consumer the growing threat to security based on income from property of any sort so exposed to every form of currency depreciation, and the risk in depending exclusively on the immediate return for labor for that security.

537 In this industrial age, the man who quite rightly accuses communism of having deprived of freedom the people over whom it holds sway should not omit to note that, in the re-

maining part of the world liberty will be a very dubious possession if man's security is not derived to a greater extent from social structures corresponding to his true nature.

538 The erroneous belief which makes security rest on the ever-mounting process of social production is a superstition, perhaps the only one, of our rationalistic age of industry; but it is also the most dangerous, because it seems to consider impossible those economic crises which always bring in their train the risk of a return to dictatorship.

539 Moreover, that superstition is in no sense suited to the setting up of a sound bulwark against communism, because the communists participate in it as well as a considerable number of the non-communists. In this erroneous belief, the two sides find a meeting ground, thus establishing a tacit agreement of such a kind as to be able to beguile the apparent realists of the West into the dream of a possible genuine co-existence.

540 In the Christmas radio message last year We set forth the mind of the Church on this topic, and We now intend to ratify it once again. We reject communism as a social system by virtue of Christ's doctrine, and We have a particular obligation to proclaim the fundamental principles of natural law. For the same reason, We likewise reject the opinion that the Christian ought today to see communism as a phenomenon or a stage in the course of history, almost a necessary point in its evolution, and consequently to accept it as if it were decreed by divine Providence.

541 But at the same time, We again warn Christians of the industrial age, in the spirit of Our immediate predecessors in the supreme pastoral and teaching office, against being satisfied with an anti-communism founded on slogan and on the defense of a liberty devoid of content. Rather We urge them to build up a society in which man's security rests on that moral order the necessity and implications of which We have often set forth, looking as it does to true human nature.

542 Now Christians, to whom We address ourselves more particularly here, ought to know better than others that the Son of God become Man is the one steadfast support of the human race in the social and historical orders as well, and that

He, by taking to Himself human nature, has borne witness to its dignity as the basis and rule of that moral order. It is therefore their primary duty to act with a view to bringing about the return of modern society structurally to the wellsprings sanctified by the Word of God made flesh. If ever Christians were to neglect this duty of theirs by leaving inactive, insofar as it lies with them, the guiding force of faith in public life, they would be committing treason against the God-Man Who appeared in visible form among us in the crib of Bethlehem. Let the seriousness and the deep motive of Christian action be an effective testimony in the world, and at the same time avail to dispel every suspicion of supposed aims of earthly power on the part of the Church.

543 If, therefore, Christians unite to this end in various institutions and organizations, they are setting before themselves no other objective than the service willed by God for the benefit of the world. From this motive and not out of weakness let Christians band themselves together. But let them—and they more so than others—remain open to every healthy undertaking and to all genuine progress, and not withdraw themselves into a sealed enclosure as if to preserve themselves from the world. Committed to promote the common welfare, let them not despise others who, particularly if they are submissive to the light of reason, both could and should accept from the teaching of Christianity at least what is based on the natural law.

544 Be on your guard against those who undervalue this Christian service to the world, and oppose to it a so-called "pure," "spiritual" Christianity. They have not understood this divine institution—to begin from its fundamental principle: Christ, true God, but also true man. The Apostle St. Paul makes known to us the complete and integral will of God made man, which aims at setting aright the mundane sphere as well, when he attributes to Him in His praise two very expressive titles, "Mediator" and "Man" (*1 Timothy,* 2:5). Yes, man, just like each of those redeemed by Him.

545 Jesus Christ is not only the steadfast support of the human race in the social and historical orders, but also in the life of the individual Christian, so that as "all things were made

through Him, and without Him was made nothing that has been made" (*John* 1, 3), so no one will ever be able to carry out works worthy of the Divine Wisdom and glory without Him. The concept of the necessary integration and stability of each life in Christ was strongly presented to the faithful from the earliest days of the Church: by St. Peter the Apostle, when, at the portico of the temple of Jerusalem, he proclaimed Christ as "*τον αρχηγον της ζωης* " (*Acts* 3, 15), that is, the "Author of life," and by the Apostle of the Gentiles, who frequently pointed out what ought to be the foundation of the new life received in Baptism. "You," he wrote, "are not carnal but spiritual if the Spirit of God dwells in you. But if anyone does not have the Spirit of Christ, he does not belong to Christ" (cfr. *Rom.* 8, 9). Everyone therefore who is redeemed, just as he is "reborn" in Christ, likewise exists through Him "unto salvation by the faith" (cfr. *John* 3, 3; *1 Peter* 1, 5).

546 How moreover could the individual, even the non-Christian, left to himself, reasonably believe in his own autonomy, completeness and stability, if reality confronts him on every side with limitations within which nature confines him, limitations which could indeed be reduced, but not entirely demolished?

547 The law of limitation is proper to life on earth nor would Jesus Christ as man withdraw Himself from its rule, for there were fixed limits to His actions according to the inscrutable designs of God and inconformity with the mysteriously conjoined workings of divine grace and human freedom. Nevertheless, while Christ as Man, limited during the period of His earthly life, consoles and strengthens us in our limitations, Christ as God fills us with a higher freedom, for He has the fullness of wisdom and power.

548 Founded on this reality, the Christian who prepares himself boldly with all natural and supernatural means for building a world in accordance with the natural and supernatural order willed by God, will constantly raise his gaze to Christ, and will confine his actions within the limits fixed by God. Not to recognize that would be to will a world contrary to the divine plan, hence a thing disastrous for social life itself.

549 We have just indicated the harmful consequences which flow from the false overvaluation of human power and from the misprising of objective reality which, with the complexes of its principles and laws—religious, moral, economic and social—sets limits and indicates the correct course of human action. Now the same errors with same results are being repeated in the field of human toil, and particularly in that of economic activity and production.

550 In the face of the astonishing development of technology, and, more often, by means of ideas received, the worker feels himself absolute lord and master of his existence, completely capable of pursuing every objective, of realizing every dream. By confining the whole of reality to the limits of the physical world he discerns in the live nature of production the means to increased human perfection. Productive society, which appears to the worker as the sole living reality and as the power which sustains everybody, becomes normative for his whole life. It is his one sure support for both the present and the future. In it he lives, and moves, and has his being. It finally grows into a substitute for religion for him. So conceived—one cannot help thinking—there will arise a new type of man, namely, a man who surrounds his work with the aureole of highest ethical value, and worships the workers' society with a kind of religious fervor.

551 The question is being put these days whether the creative power of work truly constitutes the stay of man independently of other values not purely technical, and whether in consequence it deserves to be all but divinized by moderns. Certainly not; for no power whatever nor any activity of an economic nature can be so regarded. Even in a technical era the human person, created by God and redeemed by Christ, remains elevated in his being and in his dignity; therefore his creative power and his work have a very much higher permanence. Thus firmly established, human labor is also a profound moral force; and the human race of workers a society which not only produces objects, but also glorifies God. Man can consider his work as a true instrument of his sanctification because of working he makes perfect in himself the image of God, fulfills his duty and the right to gain for

himself and his dependents the necessary sustenance, and makes himself a useful contributor to society. Bringing this order into existence will obtain for him security, and, at the same time the "peace on earth" proclaimed by the angels.

552 And yet, it is precisely against him, the religious and Christian man, that some will bring the charge that he is an obstacle to peace, that he opposes the peaceful co-existence of men, of nations, of different systems, because he does not keep unspoken in the privacy of his conscience his religious convictions, but makes them effective even in long standing and powerful organizations, in all the activities of life, both public and private. It is asserted that this kind of Christianity makes a man overbearing, biased, oversure and satisfied with himself; that it leads him to defend positions which no longer have any significance, instead of being open to everything and everybody, and having confidence that in a general co-existence interior living faith, such as "spirit and love" in the cross and in sacrifice at least, would furnish a definite contribution to the common cause.

553 In this false idea of a religion and Christianity, have we not once more before us that erroneous worship of the human subject and of his positive life-force carried to the supernatural plane? Face to face with opinions and systems opposed to the true religion, man is nevertheless ever bound by the limits established by God in the natural and supernatural orders. In obedience to this principle, Our peace program cannot approve of an indiscriminate co-existence with every one at all costs; certainly not at the cost of truth and justice. These irremovable boundary marks have the effect of demanding complete observance. Where this is so, including the question of peace today, religion is protected with certainty against abuse from the political quarter; whereas in cases where religion has been restricted to purely interior life, it is more exposed to that danger.

554 This thought leads Us naturally to the continually acute question of peace which constitutes an object of solicitude ever present to Our heart; at this moment one of its partial problems begs for special consideration. We propose to direct Our attention to a recent proposal which aims at

putting a check on experiments in nuclear weapons by means of an international agreement. There has been talk also of taking further steps toward conventions, through which the use of those weapons would be renounced and all states subjected to an effective arms control. Thus it seems to be a matter of three steps: renunciation of experimentation with atomic weapons, renunciation of the use of such, and general control of armaments.

555 The supreme importance of these proposals is tragically illustrated if one stops to consider what science thinks it can predict about such actions. This We think it useful to sum up briefly here.

556 As for *experiments* with atomic explosions, the opinion of those who fear the effects produced if they should be multiplied seem to be finding greater acceptance. Too many such explosions would in time cause an increased density of radioactive products in the atmosphere, the diffusion of which depends on elements not under man's control. Conditions very dangerous for many living beings would thereby be generated.

557 Concerning the *use*: In a nuclear explosion an enormous amount of energy equivalent to several thousand million kilowatts is developed in an exceedingly short time; this energy is composed of electromagnetic radiations of very great density, distributed over a vast gamut of wave lengths up to the most penetrating, and of tiny bodies produced by nuclear disintegration which are hurled at velocities close to that of light. This energy is transferred to the atmosphere, and within thousandths of a second increases the temperature of surrounding air masses by hundreds of degrees; their displacement is violent, propagated at the speed of sound. On the earth's surface, in an area of many square kilometers, reactions of unimaginable violence take place. Materials are volatilized and utterly destroyed by direct radiation, by heat, and by mechanical action, while an enormous amount of radioactive materials of varying life-span complete and continue the destruction through their activity.

558 This is the spectacle offered to the terrified gaze as a result of such use: entire cities, even the largest and richest in art

and history, wiped out; a pall of death over pulverized ruins covering countless victims—their limbs burnt, twisted and scattered—while others groan in their death agony. Meanwhile the specter of a radioactive cloud hinders survivors from giving any help, and inexorably advances to snuff out any remaining life. There will be no song of victory, only the inconsolable weeping of humanity which in desolation will gaze upon the catastrophe brought on by its own folly.

559 Concerning the *control*: Inspection by properly equipped planes has been suggested, for the purpose of watching over any atomic activities in large territories. Others might perhaps think of the possibility of a worldwide network of observation posts, each one staffed by experts of different countries and protected by solemn international pacts. Such centers would have to be equipped with delicate and precise meteorological and seismic instruments, with equipment for chemical analysis, with vast spectographs and such like; they would render possible the real control of many, but unfortunately not of all the activities which would antecedently have been outlawed in the field of atomic experimentation.

560 We do not hesitate to declare, as We have in previous Allocutions, that the sum total of those three precautions as an object of international agreement, is an obligation in conscience of nations and of their leaders. We said the sum total of those precautions, because the reason they are morally binding is that equal security be established for all. If, however, only the first point concerning experimentation were put into effect, the result would be that that condition would not be verified, the more so because there would be sufficient reason to doubt a sincere desire to put into effect the other two conventions. We speak so frankly as We do because the danger of insufficient proposals concerning peace depends largely on the mutual suspicions that often disturb the relations of powers concerned, each accusing the other in varying degrees of pure tactical shrewdness, even lack of sincerity in a matter basic to the fate of the whole human race.

561 For the rest, efforts toward peace must consist not only in measures aimed at restricting the possibility of waging

war, but even more in preventing or eliminating or lessening with time the quarrels between nations which might lead to war.

562 To this kind of preventive pacification statesmen imbued with a spirit of impartial justice and generosity, must devote themselves with great vigilance, within the limits of course, of a healthy realism. In last year's Christmas Message We indicated the points of dispute in relations between Europeans and those non-Europeans who aspire to full political independence. Can those disputes be allowed to run their course so to speak—a procedure which might easily increase their gravity, sow hatred in men's souls and create what are usually called traditional enmities? And might not a third party come to profit from such enmities, a third party basically unwilled by the others nor could they be expected to will it. At any rate let not those peoples be denied a fair and progressive political freedom nor hindered in its pursuit. To Europe, however, they will give credit for their advancement; to that Europe without whose influence, extended to all fields, they might be drawn by a blind nationalism to plunge into chaos or slavery.

563 On the other hand, Western peoples, especially those of Europe, should not, in the face of such problems, remain passive, in futile regret over the past or in mutual recrimination over colonialism. Rather they should set themselves constructively to work, to extend the true values of Europe and the West where it has not yet been done, values which have produced so much good fruit on other continents.

564 The more Europeans strive for this, the more will they be of assistance to the legitimate freedom of young nations, which in turn will be saved from the pitfalls of false nationalism. This in truth is their real enemy, which would pit them one day against each other, to the advantage of third parties. Such a forecast, not unfounded, cannot be neglected or forgotten by those who handle their problems of peace at Congresses where, unfortunately, there gleams the splendor of a unity that is external and predominantly negative. We think that in such considerations and in such modes of procedure there is a valuable assurance of peace, in some re-

spects even more important than an immediate prevention of war.

565 Beloved sons and daughters: if even today, the Birth of Christ spreads through the world rays of joy and quickens profound emotion in the heart, it is because the immense yearnings of generations of men are contained in the lowly crib of the Incarnate Son of God. In Him, with Him, and through Him is the salvation, the security, the temporal and eternal destiny of humankind. To each and every man the way is clear to approach that crib, to attain, through the teaching, the example, the goodness of the God-Man, his share of grace and the things necessary for this life and the life to come.

566 Where that is not done, either because of individual sloth or because of other hindrances, it would be useless to seek it elsewhere, for on all sides the darkness of error, of selfishness, of vanity and sin, of disappointment and uncertainty weighs heavily. The disappointing experiences of peoples, of systems, of individuals who were unwilling to seek from Christ the way, the truth and the life, should be seriously studied and meditated on by whoever thinks he can do all by himself. Today's humanity, cultured, powerful, dynamic, perhaps holds a greater title to earthly happiness possessed in security and peace, but will not be able to realize that happiness so long as the highest and most influential factor does not enter into its plans and discussions: God and His Christ. Let the God-Man return among men, their Lord acknowledged and obeyed, as at every Christmas He returns in spirit to the crib and offers Himself to all. Such is the wish We express today to mankind's great family, in the certainty that We are showing it the path to salvation and happiness.

567 May the Divine Infant deign to hear Our fervent prayer so that His presence in today's world may be felt almost sensibly, as in the days of His dwelling on earth. Living in the midst of men, may He enlighten the minds and strengthen the wills of those who rule over nations; to these latter may He assure justice and peace; may He encourage the zealous apostles of His divine message, sustain the good, draw

the errant to Himself, console those persecuted for His Name and for His Church, succor the poor and the oppressed, assuage the pains of the sick, the imprisoned, the exiled. May He give to all a spark of His divine love so that everywhere on earth His peaceful kingdom may triumph. Amen.

HAURIETIS AQUAS

Encyclical Letter of Pope Pius XII
on Devotion to the Sacred Heart
May 15, 1956

You shall draw waters with joy out of the Saviour's foundations."[1] These words, in which the Prophet Isaias symbolically foretold the manifold and rich gifts of God that Christianity was to reap, spontaneously come to Our mind as We recall the centenary of the proclamation in which our predecessor of immortal memory, Pius IX, gladly granting the petition of the Catholic world, ordered the celebration of the feast of the Sacred Heart throughout the whole Church.

569

2. Those heavenly blessings which devotion to the Sacred Heart of Jesus pours into the soul of the faithful, purifying them, refreshing them with heavenly consolation and urging them to acquire all virtues, cannot be counted. Mindful, therefore, of the wise words of the Apostle St. James—"Every good gift and every perfect gift is from above, coming down from the Father of Lights"[2] —We rightly see in this devotion, which everywhere grows more fervent, the inestimable gift which the Incarnate Word, our Divine Saviour, as the sole Mediator of grace and truth between the Heavenly Father and the human race, gave to the Church, His mystical bride, in recent times so that she could endure great trials and surmount difficulties. In virtue of this inestimable gift the Church is able to manifest her ardent love for her Divine Founder and in a fuller measure carry out the injunction given by Jesus Christ Himself, which St. John the Evangelist

records: "Now on the last, the great day of the feast, Jesus stood and cried out, saying, 'If anyone thirst, let him come to me and drink. He who believes in me, as the Scripture says, "From within him there shall flow rivers of living water." ' He said this, however, of the Spirit whom they who believed in him were to receive."[3]

570 3. It was certainly not hard for those who heard Jesus speak these words, in which He promised that a fountain of "living water" would flow from within Him, to recall the words of the holy prophets Isaias, Ezechiel and Zachary foretelling the messianic kingdom, and that rock from which water miraculously gushed forth when Moses struck it.[4]

571 4. Divine love has its origin in the Holy Ghost, who is the Personified Love both of the Father and the Son in the bosom of the August Trinity. Most aptly, then, does the Apostle of the Gentiles, echoing the words of Jesus Christ, attribute the infusion of charity in the souls of the faithful to this Spirit of Love. "The charity of God is poured forth in our hearts by the Holy Spirit who has been given to us."[5]

572 5. This intimate bond which, according to Sacred Scripture, exists between the divine charity that must burn in the souls of the faithful and the Holy Ghost, clearly shows to all, venerable brothers, the real nature of devotion to the Sacred Heart of Jesus Christ. For it is perfectly clear that this devotion, if we examine its proper nature, is a most excellent act of religion.

573 6. It demands the full and absolute determination of surrendering and consecrating oneself to the love of the Divine Redeemer. The wounded heart of the Saviour is the living sign and symbol of that love. It is likewise clear, even to a greater degree, that this devotion especially declares that we must repay divine love with our own love.

574 7. Indeed it flows from the very essence of love that the souls of men fully and completely submit to the rule of the Supreme Being, because the act of our love so depends upon the divine will that it forms, as it were, a certain oneness according to the words of Scripture, "He who cleaves to the Lord is one in spirit with Him."[6]

8. The Church has always held devotion to the Sacred Heart of Jesus in such high regard and continues to esteem it so greatly that she strives to have this devotion flourish throughout the world and to promote it in every way. At the same time she is vigilant to safeguard it with all her strength against the charges of naturalism and so-called sentimentalism. In spite of this vigilance, it is nevertheless a deplorable fact that in the past and in our own time this most noble devotion has not even been held in the honor it deserves by some Christians, and at times even by those who claim to be animated by zeal for the Catholic religion and the acquiring of sanctity. 575

9. "If thou didst know the gift of God."[7] venerable brothers, We, who by the hidden designs of God have been chosen as guardian and dispenser of that sacred treasure of faith and piety which the Divine Redeemer entrusted to His Church, make these words Our own. Through them, in keeping with the duty of Our office, We admonish all those of Our sons who are still led by preconceived opinions, and go so far at times as to consider devotion to the Sacred Heart of Jesus (which triumphing, as it were, over the errors and neglect of men has spread over His whole Mystical Body) as less suited—not to say detrimental—to the more pressing spiritual needs of the Church and the human race in our times. 576

10. There are some who join the very essence of this devotion with other forms of piety which the Church approves and encourages but does not command. They put it on an equal footing with those other forms of piety. They look upon this devotion as some kind of additive which each one is free to use according to his own good pleasure. 577

11. There are others, again, who assert that this devotion is burdensome and of little or no use, particularly to those who are fighting in the kingdom of God motivated by the idea of defending, teaching, and spreading Catholic truth to the utmost of their strength, resources, and time and of inculcating Christian social teaching and who strive to promote those acts of religion and undertakings which they consider much more necessary today. Then, too, there are those who, far from considering this devotion a powerful help for correctly forming and restoring Christian morals both in the 578

private life of individuals and in the family circle, consider it rather as a form of piety springing from emotions and not from reasoned convictions and more suited, therefore, for women, because they see in it something unbecoming educated men.

579 12. Others again, when they pause to think that this devotion especially demands penance, expiation and the rest of the virtues which they call passive and which have no external influence, do not consider it apt for arousing the spiritual fervor of our times. Fervor today must aim rather at visible strenuous action, the triumph of the Catholic faith and a vigorous defense of Christian moral standards.

580 13. As everyone knows these norms are flippantly attacked by the captious objections of those who are indifferent to all religion, who tear down the distinction of true and false in thought and action and who are pitifully contaminated by the principles of atheistic materialism and laicism.

581 14. Venerable brothers, who does not see that such opinions are completely contrary to the teachings which Our predecessors publicly proclaimed from this chair of truth when they approved the devotion to the Sacred Heart of Jesus? Who would dare call useless and less uitable to our time that piety which Our predecessor of immortal memory, Leo XIII, declared a "most excellent form of religion" and in which he had no doubt there was to be found a powerful remedy to cure those very same evils which today, too,–beyond doubt in an even greater and more violent manner–afflict and vex individuals and society? "This devotion," he said, "which We recommend to all, will be profitable for all."

582 15. He added these admonitions and exhortations which also apply to devotion to the Sacred Heart of Jesus: "Hence this force of evils, which so long weighs us down seriously, demands that the help of One be sought by whose power it can be driven off. Who is He, but the only begotten Son of God! For there is no other name under heaven given to men by which we must be saved. We must then flee to Him, who is the Way, the Truth and the Life."[8]

583 16. Neither did Our immediate predecessor of happy memory, Pius XI, declare this devotion less approved and suited

to foster Christian piety. In an encyclical letter he wrote: "Is not the epitome of religion, and consequently the norm of the more perfect life, contained in that form of piety which more readily leads souls to acknowledge Christ the Lord and which more effectively inclines hearts to love Him more ardently and imitate Him more closely?"[9]

17. This truth is as evident and clear to Us as it was to Our predecessors. When We became Pope and saw with pleasure that devotion to the Sacred Heart of Jesus had providentially increased among Christian peoples and was marching in triumph, so to speak, We were filled with joy at the graces which flowed to the Chuch from this devotion. We were pleased to note this in Our very first encyclical.[10] 584

18. Through the years of Our pontificate, filled not only with cares and anxieties but also with ineffable consolations, these blessings have not been diminished either in number, power or splendor, but have rather been multiplied. Various movements have providentially started which are conducive to the adding of new fervor to this devotion and most aptly suited to the needs of our times. We mean organizations to promote religion and charity, published articles which explain the historical, the ascetical or they mystical aspects which have bearing on this topic and pious works of expiation. 585

19. We mention especially the proofs of deepest peity given by the Apostleship of Prayer, under whose auspices and care homes, colleges, institutions and at times whole nations were consecrated to the most Sacred Heart of Jesus. Not infrequently by letter, public addresses, and even by radio We have extended Our paternal congratulations to these undertakings.[11] 586

20. Consequently, as We behold the rich abundance of salutary waters, that is, of heavenly gifts of divine love, flowing from the Sacred Heart of Our Redeemer and permeating countless children of the Catholic Church (under the inspiration and operation of the Holy Ghost), We cannot refrain, venerable brothers, from exhorting you paternally to join Us in giving glory and thanks to God, the Giver of all good gifts. We join Our sentiments whith those of the Apostle of the Gentiles: "Now, to him who is able to accomplish all things 587

in a measure far beyond what we ask or conceive, in keeping with the power that is at work in us—to him be glory in the Church and in Christ Jesus down through all the ages of time without end. Amen."[12]

588 21. But after We have duly thanked the Eternal God, We wish through this encyclical to urge you, and all Our dearly beloved children of the Church, to study diligently the teachings of Scripture, the Fathers and theologians—the solid foundations on which devotion to the Sacred Heart of Jesus rests.

589 22. For we are firmly convinced that only when we have thoroughly investigated the basic and profound nature of this devotion in the light of divinely revealed truth, only then, do We say, can we rightly and fully appreciate its incomparable excellence and its inexhautible store of heavenly gifts. Only after piously meditating on the countless blessings flowing from this devotion can we worthily celebrate the first centenary of the feast of the most Sacred Heart of Jesus.

590 23. To give to the minds of the faithful a salutary teaching by virtue of which they can more easily and fully understand the true nature of this devotion and reap its abundant fruits, We shall explain those passages of the Old and New Testaments in which God's infinite love for mankind is revealed and set before us. We can, of course, never really study that love sufficiently. We shall then touch upon the chief points of the teaching of the Fathers and Doctors of the Church.

591 24. Finally We shall show in its true light the close connection that exists between the kind of devotion to be shown to the heart of the Divine Redeemer and the veneration due to His love and the love of the August Trinity for all men. For We think that if the principal reasons for this noblest form of piety and the foundations on which it rests are set forth in the light of Scripture and the teaching handed down in the Church, the faithful can more easily "draw waters with joy out of the Saviour's fountains."[13]

592 25. To draw this water means to consider more fully the special importance which devotion to the Sacred Heart of Jesus has in the liturgy of the Church and in her internal and external life and activity, and to have the power to gather those spiritual fruits through which individuals can renew

their spiritual life, as the shepherds of the flock of Christ desire. That everyone may be able to understand more fully the doctrine which the passages to be cited from the Old and New Testament proclaim in regard to this devotion, they must above all clearly understand the reason why the Church adores the heart of the Divine Redeemer.

26. Now it is perfectly clear to you, venerable brothers, that there is a twofold reason. The first reason, which also applies to the rest of the most holy members of the body of Jesus Christ, rests on the teaching by which we know that His Heart, as the noblest part of human nature, is hypostatically united to the person of the Divine Word and must therefore be adored in the same way in which the Church adores the Person of the Incarnate Son of God. We deal here with an article of Catholic faith since this point was already solemnly defined in the general Council of Ephesus and the second Council of Constantinople.[14] 593

27. The second reason, which refers specifically to the Heart of the Divine Redeemer and in a special manner demands adoration, stems from the fact that His Heart, more than all the rest of the members of His body, is the natural sign and symbol of His boundless love for the human race. Our predecessor of immortal memory, Leo XIII, remarked: "In the Sacred Heart there is the symbol and the express image of the infinite love of Jesus Christ which moves us to love in return."[15] 594

28. There is no doubt that Scripture never makes express mention of special veneration paid to the physical heart of the Incarnate Word as the symbol of His most ardent love. If we must openly admit this, it cannot surprise Us nor in any way lead Us to doubt the divine love for us which is the principal reason for this devotion. This love is proclaimed and inculcated both in the Old and New Testaments in such vivid images as to greatly stir our souls. At times these images were presented in the Scripture which announced the coming of the Son of God made man. They can therefore be considered as the beginning of the sign and symbol of that divine love, that is of the most Sacred and Adorable Heart of the Divine Redeemer. 595

596 29. For our present purpose we do not consider it necessary to cite many passages from the Old Testament, which contains truths revealed by God long ago. We deem it sufficient to recall the covenant made between God and the Jewish people which was ratified with peace offerings.

597 30. Moses wrote the laws of the covenant on two tables of stone and the prophets expounded them.[16] The covenant was sealed not only by the bonds of God's supreme dominion and the obedience which men owe Him, but was also strengthened and sustained by higher considerations of love.

598 31. For to the people of Israel the weightiest reason for obeying God was not the fear of divine vengence, which the thunder and lightning flashing from the peak of Mt. Sinai struck into their souls, but rather love for God. "Hear, O Israel! The Lord is our God, the Lord alone! Therefore, you shall love the Lord, your God, with all your heart, and with all your soul, and with all your strength. Take to heart these words which I enjoin on you today."[17]

599 32. We are not surprised then if Moses and the prophets, whom the Angelic Doctor rightly calls the elders of the chosen people[18], because they knew that the foundation of the entire law was placed on this precept of love, described the dealings between God and his people in terms of the mutual love of a father and his children or of a husband and his wife, rather than in stern terms of God's supreme dominion or of our own subjection in fear.

600 33. Therefore, to cite a few examples, Moses himself, when he sang his famous canticle because of the liberation of his people from the bondage of Egypt and wanted to declare that it had been accomplished by the power of God, used these touching expressions and comparisons: "As an eagle incites its nestlings forth by hovering over its brood, so he (God) spreads his wings to receive them and bore them up on his pinions."[19]

601 34. Of the prophets perhaps none more than Osee expresses and explains so clearly and forcefully the love which God always showed His people. In the writings of this prophet, who is outstanding among the rest of the minor prophets for the austere grandeur of his diction, God manifests a holy and

solicitous love for His chosen people, a love like that of a loving and merciful father or that of a husband whose honor is offended.

35. It is a question here of a love that is so far from diminishing or ceasing on account of the perfidy of traitors or enormour crimes, that it will rather justly punish offenses, not indeed to repudiate and dismiss the estranged and faithless wife and ungrateful children, but to make amends and purify and reunite them in renewed and strengthened bonds of love. "Because Israel was a child and I loved him; and I called my son out of Egypt. . .And I was like a foster father to Ephraim, I carried them in my arms; and they knew not that I healed them. I will draw them with the cords of Adam, with the bands of love. . .I will heal their breaches, I will love them freely, for my wrath is turned away from them. I will be as the dew, Israel shall spring as the lily, and his root shall shoot forth as that of Libanus."[20] 602

36. The prophet Isaias expresses similar sentiments when he represents God Himself and His chosen people expressing, as it were, opposite views in a conversation: "And Sion said: The Lord hath forsaken men, and the Lord hath forgotten me. Can a woman forget her infant, so as not to have pity on the son of her womb? And if she should forget, yet will not I forget thee."[21] 603

37. No less touching are the words which the author of the Canticle of Canticles uses when he graphically describes the bonds of mutual love which join God and His chosen people in terms of conjugal love. "As a lily among thorns, so is my beloved among women. . .My lover belongs to me and I to him; he browses among the lilies. . .Set me as a seal on your heart, as a seal on your arm; for stern as death is love, relentless as the nether world is devotion; its flames are a blazing fire."[22] 604

38. Yet this most tender, indulgent and patient love of God, which indeed disclaimed the Jewish people as it added crime upon crime, yet never completely repudiated it, and which seems ardent indeed and sublime, was but a harbinger of the most ardent love which the promised Redeemer was to unfold for all from His Most Loving Heart. This love, was to 605

be the exemplar of our love, the foundation of the new covenant. However, only He who is the only Begotten of the Father and the World-made-Flesh "full of grace and of truth"[23] when He came among men weighed down with countless sins and miseries could in His human nature, hyostatically united with the Divine Person, open for mankind "a fountain of living water" to irrigate the parched earth and transform it into a blooming fruitful garden.

606 39. It seems that the prophet Jeremias in a way foretold this marvelous transformation to be accomplished through God's most merciful and eternal love in these words: "I have loved thee with an everlasting love, therefore have I drawn thee, taking pity on thee. . .Behold the days shall come, saith the Lord, and I will make a new covenant with the house of Israel, and with the house of Juda. . .This shall be the covenant that I will make with the house of Israel, after those days, saith the Lord: I will give my law in their bowels, and I will write it in their heart, and I will be their God, and they shall be my people. . .for I will forgive their iniquity, and I will remember their sin no more."[24]

607 40. However, only from the Gospels do we get clear and full knowledge of the new covenant between God and man. The covenant which Moses made between the people of Isarel and God was merely the symbol and token which the prophet Jeremias foretold. The new covenant, We say, is that which was established and accomplished by the Incarnate Word and divine grace reconciling us with God. This covenant must therefore be considered incomparably nobler and more lasting because it was ratified, not by the blood of goats and heifers, as was the first, but by His Most Holy Blood, which the peace offerings–irrational animals–foreshadowed as "the lamb of God, who takes away the sin of the world."[25]

608 41. The Christian convenant, much more than the old covenant, clearly shows that it was not based on submission and fear, but ratified in terms of that friendship that must exist between a father and his sons and is sustained and strengthened by a more lavish participation in divine grace and truth, according to the words of St. John the Evangelist: "and of his fullness we have all received, grace for grace. For the Law

was given through Moses; grace and truth came through Jesus Christ."[26]

42. Since we are led then to the mystery of the infinite love of the Incarnate Word by the statement of that disciple "whom Jesus loved, the one who, at the supper, had leaned back upon his breast"[27] it seems meet and just, right and availing unto salvation, venerable brothers, to linger awhile in the sweetest contemplation of that mystery. 609

43. We pause in this consideration so that, enlightened by that light which shines from the Gospel and sheds light on this mystery, We too may conceive and express the desire recorded by the Apostle of the Gentiles: "To have Christ dwelling through faith in your hearts: so that, being rooted and grounded in love, you may be able to comprehend with all the saints what is its breadth and length and height and depth, and to know Christ's love which surpasses knowledge, in order that you may be filled unto all the fullness of God."[28] 610

44. The mystery of the divine Redemption is first and foremost a mystery of love, that is, of the true love of Christ for His Heavenly Father, to whom the sacrifice offered on the Cross in loving obedience renders most abundant and infinite satisfactions for the sins of mankind. "By suffering out of love and obedience, Christ gave more to God than was required to compensate for the offense of the whole human race."[29] It is, moreover, a mystery of the merciful love of the August Trinity and the Divine Redeemer for all mankind. Since men could in no way expiate their sins,[30] Christ acquired for us by shedding His precious Blood, was able to restore and perfect the bond of friendship between God and men which had been severed first in paradise by the pitiful fall of Adam, and later by the countless sins of the chosen people. 611

45. Therefore the Divine Redeemer, as our duly constituted and perfect Mediator, because He made perfect satisfaction to divine justice for all the debts and obligations of the human race out of His most ardent love for us, effected the marvelous reconciliation between divine justice and divine mercy which constitutes the impenetrable mystery of our salvation. 612

613 46. Concerning this mystery, the Angelic Doctor wisely says: "That man should be delivered by Christ's Passion was in keeping with both His mercy and His justice. With His justice, because by His passion Christ made satisfaction for the sin of the human race; and so man was set free by Christ's justice: and with His mercy, for since man of himself could not satisy for the sin of all human nature God gave him His Son to satisfy for him.

614 47. "And this came of a more copious mercy than if He had forgiven sins without satisfaction. Hence St. Paul says: 'God, Who is rich in mercy, by reason of His very great love wherewith He has loved us even when we were dead by reason of our sins, brought us to life together with Christ.' "[31]

615 48. However, that we may be able so far as it is possible for mortal man "to comprehend with all the saints what is the breadth and length and height and depth"[32] of the fathomness love of the Incarnate Word for His Heavenly Father and for men defiled by sin, we must understand that His love was spiritual, as becomes God, because "God is Spirit."[33] But it was not only spiritual. To be sure, the love with which God loved our first parents and the Hebrew people was of a spiritual nature. The expressions of love, so human, intimate and paternal which we read in the Psalms, in the writings of the prophets and in the Canticle of Canticles, are indications and manifestations of the truest but entirely spiritual love with which God loved the human race. On the contrary, the love spoken of in the Gospel, the letters of the apostles and the pages of the Apocalypse—all of which describe the love of the heart of Jesus Christ—express not only divine love but also human sentiments of love.

616 49. This point is quite clear to all who are Catholics. For the Word of God assumed not a fictitious and empty body, as some heretics already maintained in the first century of the Christian era and who were condemned by St. John the Apostle in most severe terms: "For many deceivers have gone forth into the world, who do not confess Jesus as the Christ coming in the flesh. This is the deceiver and the Antichrist."[34] But the Word actually united to His divine person an individual, integral and perfect human nature which was conceived by

the power of the Holy Ghost in the most pure womb of the Virgin Mary.[35] Nothing, therefore, was lacking in the human nature which the Word of God joined to Himself. Indeed He assumed a human nature in no way diminished or changed in its spiritual and bodily capacities, that is, a nature endowed with intelligence and free will and the rest of the internal and external faculties of perception, sense appetites and all natural impulses.

50. The Catholic Church teaches all these doctrines as solemnly proclaimed and confirmed by the Roman Pontiffs and general councils. "Whole and entire in what is His own, whole and entire in what is ours."[36] "Perfect in his Godhead and likewise perfect in His humanity,"[37] "Complete God is man, complete man is God."[38] 617

51. Therefore, there can be no doubt that Jesus Christ took a human body having all the affections which are proper to it, among which love holds the first place. There can likewise be no doubt that He had a physical heart like ours, since without this most excellent organ human life, even as regards affections, is impossible. Wherefore, the heart of Jesus Christ, hypostatically united to the Divine Person of the Word, beyond doubt throbbed with love and the rest of the impulses of the affections which, however, were in such perfect accord and harmony with His human will filled with divine love and with the infinite love itself which the Son shares with the Father and the Holy Ghost so that there never was anything contrary or conflicting in these three kinds of love.[39] 618

52. Nevertheless, We say that the Word of God took upon Himself a "real" and perfect human nature and formed and fashioned for Himself a heart of flesh, which like ours could suffer and be pierce. We repeat that unless this teaching be considered not only in the light which is shed by the hypostatic and substantial union, but also in that of the redemption of mankind—its complement, as it were—this doctrine can be a stumbling block and foolishness to some, as Christ nailed to the Cross actually was to the Jews and Gentiles.[40] 619

53. The authoritative teaching of the Catholic faith, since it is in complete agreement with Scripture, assures us that the 620

only begotten Son of God assumed a human nature capable of suffering and dying precisely because He wished, by offering the bloody sacrifice on the Cross, to accomplish the task of man's redemption.

621 54. For the rest, the Apostle of the Gentiles teaches this doctrine in these words: "For both he who sanctifies and they who are sanctified are all from one. For which cause he is not ashamed to call them brethren, saying, 'I will declare thy name to my brethren'. . . .And again, 'Behold I and my children, whom God has given me.' Therefore, because children have blood and flesh in common, so he in like manner has shared in these. . . .Wherefore it was right that he should in all things be made like unto his brethren, that he might become a merciful and faithful high priest before God to expiate the sins of the people. For in that he himself has suffered and has been tempted, he is able to help those who are tempted."[41]

622 55. The Fathers of the Church, truthful witnesses of divinely revealed doctrine, understood most definitely what the Apostle Paul had quite clearly stated: that the mysteries of the Incarnation and Redemption were the beginning and culmination of divine love. Frequently, and in clear words, we read in their writings that Jesus Christ assumed perfect human nature, and our mortal and perishable body, to provide for our eternal salvation and to show us His infinite, even sensible, love.

623 56. Echoing the words of the Apostle of the Gentiles, St. Justin writes: "We adore and love the Word born of the unbegotten and ineffable God since He became Man for our sake, so that having become partaker of our sufferings He might provide a remedy for them."[42] St. Basil, the greatest of the three Cappadocian Fathes, teaches that the affections of the senses in Christ were at one and the same time real and holy. "It is clear that the Lord indeed did assume natural affections as a proof of His real and not imaginary Incarnation and that He rejected as unworthy of the Godhead corrupt affections which defile the purity of our life."[43] In like manner the light of the church of Antioch, St. John Chrysostom, states that the affections of the senses to which the Divine

Redeemer was susceptible prove beyond doubt that He assumed a complete human nature. "For if He had not shared our nature He would not have repeatedly been seized with grief."[44]

57. Of the Latin Fathers We select for mention those whom the Church today honors as the greatest. St. Ambrose testifies that the movements of the senses and the affections, from which the Incarnate Word was not free, are rooted in the hypostatic union as in a natural principle: "And therefore he assumed a soul and the passions of the soul; for God precisely because He is God could not have been disturbed nor could He have died."[45] 624

58. From these affections St. Jerome draws his chief proof that Christ assumed human nature: "To prove that He really assumed human nature, he really became sorrowful."[46] St. Augustine in a special manner calls attention to the relations between the affections of the Incarnate Word and the purpose of the redemption of the human race. "These affections of human infirmity, just as the human body itself and death, the Lord Jesus assumed not out of necessity but freely out of compassion so that He might transform in Himself His body, which is the Church of which He deigned to be the Head, that is, His members who are among the faithful and the saints so that if any of them in trials of this life should be saddened and afflicted, they should not therefore think that they are deprived of His grace; nor should they consider this sorrow a sin, but a sign of human weakness; like a choir singing in harmony with the note that has been sounded, so should his body learn from its Head."[47] 625

59. In less ornate but nevertheless forceful words, the following passages from St. John Damascene set forth the clear teaching of the Church: "Complete God assumed complete man, and complete man is united to complete God so that He might bring salvation to complete man. For what was not assumed could not be healed."[48] "He therefore assumed all that He might sanctify all."[49] 626

60. We must, however, bear in mind that these quotations from scripture and the Fathers and not a few similar ones which We did not cite, although they clearly attest that there 627

were in Jesus Christ movements of the senses and affections and that he assumed human nature to accomplish our eternal salvation, they never refer to His physical heart in such a manner as to clearly indicate it as the symbol of his infinite love.

628 61. "But if the evangelists and the rest of the sacred writers do not clearly describe the heart of our Redeemer as responding to feelings and emotions no less than ours and as throbbing and palpitating on account of the various movements and affections of his soul and of the most ardent love of His human and divine wills, they do frequently, however, clearly record His divine love and those movements of the emotions connected with them, namely, desire, joy, sadness, fear and anger as they are reflected in His countenance, words and manner of acting.

629 62. The countenance of our adorable Saviour was an indication and perfect mirror of those affections which, in various ways, moved His soul, and of the reactions which reached and touched His Most Sacred Heart. The observation based on common experience which the Angelic Doctor made concerning human psychology and what follows from it is pertinent to this matter: "The disturbance of anger reaches to the outward members and chiefly to those members which reflect more distinctly the emotions of the heart, such as the eyes, face and tongue."[50]

630 63. Wherefore the heart of the Incarnate Word is rightly considered the chief index and symbol of the threefold love with which the Divine Redeemer continuously loves the Eternal Father and the Whole human race. It is the symbol of that divine love which He shares with the Father and the Holy Ghost, but which in Him alone, in the Word namely that was made Flesh, is it manifested to us through His mortal human body, since "in Him dwells the fullness of the Godhead bodily."[51]

631 64. It is moreover the symbol of that most ardent love, which, infused into His soul, sanctifies the human will of Christ and whose action is enlightened and directed by a twofold most perfect knowledge, namely the beatific and infused.[52]

65. Finally, in a more direct and natural manner, it is a symbol also of sensible love, since the body of Jesus Christ, formed through the operation of the Holy Ghost in the womb of the Virgin Mary, has a most perfect capacity for feeling and perception, much more than the bodies of all other men.[53] 632

66. Since Scripture and the teachings of the Catholic Faith affirm that there is the highest possible harmony and agreement in the Most Holy Soul of Jesus Christ, and that He clearly directed His threefold love to accomplish our redemption, it is therefore obvious that we can most correctly consider and venerate the heart of the Divine Redeemer as signifying the image of His love, the proof of our redemption and the mystical ladder by which we climb to the embrace of "God our Saviour."[54] 633

67. Wherefore His words, actions, teachings, miracles, and in particular those deeds which more clearly testify this love for us—the institution of the Holy Eucharist, His most bitter passion and death, His Most Holy Mother whom He lovingly gave to us, the founding of the Church and the sending of the Holy Ghost upon the apostles and upon us—all these we must regard as proofs of His threefold love. 634

68. In like manner we must lovingly meditate on the pulsations of His most Sacred Heart by which, so to say, He Himself kept on measuring the time of His sojourn on earth up to the last moment when as the evangelists testify "crying out in a loud voice 'It is consummated,' and, bowing his head, gave up his spirit.[55] 635

69. Then the beating of His heart stopped, and His sensible love was interrupted until He arose from the tomb in triumph over death. 636

70. But after His glorified body was again united to the soul of the Divine Redeemer, the Conqueror of death, His Most Sacred Heart never ceased, and never will cease, to beat with imperturbable and calm pulsation. It will likewise never cease to signify His threefold love by which the Son of God is bound to His heavenly Father and the whole human race, of which He is by perfect right the mystical head. 637

638 71. But now, venerable brethren, in order that we may gather rich and salutary fruits form these considerations, let us briefly meditate on and contemplate the manifold affections, human and divine, of Our Saviour, Jesus Christ. These indeed His Heat manifested through the course of His mortal life.

639 72. These affections He now manifests and will continue to do so forever. Especially from the pages of the Gospel does light shine forth to us. Illumined and strengthened by this light, we can enter into the tabernacle of His Divine Heart. Together with the Apostle of the Gentiles we can wonder at "the riches of grace in kindness towards us in Christ Jesus."[56]

640 73. The adorable Heart of Jesus Christ beats with human and divine love since the Virgin Mary pronounced that great-souled "Fiat" and the Word of God, as the Apostle observes, "coming into the world, he says, "Sacrifice and oblation thou wouldst not, but a body thou hast fitted to me: in holocausts and sin-offerings thou hast had no pleasure. Then said I, "Behold, I come"!. . .It is in this 'will' that we have been sanctified through the offering of the body of Jesus Christ once for all."[57]

641 74. In the same way was He moved by love in perfect accord with the affections of His human will and divine love when in the home at Nazareth He engaged in heavenly discourse with His most sweet Mother and with His foster-father, Joseph. He was obedient to him and He toiled with him in the carpenter's trade and, with the triple love of which We have spoken, He was driven on during the lengthy apostolic journeys which He undertook, in the innumerable miracles which He wrought and by which He recalled the dead from the tomb or bestowed health on those ill with every sort of disease. He was moved by this triple love during the labors He endured, in the sweat, hunger and thirst He suffered and in the nocturnal vigils in which He most lovingly prayed to His Heavenly Father.

642 75. And finally He was moved by this triple love in the discourses He held and in the parables which He spoke and explained. This is especially true of the parables which treat of His mercy, such as those which tell of the lost drachma, the

lost sheep, the prodigal son. In these parables, both by their subject matter and by words, the very Heart of God is expressly laid bare to us, as Gregory the Great observed: "Learn of the Heart of God in the words of God, so that you may more ardently long for eternal things."[58]

76. But the Heart of Christ was moved by an even greater charity when words full of love fell from His lips. Let Us cite some examples. When He saw the crowds tired and hungry, He exclaimed, "I have compassion on the crowd."[59] And when He gazed upon Jerusalem, his most beloved City, blinded by her sins and therefore destined for complete destruction, He said: "Jerusalem, Jerusalem! Thou who killest the prophets, and stonest those who are sent to thee! How often would I have gathered thy children together, as a hen gathers her young under her wings, but Thou wouldst not!"[60] 643

77. But, because of love for His Father and holy indignation, His Heart beat violently when He beheld the sacrilegious buying and selling in the temple, and He rebuked the profaners of the temple with these words: "It is written, 'My house shall be called a house of prayer; but you have made it a den of thieves.' "[61] 644

78. But His Heart was moved by a special love and fear when He saw that the hour of His most cruel sufferings was now at hand. He felt a natural repugnance for death and those sorrows which were rushing upon Him and cried out: "Father, if it is possible, let this cup pass away from me."[62] But with love unconquered by the greatest grief when He received a kiss from the traitor, He addressed him with these words, which seem to be the last invitation of His Most Merciful Heart to a friend who was about to betray Him to His executioners with an impious, faithless and most hardened heart: "Friend, for what purpose hast thou come? Doest thou betray the Son of Man with a kiss?"[63] 645

79. In truth, He spoke with exceedingly great love and pity when He said to the pious women weeping for Him as He was about to suffer the underserved death of the Cross: "Daughters of Jerusalem, do not weep for me, but weep for yourselves and for your children. . .for if in the case of green wood they do these things, what is to happen in the case of the dry?"[64] 646

647 80. And finally, our Divine Redeemer, hanging on the Cross felt His Heart on fire with varied and vehement affections, affections of the most ardent love, of dismay, of mercy, of a most intense longing, of serene calm, which affections are indeed most strikingly expressed by the following words: "Father, forgive them, for they do not know what they are doing."[65] "My God, my God, why hast Thou forsaken Me?"[66] "Amen I say to thee, this day thou shalt be with Me in Paradise."[67] "I thirst."[68] "Father, into Thy hands I commend My spirit."[69]

648 81. Who in truth could describe in a worthy manner those beatings of the Divine Heart, the indications of His infinite love, when He bestowed His greatest gifts on man, that is, Himself in the sacrament of the Eucharist, His Most Holy Mother and the priestly office communicated to us?

649 82. Even before He ate the Last Supper with His disciples, when He knew that He was going to institute the sacrament of His Body and Blood by the shedding of which the new covenant was to be consecrated, He felt His Heart stirred by strong emotions, which He made known to the Apostles in these words: "I have greatly desired to eat this passover with you before I suffer."[70] These same emotions were even stronger, without doubt, when "having taken bread, He gave thanks and broke it and gave it to them saying: "This is My Body which is being given for you; do this in remembrance of me.' In like manner, he took also the cup after the supper, saying: "This cup is the new covenant in my blood, which shall be shed for you.'[71]

650 83. Rightly, therefore, one may affirm that the Divine Eucharist, both as a sacrament and as a sacrifice–the one He bestowed on men, the other He Himself continually offers "from the rising of the sun even to the going down"[72]–and the priesthood are all really the gifts of the Most Sacred Heart of Jesus.

651 84. Indeed another most precious gift of His Most Sacred Heart is, as We have said, Mary, the sweet Mother of God and the most loving Mother of us all. For she was the Mother of Our Redeemer according to the flesh and His associate in recalling the children of Eve to the life of divine grace. And

so she is rightly hailed as the spiritual Mother of Mankind. Wherefore St. Augustine, in writing of her says:

85. "Indeed she is the Mother of the members of the Saviour, which we are because she cooperated by love so that the faithful who are the members of that head might be born in the Church."[73] 652

86. And to the unbloody gift of Himself, under the appearance of bread and wine, Our Saviour, Jesus Christ, wished, as a special proof of His intimate and infinite love to add the bloody sacrifice of the Cross. Indeed, in His way of acting, He gave an example of that sublime charity which He set before His disciples as the highest measure of love: "Greater love than this no one has, that one lay down his life for his friends."[74] 653

87. Wherefore, the love of Jesus Christ, the Son of God, by the Sacrifice of Golgotha, clearly and richly proves the love of God himself: "In this we have come to know His love that He laid down his life for us; and we likewise ought to lay down our life for the brethren."[75] 654

88. And in fact Our Divine Redeemer was nailed to the Cross more by His love than by the force of the executioners. His voluntary holocaust is the supreme gift which He bestowed on each man according to the concise words of the Apostle: "Who loved me, and gave Himself up for me."[76] 655

89. Therefore, there can be no doubt that the Most Sacred Heart of Jesus, since it is most intimately the sharer of the life of the Incarnate Word, and since it was assumed as an instrument of the Divinity, no less than the other members of His human nature in accomplishing the works of divine grace and omnipotence,[77] is the true symbol of the boundless love by which Our Saviour, through the shedding of His blood, contracted a mystical marriage with the Church. "Through charity He suffered for the Church who was to be united to Him as His spouse."[78] 656

90. Therefore, from the wounded heart of Our Redeemer, the Church, the dispenser of the blood of the Redeemer, was born. From this wounded Heart the grace of the sacraments, from which the children of the Church draw supernatural life, flowed most profusely, as we read in the sacred liturgy: 657

"From the pierced Heart, the Church, joined to Christ is born. . .Who pourest forth grace from Thy Heart."[79] By reason of this symbol, which was not, indeed, unknown even to the ancient Fathers of the Church and ecclesiastical writers, the Common Doctor, as if reechoing these same sentiments writes: "Water flowed from Christ's side to wash us; blood to redeem us. Wherefore blood belongs to the sacrament of the Eucharist, while water belongs to the sacrament of Baptism. Yet this latter sacrament derives its cleaning virtue from the power of Christ's blood."[80]

658 91. What is written here concerning the side of Christ, wounded and opened by a soldier, must likewise be said of His Heart, which the lance actually touched with its stroke, inasmuch as the soldier pierced it so that he might be clearly certain of the death of Jesus Christ fixed to the Cross.

659 92. Wherefore the wound of the Most Sacred Heart of Jesus, which had now completed the course of this mortal life, is down through the ages the living image of that love freely bestowed by which God gave His only begotten Son for the redemption of man, and with which Christ loved us all so intensely that He offered Himself for us as a bloody victim on Calvary: "Christ also loved us and delivered Himself up for us as an offering and a sacrifice to God to ascend in fragrant odor."[81]

660 93. After Our Saviour ascended into Heaven, with His body adorned with the splendor of eternal glory, and sat at the right hand of the Father, His Heart beat with the most ardent love and He did not cease to manifest His love for His spouse, the Church. Indeed in His hands and feet and side He bears in majesty the glowing marks of the wounds which represent the triple victory gained by Him over the devil, sin and death.

661 94. He likewise has in His Heart, placed, as it were, in a most precious shrine, that treasure of merit, the fruit of His triple triumph. These He bestows generously on redeemed mankind. This is a truth full of consolation, which the Apostle of the Gentiles stated in these words: "According on high, He led away captives; he gave gifts to men. He who descended, He it is who ascended also above all the heavens, that He might fill all things."[82]

95. The gift of the Holy Spirit to His disciples is the first clear sign of His munificent charity after His triumphal ascent to the right hand of the Father. Indeed after ten days the Spirit, the Paraclete, given by the Heavenly Father, descended upon them gathered in the Cenacle, as He had promised them at the Last Supper: "I will ask the Father and He will give you another Advocate to dwell with you forever."[83] 662

96. This Spirit, the Paraclete, since He is the personified mutual love of the Father for the Son and of the Son for the Father, is sent indeed by both. Assuming the appearance of tongues of fire, He poured the abundance of divine love and other heavely gifts into their souls. The infusion of this divine love also sprang from the Heart of our Saviour "in whom are hidden all the treasures of wisdom and knowledge."[84] 663

97. Indeed, this love is the gift of the Heart of Jesus and His Spirit, who is indeed the Spirit of the Father and the Son and from whom both the rise of the Church and its remarkable spread is unfolded for all the pagan nations which the worship of idols, hatred of brothers, and corruption of morals as well as violence had befouled. 664

98. Ths divine love is the most precious gift of the Heart of Christ and of His Spirit. This love gave the apostles and martyrs that fortitude with which they were strengthened to fight even to the point of death, which they met with heroic spirit, to preach the truth of the gospel and to testify to it with their blood. This love gave to the Doctors of the Church a most ardent desire to teach and defend the Catholic Faith. 665

99. It was this love which nourished the virtues of the confessors and urged them to accomplish eminently useful and marvelous deeds, profitable for their own eternal and temporal welfare and that of others. This was the love which persuaded virgins to abstain, willingly and joyfully, from sensual pleasures, and to consecrate themselves entirely to the love of their heavenly Spouse. This love, pouring forth from the Heart of the Incarnate Word, is infused by the Holy Spirit into the souls of all the faithful. 666

100. It brought forth that hymn of victory for the Apostle of the Gentiles, who proclaimed the triumph of the members 667

of the Mystical Body and of Jesus Christ, its Head, and the restoration of the divine kingdom of love among men, no matter how they might try to prevent it: "Who shall separate us from the love of Christ? Shall tribulation, or distress, or persecution, or hunger, or nakedness, or danger, or the sword? But in all these things we overcome because of him who has loved us. For I am sure that neither death, nor life, nor angels, nor principalities, nor things present, nor things to come, nor powers, nor height, nor depth, nor any other creature will be able to separate us from the love of God which is in Christ Jesus our Lord."[85]

668 101. There is nothing, then, which forbids us to adore the Most Sacred Heart of Jesus, since it participates in and is the natural and most expressive symbol of that inexhaustible love with which Our Divine Redeemer still loves mankind. That Heart indeed, even if it is no longer liable to the disturbances of this mortal life, still lives and beats. It is now inseparably joined with the Person of the Divine Word, and in it and through it with His divine will.

669 102. Wherefore, since the Heart of Christ overflows with divine and human love, and since it is abundantly rich with treasures of all graces which Our Redeemer acquired by His life and His sufferings, it is truly the unfailing fountain of that love which His Spirit pours forth into all the member of His Mystical Body.

670 103. Therefore the Heart of Our Saviour to some degree expresses the image of the Divine Person of the Word and His two-fold nature, human and divine. In it we can contemplate not only the symbol, but also, as it were, the sum of the whole mystery of our redemption.

671 104. When we adore the Most Sacred Heart of Jesus Christ, we adore in it and through it both the uncreated love of the Divine Word and His human love and all His other affections and virtues. This is so because both loves moved Our Redeemer to sacrifice Himself for us and for the whole Church, His Spouse. As the Apostle says: "Christ also loved the Church and delivered Himself up for her, that He might sanctify her, cleansing in the bath of water by means of the Word, in order that he might present to Himself the Church in all her glory,

not having spot or wrinkle or any such thing, but that she might be holy and without blemish."[86]

105. As Christ loved the Church with that triple love of which We have spoken, He still loves her most deeply. This love moves Him as Our Advocate[87] to gain grace and mercy for us from the Father, "since he lives always to make intercession for them."[88] The prayers which come forth from His inexhaustible love and which are directed to the Father are never interrupted. As "in the days of His earthly life"[89] so now triumphant in heaven He beseeches the Father with no less efficacy. 672

106. He shows His living Heart to Him who "so loved the world that he gave His only-begotten Son, that those who believe in Him may not perish, but may have life everlasting."[90] His Heart is, as it were, wounded and burning with even greater love than when it was pierced at death by the lance of a Roman soldier. "Wherefore (Thy Heart) was wounded so that through the visible wound we might see the invisible wound of love."[91] 673

107. It is then absolutely certain that the Heavenly Father "who has not spared even his own Son, but has delivered him for us all"[92] when He has been asked by so powerful an Advocate and with such ardent love, will never at any time, diminish the rich flow of divine graces to all men. 674

108. It has been Our wish, venerable brothers, to explain to you and to the faithful the real nature of devotion to the most Sacred Heart of Jesus in the light of divine revelation, its chief source, and the graces which flow from it. 675

109. We think that Our statements, confirmed by the teaching of the Gospel, have made it clear that essentially this devotion is nothing else than devotion to the human and divine love of the Incarnate Word and to the love which the Heavenly Father and the Holy Ghost have for sinful men. 676

110. For, as the Angelic Doctor teaches, the first cause of man's redemption is the love of the August Trinity. This love pouring forth abundantly into the human will of Jesus Christ and His Adorable Heart, moved Him to shed His blood to redeem us from the captivity of sin.[93] "I have a baptism to be baptized with; and how distressed I am until it is accomplished!"[94] 677

678 111. We know, therefore, that the devotion whereby we pay homage to Jesus Christ's love for men through the august sign of the Wounded Heart of the Redeemer nailed to the Cross has never been entirely unknown to Christian piety. In more recent times, however, this devotion has become better known and wondrously spread throughout the Church, particularly after the Lord Himself privately revealed this divine mystery to some of His children, richly endowed with an abundance of heavenly graces, and chose them as the messengers and heralds of this devotion.

679 112. Indeed, there always have been souls especially dedicated to God, who imitating the example of the holy Mother of God, the Apostles and the illustrious Fathers of the Church, have adored, thanked and loved Christ's most sacred human nature, especially the wounds inflicted on His body during His salutary Passion.

680 113. Furthermore, do not these very words, "My Lord and my God,"[95] spoken by the Apostle Thomas signifying a person changed from an unbeliever into a faithful follower, contain a clear profession of faith, adoration and love rising from the wounded humanity of the Lord to the majesty of the Divine Person?

681 114. But if men were always strongly moved by the wounded heart of the Redeemer to venerate the infinite love with which He loves the human race, since the words of the Prophet Zacharias applied by St. John the Evangelist to Christ on the Cross, "They shall look upon him whom they have pierced,"[96] were addressed to the faithful of all ages, we must nevertheless admit that only gradually and by degrees was the homage of special devotion paid to His Heart as the image of the human and divine love in the Incarnate Word.

682 115. If we wish to sketch the significient states in the progress of this devotion through the years, there immediately comes to mind the names of some who have gained special renown in this respect and who are to be considered the standard-bearers of this devotion which gradully gained momentum privately in religious communities.

683 116. We mention, by way of example, the names of those who achieved special distinction in establishing and promoting

devotion to the Most Sacred Heart of Jesus: St. Bonaventure, St. Albert the Great, St. Gertrude, St. Catherine of Siena, Blessed Henry Suso, St. Peter Canisius, St. Francis de Sales and St. John Eudes, author of the first liturgical office to be celebrated in honor of the Most Sacred Heart of Jesus.

117. With the approval of many bishops of France, this solemn feast was celebrated for the first time on October 20, 1672. 684

118. Among those who have promoted this most excellent devotion, St. Margaret Mary Alacoque occupies the chief place of honor. Inflamed with great zeal and with the aid of her spiritual director, Blessed Claude de la Colombiere, she succeeded in her efforts, not without the great admiration of the faithful, to have this devotion rich in spiritual blessings established and clearly distinguished from other forms of Christian piety by the special nature of its acts of love and reparation.[97] 685

119. A review of the history of the period in which this devotion to the Most Sacred Heart of Jesus began is enough to increase our clear understanding that its marvelous progress is due to the fact that this devotion is in perfect accord with the nature of the Christian religion, which is indeed a religion of love. 686

120. Therefore, we must not say that this devotion began because it was privately revealed by God or that it suddenly came into existence in the Church, but rather that it is the spontaneous flowering of a living and fervent faith by which men filled with supernatural grace were led to adore the Redeemer and His glorious wounds as symbols of His boundless love which stirred their souls to the very depths. 687

121. Consequently, as it is obvious, the revelations made to St. Margaret Mary added nothing new to Catholic doctrine. The significance of these revelations lies in this, that Christ the Lord—showing His Most Sacred Heart—willed in an extraordinary and special way to call the minds of men to the contemplation and veneration of the mystery of God's most merciful love for the human race. 688

122. And so in this special manifestation, in repeated and clear words, Christ pointed to His Heart as the symbol by 689

which men are drawn to recognize and acknowledge His love, and at the same time constituted it as the sign and pledge of His mercy and His grace for the needs of the Church in our time.

690 123. Moreover, the fact that this devotion stems from the principles of Christian doctrine is clearly demonstrated by the fact that the Apostolic See approved the liturgical feast before it approved the writings of St. Margaret Mary. For, paying no specific attention to any private divine revelation, but graciously granting the petitions of the faithful, the Sacred Congregation of Rites in a decree of January 25, 1765, approved by Our predecessor, Clement XIII, on February 6 of the same year, granted the celebration of a liturgical feast to the Bishops of Poland and to the Roman Archconfraternity of the Sacred Heart.

691 124. The Apostolic See granted this petition to extend an already existing and flourishing devotion whose purpose was "symbolically to renew the memory of that divine love."[98] by which our Redeemer was impelled to offer Himself as a propitiatory victim for the sins of men.

692 125. This first approbation was granted in the form of a privilege and was restricted to definite regions. After almost a century, another approbation followed of far greater importance, and phrased in more solemn words. We are referring, as We previously mentioned, to the decree of the Sacred Congregation of Rites issued August 23, 1856. By it Our predecessor of immortal memory Pius XI, acceding to the petitions of the Bishops of France and of almost the whole Catholic world ordered the feast of the Most Sacred Heart of Jesus to be extended to the entire Church and to be duly celebrated.[99] The faithful should always remember this decree, for, as we read in the liturgy of this feast, "Since that time devotion to the Most Sacred Heart, gushing forth like a mighty stream, has spread throughout the world, washing away every obstruction in its course."

693 126. From the explanations which We have given, venerable brothers, it is perfectly clear that the faithful must trace devotion to the Most Sacred Heart of Jesus back to Sacred Scripture, tradition and the liturgy, if they wish to understand

its real meaning and through pious meditation, receive food to nourish and increase their religious fervor.

127. If this devotion is constantly practiced with this knowledge and understanding, the souls of the faithful cannot but attain to the sweet knowledge of the love of Christ which is the acme of Christian life as the Apostle, who knew this from personal experience, teaches: "For this reason I bend my knees tothe Father of our Lord Jesus Christ. . .that he may grant you from His glorious riches to be strengthened with power through his Spirit unto the progress of the inner man; and to have Christ dwelling through faith in your hearts: so that, being rooted and grounded in love. . .you know Christ's love which surpasses knowledge, in order that you may be filled unto all the fullness of God."[100] 694

128. The heart of Christ is the clearest image of this fullness of God embracing all things. By this We mean the fullness of mercy, which is the special characteristic of the New Testament in which "the goodness and kindness of God our Saviour appeared."[101] "For God did not send his Son into the world in order to judge the world, but that the world might be saved through him."[102] 695

129. From the very day on which she issued the first decree concerning devotion to the Most Sacred Heart of Jesus, the Church, the teacher of mankind, has always been certain that the essential characteristic of this devotion—that is acts of love and reparation by which God's infinite love for mankind is venerated—is in no way infected with the poison of materialism or superstition. 696

130. On the contrary, this devotion is a form of piety by which the soul clearly discharges religious obligations and a perfectly true worship which the Saviour Himself foretold in His conversation with the Samaritan woman: "But the hour is coming, and is now here, when the true worshippers will worship the Father in spirit and in truth. For the Father also seeks such to worship him. God is spirit, and they who worship him must worship in spirit and in truth."[102] 697

131. It is therefore wrong to say that contemplation of the physical heart of Jesus is a hindrance to attaining intimate love of God, and that it impedes the soul in its progress to the highest virtues. 698

699 132. The Church completely condemns this false mysticism, just as she did when she spoke through Our predecessor of happy memory, Innocent XI, who condemned the errors of those who idly maintained: "Nor must they (souls of the interior way) elicit acts of love for the Blessed Virgin, or the saints or the humanity of Christ for, since these are sensible objects love for them is of the same nature. No creature, neither the Blessed Virgin nor the saints, must have a place in our heart; because God wishes to occupy and possess it."[104]

700 133. It is evident that those who hold such opinions think that the image of the Heart of Christ represents nothing nobler than His sensible love and that this image is not of such a nature as to be a new basis for adoration, which is given only to that which is by its nature divine.

701 134. There is no one who does not see that this interpretation of sacred images is entirely false. It confines their meaning, which is much broader, within too narrow limits. Catholic theologians, among them St. Thomas, write: "The worship of religion is paid to images not as considered in themselves, nor as things, but as images leading us to God Incarnate. Now, movement to an image as image does not stop at the image, but goes on to the thing it represents. Hence, neither latria nor the virtue of religion is differentiated by the fact that religious worship is paid to the images of Christ."[105]

702 135. The veneration paid to images, whose excellence must be determined what is venerated, or to relics of the bitter sufferings which Our Saviour endured for us or to the picture of the pierced heart of Christ hanging on the Cross, which surpasses everything in force and meaning, is paid to the very person of the Incarnate Word as its final object.

703 136. Therefore, from the physical thing which the heart of Christ is, and from its natural signification, we can and must, supported by Christian faith, rise not only to contemplate His love, which is perceived through the senses, but even to meditate on and adore the most sublime infused love and finally the divine love of the Incarnate Word.

704 137. By faith, through which we believe that the human and the divine nature were united in the Person of Christ, we

can see the closest bonds between the sensible love of the physical heart of Jesus and the two-fold spiritual love namely, human and divine.

138. We must not only say that these two loves were simultaneously present in the adorable Person of the Divine Redeemer, but also that they were joined by natural bond so that the human and sensible loves are subject to the divine and bear its analogical resemblance. We do not, however, maintain that the Heart of Jesus is to be understood in such a way that in it we have and adore a formal image, as they say, or a perfect and absolute sign of His divine love, since the essence of this love can in no way be adequately expressed by any created image whatsoever. 705

139. But the Christian, in honoring the Heart of Jesus together with the Church, adores the sign and manifestation of divine love which went so far as to love through the heart of the Incarnate Word the human race defiled with countless sins. 706

140. It is therefore necessary, at this central point of a teaching which is so important and profound, that everyone bear in mind that the truth of the natural symbol by which the physical heart of Jesus is referred to the Person of the Word, rests completely on the fundamental doctrine of the hypostatic union. 707

141. Whoever denies that this doctrine is true would renew false teachings, repeatedly condemned by the Church, which deny that there is one Person in Christ with two distinct and complete natures. 708

142. With this fundamental truth firmly established, we understand that the heart of Jesus is the heart of a Divine Person, that is of the Incarnate Word, and that by it all the love with which He loved, and even now continues to love us is represented and, so to speak, placed before our very eyes. 709

143. Therefore, devotion to the Most Sacred Heart is so important that it may be considered, so far as practice is concerned, the perfect profession of the Christian religion. 710

144. For this is the religion of Jesus which rests entirely on a Mediator who is man and God, so that no one can come to the heart of God except through the heart of Christ, as He 711

Himself says: "I am the way, and the truth, and the life. No one comes to the Father but through me."[106]

712 145. Since this is true, we readily understand that devotion to the Most Sacred Heart of Jesus is essentially devotion to the love with which God loved us through Jesus and is at the same time an enlivening of our love for God and man. Or, to put it in other words, this devotion is directed to God's love for us in order to adore Him, to thank Him and to spend our lives imitating Him.

713 146. It seeks to lead us, in attaining this goal, to a strengthening of the bonds of love, with which we are bound to God and our fellow men, by daily observing more eagerly the new commandment which the Divine Master gave to His disciples as a sacred inheritance when He said: "A new commandment I give you, that you love one another: as I have loved you. . .This is my commandment, that you love one another as I have loved you."[107]

714 147. This commandment is indeed new and Christ's very own. As St. Thomas says, "The difference between the Old and New Testament is told in a few words, for as Jeremias says, 'I will make a new covenant with the house of Israel'[108] However, because the commandment was in the old law not as something that belonged to it but as a preparation for the new law."[109]

715 148. We have presented for your consideration the real nature and excellence of this devotion—beautiful teachings filled with consolation. But before We close this letter, mindful of Our apostolic office, which was first entrusted to St. Peter after his three-fold protestation of love for Christ the Lord, We deem it fitting to exhort you again, venerable brothers, and through you all of Our dearly beloved children in Christ, to strive ever more earnestly to promote this most gratifying devotion.

716 149. We are confident that in Our day, as in others, a great many blessings will flow from it.

717 150. Indeed, if the evidence on which devotion to the Wounded Heart of Jesus rests is rightly weighed, it is clear to all that we are dealing here, not with an ordinary form of piety which anyone may at his discretion slight in favor of

other devotions, or esteem lightly, but with a duty of religion most conductive to Christian's perfection.

151. For if devotion, according to the common theological definition which the Angelic Doctor gives, "is apparently nothing else but the will to give oneself readily to things concerning the service of God."[110] can there be a service to God more required and necessary—and at the same time nobler and more pleasant—than that which pays homage to His love? 718

152. What is more pleasing and acceptable to God than that service which submits to divine love and is rendered for the sake of love? 719

153. For every service freely rendered is in a sense a gift, and love "has the nature of a first gift in strength whereof all free gifts are given."[111] 720

154. That form of religion must be held in highest honor by which man honors and loves God more and more easily, and by which he more readily consecrates himself to divine love, which Our Redeemer Himself deigned to propose and recommend to Christianity and which the Sovereign Pontiffs have defended in their writings and extolled with highest praise. 721

155. Therefore, whoever considers of little value this outstanding gift of Jesus Christ to His Church, does a rash and harmful thing and offends God Himself. 722

156. There is, then, no doubt that the faithful, in honoring the Most Sacred Heart of the Redeemer, fulfill a most serious obligation by which they are bound to serve God and dedicate themselves and all they have, including their most secret thoughts and actions, to their Creator and Redeemer, and in this way obey the divine commandment: "Thou shalt love the Lord thy God with thy whole heart, and with thy whole soul, and with thy whole mind, and with thy whole strength."[112] 723

157. The faithful know with certainty that they are primarily led to worship God not for their own spiritual or physical, temporal or eternal advantage, but on account of the goodness of God, whom they seek to serve by loving Him in return, by adoring Him and thanking Him. 724

725 158. If this were not true, devotion to the Sacred Heart of Jesus would not be in accord with the true nature of the Christian religion, since by such devotion divine love is not primarily venerated. And, so, those who incorrectly understand the nature of this devotion and practice it in the wrong way, are not unjustly, as sometimes happens, accused of excessive love and concern for themselves.

726 159. Let all therefore be firmly convinced that in showing devotion to the Most August Heart of Jesus, external acts of Piety do not play the first and foremost role.

727 160. The reason for this devotion is not primarily to be sought in the blessings which Christ the Lord promised in private revelations. Rather it is that men should fulfill more fervently the principal duties of the Catholic faith, namely the obligations of love and expiation, and so also contribute greatly to their own spiritual advancement.

728 161. We therefore urge all Our sons in Christ eagerly to cherish this devotion, both those who already are accustomed to draw salutary waters from the Heart of the Redeemer, and especially those who, in the idle manner of spectators, look on from a distance with misgivings.

729 162. Let them seriously consider that We speak of a devotion, as We have already said, which has long been in the Church and is firmly based on the Gospel and which tradition and the sacred liturgy openly encourage.

730 163. The Roman pontiffs themselves praised it most highly on numerous occasions, and were not content merely to institute a feast in honor of the Sacred Heart and extend it to the universal Church, but also solemnly consecrated and dedicated the whole human race to the Most Sacred Heart.[113]

731 164. Finally, We add the rich and most pleasing fruits of this devotion for the Church: the return of countless souls to the religion of Christ, the reanimated faith of many people and the closer union of the faithful with our most loving Redeemer, all of which, especially in these past few decades, have happened before Our eyes in an ever increasing and richer profusion.

732 165. As we look upon this marvelous spectacle of devotion to the Most Sacred Heart of Jesus so widely spread and so

ardent among all classes of the faithful, We are filled with joyous sentiments of gratitude.

166. After rendering fitting thanks to Our Redeemer, who is the infinite treasure of goodness, We cannot refrain from extending Our paternal congratulations to all, both of the clergy and of the laity, who have actively contributed to the spreading of this devotion. 733

167. Although devotion to the Most Sacred Heart of Jesus has everywhere produced the salutary fruits of Christian living, everyone knows, venerable brothers, that the Church Militant here on earth, and especially civil society, have not yet achieved that full and complete measure of perfection which corresponds to the wishes and desires of Jesus Christ, the Mystical Spouse of the Church and the Redeemer of the human race. 734

168. Not a few of the Church's children mar the beauty of their mother's countenance, which they reflect in themselves with too many blemishes and wrinkles. Not all the faithful are resplendent with that sanctity of life to which they have been called by God. 735

169. All sinners have not returned to the Father's house, which they left through sin, there to put on once more the "best robe"[114], and to receive for their finger a ring, the sign of fidelity to the Spouse of their soul. 736

170. Not all of the pagans, not even a goodly number, have yet been joined to the Mystical Body of Christ. For if the languishing faith of the good, in whose souls, led astray by the deceptive desire for wordly possession, the fervor of charity grows cold and is gradully extinguished, causes Us bitter grief, the machinations of the wicked wrack Us with even greater pain. 737

171. As if goaded on by the infernal enemy, these men, especially now, are on fire with an implacable and open hatred for God, the Church and especially for him who takes the place of the Divine Redeemer on earth and represents His love for men according to the memorable words of St. Ambrose: "For (Peter) is questioned in a matter about which he feels uncertain; but the Lord who put the question has no doubt. He asked not to find out, but to appoint before His 738

ascension Him whom He left us as the Vicar of His love."[115]

739 172. Indeed hatred of God and those who lawfully take His place is so great a sin that man, created in the image and likeness of God and destined to enjoy His friendship which is to last forever in heaven, can commit none greater.

740 173. By hatred of God, man is separated completely from the highest good and driven to cast from himself and his fellow men whatever comes from God, whatever joins us to God and whatever leads us to enjoy God, that is to reject truth, virtue, peace and justice.[116]

741 174. Unfortunately, since it is possible to see increasing everywhere the number of those who glory in being enemies of God, the false tenets of materialism being propagated in practice and theory, unbridled freedom of lust everywhere extolled, what wonder if charity—the supreme law of the Christian religion, the surest foundation of true and perfect justice, the chief source of peace and chaste pleasure—grow cold in the souls of many? For, as Our Saviour warned, "because iniquity will abound, the charity of the many who will grown cold."[117]

742 175. Faced with so many evils which today more than ever deeply disturbed individuals, homes, nations and the whole world, where, venerable brothers, is a remedy to be found?

743 176. Is there a devotion more excellent than that to the Most Sacred Heart of Jesus, one which is more in accord with the real nature of the Catholic faith or which better meets the needs of the Church and the human race today? What act of religion is nobler, more suitable, sweeter and more conducive to salvation, since this devotion is wholly directed to the love of God Himself?[118]

744 177. Finally, what is more powerful than the love of Christ, which devotion to the Most Sacred Heart daily increases and fosters?

745 178. This love can truly bring the faithful to live the law of the Gospel.

746 179. If this law is rejected, is it possible to have genuine peace among men? For as the words of the Holy Ghost clearly teach, "The work of justice shall be peace."[119]

180. Therefore, following the example of Our immediate predecessor, We choose to address again all Our beloved sons in Christ in the words of admonition which Leo XIII of immortal memory spoke to all the faithful at the end of the last century. 747

181. We likewise address these words to all who have a genuine concern for their own salvation and that of civil society. "Behold another most auspicious and divine standard presented to our view today: the Most Sacred Heart of Jesus gleaming with dazzling light surrounded by flames. In it all hopes must be placed, in it man's salvation must be sought and looked for."[120] 748

182. It is also Our most ardent desire that all who glory in the name of Christian and who zealously strive to establish the Kingdom of Christ on earth, consider devotion to the Heart of Jesus as the standard and the source of unity, salvation and peace. 749

183. Nevertheless, let no one think that this devotion detracts anything from other devotions with which Christian people, under the leadership of the Church, honor the Divine Redeemer. 750

184. On the contrary, ardent devotion to the Heart of Jesus will without doubt encourage and promote devotion to the Most Holy Cross and love for the Most August Sacrament of the Altar. For We can definitely state a fact which the revelations made by Jesus Christ to St. Gertrude and St. Margaret marvelously confirm: that no one ever fittingly loves Christ hanging on the Cross but he to whom the mystical secrets of His Sacred Heart have been unfolded. 751

185. Nor will it be easy to grasp the force of that love by which Christ was impelled to give us himself as our spiritual food except by fostering a special devotion to the Eucharistic Heart of Jesus. 752

186. The purpose of this devotion, to use the words of Our predecessor of happy memory, Leo XIII, is to recall to our minds "that supreme act of love by which Our Redeemer, pouring forth all the riches of His Heart, instituted the adorable sacrament of the Eucharist to remain in our midst to the end of time."[121] 753

754 187. For "the Eucharist is not the smallest portion of His Heart which He gave us from the overflowing love of His heart."[122]

755 188. Finally, greatly impelled by the desire to set up a firm defence against the wicked machinations of the enemies of God and His Church, and at the same time to lead back domestic and civil society to the love of God and neighbor, We do not hesitate to state emphatically that devotion to the Sacred Heart of Jesus is the most effective school of divine charity, on which the Kingdom of God to be established in the souls of individuals, in families and in nations must rest.

756 189. As Our same predecessor of blessed memory most wisely teaches: "The kingdom of Jesus Christ draws its power and distinctive characteristic from divine love; its foundation and chief doctrine is to love holily and in proper order. From this it necessarily follows that we must fulfill obligations faithfully, not infringe on the rights of others, consider human matters inferior to divine and place love of God above everything else."[123]

757 190. That graces for the Christian family and for the whole human race may flow more abundantly from devotion to the Sacred Heart, let the faithful strive to join it closely with devotion to the Immaculate Heart of the Mother of God.

758 191. By the will of God, the Most Blessed Virgin Mary was inseparably joined with Christ in accomplishing the work of man's redemption, so that our salvation flows from the love of Jesus Christ and His sufferings, intimately united with the love and sorrows of His mother.

759 192. It is, then, highly fitting that after due homage has been paid to the Most Sacred Heart of Jesus, Christian people who have obtained divine life from Christ through Mary, manifest similar piety and the love of their grateful souls for the most loving heart of our heavenly Mother.

760 193. The memorable act of consecration by which We Ourselves, in the wise and loving dispositions of Divine Providence, solemnly dedicated the Church and the whole world to the Immaculate Heart of the Blessed Virgin Mary, is in perfect accord with devotion to the Sacred Heart.[124]

194. Since in the course of the present year, as previously mentioned, We are joyfully completing the first century since Our predecessor of happy memory, Pius IX, ordered the celebration of the feast of the Most Sacred Heart of Jesus throughout the entire Church, it is Our fervent desire, venerable brothers, that this centenary be solemnly celebrated by the faithful everywhere with public acts of adoration, thanksgiving and reparation to the Divine Heart of Jesus. 761

195. With all the faithful united in bonds of love and common prayer, these festivals of Christian joy and piety will be celebrated with special religious fervor in that country where by God's special providence St. Margaret Mary, the promoter and indefatigable herald of this devotion, was born. 762

196. In the meantime, strengthened with new hope and in spirit already gathering the spiritual fruits which We are certain will grow abundantly in the Church from devotion to the Sacred Heart, if correctly understood according to Our explanation and zealously practiced, We humbly pray God lovingly to grant His grace for the fulfillment of Our most ardent desire. 763

197. With God's help may this year's celebration increase from day to day the love of the faithful for the Most Sacred Heart of Jesus. And may His kingdom, "a kingdom of truth and life, a kingdom of holiness and grace, a kingdom of justice, love and peace,"[125] be extended further to all in the whole world. 764

198. As a pledge of these heavenly graces, We most lovingly impart to each of you, venerable brothers, to the clergy and people entrusted to your care, and in particular to those who zealously encourage and promote devotion to the Most Sacred Heart of Jesus, Our apostolic benediction. 765

199. Given at Rome from St. Peter's, May 15, 1956, in the eighteenth year of Our pontificate. 766

AETERNA DEI SAPIENTIA

Encyclical Letter of Pope John XXIII
Commemorating the Fifteenth Centenary of the Death
of St. Leo the Great, Pope and Doctor of the Church
November 11, 1961

God's Eternal Wisdom "reacheth from end to end mightily and ordereth all things sweetly."[1] Its light shone with exceptional brilliance in the soul of Pope St. Leo I, for it would seem to have burned into the very image of itself; so fearless the moral courage displayed by this Pope—"the greatest among the great." as Our late predecessor Pius XII rightly called him[2]—yet so gentle his fatherly concern.

768 The wisdom of his government, the wealth and scope of his teaching, the loftiness of his mind, his unfailing charity—these are the things which St. Leo the Great brought to enhance the fame of Peter's See, to which Almighty God in His providence has also raised Us. And now, on this fifteenth centenary of his death, We feel it incumbent upon Us to highlight his virtues and his immortal merits, confident that these can be of great spiritual value to us all, and increase the prestige and promote the spread of the Catholic Faith.

769 Wherein, then, lies the true greatness of this Pope? In moral courage?—in what moral courage which he showed when, at the River Mincius in 452, with no other armor to protect him than his high-priestly majesty, he bodly confronted the barbarous king of the Huns, Attila, and persuaded him to retreat with his armies across the Danube? That was certainly an heroic act and one which accorded well with the Roman pontificate's mission of peace. Yet we must think of

it as but one isolated instance of a life-long activity of remarkable brilliance devoted to the religious and social welfare, not merely of Rome and of Italy, but of the whole Church throughout the world.

770 "The path of the just, as a shining light, goeth forwards and increaseth even to perfect day."[3] These words of Holy Scripture may well be applied to the life and activity of St. Leo. To be convinced of this we have but to consider St. Leo in his three main characteristic roles: (1) as a man singularly dedicated to the service of the Apostolic See, (2) as Christ's chief Vicar on earth, and (3) as Doctor of the Universal Church.

771 Leo was born towards the end of the fourth century. The *Liber Pontificalis* informs us that he was "of Tuscan nationality from his father Quintian."[4] Since, however, he spent his early years in Rome, he not unnaturally called this city his *patria* [homeland].[5] While still a young man he joined the ranks of the Roman clergy and in the course was ordained deacon. In this capacity he rendered signal service to Pope Sixtus III between the years 430 and 439, and played a considerable part in the conduct of Church affairs. Among the many friends he made at this time were St. Propser, bishop of Aquitania, and Cassian, founder of the celebrated Abbey of St. Victor in Marseilles. Cassian, whom he persuaded to write. *De Incarnatione Domini*[6] against the Nestorians, proclaimed him "the glory of the Church and the sacred ministry"[7]—praise indeed for a simple deacon!

772 At the request of the court of Ravenna the Pope sent St. Leo to Gaul to settle a dispute between the patrician Aetius and the prefect Albinus. It was while Leo was engaged on this mission that Sixtus III died. Recognizing Leo's unrivalled theological learning and practical wisdom in diplomacy and the conduct of affairs, the Roman Church could think of no more worthy candidate for Christ's vicarious power on earth than this deacon.

773 Hence on September 29th, 440, he was consecrated bishop and entered upon his sovereign pontificate. He discharged this office with such mastery ability that he must be reckoned among the most illustrious of the early popes, few of whom

reigned longer than he. He died in November, 461, and was buried in the porch of the Vatican Church. In 688, by order of Pope St. Sergius I, his body was removed to "Peter's Citadel" and later, on the building of the new basilica, found a resting-place in the altar dedicated to his name.

774 What then were the more notable achievements of his life? To this question We must reply that rarely in her history as Christ's Church won such victories over her foes as in the pontificate of Leo the Great. He shone in the middle of the fifth centruy like a brilliant star in the Christian firmament.

775 To be convinced of this we have but to consider the way in which he discharged his office as teacher of the Catholic Faith. In this field he won for himself a name equal to that of St. Augustine of Hippo and St. Cyril of Alexandria. St. Augustine, as we know, in defending the Faith against the Pelagians, insisted on the absolute necessity of divine grace for right living and the attainment of eternal salvation. St. Cyril, faced with the errors of Nestorius, upheld Christ's Divinity and the fact that the Virgin Mary is truly the Mother of God. These truths lie at the very heart of our Catholic Faith, and St. Leo, who entered into the doctrinal inheritance of both these men of learning, the brightest luminaries of the Eastern and Western Church, was among all his contemporaries by far the most fearless protagonist of them.

776 St. Augustine, then, is celebrated in the universal Church as "Doctor of divine grace," and St. Cyril as "Doctor of the Incarnate Word." By the same token St. Leo is universally proclaimed as "Doctor of the Church's unity."

777 For the integrity of doctrine was not his only concern. We have but to cast a cursory glance over the great volume of evidence of his amazing industry as pastor and writer to realize that he was equally concerned with the upholding of moral standards and the defense of the Church's unity.

778 Consider, too, the field of liturgical composition and the due regard which this religious and saintly Pope had for the unity of worship. Many of the principal prayers contained in the *Leonine Sacramentary*[8] were either written by him or modelled on his compositions.

Most noteworthy, perhaps, is his timely and authoritative intervention in the controversy as to whether there was in Jesus Christ a human nature in addition to the divine nature. His efforts were responsible for the magnificent triumph of the true doctrine concerning the incarnation of the Word of God. This fact alone would assure him his place in hisotry. 779

Our principal evidence for it is his Epistle to Flavian, Bishop of Constantinople, in which he expounds the dogma of the Incarnation with remarkable clarity and precision, showing how it accords with the teaching of the Prophets, the Gospel, the apostolic writings, and the Creed.[9] 780

Let Us quote a significant passage from this Epistle: "Without detriment, therefore, to the properties of either of the two natures and substances which are joined in the one person, majesty took on humility; strength, weakness; eternity, mortality; and, in order to pay off the debt which attached to our condition, inviolable nature was united with passible nature, so that, as suited the cure of our ills, one and the same Mediator between God and men, the Man Jesus Christ, could die with the one nature and not die with the other. Thus true God was born in the whole and perfect nature of true man; complete in what was His own, complete in what was ours."[10] 781

Not content with this, St. Leo, having made perfectly clear "what the Catholic Church universally believes and teaches concerning the mystery of the Lord's incarnation,"[11] followed up this Epistle to Flavian with a condemnation of the Ephesine Council of 449. At this council the supporters of Eutyches had, by violent and unconstitutional means, done all they could to impose the goundless dogmatic assertions of this "very foolish and exceedingly ignorant man,"[12] who obstinately maintained that there was only one nature in Christ, the divine nature. 782

The Pope, with evident justification, branded this "a robber council."[13] In violation of the express commands of the Apostolic See, it had presumed by every means at its disposal to arrogate to itself no less a task than "the breaking down of the Catholic Faith"[14] and "the strengthening of execrable heresy."[15] 783

784 But St. Leo's principal title to fame is the Council of Chalcedon, held in 451. In spite of pressure from the Emperor Marcian, the Pope refused to allow it to be summoned except on condition that his own legates should preside over it.[16] It proved, Venerable Brethren, to be one of the greatest events in the history of the Church, renowned alike for its solemn definition of the doctrine of the two natures in God's Incarnate Word, and its recognition of the magisterial primacy of the Roman Pontiff. We need not, however, enter into any more detailed discussion of it here, for Our predecessor Pius XII has already dealt with it in an important Encyclical addressed to the entire Catholic world on the fifteenth centenary of its convocation.[17]

785 St. Leo's delay in ratifying the acts of this council is further proof of his genuine concern for the Church's unity and peace. We cannot attribute this delay to any remissness on his part, or to any cause of a doctrinal character. Obviously his intention—as he himself explains—was to thwart the twenty-eighth canon, which voiced the agreement of the Fathers of the council to the primacy of the See of Constantinople over all the churches of the East.

786 Whether or not this canon was inserted in defiance of the protests of the papal legates, or to win the favor of the Byzantine Emperor, is not clear. To St. Leo, it appeared to undermine the prerogatives of other more ancient and more illustrious churches, prerogatives which had been recognized by the Fathers of the Council of Nicea. He also saw it as detracting somewhat from the authority of the Apostolic See itself. His misgivings were occasioned not so much by the word- of the twenty-eighth canon as by the policies of those who framed it.

787 Two letters illustrate this point: one sent by the bishops of the council,[18] and the other written by Leo himself in refutation of their arguments and sent to the Emperor Marcian. This letter contains the following admonition:—

788 "Things secular stand on a different basis from things divine, and there can be no sure building save on that rock which the Lord has set as the foundation (Matt. 16, 18). He who covets what is not his due, loses what is rightfully his."[19]

The sad history of the schism that was later to separate so many illustrious Eastern churches from the church of Rome bears striking testimony to the accuracy of St. Leo's prophetic vision, here expressed, and to his presentiment of the future disruption of Christian unity. 789

To complete this account We would mention in passing two further instances of St. Leo's unfailing solicitude for the defense of the Catholic Church's unity: his intervention in the dispute concerning the date of Easter, and his great efforts to create an atmosphere of mutual respect, trust and cordiality in the Holy See's public relations wtih Christian princes. To see the Church at peace was the dearest desire of his heart. He frequently prevailed upon these princes to join forces with the bishops and lend them for the support of their counself "for the concord of Catholic unity."[20] so as to win from Almighty God "a priestly palm, besides a kingly crown."[21] 790

Besides being a watchful shepherd of Christ's flock and a stout-hearted defender of the true faith, St. Leo is honored also as a Doctor of the Church, one, that is, who excelled in expounding and sponsoring those divine truths which every Roman Pontiff safeguards and proclaims. 791

In support of this We quote that magnificent eulogy of St. Leo written by Pope Benedict XIV in his Apostolic Constitution *Militantis Ecclesiae*, October 12, 1754, when he made him a Doctor of the Church:— 792

"It was due to his excelling virtue, his teaching, and his most vigilant zeal as shepherd of his people, that he won from our forefathers the title Great. In expounding the deeper mysteries of our faith and vindicating it against the errors that assail it, in imparting disciplinary rules and moral precepts, the excellence of his teachig is so radiant with the majestic richness of priestly eloquence and has so won the admiration of the world and the enthusiasm alike of Councils, Fathers and writers of the Church, that the fame and reptution of this wisest of popes can hardly be rivalled by any other of the Church's holy doctors."[22] 793

It is through his many extant Sermons and Epistles that he principally lays claim to the title of Doctor. The *Sermons* 794 cover a great variety of subjects, nearly all of which have some connection with the liturgical cycle. In all these writings he is not just the exegete elucidating a Book of Sacred Scripture, not just the theologian at pains to investigate some divinely revealed truth. He is the siantly exponent of the Christian mysteries. He explains them with clarity and with a wealth of detail, in accordance with the faith of the councils, the Fathers, and the popes who preceded him.

795 His style is simple, majestic, lofty, persuasive, a model of classic eloquence. But in declaring the truth he never sacrificed precision to mere rhetoric. He did not speak or write to be admired, but to enlighten the minds of his hearers, and to awaken in them the desire to live lives in conformity with the truths they professed.

796 The *Epistles* are the letters he wrote as Sovereign Pontiff to the princes, priests, deacons and religious *of the universal Church*. They display his exceptional qualities of leadership. They show him as a man of keen intellect, yet full of practical good sense; a man of character who kept to his decisions, yet a father most ready to forgive; on fire with the charity which St. Paul, indicated to all Christians as "a more excellent way."[23]

797 For that blend of justice and mercy, of strength and gentleness, which we observe in his character is surely attribuable to that same charity which Jesus Christ demanded of Peter when He made him a shepherd to feed His lambs and His sheep.[24]

798 In very truth St. Leo's life-long endeavor was to appear before the world in the character of Christ, the Good Shepherd. In evidence of this, We may quote the following passage from the Epistles:—

799 "We are encompassed by both the gentleness of mercy and the strictness of justice. And because 'all the ways of the Lord are mercy and truth' (Ps. 24:10), We are forced according to Our loyalty to the Apostolic See so to moderate Our opinions as to weigh men's misdeeds in the balance (for, of course, they are not all of one measure), and to reckon some as to a certain degree pardonable, but others as altogether reprehensible."[25]

All in all, these Epistles and Sermons are an eloquent testimony to St. Leo's passionate devotion, in thought and feeling, word and action, to the welfare of the Catholic Church and the cause of truth, harmony and peace. 800

Venerable Brethren, the time is drawing near for the Second General Council of the Vatican. Surrounding the Roman Pontiff and in close communion with him, you, the Bishops, will present to the world a wonderful spectacle of Catholic unity. Meanwhile We, for Our part, will seek to give instruction and comfort by briefly recalling to mind St. Leo's high ideals regarding the Church's unity. Our intention in so doing is indeed to honor the memory of a most wise Pope, but at the same time to give the faithful profitable food for thought on the eve of this great event. 801

First, St. Leo teaches that the Church must be one because Jesus Christ, her Bridegroom, is one. "For the Church is that virgin, the spouse of one husband, Christ, who does not allow herslf to be corrupted by any error. Thus throughout the whole world we are to have one entire and pure communion."[26] 802

In St. Leo's view, this remarkable unity of the Church has its well-spring in the birth of God's Incarnate Word. "For Christ's birth is the source of life for Christian people; the birthday of the Head is the birthday of the Body. Although every individual is called in his own turn, and all the Church's sons are separated from one another by intervals of time, yet the entire body of the faithful, born in the baptismal font, is born with Christ in His nativity, just as all are crucified with Him in His passion, raised again in His resurrection, and set at the Father's right hand in His ascension."[27] 803

It was Mary who participated most intimately in this secret birth "of the body, the Church,"[28] because the Holy Spirit gave fruitfulness to her virginity. St. Leo praises Mary as "the Lord's virgin, handmaid and mother,"[29] "she who gave God birth" [*De genitrix*],[30] "a virgin for ever."[31] 804

Furthermore, the sacrament of Baptism—as St. Leo rightly claims—makes those who are washed in the sacred font not only members of Christ, but also sharers in His kingship and His priesthood. "All those who are reborn in Christ, the sign 805 of the cross makes kings; the Holy Spirit's anointing consecrates them priests."[32] Confirmation, called by St. Leo "sanctification by chrism,"[33] strengthens their assimilation to Jesus Christ, the Head of His body, the Church, and the sacrament of the Eucharist perfects this union. "For," as St. Leo says, "the reception of Christ's Body and Blood does nothing less than transform us into that which we consume, and henceforth we bear in soul and body Him in whose fellowship we died, were buried, and are risen again."[34]

806 But mark this well: unless the faithful remain bound together by the same ties of virtue, worship and sacrament, and all hold fast to the same belief, they cannot be perfectly united with the Divine Redeemer, the universal Head, so as to form with Him one visible and living body. "A whole faith," says St. Leo, "a true faith, is a mighty bulwark. No one can add anything to it, no one can take anything away from it; for unless it is one, it is no faith at all."[35]

807 To preserve this unity of faith, all teachers of divine truths —all bishops, that is—must necessarily speak with one mind and one voice, in communion with the Roman Pontiff. "It is the union of members in the body as a whole which makes all alike healthy, all alike beautiful, and this union of the whole body requires unanimity. It calls especially for harmony among the priest. They have a common dignity, yet they have not uniform rank, for there was a distinction of power even among the blessed apostles, notwithstanding the similarity of their honorable state, and while the election of them all was to equal, yet it was given to one to take the lead over the rest."[36]

808 St. Leo, therefore, maintained that the Bishop of Rome, as Peter's successor and Christ's Vicar on earth, is the focal center of the entire visible unity of the Catholic Church. And St. Leo's opinion is clearly supported by the evidence of the Gospels and by ancient Catholic tradition, as these words show: "Out of the whole world one man is chosen, Peter. He is set before all the elect of every nation, before all the apostles and all the Fathers of the Church; so that although there are among God's people many priests and many pastors, Peter governs by personal commission all whom Christ rules

by His supreme authority. Great and wonderful, beloved, is the share in its own power which the Divine Condescension assigned to this man. And if it desired other princes to share anything in common with him, never except through him did it accord what it did not deny to others."[37]

809 And since St. Leo regarded this indissoluble bond between Peter's divinely-given authority and that of the other apostles as fundamental to Catholic unity, he was never tired of insisting that "this authority [to bind and to loose] was also passed on to the other apostles, and what was established by this decree found its way to all the princes of the Church. But there was good reason for committing what was intended for all to the care of one in particular. And so it was entrusted to Peter individually because the figure of Peter was to be put ahead of all those in charge of the Church."[38]

810 There is, moreover, another essential safeguard of the Church's visible unity which did not escape the notice of this saintly Pope: that supreme authority to teach infallibly, which Christ gave personally to Peter, the prince of the apostles, and to his successors. Leo's words are quite unequivocal: "The Lord takes special care of Peter; He prays especially for Peter's faith, for the state of the rest will be more secure if the mind of their chief be not overthrown. Hence the strength of all the rest is made stronger in Peter, and the assistance of divine grace is so ordained that the stability which through Christ is given to Peter, should through Peter be transmitted to the other apostles."[39]

811 Applied to St. Peter this pronouncement is clear and emphatic enough; yet unhesitatinly St. Leo claims the same prerogative for himself. Not that he wanted worldly honor, but he had no doubt whatever that he was just as much Christ's vicar as was the Prince of the Apostles. Consider, for example, this passage from his Sermons:—

812 "Mindful, then, of Our God given responsibility, We find no reason for pride in solemnly celebrating the anniversary of Our priesthood, for we acknowledge with all sincerity and truth that it is Christ who does the work of Our ministry in all that We do rightly. We do not glory in Him who is all Our power."[40]

813 By that he did not mean that St. Peter had no further influence on the government of Christ's Church. While he trusted in the continued activity of the Church's Divine Founder, he trusted too in the protection of the Apostle Peter whose heir and successor he claimed to be, and whose office of authority "he in his turn discharged."[41] He attributed the success of his universal ministry more to the merits of the Apostle than to his own industry. Many passages from his writings might be quoted in support of this statement. We choose the following':—

814 "And so if anything is rightly done and rightly decreed by Us, if anything is won from the mercy of God by Our daily supplications, it is due to his [Peter's] works and merits, whose power lives and whose authority prevails in his See."[42]

815 Nor must we think that St. Leo was preaching a doctrine that had never before been taught. For, that his supreme office as universal pastor came from Christ Himself was also the teaching of his predecessors St. Innocent I[43] and St. Boniface I,[44] and was in full accord with those passages of the Gospels which he so often expounded (*Matt.* 16:17-18; *Luke* 22:31-32; *John* 21:15-17). He frequently referred to "the care which, principally by divine mandate, We must have for all the churches."[45]

816 Small wonder then that St. Leo habitually combines the praises of Rome with those of the Prince of the Apostles. He begins one of his Sermons on the Apostles Peter and Paul by apostrophizing the City in these words:—

817 "It was through these men, O Rome, that the light of Christ's gospel shone upon you. . .It was they who promoted you to such glory, making you a holy nation, a chosen people, a priestly and royal state, the capital of the world through Peter's holy See. By the worship of God you gained a wider empire than you did by earthly government. For although your boundaries were extended by your many victories and you stretched your rule over land and ocean, yet your labors in war gained you less subjects than have been won for you by the peace of Christ."[46]

818 Recalling St. Paul's magnificent testimony to the faith of the first Christians in Rome, this great Pope bids the Romans

preserve the faith whole and entire and without flaw. These are the words of fatherly encouragement he uses:—

"You, therefore, beloved of God and honored by apostolic approval—for it is to you that the teacher of the Gentiles, the blessed Apostle Paul, says: 'Your faith is spoken of in the whole world' (*Rom.* 1:8)—preserve in yourselves that which you know to have been the cause of this great preacher's good opinion of you. Let not a man of you make himself undeserving of this praise, or allow so much as a taint of Eutyches' impious doctrine to infect a people that has remained for so long untouched by heresy, taught by the Holy Spirit."[47] 819

St. Leo's heroic efforts to safeguard the authority of the Church of Rome were not in vain. It was principally due to his personal prestige that "the citadel of the apostolic rock" was extolled and venerated not only by the Western bishops who took part in the councils held at Rome, but by more than five hundred Eastern bishops assembled at Chalcedon,[48] and even by the Byzantine emperors.[49] 820

We might also quote that magnificent tribute paid by Theodoret, Bishop of Cyrus, to the Roman Biship and his privileged flock. Writing in 449, before the famous Council of Chalcedon, Theodoret says:— 821

"It is fitting that you should in all things have the preeminence, in view of the many peculiar privileges possessed by your See. Other cities are distinguished for their size or beauty or population. . .but your city has the greatest abunddance of good things from the Giver of all good. It is of all cities the greatest and most famous, the mistress of the world and teeming with population. . .It has, too, the tombs of our common gathers and teachers of the Truth, Peter and Paul, to illumine the souls of the faithful. These two saintly men did indeed have their rising in the East, but they shed their light in all directions, and voluntarily under went the sunset of life in the West, from whence now they illumine the whole world. It is they who have made your See so glorious. This is the foremost of all your goods. Their See is still blessed by the light of God's presence, for He has placed Your Holiness in it to shed abroad the rays of the one true Faith."[50] 822

823 Nor did these great honors paid to Leo by the official representatives of the Eastern Churches terminate with his death. The Byzantine liturgy keeps the 18th of February as his feast day, and most truly proclaims him as "leader of orthodoxy, teacher renowed for his holiness and majesty, star of the world, glory and light of Christians, lyre of the Holy Spirit."[51]

824 The Gelasian Menology reechoes these praises: "As bishop of great Rome, this father of ours, Leo, whom we admire for his selfmastery and purity and his many other virtues, gained by these virtues many notable achievements, but his most brilliant achievements are those which concern the true Faith."[52]

825 Our purpose, Venerable Brethren, in focusing attention on these facts has been to establish beyond doubt that in ancient times East and West alike were united in the generosity of their tribute to the holiness of St. Leo the Great. Would that it were so today; that those who are separated from the Church of Rome yet still have the welfare of the Church at heart, might bear witness once more to that ancient, universal esteem for St. Leo.

826 For if only they will settle their differences—those lamentable differences concerning the teaching and pastoral activity of this great Pope—then the Faith in which they believe will shine forth with renewed splendor; namely, that "there is one God, and one mediator of God and men, the man Christ Jesus."[53]

827 We are St. Leo's successor in Peter's See of Rome. We share his firm belief in the divine origin of that command which Jesus Christ gave to the apostles and their successors to preach the gospel and bring eternal salvation to the whole world. We cherish, therefore, St. Leo's desire to see all men enter the way of truth, charity and peace.

828 It is to render the Church better able to fulfill this high mission of hers that We have resolved to summon the Second General Council of the Vatican. We are fully confident that this solemn assembly of the Catholic Hierachy will not only reinforce that unity in faith, worship and discipline which is a distinguishing mark of Christ's true Church,[54] but will

also attract the gaze of the great majority of Christians of every demonination, and induce them to gather around "the great Pastor of the sheep"[55] who entrusted His flock to the unfailing guardianship of Peter and his successors.[56]

829 Our fervent appeal for unity is intended, therefore, to be the echo of that which was made many times by St. Leo in the fifth century. We wish, too, to make Our own those words which St. Irenaeus addressed to the faithful of all the churches, when God's Providence called him from Asia to rule the See of Lyons and confer on it the fame of his martyrdom. Recognizing that the Bishops of Rome were heirs to that power which had been handed down for uninterrupted succession from the two Princes of the Apostles,[57] he went on to address the following appeal to all Christians:—

830 "For with this church, by reason of its pre-eminent superiority, all the churches—that is, all Christians everywhere—must be united; and it is through communion with it that all these faithful (*or* those who preside over the churches) have preserved the apostolic tradition."[58]

831 But our greatest desire is that this Our call to unity shall reecho the saviour's prayer to His Father at the Last Supper: "That they all may be one, as thou, father, in me, and I in thee; that they also may be one in us."[59]

832 Are we to say that this prayer went unheeded by the heavenly Father, who yet accepted the sacrifice of Christ's blood on the Cross? Did not Christ say that His Father never failed to hear Him?[60] He prayed for the Church; He sacrificed Himself on the Cross for it, and promised it His unfailing presence. Assuredly, then, we must believe that this Church has always been, and still is, *one, holy, catholic and apostolic*; for thus was it founded.

833 Unfortunately, however, the sort of unity whereby all believers in Christ profess the same faith, practice the same worship and obey the same supreme authority, is no more evident among the Christians of today than it was in bygone ages. We do, however, see more and more men of good will in various parts of the world earnestly striving to bring about this visible unity among Christians, a unity which truly accords with the Divine Saviour's intentions, commands and

desires; and this to Us is a source of joyous consolation and ineffable hope. This desire for unity, We know, is fostered in them by the Holy Spirit, and it can only be realized in the way in which Jesus Christ has prophesied it: "There will be one fold and one shepherd."[61]

834 We therefore beg and implore Christ Our Mediator and Advocate with the Father[62] to give all Christians the grace to recognize those marks by which His true Church is distinguished from all others, and to become its devoted sons. May God in His infinite kindness hasten the dawn of that long awaited day of joyful, universal reconciliation. Then will all Christ's redeemed, united in a single family, join in praising the divine Mercy, singing in joyous harmony those words of the psalmist of old: "Behold, how good and how pleasant it is for brethren to swell together in unity."[63]

835 That day of peace and reconciliation between sons of the same heavenly Father and co-heirs of the same eternal happiness, will indeed be a day of triumph for the Mystical Body of Jesus Christ.

836 Venerable Brethren, the fifteenth centenary of the death of St. Leo the Great finds the Catholic Church in much the same plight as she was at the turn of the fifth century. The same waves of bitter hostility break upon her. How many violent storms does she not encounter in these days of ours—storms which trouble Our fatherly heart, even though our Divine Redeemer clearly forewarned us of them!

837 On every side We see "the faith of the gospel"[64] imperilled. In some quarters an attempt is being made—usually to no avail—to induce bishops, priests and faithful to withdraw their allegiance from this See of Rome, the stronghold of Catholic unity.

838 To rid the Church of these dangers We confidently invoke the patronage of that most vigilant of Popes who labored and wrote and suffered so much for the cause of Catholic unity.

839 To those of you who suffer patiently in the cause of truth and justice, We speak the consoling words which St. Leo once addressed to the clergy, public officials and people of Constantinople: "Be steadfast, therefore, in the spirit of

Catholic truth, and receive apostolic exhortation through Our ministry. 'For unto you it is given for Christ, not only to believe in him, but also to suffer for him' (*Phil.* 1:29)"[65]

840 We pray, too, for those of you who have the security and stability of Catholic unity. Unworthy as We are, We are nonetheless the Divine Redeemer's Vicar, and Our prayer for you is the same as that which Christ prayed to the heavenly Father for His own beloved disciples and for those who would believe in Him: "Holy Father. . .I pray. . .that they may be made perfect in one."[66]

841 That perfection and consummation of unity which We most earnestly beg God to grant to all the Church's sons, can be achieved only through charity. For charity is "the bond of perfection."[67] It is charity alone that makes it possible for us to love God above all else, and makes us ready and glad to do all the good we can to others in a spirit of generosity. It is charity alone which makes "the temple of the living God",[68] the holy Church, and all her sons throughout the world, radiant with supernatural beauty.

842 These sons of the Church, therefore, We counsel once more in the words of St. Leo: "The faithful, wholly and singly, are God's temple; and just as His temple is perfect in the whole, so must it be perfect in the individual. For although all the members are not equally beautiful, nor can there be parity of merits in so great a variety of parts, nevertheless the bond of charity makes them all alike sharers in the beauty of the whole. For they are all united in the fellowship of holy love, and though they do not all make use of the same gifts of grace, they nevertheless rejoice with one another in the good things which are theirs. Nor can the object of their love be anything which bears no relation to themselves, for in the very fact of rejoicing in another's progress they are enriched by their own growth."[69]

843 We cannot end this Encyclical, Venerable Brethren, without once more to Our own and St. Leo's most ardent longing: to see the whole company of the redeemed in Jesus Chrsit's precious blood reunited around the single standard of the militant Church. Then let the battle commence in earnest, as we strive with mighty and main to resist the adversary's

assults who in so many parts of the world is threatening to annihilate our Chrsitian faith.

844 "Then are God's people strongest," said St. Leo, "when the hearts of all the faithful unite in one common act of holy obedience; when in the camp of the Christian army the same preparation is made on all sides for the fight and for defence."[70]

845 For in the Church of Chrsit, if love is queen, no prince of darkness can prevail. "The devil's works are then most effectually destroyed, when men's hearts are reunited in the love of God and the love of one another."[71]

846 In furtherance of this expectation, Venerable Brethren, We lovingly impart to each and every one of you, and to the flocks committed to your watchful care, that earnest of the blessings of heaven, Our Apostolic Benediction.

847 Given at Rome, at St. Peter's, on the eleventh day of November in the year 1961, the fourth of Our Pontificate.

SACROSANCTUM CONCILIUM
General Principles for the Restoration
and Promotion of the Sacred Liturgy
December 4, 1963

I. The Nature of the Sacred Liturgy and Its Importance in the Life of the Church

God who "wills that all men be saved and come to the knowledge of the truth" (*1 Tim.* 2:4), "who in many times and various ways spoke of old to the fathers through the prophets" (*Heb.* 1:1), when the fullness of time had come sent his Son, the Word made flesh, anointed by the Holy Spirit, to preach the Gospel to the poor, to heal the contrite of heart,[1] to be a bodily and spiritual medicine:[2] the Mediator between God and man.[3] For his humanity united with the Person of the Word was the instrument of our salvation. Therefore, "in Christ the perfect achievement of our reconciliation came forth and the fullness of divine worship was given to us."[4]

849 The wonderful works of God among the people of the Old Testament were but a prelude to the work of Christ Our Lord in redeeming mankind and giving perfect glory to God. He achieved his task principally by the paschal mystery of his blessed passion, resurrection from the dead, and glorious ascension, whereby "dying, he destroyed our death, and rising, restored our life."[5] For it was from the side of Christ as he slept the sleep of death upon the cross that there came forth "the wondrous sacrament of the whole Church."[6]

850 Accordingly, just as Christ was sent by the Father so also he sent the apostles, filled with the Holy Spirit. This he did so that they might preach the Gospel to every creature[7] and proclaim that the Son of God by his death and resurrection had freed us from the power of Satan[8] and from death, and brought us into the Kingdom of his Father. But he also willed that the work of salvation which they preached should be set in train through the sacrifice and sacraments, around which the entire liturgical life revolves. Thus by Baptism men are grafted into the paschal mystery of Christ; they die with him, are buried with him, and rise with him.[9] They receive the spirit of adoption as sons "in which we cry, Abba, Father" (*Rom.* 8:15) and thus become true adorers such as the Father seeks.[10] In like manner as often as they eat the Supper of the Lord they proclaim the death of the Lord until he comes.[11] That was why on the very day of Pentecost when the Church appeared before the world those "who receieved the word" of Peter "were baptized." And "they continued steadfastly in the teaching of the apostles and in the communion of the breaking of bread and in prayers . . . praising God and being in favor with all the people" (*Acts* 2:41-47). From that time onward the Church has never failed to come together to celebrate the paschal mystery, reading those things "which were in all the scriptures concerning him" (*Lk.* 24:27), celebrating the Eucharist in which "the victory and triumph of his death are again made present,"[12] and at the same time "giving thanks to God for his inexpressible gift" (*2 Cor.* 9:15) in Christ Jesus, "in praise of his glory" (*Eph.* 1:12) through the power of the Holy Spirit.

851 To accomplish so great a work Christ is always present in his Church, especially in her liturgical celebrations. He is present in the Sacrifice of the Mass not only in the person of his minister, "the same now offering, through the ministry of priests, who formerly offered himself on the cross,"[13] but especially in the eucharistic species. By his power he is present in the sacraments so that when anybody baptizes it is really Christ himself who baptizes.[14] He is present in his word since it is he himself who speaks when the holy scriptures are read in the Church. Lastly, he is present when

the Church prays and sings, for he has promised "where two or three are gathered together in my name there am I in the midst of them" (*Mt.* 18:20).

Christ, indeed, always associates the Church with himself in this great work in which God is perfectly glorified and men are sanctified. The Church is his beloved Bride who calls to her Lord, and through him offers worship to the eternal Father. 852

The liturgy, then, is rightly seen as an exercise of the priestly office of Jesus Christ. It involves the presentation of man's sanctification under the guise of signs perceptible by the senses and its accomplishment in ways appropriate to each of these signs. In it full public worship is performed by the Mystical Body of Jesus Christ, that is, by the Head and his members. 853

From this it follows that every liturgical celebration, because it is an action of Christ the Priest and of his Body, which is the Church, is a sacred action surpassing all others. No other action of the Church can equal its efficacy by the same title and to the same degree. 854

In the earthly liturgy we take part in a foretaste of that heavenly liturgy which is celebrated in the Holy City of Jerusalem toward which we journey as pilgrims, where Christ is sitting at the right hand of God, Minister of the holies and of the true tabernacle.[15] With all the warriors of the heavenly army we sing a hymn of glory to the Lord; venerating the memory of the saints, we hope for some part and fellowship with them; we eagerly await the Saviour, Our Lord Jesus Christ, until he our life shall appear and we too will appear with him in glory.[16] 855

The sacred liturgy does not exhaust the entire activity of the Church. Before men can come to the liturgy they must be called to faith and to conversion. "How then are they to call upon him in whom they have not believed? And how are they to believe in him of whom they have not heard? And how are they to hear without a preacher? And how are men to preach unless they be sent?" (*Rom.* 10:14-15). 856

857 Therefore the Church announces the good tidings of salvation to those who do not believe, so that all men may know the one true God and Jesus Christ whom he has sent and may be converted from their ways, doing penance.[17] To believers also the Church must ever preach faith and penance; she must prepare them for the sacraments, teach them to observe all that Christ has commanded,[18] and encourage them to engage in all the works of charity, piety and the apostolate, thus making it clear that Christ's faithful, though not of this world, are to be the lights of the world and are to glorify the Father before men.

858 Nevertheless the liturgy is the summit toward which the activity of the Church is directed; it is also the fount from which all her power flows. For the goal of apostolic endeavor is that all who are made sons of God by faith and baptism should come together to praise God in the midst of his Church, to take part in the Sacrifice and to eat the Lord's Supper.

859 The liturgy, in its turn, moves the faithful filled with "the paschal sacraments" to be "one in holiness";[19] it prays that "they hold fast in their lives to what they have grasped by their faith."[20] The renewal in the Eucharist of the covenant between the Lord and man draws the faithful and sets them aflame with Christ's insistent love. From the liturgy, therefore, and especially from the Eucharist, grace is poured forth upon us as from a fountain, and the sanctification of men in Christ and the glorification of God to which all other activities of the Church are directed, as toward their end, are achieved with maximum effectiveness.

860 But in order that the liturgy may be able to produce its full effects it is necessary that the faithful come to it with proper dispositions, that their minds be attuned to their voices, and that they cooperate with heavenly grace lest they receive it in vain.[21] Pastors of souls must, therefore, realize that, when the liturgy is celebrated, something more is required than the laws governing valid and lawful celebration. It is their duty also to ensure that the faithful take part fully aware of what they are doing, actively engaged in the rite and enriched by it.

The spiritual life, however, is not limited solely to participation in the liturgy. The Christian is indeed called to pray with others, but he must also enter into his bedroom to pray to his Father in secret;[22] furthermore, according to the teaching of the apostle, he must pray without ceasing.[23] We also learn from the same apostle that we must always carry around in our bodies the dying of Jesus, so that the life also of Jesus may be made manifest in our mortal Flesh.[24] That is why we beg the Lord in the Sacrifice of the Mass that "receiving the offering of the Spiritual Victim" he may fashion us for himself "as an eternal gift."[25] 861

Popular devotions of the Christian people, provided they conform to the laws and norms of the Church, as to be highly recommended, especially where they are ordered by the Apostolic See. 862

Devotions proper to individual churches also have a special dignity if they are undertaken by order of the bishops according to customs or books lawfully approved. 863

But such devotions should be so drawn up that they harmonize with the liturgical seasons, accord with the sacred liturgy, are in some way derived from it, and lead the people to it, since in fact the liturgy by its very nature is far superior to any of them. 864

II. The Promotion of Liturgical Instruction and Active Participation

Mother Church earnestly desires that all the faithful should be led to that full, conscious, and active participation in liturgical celebrations which is demanded by the very nature of the liturgy, and to which the Christian people, "a chosen race, a royal priesthood, a holy nation, a redeemed people" (*1 Pet.* 2:9, 4-5) have a right and obligation by reason of their baptism. 865

In the restoration and promotion of the sacred liturgy the full and active participation by all the people is the aim to be considered before all else, for it is the primary and indispensable source from which the faithful are to derive the true Christian spirit. Therefore, in all their apostolic activity, 866 pastors of souls should energetically set about achieving it through the requisite pedagogy.

867 Yet it would be futile to entertain any hope of realizing this unless pastors of souls, in the first place, themselves become fully imbued with the spirit and power of the liturgy and capable of giving instruction about it. Thus it is absolutely essential, first of all, that steps be taken to ensure the liturgical training of the clergy. For that reason the sacred Council has decided on the following enactments:

868 Professors who are appointed to teach liturgy in seminaries, religious houses of studies, and theological faculties, must be properly trained for their work in institutes which specialize in this subject.

869 The study of sacred liturgy is to be ranked among the compulsory and major courses in seminaries and religious houses of studies. In theological faculties is it to rank among the principal courses. It is to be taught under its theological, historical, spiritual, pastoral, and juridical aspects. In addition, those who teach other subjects, especially dogmatic theology, should—each of them submitting to the exigencies of his own discipline—expound the mystery of Christ and the history of salvation in a manner that will clearly set forth the connection between their subjects and the liturgy, and the unity which underlies all priestly training.

870 In seminaries and religious houses, clerics shall be given a liturgical formation in their spiritual lives. For this they will need a proper initiation, enabling them to understand the sacred rites and participate in them wholeheartedly. They will also need to celebrate the sacred mysteries and popular devotions which are imbued with the spirit of the sacred liturgy. Likewise they must learn to observe the liturgical laws so that life in seminaries and religious institutes may be thoroughly influenced by the liturgical spirit.

871 Priests, both secular and religious, who are already working in the Lord's vineyard, are to be helped by every suitable means to a fuller understanding of what they are about when they perform sacred rites, to live the liturgical life and to share it with the faithful entrusted to their care.

With zeal and patience pastors of souls must promote the liturgical instruction of the faithful and also their active participation, both internal and external, taking into account their age, condition, way of life and standard of religious culture. By so doing pastors will be fulfilling one of the chief duties of a faithful dispenser of the mysteries of God, and in this matter they must lead their flock not only by word but also by example. 872

Transmission of the sacred rites by radio and television, especially in the case of Mass, shall be done with delicacy and dignity. A suitable person, appointed by the bishops, should direct it and have the responsibility for it. 873

III. The Reform of the Sacred Liturgy

In order that the Christian people may more certainly derive an abundance of graces from the sacred liturgy, holy Mother Church desires to undertake with great care a general restoration of the liturgy itself. For the liturgy is made up of unchangeable elements divinely instituted, and of elements subject to change. These latter not only may be changed but ought to be changed with the passage of time, if they have suffered from the intrusion of anything out of harmony with the inner nature of the liturgy or have become less suitable. In this restoration both texts and rites should be drawn up so as to express more clearly the holy things which they signify. The Christian people, as far as is possible, should be able to understand them with ease and take part in them fully, actively, and as a community. 874

Therefore, the sacred Council establishes the following general norms: 875

(1) Regulation of the sacred liturgy depends solely on the authority of the Church, that is, on the Apostolic See, and, as laws may determine, on the bishop.

(2) In virtue of power conceded by law, the regulation of the liturgy within certain defined limits belongs also to various kinds of bishops' conferences, legitimately established, with competence in given territories.

(3) Therefore no other person, not even a priest, may add, remove, or change anything in the liturgy on his own authority.

876 In order that sound tradition be retained, and yet the way remain open to legitimate progress, a careful investigation—theological, historical, and pastoral—should always be made into each part of the liturgy which is to be revised. Furthermore the general laws governing the structure and meaning of the liturgy must be studied in conjunction with the experience derived from recent liturgical reforms and from the indults granted to various places.

877 Finally, there must be no innovations unless the good of the Church genuinely and certainly requires them, and care must be taken that any new forms adopted should in some way grow organically from forms already existing.

878 As far as possible, notable differences between the rites used in adjacent regions should be avoided.

879 Sacred scripture is of the greatest importance in the celebration of the ligurgy. For it is from it that lessons are read and explained in the homily, and psalms are sung. It is from the scriptures that the prayers, collects, and hymns draw their inspiration and their force, and that actions and signs derive their meaning. Hence in order to achieve the restoration, progress, and adaptation of the sacred liturgy it essential to promote that sweet and living love for sacred scripture to which the venerable tradition of Eastern and Western rites gives testimony.

880 The liturgical books are to be revised as soon as possible. Experts are to be employed on this task, and bishops from various parts of the world are to be consulted.

881 Liturgical services are not private functions but are celebrations of the Church which is "the sacrament of unity," namely, "the holy people united and arranged under their bishops."[26]

882 Therefore, liturgical services pertain to the whole Body of the Church. They manifest it, and have effects upon it. But they also touch individual members of the Church in different ways, depending on their orders, their role in the liturgical services, and their actual participation in them.

It must be emphasized that rites which are meant to be celebrated in common, with the faithful present and actively participating, should as far as possible be celebrated in that way rather than by an individual and quasi-privately. 883

This applies with special force to the celebration of Mass (even though every Mass has of itself a public and social nature) and to the administration of the sacraments. 884

In liturgical celebrations each person, minister, or layman who has an office to perform, should carry out all and only those parts which pertain to his office by the nature of the rite and the norms of the liturgy. 885

Services, readers, commentators, and members of the choir also exercise a genuine liturgical function. They ought, therefore, to discharge their offices with the sincere piety and decorum demanded by so exalted a ministry and rightly expected of them by God's people. 886

Consequently they must all be deeply imbued with the spirit of the liturgy, each in his own measure, and they must be trained to perform their functions in a correct and orderly manner. 887

To promote active participation, the people should be encouraged to take part by means of acclamations, responses, psalms, antiphons, hymns, as well as by actions, gestures and bodily attitudes. And at the proper time a reverent silence should be observed. 888

When the liturgical books are being revised, the people's parts must be carefully indicated by the rubrics. 889

In the liturgy, apart from the distinctions arising from liturgical function or sacred orders and apart from the honors due to civil authorities in accordance with liturgical law, no special exception is to be made for any private persons or classes of persons whether in the ceremonies or by external display. 890

Although the sacred liturgy is principally the worship of the divine majesty it likewise contains much instruction for the faithful.[27] For in the liturgy God speaks to his people, and Christ is still proclaiming his Gospel. And the people reply to God both by song and prayer. 891

892 Moreover the prayers addressed to God by the priest who, in the person of Christ, presides over the assembly, are said in the name of the entire holy people and of all present. And the visible signs which the sacred liturgy uses to signify invisible divine things have been chosen by Christ or by the Church. Thus not only when things are read "which were written for our instruction" (*Rom.*15:4), but also when the Church prays or sings or acts, the faith of those taking part is nourished, and their minds are raised to God so that they may offer him their spiritual homage and receive his grace more abundantly.

893 Therefore in the revision of the liturgy the following general norms should be observed:

894 The rites should be distinguished by a noble simplicity. They should be short, clear, and free from useless repetitions. They should be within the people's powers of comprehension, and normally should not require much explanation.

895 That the intimate connection between rite and words may be apparent in the liturgy:

(1) In sacred celebrations a more ample, more varied, and more suitable reading from sacred scripture should be restored.

(2) The most suitable place for a sermon ought to be indicated in the rubrics, for a sermon is part of the liturgical action whenever a rite involves one. The ministry of preaching is to be fulfilled most faithfully and carefully. The sermon, moreover, should draw its content mainly from scriptural and liturgical sources, for it is the proclamation of God's wonderful works in the history of salvation, which is the mystery of Christ ever made present and active in us, especially in the celebration of the liturgy.

(3) Instruction which is more explicitly liturgical should also be given in a variety of ways. If necessary, short directives to be spoken by the priest or competent minister should be provided within the rites themselves. But they should be given only at suitable moments and in prescribed words or their equivalent.

(4) Bible services should be encouraged, especially on the vigils of the more solemn feasts, on some weekdays of Advent

and Lent, and on Sundays and Holydays, especially in places where no priest is available. In this case a deacon or some other person authorized by the bishop should preside over the celebration.

§ 1. The use of the Latin language, with due respect to particular law, is to be preserved in the Latin rites.

§ 2. But since the use of the vernacular, whether in the Mass, the administration of the sacraments, or in other parts of the liturgy, may frequently be of great advantage to the people, a wider use may be made of it, especially in readings, directives and in some prayers and chants. Regulations governing this will be given separately in subsequent chapters.

§ 3. These norms being observed, it is for the competent territorial ecclesiastical authority mentioned in Article 22:2, to decide whether, and to what extent, the vernacular language is to be used. Its decress have to be approved, that is, confirmed, by the Apostolic See. Where circumstances warrant it, it is to consult with bishops of neighboring regions which have the same language.

§ 4. Translations from the Latin for use in the liturgy must be approved by the competent territorial ecclesiastical authority already mentioned.

896 Even in the liturgy the Church does not wish to impose a rigid uniformity in matters which do not involve the faith or the good of the whole community. Rather does she respect and foster the qualities and talents of the various races and nations. Anything in these poeple's way of life which is not indissolubly bound up with superstition and error she studies with sympathy, and, if possible, preserves intact. She sometimes even admits such things into the liturgy itself, provided they harmonize with its true and authentic spirit.

897 Provided that the substantial unity of the Roman rite is preserved, provision shall be made, when revising the liturgical books, for legitimate variations and adaptations to different groups, regions and peoples, especially in mission countries. This should be borne in mind when drawing up the rites and determining rubrics.

898 Within the limits set by the typical editions of the liturgical books it shall be for the competent territorial ecclesiasti-

cal authority mentioned in Article 22:2, to specify adaptations, especially as regards the administration of the sacraments, sacramentals, processions, liturgical language, sacred music and the arts, according, however, to the fundamental norms laid down in this Constitution.

899 In some places and circumstances, however, an even more radical adaptation of the liturgy is needed, and this entails greater difficulties. For this reason:

(1) The competent territorial ecclesiastical authority mentioned in Article 22:2, must in this matter, carefully and prudently consider which elements from the traditions and cultures of individual peoples might appropriately be admitted into divine worship. Adaptations which are considered useful or necessary should then be submitted to the Holy See, by whose consent they may be introduced.

(2) To ensure that adaptations may be made with all the circumspection necessary, the Apostolic See will grant power to this same territorial ecclesiastical authority to permit and to direct, as the case requires, the necessary preliminary experiments over a determined period of time among certain groups suitable for the purpose.

(3) Because liturgical laws usually provide special difficulties with respect to adaptation, especially in mission lands, men who are experts in the matters in question must be employed to formulate them.

900 The bishop is to be considered as the High Priest of his flock from whom the life in Christ of his faithful is in some way derived and upon whom it in some way depends.

901 Therefore all should hold in the greatest esteem the liturgical life of the diocese centered around the bishops, especially in his cathedral church. They must be convinced that the principal manifestation of the Church consists in the full, active participation of all God's holy people in the same liturgical celebrations, especially in the same Eucharist, in one prayer, at one altar, at which the bishop presides, surrounded by his college of priests and by his ministers.[28]

902 But as it is impossible for the bishop always and everywhere to preside over the whole flock in his church, he must of necessity establish groupings of the faithful; and, among

these, parishes, set up locally under a pastor who takes the place of the bishop, are the most important, for in some way they represent the visible Church constituted throughout the world.

Therefore the liturgical life of the parish and its relation to the bishop must be fostered in the spirit and practice of the laity and clergy. Efforts must also be made to encourage a sense of community within the parish, above all in the common celebration of the Sunday Mass. 903

Zeal for the promotion and restoration of the sacred liturgy is rightly held to be a sign of the providential dispositions of God in our time, and as a movement of the Holy Spirit in his Church. It is today a distinguishing mark of the life of the Church, and, indeed, of the whole tenor of contemporary religious thought and action. 904

Therefore, so that this pastoral liturgical action may become still more vigorous in the Church the sacred Council decrees: 905

It is desirable that the competent territorial ecclesiastical authority mentioned in Article 22:2 set up a liturgical commission to be assisted by experts in liturgical science, sacred music, art and pastoral practice. As far as possible the commission should be aided by some kind of Institute for Pastoral Liturgy, consisting of people who are eminent in these matters, not excluding laymen, if circumstances so demand. It will be the task of this commission, under the direction of the above-mentioned competent territorial ecclesiastical authority (see Article 22:2), to regulate pastoral liturgical action throughout the territory, and to promote studies and necessary experiments whenever there is a question of adaptations to be proposed to the Holy See. 906

For the same reason every diocese is to have a commission on the sacred liturgy, under the direction of the bishop, for promoting the liturgical apostolate. 907

Sometimes it may be expedient that several dioceses should form between them one single commission which will be able to promote the liturgy by common consultation. 908

In addition to the commission on sacred liturgy, every diocese, as far as possible, should have commissions for sacred music and sacred art. 909

910 These three commissions must work in the closest collaboration. Indeed it will often be best to fuse the three of them into one single commission.

LUMEN GENTIUM
The Dogmatic Constitution on the Church
November 21, 1964

THE MYSTERY OF THE CHURCH

Christ is the light of nations. Therefore this sacred Council gathered together in the Holy Spirit eagerly desires, by proclaiming the Gospel to every creature (cf. *Mk* 16,15), to enlighten all men with the light of Christ which shines resplendently on the countenance of the Church. The Church exists in Christ as a sacrament or sign and an instrument of intimate union with God and of the unity of the whole human race; so now, adhering faithfully to the teachings of previous councils, it proposes to present to the faithful and to the entire world a more concise explanation of its nature and its universal mission. Present-day conditions lend an urgency to this task if all men, who are already linked more closely together by social, technological and cultural ties, are to achieve full unity in Christ as well.

The Father's plan

2. Following the free and secret designs of His own wisdom and goodness, the eternal Father created the whole world and willed to raise men to a participation in the divine life. When they fell in Adam, He did not abandon them. He kept offering them helps to salvation in view of Christ, the Redeemer, "who is the image of the invisible God, the firstborn of every creature" (*Col* 1, 15). All the elect before time 912

began, the Father "foreknew and predestined to become conformed to the image of his Son, that he should be the firstborn among many brethren" (*Rom* 8, 29). He chose to gather all those who believe in Christ into the holy Church, which was prefigured from the very beginning of the world. The preparatory stages for this Church were worked out in marvelous fashion in the history of the Israelite people and through the Old Covenant.[1] In the final epoch of time it was established, and made manifest by the outpouring of the Spirit. At the end of time it will attain its glorious consummation. Then, as we read in the Fathers of the Church, all the just from Adam on, "from Abel, the just one, to the last of the elect,"[2] will be gathered to the Father's presence in the universal Church.

Christ's mission

913 3. And so the Son came, sent by the Father. It was in Him that the Father chose us before the foundation of the world and predestined us to be His adopted children, because in Him it pleased the Father to establish all things anew (cf. *Eph* 1, 4-5, 10). To carry out the Father's will, Christ inaugurated the kingdom of heaven on earth, revealed the mystery of that kingdom to us, and brought about redemption by His obedience. The Church, or, in other words, the kingdom of Christ now present in the form of a mystery, undergoes visible growth in the world through the power of God. This birth and growth are symbolized by the blood and water which flowed from the open side of the crucified Christ (cf. *Jn* 19, 34); and they are foretold in the Lord's words concerning His death on the cross: "And I, if I be lifted up from the earth, will draw all things to myself" (*Jn* 12, 32 Gk). Every time the sacrifice of the cross—in which "Christ, our passover, has been sacrificed" (*1 Cor* 5, 7)—is celebrated on the altar, the work of our redemption is carried out. At the very same time the sacrament of the Eucharistic bread expresses and brings about the unity of the faithful who form one body in Christ (cf. *1 Cor* 10, 17). All men are called to this union with Christ, the light of the world, the source from which we come, the means whereby we live, the goal toward which we strive.

The Holy Spirit's mission

4. When the Son finished the work which the Father had commissioned Him to do on earth (cf. *Jn* 17, 4), the Holy Spirit was sent on the day of Pentecost. He was to sanctify the Church unceasingly and thus enable all believers to have access to the Father through Christ and in one Spirit (cf. *Eph* 2, 18). He is the Spirit of life, a fountain of water springing up into life eternal (cf. *Jn* 4, 14; 7, Through Him the Father restores life to men who are dead through sin, until the time comes to resurrect their mortal bodies in Christ (cf. *Rom* 8, 10-11). The Spirit dwells in the Church and in the hearts of the faithful, as in a temple (cf. 1 *Cor* 3, 16; 6, 19); in them He prays and bears witness to their filial adoption (cf. *Gal* 4, 6; Rom 8, 15-16, 26). As for the Church; He introduces it to every truth (cf. *Jn* 16, 13), makes it one in its communion and ministry, provides it with various hierarchical and charismatic gifts, directing it through them, and adorns it with His fruits (cf. *Eph* 4, 11-12; 1 *Cor* 12, 4; *Gal* 5, 22). Through the power of the Gospel He keeps the Church ever young and refreshed, and leads it toward perfect union with its spouse.[3] For the Spirit and the Bride say to the Lord Jesus: "Come" (cf. *Ap* 22, 17). 914

Thus the universal Church is seen to be "a people made one with the unity of the Father, the Son, and the Holy Spirit."[4] 915

The kingdom made manifest

5. The mystery of the holy Church is clearly apparent in its very foundation. The Lord Jesus began His Church by preaching the good news, the arrival of the kingdom of God promised for ages in the Scriptures: "The time is fulfilled, and the kingdom of God is at hand" (*Mk* 1, 15; cf. *Mt* 4, 17). This kingdom shines forth for men in the words, the deeds, and the very presence of Christ. The Lord's Word is compared to a seed sown in a field (*Mk* 4, 14); those who hear it with faith and are numbered among Christ's little flock (*Lk* 12, 32) have received the kingdom itself. The seed then sprouts and grows under its own power 916

until harvest time (cf *Mk* 4, 26-29). Jesus' miracles also confirm the fact that the kingdom has already arrived on earth: "If I cast out devils by the finger of God, then the kingdom of God has come upon you" (*Lk* 11, 20); cf. *Mt* 12, 28). but the clearest manifestation of the kingdom is the very person of Christ, Son of God and Son of Man, who came "to serve and to give His life as a ransom for many." (*Mk* 10, 45).

917 Now when Christ rose, after suffering the death of the cross for men's sake, He appeared as the one who had been constituted Lord and Christ and Priest in perpetuity (cf. *Acts* 2, 36; *Heb* 5, 6; 7, 17-21); and He poured out on His disciples the Spirit which had been promised by the Father (cf. *Acts* 2, 33). It is from this source that the Church, bolstered by its founder's gifts and adhering faithfully to His precepts of charity, humility and self-sacrifice, receives the mission to proclaim the kingdom of Christ and of God and to establish it among all nations. It is from this source that the Church is constituted as the seed, the first bud, of this kingdom on earth. Slowly it continues to grow, ardently longing for the kingdom to reach its complete measure, hoping with all its strength to be united with its king in glory.

Figurative descriptions of the Church

918 6. In the Old testament the revelation of the kingdom is often put forward in figures of speech. In a similar vein the inner nature of the Church is now made known to us by a variety of images, taken from pastoral or farm life, from building, or even from family and married life. These images were first shaped in the books of the Prophets.

919 The Church is a sheepfold, and its sole, necessary entrance-way is Christ (*Jn* 10, 1-10). It is also a flock, and God foretold that He Himself would be its shepherd (cf. *Is* 40, 11; *Ez* 34, 11 ff). Its sheep, though tended by human shepherds, are ever guided and nourished by Christ Himself, the good shepherd and the prince of shephereds (cf. *Jn* 10, 11; 1 *Pt* 5, 4) who gave up His life for His sheep (cf. *Jn* 10, 11-15).

The Church is a piece of land under cultivation, God's tillage (1 *Cor* 3, 9). On it grows the ancient olive tree whose sacred roots were the patriarchs, the tree in which the reconciliation of Jews and Gentiles has been and will be achieved (*Rom* 11, 13-26). This plot of land has been planted as a choice vineyard by the heavenly vine-dresser (*Mt* 21, 33-43; cf. *Is* 5, 1 ff). The true vine is Christ, who gives life and fertility to us, the branches. Through the Church we continue to abide in Christ without whom we can do nothing (*Jn* 15, 1-4). 920

More often the Church is called *God's building* (*1 Cor* 3, 9). The Lord compared Himself to the stone which was rejected by the builders but became the cornerstone (*Mt* 21, 42; cf. *Acts* 4, 11; 1 *Pt* 2, 7; *Ps* 117, 22). This is the foundation upon which the Church is built by the Apostles (cf. 1 *Cor* 3, 11), from which it acquires solidity and cohesiveness. This edifice has a variety of names to describe it; the house of God (1 *Tm*3, 15), in which His *family* dwells; a dwelling place for God in the spirit (*Eph* 2, 19-22); the tabernacle of God among men (*Ap* 21, 3). In particular it is the holy *temple.* The Fathers of the Church found its image in sanctuaries made of stone and had words of praise for it. And in the liturgy it is quite rightly compared to the Holy City, the New Jerusalem.[5] Here on earth we are, as it were, living stones being built into it (*1 Pt* 2, 5). And John casts his gaze on this holy city coming down out of heaven from God at the re-creation of the world, adorned like a bride for her husband (*Ap* 21, 1 ff). 921

The Church is also called "that Jerusalem which is above" and "our mother" (*Gal* 4, 26; cf. *Ap* 12, 17). It is described as the spotless *bride* of the spotless Lamb (*Ap* 19, 7; 21. 2.9; 22, 17), whom Christ "loved and for whom he delivered himself up that he might sanctify her" (*Eph* 5, 26). He joined it to Himself in an unbreakable covenant. He "nourishes and cherishes" it unceasingly (*Eph* 5, 29). He willed to purify it and to unite it to Himself; to subject it to Himself in love and fidelity (cf. *Eph* 5, 24); and, finally, to flood it with divine gifts for all eternity so that we might 922 comprehend the love of God and Christ for us, a love which surpasses all knowledge (cf. *Eph* 3, 19). While it journeys on this earth, apart from the Lord (cf. *2 Cor* 5, 6), it regards itself as an exile. So it longs and yearns for the things above, where Christ sits at the right hand of the Father, where the life of the Church lies hidden with Christ in God until it appears in glory with its spouse (cf. *Col* 3, 1-4).

The Mystical Body

923 7. The Son of God united a human nature to Himself and overcame death by His own death and resurrection. Thus He redeemed man and transformed him into a new creature (cf. *Gal.* 6, 15; *2 Cor.* 5, 17). He assembled His brethren out of every nation and, by communicating His Spirit, mystically constituted them as His body.

924 In this body the life of Christ is poured out on believers. Through the Sacraments they are united in a hidden yet real way to the Christ who underwent suffering and was glorified.[6] Through Baptism we are shaped in the image of Christ: "For in one Spirit we were all baptized into one body" (*1 Cor.* 12, 13). In this sacred rite, fellowship with Christ's death and resurrection is symbolized and actually brought about: "For we were buried with him by means of baptism into death"; but if "we have been united with him in the likeness of his death, we shall be so in the likeness of his resurrection also" (*Rom.* 6, 4-5).

925 In the breaking of the eucharistic bread we really partake of the Lord's body; and we are raised into communion with Him and with each other. "Because the bread is one, we though many, are one body, all of us who partake of the one bread" (1 *Cor* 10, 17). In this way we are all made members of His body (cf. 1 *Cor,* 12, 27), "but severally members of one another" (*Rom* 12, 5).

926 All the members of the human body, though they are many, form one body. so it is with the faithful in Christ (cf. 1 *Cor* 12, 12). In the build-up of Christ's body too there is a variety of members and functions. There is one Spirit who dispenses His varied gifts for the benefit of the Church, according to His own store of riches and the needs of the ministries (cf. 1 *Cor* 12, 1-11). Among these gifts the grace

of the Apostles stands out. To their authority the Spirit Himself subjects even those who are endowed with charismatic gifts (cf. 1 *Cor* 14). Giving unity to the body through His person, His power, and the internal cohesion of the members, this same Spirit produces and fosters charity among the faithful. So if one member suffers anything, all the members suffer with it, if one member is honored, all the members rejoice with it (cf. 1 *Cor* 12, 26).

927 The head of this body is Christ. He is the image of the invisible God; in Him all things were established. He is before all, and all things hold together in Him. He is the head of that body which is the Church. He is the beginning, the first-born from the dead, that in all things He may have the first place (cf. *Col* 1, 15-18). By the greatness of His power he rules the things in heaven and on earth; and with His all-surpassing perfection and activity He fills the whole body with the riches of His glory (cf. *Eph* 1, 18-23).[7]

928 All the members ought to be molded in His likeness, until Christ is formed in them (cf. *Gal* 4, 19). That is why we are taken up into the mysteries of His life, molded to His image, buried and resurrected with Him—until we come to reign with Him (cf. *Phil* 3, 21; *2 Tim 2*, 11; *Eoh* 2, 6; *Col* 2, 12 etc.) For the present, we travel as wayfarers here on earth, following His footsteps in tribulation and persecution, liked to His sufferings as the body is to the head. We share glory with Him (cf. *Rom* 8, 17).

929 From Him "the whole body, supplied and built up by joints and ligaments, attains a growth that is of God" (*Col* 2, 19). In His body, the Church, He continually distributes gifts of services. Through His power we can use them to help each other toward salvation. Thus we are able to practice truth in the spirit of charity and, in all things, grow up in Him who is our head (cf. *Eph* 4, 11-16 Gk).

930 In order that we might be renewed unceasingly in Him (cf. *Eph.* 4, 23), He shared His Spirit with us. This Spirit exists as one and the same in the head and the members, gives life, unity, and motive power to the whole body. Thus the Fathers of the Church could compare His function to that of the life-principle, the soul, in the human body.[8]

931 Christ really loves the Church as His bride. He has become the model of a man who loves his wife as his own body (cf. *Eph* 5, 25-28). And the Church is truly subject to its head (*Eph* 5, 23-24). "Because in him dwells all the fullness of the Godhead bodily" (*Col* 2, 9), He fills the Church with His divine gifts (cf. *Eph* 1, 22-23); for it is His body and His plenitude. In this way it may grow and arrive at all the fullness of God (cf. *Eph* 3, 19).

The Church's mission

932 8. Christ, the one and only Mediator, has established the Church, His holy community of faith, hope and charity, as a visible structure on this earth; and He gives it unfailing support.[9] Through it He diffuses truth and grace to all. But the hierarchical society and the Mystical Body of Christ, the visible assembly and the spiritual community, the Church on earth and the Church enriched with heavenly favors—these are not to be regarded as two realities. Rather, they form one complex reality compounded of a human and a divine element.[10] For this reason, there is much to be said for the analogy which likens the church to the mystery of the incarnate Word. The nature assumed by the divine Word and indissolubly united to Him, serves as a living instrument of salvation; so, in a similar way, the social structure of the Church serves the Spirit of Christ, who vivifies it, in the building-up of His body (cf. *Eph* 4, 16).[11]

933 This is the one and only Church of Christ, which we, in the Creed, proclaim to be one, holy, catholic and apostolic,[12] which our Savior, after His Resurrection, entrusted to Peter's pastoral care (*Jn* 21, 17); which He commissioned Peter and the other Apostles to spread and to rule (cf. *Mt* 28, 18 ff); which He erected in perpetuity as "the pillar and the mainstay of the truth" (1 *Tm* 3, 15). This Church, set up and structured as a society in this world, perdures in the Catholic Church under the government of Peter and the bishops in communion with him[13]—even though many elements of sactification and truth may be found outside its structure, elements which are an impetus

to universal unity insofar as they are gifts proper to the Church of Christ.

Just as Christ carried out the work of redemption in poverty and under oppression, so the Church is called to follow that same road in order to communicate the fruits of salvation to men. Christ Jesus "though he was by nature God . . . empties himself, taking the nature of a slave" (*Phil* 2, 6, 7) and "being rich, became poor" (*2 Cor* 8, 9) for our sakes. Even so the Church too, though it needs human resources in carrying out its mission, is not set up to seek earthly glory but to proclaim poverty and self-denial by its own example. Christ was sent by the Father "to bring good news to the poor . . . to heal the broken-hearted" (*Lk* 4, 18), "to seek and to save what was lost" (*Lk* 19, 10). In like manner the Church lovingly embraces all those afflicted with human frailty. Indeed it sees the image of its poor, suffering founder in all those who are poor and who suffer. It makes an effort to alleviate their wants and strives to serve Christ in them. While Christ, "holy, innocent, undefiled" (*Heb* 7, 26), did not know sin (*2 Cor* 5, 21) and came to expiate only the sins of the people (cf. *Heb* 2, 17), the Church, holy and yet always in need of purification, embraces sinners in its bosom and enlessly pursues the way of penance and renewal. 934

"Like a wayfarer," the Church "moves forward amid the persecution of the world and God's consolation,"[14] proclaiming the Lord's cross and His death until He comes (cf. 1 *Cor* 11, 26). It is strengthened by the power of the risen Lord so that by patience and love it may overcome its afflictions and problems—both internal and external—so that it may faithfully reveal His mystery in the world—though in a shadowy way—until that mystery is manifested in full light at the end. 935

MYSTERIUM FIDEI

Encyclical Letter of Pope Paul VI
on the Doctrine and Worship of the Holy Eucharist
September 3, 1965

The mystery of Faith, that is, the ineffable gift of the Eucharist that the Catholic Church received from Christ, her Spouse, as a pledge of His immense love, is something that she has always devoutly guarded as her most precious treasure, and during the Second Vatican Council she professed her faith and veneration in a new and solemn declaration. In dealing with the restoration of the sacred liturgy, the Fathers of the Council were led by their pastoral concern for the whole Church to regard it as a matter of highest importance to urge the faithful to participate actively, with undivided faith and the utmost devotion, in the celebration of this Most Holy Mystery, to offer it to God along with the priest as a sacrifice for their own salvation and that of the whole world, and to use it as spiritual nourishment.

937 2. For if the sacred liturgy holds first place in the life of the Church, then the Eucharistic Mystery stands at the heart and center of the liturgy, since it is the font of life that cleanses us and strengthens us to live not for ourselves but for God and to be united to each other by the closest ties of love.

938 3. In order to make the indissoluble bond that exists between faith and devotion perfectly clear, the Fathers of the Council decided, in the course of reaffirming the doctrine that the Church has always held and taught and that was solemnly defined by the Council of Trent, to offer the fol-

lowing compendium of truths as an introduction to their treatment of the Most Holy Mystery of the Eucharist:

4. "At the Last Supper, on the night when He was betrayed, our Savior instituted the Eucharistic Sacrifice of His Body and Blood. He did this in order to perpetuate the Sacrifice of the Cross throughout the centuries until He should come again, and so to entrust to His beloved Spouse, the Church, a memorial of His Death and Resurrection: a sacrament of love, a sign of unity, a bond of charity, a paschal banquet in which Christ is eaten, the mind is filled with grace, and a pledge of future glory is given to us."[1] 939

5. These words highlight both the sacrifice, which pertains to the essence of the Mass that is celebrated daily, and the sacrament in which those who participate in it through holy Communion eat the flesh of Christ and drink the blood of Christ, and thus receive grace, which is the beginning of eternal life, and the "medicine of immortality" according to Our Lord's words: "The man who eats my flesh and drinks my blood enjoys eternal life, and I will raise him up on the last day."[2] 940

6. And so We earnestly hope that the restoration of the sacred liturgy will produce abundant fruits in the form of Eucharistic devotion, so that the Holy Church may, with this salvific sign of piety raised on high, make daily progress toward the full achievement of unity,[3] inviting all Christians to a unity of faith and love and drawing them to it gently, through the action of divine grace. 941

7. We seem to have a preview of these fruits and a first taste of them in the outpouring of joy and eagerness that has marked the reception the sons of the Catholic Church have accorded to the Constitution on the Sacred Liturgy and to the restoration of the liturgy; and we find these fruits too in the large number of carefully-edited publications that make it their purpose to go into the doctrine of the Holy Eucharist more profoundly and to come to a more fruitful understanding of it, especially in terms of its relationship to the mystery of the Church. 942

8. All of this brings Us deep consolation and joy. And it gives Us great pleasure to inform you of this, Venerable 943

Brothers, so that you may join with Us in giving thanks to God, the bestower of all gifts, who rules the Church and makes her grow in virtue through His Spirit.

944 9. There are, however, Venerable Brothers, a number of reasons for serious pastoral concern and anxiety in this very matter that we are now discussing, and because of Our consciousness of Our Apostolic office, We cannot remain silent about them.

945 10. For We can see that some of those who are dealing with this Most Holy Mystery in speech and writing are disseminating opinions on Masses celebrated in private or on the dogma of transubstantiation that are disturbing the minds of the faithful and causing them no small measure of confusion about matters of faith, just as if it were all right for someone to take doctrine that has already been defined by the Church and consign it to oblivion or else interpret it in such a way as to weaken the genuine meaning of the words or the recognized force of the concepts involved.

946 11. To give an example of what We are talking about, it is not permissible to extol the so-called "community" Mass in such a way as to detract from Masses that are celebrated privately; or to concentrate on the notion of sacramental sign as if the symbolism—which no one will deny is certainly present in the Most Blessed Eucharist—fully expressed and exhausted the manner of Christ's presence in this Sacrament; or to discuss the mystery of transubstantiation without mentioning what the Council of Trent had to say about the marvelous conversion of the whole substance of the bread into the Body and the whole substance of the wine into the Blood of Christ, as if they involve nothing more than "transignification," or "transfinalization" as they call it; or, finally, to propose and act upon the opinion that Christ Our Lord is no longer present in the consecrated Hosts that remain after the celebration of the sacrifice of the Mass has been completed.

947 12. Everyone can see that the spread of these and similar opinions does great harm to belief in and devotion to the Eucharist.

948 13. And so, with the aim of seeing to it that the hope to which the Council has given rise—that a new wave of Eucha-

ristic devotion will sweep over the Church—not be reduced to nil through the sowing of the seeds of false opinions, We have decided to use Our apostolic authority and speak Our mind to you on this subject, Venerable Brothers.

14. We certainly do not deny that those who are spreading these strange opinions are making a praiseworthy effort to investigate this lofty Mystery and to set forth its inexhaustible riches and to make it more understandable to the men of today; rather, We acknowledge this and We approve of it. But We cannot approve the opinions that they set forth, and We have an obligation to warn you about the grave danger that these opinions involve for true faith. 949

15. First of all, We want to recall something that you know very well but that is absolutely necessary if the virus of every kind of rationalism is to be repelled; it is something that many illustrious martyrs have witnessed to with their blood, something that celebrated Fathers and Doctors of the Church have constantly professed and taught. We mean the fact that the Eucharist is a very great mystery—in fact, properly speaking and in the words of the Sacred Liturgy, *the mystery of faith*. "It contains within it," as Leo XIII, Our predecessor of happy memory, very wisely remarked, "all supernatural realities in a remarkable richness and variety of miracles."[4] 950

16. And so we must approach this mystery in particular with humility and reverence, not relying on human reasoning, which ought to hold its peace, but rather adhering firmly to divine Revelation. 951

17. St. John Chrysostom who, as you know, dealt with the Mystery of the Eucharist in such eloquent language and with such insight born of devotion, had these most fitting words to offer on one occasion when he was instructing his faithful about this mystery: "Let us submit to God in all things and not contradict Him, even if what He says seems to contradict our reason and intellect; let His word prevail over our reason and intellect. Let us act in this way with regard to the Eucharistic mysteries, and not limit our attention just to what can be perceived by the senses, but instead hold fast to His words. For His word cannot deceive."[5] 952

953 18. The scholastic Doctors made similar statements on more than one occasion. As St. Thomas says, the fact that the true body and the true blood of Christ are present in this Sacrament "cannot be apprehended by the senses but only by faith, which rests upon divine authority. This is why Cyril comments upon the words, *This is my body which is delivered up for you,* in *Luke* 22,19, in this way: Do not doubt that this is true; instead accept the words of the Savior in faith; for since He is truth, He cannot tell a lie."[6]

954 19. Hence the Christian people often follow the lead of St. Thomas and sing the words: "Sight, touch and taste in Thee are each deceived; The ear alone most safely is believed. I believe all the Son of God has spoken; Than truth's own word, there is no truer token."

955 20. And St. Bonaventure declares: "There is no difficulty over Christ's being present in the sacrament as in a sign; the great difficulty is in the fact that He is really in the sacrament, as He is in heaven. And so believing this is especially meritorious."[7]

956 21. Moreover, the Holy Gospel alludes to this when it tells of the many disciples of Christ who turned away and left Our Lord, after hearing Him speak of eating His flesh and drinking His blood. "This is strange talk," they said. "Who can be expected to listen to it?" Peter, on the contrary, replied to Jesus' question as to whether the twelve wanted to go away too by promptly and firmly expressing his own faith and that of the other Apostles in these marvelous words: "Lord, to whom should we go? Thy words are the words of eternal life."[8]

957 22. It is only logical, then, for us to follow the magisterium of the Church as a guiding star in carrying on our investigations into this mystery, for the Divine Redeemer has entrusted the safeguarding and the explanation of the written or transmitted word of God to her. And we are convinced that "whatever has been preached and believed throughout the whole Church with true Catholic faith since the days of antiquity is true, even if it not be subject to rational investigation, and even if it not be explained in words."[9]

23. But this is not enough. Once the integrity of the faith has been safeguarded, then it is time to safeguard the proper way of expressing it, lest our careless use of words give rise, God forbid, to false opinions regarding faith in the most sublime things. St. Augustine gives a stern warning about this when he takes up the matter of the different ways of speaking that are employed by the philosophers on the one hand and that ought to be used by Christians on the other. "The philosophers," he says, "use words freely, and they have no fear of offending religious listeners in dealing with subjects that are difficult to understand. But we have to speak in accordance with a fixed rule, so that a lack of restraint in speech on our part may not give rise to some irreverent opinion about the things represented by the words."[10] 958

24. And so the rule of language which the Church has established through the long labor of centuries, with the help of the Holy Spirit, and which she has confirmed with the authority of the Councils, and which has more than once been the watchword and banner of orthodox faith, is to be religiously preserved, and no one may presume to change it at his own pleasure or under the pretext of new knowledge. Who would ever tolerate that the dogmatic formulas used by the ecumenical councils for the mysteries of the Holy Trinity and the Incarnation be judged as no longer appropriate for men of our times, and let others be rashly substituted for them? In the same way, it cannot be tolerated that any individual should on his own authority take something away from the formulas which were used by the Council of Trent to propose the Eucharistic Mystery for our belief. These formulas—like the others that the Church uses to propose the dogmas of faith—express concepts that are not tied to a certain specific form of human culture, or to a certain level of scientific progress, or to one or another theological school. Instead they set forth what the human mind grasps of reality through necessary and universal experience and what it expresses in apt and exact words, whether it be in ordinary or more refined language. For this reason, these formulas are adapted to all men of all times and all places. 959

960 25. They can, it is true, be made clearer and more obvious; and doing this is of great benefit. But it must always be done in such a way that they retain the meaning in which they have been used, so that with the advance of an understanding of the faith, the truth of faith will remain unchanged. For it is the teaching of the First Vatican Council that "the meaning that Holy Mother the Church has once declared, is to be retained forever, and no pretext of deeper understanding ever justifies any deviation from that meaning."[11]

961 26. For the joy and edification of everyone, We would like to review with you, Venerable Brothers, the doctrine on the Mystery of the Eucharist that has been handed down, and that the Catholic Church holds and teaches with unanimity.

962 27. It is a good idea to recall at the very outset what may be termed the heart and core of the doctrine, namely that, by means of the Mystery of the Eucharist, the Sacrifice of the Cross which was once carried out on Calvary is re-enacted in wonderful fashion and is constantly recalled, and its salvific power is applied to the forgiving of the sins we commit each day."[12]

963 28. Just as Moses made the Old Testament sacred with the blood of calves,[13] so too Christ the Lord took the New Testament, of which He is the Mediator, and made it sacred through His own blood, in instituting the Mystery of the Eucharist. For, as the Evangelists narrate, at the Last Supper "he took bread, and blessed and broke it, and gave it to them, saying, This is my body, given for you; do this for a commemoration of me. And so with the cup, when supper was ended, This cup, he said, is the new testament, in my Blood which is to be shed for you."[14] And by bidding the Apostles to do this in memory of Him, He made clear that He wanted it to be forever repeated. This intention of Christ was faithfully carried out by the primitive Church through her adherence to the teaching of the Apostles and through her gatherings to celebrate the Eucharistic Sacrifice. As St. Luke is careful to point out, "They occupied themselves continually with the Apostoles' teaching, their fellowship in the breaking of bread, and the fixed times of prayer."[15] The faithful used to derive such spiritual fervor from this practice that it was

said of them that "there was one heart and soul in all the company of the believers."[16]

29. Moreover, the Apostle Paul, who faithfully transmitted to us what he had received from the Lord,[17] is clearly speaking of the Eucharistic Sacrifice when he points out that Christians ought not take part in pagan sacrifices, precisely because they have been made partakers of the table of the Lord. "Is not this cup we bless," he says, "a participation in Christ's Blood? Is not the Bread we break a participation in Christ's Body? . . . To drink the Lord's cup, and yet to drink the cup of evil spirits, to share the Lord's feast, and to share the feast of evil spirits, is impossible for you."[18] Foreshadowed by Malachias,[19] this new oblation of the New Testament has always been offered by the Church, in accordance with the teaching of Our Lord and the Apostles, "not only to atone for the sins and punishments and satisfactions of the living faithful and to appeal for their other needs, but also to help those who have died in Christ but have not yet been completely purified."[20] 964

30. We will pass over the other citations and rest content with recalling the testimony offered by St. Cyril of Jerusalem, who wrote the following memorable words for the neophytes whom he was instructing in the Christian faith: "After the spiritual sacrifice, the unbloody act of worship, has been completed, we bend over this propitiatory offering and beg God to grant peace to all the Churches, to give harmony to the whole world, to bless our rulers, our soldiers and our companions, to aid the sick and afflicted, and in general to assist all those who stand in need; we all pray for all these intentions and we offer this victim for them . . . and last of all for our deceased holy forefathers and bishops and for all those who have lived among us. For we have a deep conviction that great help will be afforded those souls for whom prayers are offered while this holy and awesome victim is present." In support of this, this holy Doctor offers the example of a crown made for an emperor in order to win a pardon for some exiles, and he concludes his talk with these words: "In the same fashion, when we offer our prayers to God for the dead, even those who are sinners, we are not just 965

making a crown but instead are offering Christ who was slaughtered for our sins, and thus begging the merciful God to take pity both on them and on ourselves."[21] St. Augustine attests that this custom of offering the "sacrifice which ransomed us" also for the dead was observed in the Church at Rome,[22] and he mentions at the same time that the universal Church observed this custom as something handed down from the Fathers.[23]

966 31. But there is something else that We would like to add that is very helpful in shedding light on the mystery of the Church; We mean the fact that the whole Church plays the role of priest and victim along with Christ, offering the Sacrifice of the Mass and itself completely offered in it. The Fathers of the Church taught this wondrous doctrine.[24] A few years ago Our predecessor of happy memory, Pius XII, explained it.[25] And only recently the Second Vatican Council reiterated it in its Constitution on the Church, in dealing with the people of God.[26] To be sure, the distinction between the universal priesthood and the hierarchical priesthood is something essential and not just a matter of degree, and it has to be maintained in a proper way.[27] Yet We cannot help being filled with an earnest desire to see this teaching explained over and over until it takes deep root in the hearts of the faithful. For it is a most effective means of fostering devotion to the Eucharist, of extolling the dignity of all the faithful, and of spurring them on to reach the heights of sanctity, which means the total and generous offering of oneself to the service of the Divine Majesty.

967 32. It is also only fitting for us to recall the conclusion that can be drawn from this about "the public and social nature of each and every Mass."[28] For each and every Mass is not something private, even if a priest celebrates it privately; instead, it is an act of Christ and of the Church. In offering this sacrifice, the Church learns to offer herself as a sacrifice for all and she applies the unique and infinite redemptive power of the sacrifice of the Cross to the salvation of the whole world. For every Mass that is celebrated is being offered not just for the salvation of certain people, but also for the salvation of the whole world. The conclusion from this is that

even though active participation by many faithful is of its very nature particularly fitting when Mass is celebrated, still there is no reason to criticize but rather only to approve a Mass that a priest celebrates privately for a good reason in accordance with the regulations and legitimate traditions of the Church, even when only a server to make the responses is present. For such a Mass brings a rich and abundant treasure of special graces to help the priest himself, the faithful, the whole Church and the whole world toward salvation—and this same abundance of graces is not gained through mere reception of Holy Communion.

33. And so, We recommend from a paternal and solicitous heart that priests, who constitute Our greatest joy and Our crown in the Lord, be mindful of the power they have received from the bishop who ordained them—the power of offering sacrifice to God and of celebrating Mass for the living and for the dead in the name of the Lord.[29] We recommend that they celebrate Mass daily in a worthy and devout fashion, so that they themselves and the rest of the faithful may enjoy the benefits that flow in such abundance from the Sacrifice of the Cross. In doing so, they will also be making a great contribution toward the salvation of mankind. 968

34. The few things that We have touched upon concerning the Sacrifice of the Mass encourage Us to say something about the Sacrament of the Eucharist, since both Sacrifice and Sacrament pertain to the same mystery and cannot be separated from each other. The Lord is immolated in an unbloody way in the Sacrifice of the Mass and He re-presents the sacrifice of the Cross and applies its salvific power at the moment when he becomes sacramentally present—through the words of consecration—as the spiritual food of the faithful, under the appearances of bread and wine. 969

35. All of us realize that there is more than one way in which Christ is present in His Church. We want to go into this very joyful subject, which the Constitution on the Sacred Liturgy presented briefly,[30] at somewhat greater length. Christ is present in His Church when she prays, since He is the one who "prays for us and prays in us and to whom we pray: He prays for us as our priest, He prays in us as our 970

head, He is prayed to us by us as our God"[31]; and He is the one who has promised, "Where two or three are gathered together in my name, I am there in the midst of them."[32] He is present in the Church as she performs her works of mercy, not just because whatever good we do to one of His least brethren we do to Christ Himself,[33] but also because Christ is the one who performs these works through the Church and who continually helps men with His divine love. He is present in the Church as she moves along on her pilgrimage with a longing to reach the portals of eternal life, for He is the one who dwells in our hearts through faith,[34] and who instills charity in them through the Holy Spirit whom He gives to us.[35]

971 36. In still another very genuine way, He is present in the Church as she preaches, since the Gospel which she proclaims is the word of God, and it is only in the name of Christ, the Incarnate Word of God, and by His authority and with His help that it is preached, so that there might be "one flock resting secure in one shepherd."[36]

972 37. He is present in His Church as she rules and governs the People of God, since her sacred power comes from Christ and since Christ, the "Shepherd of Shepherds,"[37] is present in the bishops who exercise that power, in keeping with the promise He made to the Apostles.

973 38. Moreover, Christ is present in His Church in a still more sublime manner as she offers the Sacrifice of the Mass in His name; He is present in her as she administers the sacraments. On the matter of Christ's presence in the offering of the Sacrifice of the Mass, We would like very much to recall what St. John Chrysostom, overcome with awe, had to say in such accurate and eloquent words: "I wish to add something that is clearly awe-inspiring, but do not be surprised or upset. What is this? It is the same offering, no matter who offers it, be it Peter or Paul. It is the same one that Christ gave to His disciples and the same one that priests now perform: the latter is in no way inferior to the former, for it is not men who sanctify the latter, but He who sanctified the former. For just as the words which God spoke are the same as those that the priest now pronounces, so too the offering is the

same."[38] No one is unaware that the sacraments are the actions of Christ who administers them through men. And so the sacraments are holy in themselves and they pour grace into the soul by the power of Christ, when they touch the body.

These various ways in which Christ is present fill the mind with astonishment and offer the Church a mystery for her contemplation. But there is another way in which Christ is present in His Church, a way that surpasses all the others. It is His presence in the Sacrament of the Eucharist, which is, for this reason, "a more consoling source of devotion, a lovelier object of contemplation and holier in what it contains"[39] than all the other sacraments; for it contains Christ Himself and it is "a kind of consummation of the spiritual life, and in a sense the goal of all the sacraments.[40] 974

39. This presence is called "real" not to exclude the idea that the others are "real" too, but rather to indicate presence par excellence, because it is substantial and through it Christ becomes present whole and entire, God and man.[41] And so it would be wrong for anyone to try to explain this manner of presence by dreaming up a so-called "pneumatic" nature of the glorious body of Christ that would be present everywhere; or for anyone to limit it to symbolism, as if this most sacred Sacrament were to consist in nothing more than an efficacious sign "of the spiritual presence of Christ and of His intimate union with the faithful, the members of His Mystical Body."[42] 975

40. It is true that the Fathers and Scholastics had a great deal to say about symbolism in the Eucharist, especially with regard to the unity of the Church. The Council of Trent, in re-stating their doctrine, taught that our Savior bequeathed the Eucharist to His Church "as a symbol . . . of the unity and charity with which He wished all Christians to be joined among themselves," "and hence as a symbol of that one *Body* of which He *is the head*."[43] 976

41. When Christian literature was still in its infancy, the unknown author of the work called the "Didache or Teaching of the Twelve Apostles" had this to write on the subject: "As far as the Eucharist is concerned, give thanks in this 977

manner: . . . just as this bread had been broken and scattered over the hills and was made one when it was gathered together, so too may your church be gathered into your kingdom from the ends of the earth."[44]

978 42. St. Cyprian too, in the course of laying stress on the Church's unity in opposition to schism, said this: "Finally the Lord's sacrifices proclaim the unity of Christians who are bound together by a firm and unshakeable charity. For when the Lord calls the bread that has been made from many grains of wheat His Body, He is describing our people whose unity He has sustained; and when He refers to wine pressed from many grapes and berries as His Blood, once again He is speaking of our flock which has been formed by fusing many into one."[45]

979 43. But before all of these, St. Paul had written to the Corinthians: "The one bread makes us one body, though we are many in number; the same bread is shared by all."[46]

980 44. While Eucharistic symbolism is well suited to helping us understand the effect that is proper to this Sacrament—the unity of the Mystical Body—still it does not indicate or explain what it is that makes this Sacrament different from all the others. For the constant teaching that the Catholic Church has passed on to her catechumens, the understanding of the Christian people, the doctrine defined by the Council of Trent, the very words that Christ used when He instituted the Most Holy Eucharist, all require us to profess that "the Eucharist is the flesh of Our Savior Jesus Christ which suffered for our sins and which the Father in His loving kindness raised again."[47] To these words of St. Ignatius, we may well add those which Theodore of Mopsuestia, who is a faithful witness to the faith of the Church on this point, addressed to the people: "The Lord did not say: This is a symbol of my body, and this is a symbol of my blood, but rather: *This is my body and my blood.* He teaches us not to look to the nature of what lies before us and is perceived by the senses, because the giving of thanks and the words spoken over it have changed it into flesh and blood."[48]

981 45. The Council of Trent, basing itself on this faith of the Church, "openly and sincerely professes that after the conse-

cration of the bread and wine, Our Lord Jesus Christ, true God and man, is really, truly and substantially contained in the Blessed Sacrament of the Holy Eucharist under the outward appearances of sensible things." And so Our Savior is present in His humanity not only in His natural manner of existence at the right hand of the Father, but also at the same time in the sacrament of the Eucharist "in a manner of existing that we can hardly express in words but that our minds, illumined by faith, can come to see as possible to God and that we must most firmly believe."[49]

46. To avoid any misunderstanding of this type of presence, which goes beyond the laws of nature and constitutes the greatest miracle of its kind,[50] we have to listen with docility to the voice of the teaching and praying Church. Her voice, which constantly echoes the voice of Christ, assures us that the way in which Christ becomes present in this Sacrament is through the conversion of the whole substance of the bread into His body and of the whole substance of the wine into His blood, a unique and truly wonderful conversion that the Catholic Church fittingly and properly calls transubstantiation.[51] As a result of transubstantiation, the species of bread and wine undoubtedly take on a new signification and a new finality, for they are no longer ordinary bread and wine but instead a sign of something sacred and a sign of spiritual food; but they take on this new signification, this new finality, precisely because they contain a new "reality" which we can rightly call *ontological.* For what now lies beneath the aforementioned species is not what was there before, but something completely different; and not just in the estimation of Church belief but in reality, since once the substance or nature of the bread and wine has been changed into the body and blood of Christ, nothing remains of the bread and the wine except for the species–beneath which Christ is present whole and entire in His physical "reality," corporeally present, although not in the manner in which bodies are in a place. 982

47. This is why the Fathers felt they had a solemn duty to warn the faithful that, in reflecting upon this most sacred Sacrament, they should not pay attention to the senses, 983

which report only the properties of bread and wine, but rather to the words of Christ, which have power great enough to change, transform, "transelementize" the bread and wine into His body and blood. As a matter of fact, as the same Fathers point out on more than one occasion, the power that does this is the same power of almighty God that created the whole universe out of nothing at the beginning of time.

984 48. "Instructed as you are in these matters," says St. Cyril of Jerusalem, at the end of a sermon on the mysteries of the faith, "and filled with an unshakeable faith that what seems to be bread is not bread—though it tastes like it—but rather the Body of Christ; and that what seems to be wine is not wine—even though it too tastes like it—but rather the Blood of Christ . . . draw strength from receiving this bread as spiritual food and your soul will rejoice."[52]

985 49. St. John Chrysostom insists upon the same point with these words: "It is not man who makes what is put before him the Body and Blood of Christ, but Christ Himself who was crucified for us. The priest standing there in the place of Christ says these words, but their power and grace are from God. *This is my Body*, he says, and these words transform what lies before him."[53]

986 50. Cyril, the Bishop of Alexandria, is in wonderful harmony with John, the Bishop of Constantinople, when he writes in his commentary on the Gospel of St. Matthew: "He said *This is my body* and *this is my blood* in a demonstrative fashion, so that you might not judge that what you see is a mere figure; instead the offerings are truly changed by the hidden power of God almighty into Christ's body and blood, which bring us the life-giving and sanctifying power of Christ when we share in them."[54]

987 51. Ambrose, the Bishop of Milan, in a clear statement on the Eucharistic conversion, has this to say: "Let us be assured that this is not what nature formed but what the blessing has consecrated; and there is greater power in the blessing than in nature, since nature itself is changed through the blessing." To confirm the truth of this mystery, he recounts many of the miracles described in the Sacred Scriptures, including Christ's birth of the Virgin Mary, and then he turns his mind

to the work of creation, concluding this way: "Surely the word of Christ, who could make something that did not exist out of nothing, can change things that do exist into something they were not before. For it is no less extraordinary to give new natures to things than it is to change nature."[55]

52. But this is no time for assembling a long list of evidence. Instead, We would rather recall the firmness of faith and complete unanimity that the Church displayed in opposing Berengarius who gave in to certain difficulties raised by human reasoning and first dared to deny the Eucharistic conversion. More than once she threatened to condemn him unless he retracted. Thus it was that Our predecessor, St. Gregory VII, commanded him to swear to the following oath: "I believe in my heart and openly profess that the bread and wine that are placed on the altar are, through the mystery of the sacred prayer and the words of the Redeemer, substantially changed into the true and proper and life-giving flesh and blood of Jesus Christ our Lord, and that after the consecration they are the true body of Christ—which was born of the Virgin and which hung on the Cross as an offering for the salvation of the world—and the true blood of Christ—which flowed from His side—and not just as a sign and by reason of the power of the sacrament, but in the very truth and reality of their substance and in what is proper to their nature."[56] 988

53. We have a wonderful example of the stability of the Catholic faith in the way in which these words meet with such complete agreement in the constant teaching of the Ecumenical Councils of the Lateran, Constance, Florence and Trent on the mystery of the Eucharistic conversion, whether it be contained in their explanations of the teaching of the Church or in their condemnations of error. 989

54. After the Council of Trent, Our predecessor, Pius VI, issued a serious warning, on the occasion of the errors of the Synod of Pistoia, that parish priests not neglect to speak of transubstantiation, which is listed among the articles of the faith, in the course of carrying out their office of teaching.[57] Similarly, Our Predecessor of happy memory, Pius XII, recalled the bounds beyond which those who were carrying on 990

subtle discussion of the mystery of transubstantiation might not pass;[58] and We Ourself, at the National Eucharistic Congress that was recently celebrated at Pisa, bore open and solemn witness to the faith of the Church, in fulfillment of Our apostolic duty.[59]

991 55. Moreover, the Catholic Church has held firm to this belief in the presence of Christ's Body and Blood in the Eucharist not only in her teaching but in her life as well, since she has at all times paid this great Sacrament the worship known as "latria," which may be given to God alone. As St. Augustine says: "It was in His flesh that Christ walked among us and it is His flesh that He has given us to eat for our salvation; but no one eats of this flesh without having first adored it . . . and not only do we not sin in thus adoring it, but we would be sinning if we did not do so."[60]

992 56. The Catholic Church has always displayed and still displays this latria that ought to be paid to the Sacrament of the Eucharist, both during Mass and outside of it, by taking the greatest possible care of consecrated Hosts, by exposing them to the solemn veneration of the faithful, and by carrying them about in processions to the joy of great numbers of the people.

993 57. The ancient documents of the Church offer many evidences of this veneration. The bishops of the Church always urged the faithful to take the greatest possible care of the Eucharist that they had in their homes. "The Body of Christ is meant to be eaten by the faithful, not to be treated with irreverence," is the serious warning of St. Hippolytus.[61]

994 58. In fact, the faithful regarded themselves as guilty, and rightly so as Origen recalls, if, after they had received the body of the Lord and kept it with all reverence and caution, some part of it were to fall to the ground through negligence.[62]

995 59. These same bishops were severe in reproving any lack of due reverence that might occur. We have evidence of this from the words of Novatian, whose testimony is trustworthy in this matter; He felt that anybody deserved to be condemned who "came out after Sunday service bringing the Eucharist with him, as was the custom, . . . and carried the

holy body of the Lord around with him," going off to places of amusement instead of going home.[63]

60. In fact, St. Cyril of Alexandria denounced as mad the opinion that the Eucharist was of no use to sanctification if some of it were left over for another day. "For Christ is not altered," he says, "and His holy body is not changed; instead the power and force and life-giving grace of the blessing remain in it forever."[64] 996

61. Nor should we forget that in ancient times the faithful—whether being harassed by violent persecutions or living in solitude out of love for monastic life—nourished themselves even daily on the Eucharist, by receiving Holy Communion from their own hands when there was no priest or deacon present.[65] 997

62. We are not saying this with any thought of effecting a change in the manner of keeping the Eucharist and of receiving Holy Communion that has been laid down by subsequent ecclesiastical laws still in force; Our intention is that we may rejoice over the faith of the Church which is always one and the same. 998

63. This faith also gave rise to the feast of Corpus Christi, which was first celebrated in the diocese of Liege—especially through the efforts of the servant of God, Blessed Juliana of Mount Cornelius—and which Our predecessor, Urban IV, established for the universal Church. It has also given rise to many forms of Eucharistic devotion that have, through the inspiration of God's grace, grown with each passing day. Through them the Catholic Church is eagerly striving to pay honor to Christ and to thank Him for such a great gift and to beg His mercy. 999

64. And so We beseech you, Venerable Brothers, to take this faith, which means nothing less than maintaining complete fidelity to the words of Christ and the Apostles, and preserve it in its purity and integrity among the people entrusted to your care and vigilance, with all false and pernicious opinions being completely rejected; and We beseech you to foster devotion to the Eucharist, which should be the focal point and goal of all other forms of devotion. 1000

1001 65. May the faithful, thanks to your constant efforts, come to realize and experience more and more that: "He who wants to live can find here a place to live in and the means to live on. Let him approach, let him believe, let him be incorporated so that he may receive life. Let him not shy away from union with the members, let him not be a rotten member that deserves to be cut away, nor a distorted member to be ashamed of: let him be beautiful, let him be fitting, let him be healthy. Let him adhere to the body; let him live for God on God: let him labor now upon earth, so that he may afterwards reign in heaven."[66]

1002 66. It is desirable to have the faithful in large numbers take an active part in the sacrifice of the Mass each and every day and receive the nourishment of Holy Communion with a pure and holy mind and offer fitting thanks to Christ the Lord for such a great gift. They should remember these words: "The desire of Jesus Christ and of the Church to see all the faithful approach the sacred banquet each and every day is based on a wish to have them all united to God through the sacrament and to have them draw from it the strength to master their passions, to wash away the lesser sins that are committed every day and to prevent the serious sins to which human frailty is subject."[67] And they should not forget about paying a visit during the day to the Most Blessed Sacrament in the very special place of honor where it is reserved in churches in keeping with the liturgical laws, since this is a proof of gratitude and a pledge of love and a display of the adoration that is owed to Christ the Lord who is present there.

1003 67. No one can fail to see that the divine Eucharist bestows an incomparable dignity upon the Christian people. For it is not just while the Sacrifice is being offered and the Sacrament is being confected, but also after the Sacrifice has been offered and the Sacrament confected—while the Eucharist is reserved in churches or oratories—that Christ is truly Emmanuel, which means "God with us." For He is in the midst of us day and night; He dwells in us with the fullness of grace and of truth.[68] He raises the level of morals, fosters virtue, comforts the sorrowful, strengthens the weak and stirs up all those who draw near to Him to imitate Him, so that they may learn from his example to be meek and humble of heart, and to seek not their own interests but those of God. Anyone who has a special devotion to the sacred Eucharist and who tries to repay Christ's infinite love for us with an eager and unselfish love of his own, will experience and fully understand—and this will bring great delight and benefit to his soul—just how precious is a life hidden with Christ in God[69] and just how worthwhile it is to carry on a conversation with Christ, for there is nothing more consoling here on earth, nothing more efficacious for progress along the paths of holiness.

68. You also realize, Venerable Brothers, that the Eucharist is reserved in churches or oratories to serve as the spiritual center of a religious community or a parish community, indeed of the whole Church and the whole of mankind, since it contains, beneath the veil of the species, Christ the invisible Head of the Church, the Redeemer of the world, the center of all hearts, "by whom all things are and by whom we exist."[70] 1004

69. Hence it is that devotion to the divine Eucharist exerts a great influence upon the soul in the direction of fostering a "social" love,[71] in which we put the common good ahead of private good, take up the cause of the community, the parish, the universal Church, and extend our charity to the whole world because we know that there are members of Christ everywhere. 1005

70. Because, Venerable Brothers, the Sacrament of the Eucharist is a sign and cause of the unity of Christ's Mystical Body, and because it stirs up an active "ecclesial" spirit in those who are more fervent in their Eucharistic devotion, never stop urging your faithful, as they approach the Mystery of the Eucharist, to learn to embrace the Church's cause as their own, to pray to God without slackening, to offer themselves to God as an acceptable sacrifice for the peace and unity of the Church; so that all the sons of the Church may be united and feel united and there may be no divisions among them but rather unity of mind and intention, as the Apostle commands.[72] May all those who are not yet in perfect communion with the Catholic Church and who glory in 1006

the name of Christian despite their separation from her, come as soon as possible to share with us, through the help of God's grace, in that unity of faith and communion that Christ wanted to be the distinctive mark of His disciples.

1007 71. This zeal at prayer and at devoting oneself to God for the sake of the unity of the Church is something that religious, both men and women, should regard as very specially their own, since they are bound in a special way to adoration of the Blessed Sacrament, and they have, by virtue of the vows they have pronounced, become a kind of crown set around it here on earth.

1008 72. The Church in the past has felt and still feels that nothing is more ancient and more pleasing than the desire for the unity of all Christians, and We want to express this in the very same words that the Council of Trent used to conclude its decree on the Most Holy Eucharist: "In conclusion, the Council with paternal love admonishes, exhorts, begs and implores 'through the merciful kindness of our God'[73] that each and every Christian may come at last to full agreement in this *sign of unity*, in this *bond of charity*, in this *symbol of harmony*; that they may be mindful of the great dignity and the profound love of Our Lord Jesus Christ, who gave up His precious life as the price of our salvation and who gave us *His flesh to eat*[74]; and that they may believe and adore these sacred mysteries of His body and blood with such firm and unwavering faith, with such devotion and piety and veneration that they will be able to receive that supersubstantial[75] bread often and it will truly be the life of their souls and the unfailing strength of their minds, so that 'fortified by its vigor,'[76] they may be able to move on from this wretched earthly pilgrimage to their heavenly home where, without any veil, they will eat the 'bread of angels'[77] that they now eat beneath the sacred veils."[78]

1009 73. May the all-merciful Redeemer, who shortly before His death prayed to the Father that all who were to believe in Him might be one, just as He and the Father are one,[79] deign to hear this most ardent prayer of Ours and of the whole Church as quickly as possible, so that we may all celebrate the Eucharistic Mystery with one voice and one faith, and through sharing in the Body of Christ become one body,[80] joined together by the same bonds that Christ wanted it to have.

74. We also want to address with fraternal affection those who belong to the venerable Churches of the East, which have had so many glorious Fathers whose testimony to belief in the Eucharist We have been so glad to cite in this present letter of Ours. Our soul is filled with great joy as We contemplate your belief in the Eucharist, which is ours as well, as we listen to the liturgical prayers you use to celebrate this great mystery, as we behold your Eucharistic devotion, as we read your theological works explaining or defending the doctrine of this most sacred Sacrament. 1010

75. May the most blessed Virgin Mary, from whom Christ the Lord took the flesh that "is contained, offered, received"[81] in this Sacrament under the appearances of bread and wine, and may all the saints of God and especially those who were more inflamed with ardent devotion toward the divine Eucharist, intercede with the Father of mercies so that this common belief in the Eucharist and devotion to it may give rise among all Christians to a perfect unity of communion that will continue to flourish. Lingering in Our mind are the words of the holy martyr Ignatius warning the Philadelphians against the evil of divisions and schisms, the remedy for which is to be found in the Eucharist. "Strive then," he says, "to make use of one single thanksgiving. For there is only one flesh of Our Lord Jesus Christ, and only one chalice unto the union of His blood, only one altar, only one bishop . . ."[82] 1011

76. Fortified by the most consoling hope of blessings that will accrue to the whole Church and to the whole world from an increase in devotion to the Eucharist, as a pledge of heavenly blessings We lovingly impart Our apostolic blessings to you, Venerable Brothers, and to the priests, religious and all who are helping you, as well as to all the faithful entrusted to your care. 1012

Given at St. Peter's, Rome, on the third day of September, the feast of Pope St. Pius X, in the year 1965, the third of Our Pontificate. 1013

DEI VERBUM

Dogmatic Constitution on Divine Revelation

November 18, 1965

PROLOGUE

Hearing the Word of God with reverence, and proclaiming it with faith, the sacred Synod assents to the words of St. John, who says: "We proclaim to you the eternal life which was with the Father and was made manifest to us—that which we have seen and heard we proclaim also to you, so that you may have fellowship with us; and our fellowship is with the Father and with his Son Jesus Christ." (1 *Jn.* 1:2-3). Following, then, in the steps of the Councils of Trent and Vatican I, this Synod wishes to set forth the true doctrine on divine Revelation and its transmission. For it wants the whole world to hear the summons to salvation, so that through hearing it may believe, through belief it may hope, through hope it may come to love.[1]

Chapter I

DIVINE REVELATION ITSELF

1015 2. It pleased God, in his goodness and wisdom, to reveal himself and to make known the mystery of his will (cf. *Eph.* 1:9). His will was that men should have access to the Father, through Christ, the Word made flesh, in the Holy Spirit, and thus become sharers in the divine nature (cf. *Eph.* 2:18; 2 *Pet.* 1:4). By this revelation, then, the invisible God (cf. *Col.* 1:15; 1 *Tim.* 1:17), from the fullness of his love, addresses men as his friends (cf. *Ex.* 33:11; *Jn.* 15; 14-15), and moves among them (cf. *Bar.* 3:38), in order to invite and receive them into his own company. This economy of Revelation is realized by deeds and words, which are intrinsically bound up with each other. As a result, the works performed by God in the history of salvation show forth and bear out the doctrine and realitites signified by the words; the words, for their part, proclaim the works, and bring to light the mystery they contain. The most intimate truth which this revelation gives us about God and the salvation of man shines forth in Christ, who is himself both the mediator and the sum total of Revelation.[2]

1016

3. God, who creates and conserves all things by his Word, (cf. *Jn.* 1:3), provides men with constant evidence of himself in created realities (cf. *Rom.* 1:19-20). And furthermore, wishing to open up the way to heavenly salvation, he manifested himself to our first parents from the very beginning. After the fall, he buoyed them up with the hope of salvation, by promising redemption (cf. *Gen.* 3:15); and he has never ceased to take care of the human race. For he wishes to give eternal life to all those who seek salvation by patience in well-doing (cf. *Rom.* 2:6-7). In his own time God called Abraham, and made him into a great nation (cf. *Gen.* 12:2). After the era of the patriarchs, he taught this nation, by Moses and the prophets, to recognize him as the only living and true God, as a provident Father and just judge. He taught them, too, to look for the promised Saviour. And so, throughout the ages, he prepared the way for the Gospel.

1017

4. After God had spoken many times and in various ways through the prophets, "in these last days he has spoken to us by a Son" (*Heb.* 1:1-2). For he sent his Son, the eternal Word who enlightens all men, to dwell among men and to tell them about the inner life of God. Hence, Jesus Christ, sent as "a man among men,"[3] " speaks the words of God" (*Jn.* 3:34), and accomplishes the saving work which the Father gave him to do (cf. *Jn.* 5:36; 17:4). As a result, he himself—to see whom is to see the Father (cf. *Jn.* 14:9)—completed and perfected Revelation and confirmed it with divine guarantees. He did this by the total fact of his presence and self-manifes-

tation—by words and works, signs and miracles, but above all by his death and glorious resurrection from the dead, and finally by sending the Spirit of truth. He revealed that God was with us, to deliver us from the darkness of sin and death, and to raise us up to eternal life.

1018 The Christian economy, therefore, since it is the new and definite covenant, will never pass away; and no new public revelation is to be expected before the glorious manifestation of our Lord, Jesus Christ (cf. *1 Tim.* 6:14 and *Tit.* 2:13).

1019 5. "The obedience of faith" (*Rom.*16:26; cf. *Rom.* 1:5; *2 Cor.* 10:5-6) must be given to God as he reveals himself. By faith man freely commits his entire self to God, making "the full submission of his intellect and will to God who reveals,"[4] and willingly assenting to the Revelation given by him. Before this faith can be exercised, man must have the grace of God to move and assist him; he must have the interior helps of the Holy Spirit, who moves the heart and converts it to God, who opens the eyes of the mind and "makes it easy for all to accept and believe the truth."[5] The same Holy Spirit constantly perfects faith by his gifts, so that Revelation may be more and more profoundly understood.

1020 6. By divine Revelation God wished to manifest and communicate both himself and the eternal decrees of his will concerning the salvation of mankind. He wished, in other words, "to share with us divine benefits which entirely surpass the powers of the human mind to understand."[6]

1021 The sacred Synod professes that "God, the first principle and last end of all things, can be known with certainty from the created world, by the natural light of human reason" (cf. *Rom.* 1:20). It teaches that it is to his Revelation that we must attribute the fact "that those things, which in themselves are not beyond the grasp of human reason, can, in the present condition of the human race, be known by all men with ease, with firm certainty, and without the contamination of error."[7]

Chapter II

THE TRANSMISSION OF DIVINE REVELATION

7. God graciously arranged that the things he had once revealed for the salvation of all peoples should remain in their entirety, throughout the ages, and be transmitted to all generations. Therefore, Christ the Lord, in whom the entire Revelation of the most high God is summed up (cf. 2 *Cor.* 1:20; 3:16-4, 6) commanded the apostles to preach the Gospel which he fulfilled in his own person and promulgated with his own lips. In preaching the Gospel they were to communicate the gifts of God to all men. This Gospel was to be the source of all saving truth and moral discipline.[8] This was faithfully done: it was done by the apostles who handed on, by the spoken word of their preaching, by the example they gave, by the institutions they established, what they themselves had received—whether from the lips of Christ, from his way of life and his works, or whether they had learned it at the prompting of the holy Spirit; it was done by those apostles and other men associated with the apostles who, under the inspiration of the same Holy Spirit, committed the message of salvation to writing.[9] 1022

In order that the full and living Gospel might always be preserved in the Church the apostles left bishops as their successors. They gave them "their own position of teaching authority."[10] This sacred Tradition, then, and the sacred Scripture of both Testaments, are like a mirror, in which the Church, during its pilgrim journey here on earth, contemplates God, from whom she receives everything, until such time as she is brought to see him face to face as he really is (cf. *Jn.* 3:2). 1023

8. Thus, the apostolic preaching, which is expressed in a special way in the inspired books, was to be preserved in a continuous line of succession until the end of time. Hence the apostles, in handing on what they themselves had received, warned the faithful to maintain the traditions which they had 1024

learned either by word of mouth or by letter (cf. 2 *Th.* 2:15); and they warn them to fight hard for the faith that had been handed on to them once and for all (cf. *Jude* 3).[11] What was handed on by the apostles comprises everything that serves to make the People of God live their lives in holiness and increase their faith. In this way the Church, in her doctrine, life and worship, perpetuates and transmits to every generation all that she herself is, all that she believes.

1025 The Tradition that comes from the apostles makes progress in the Church, with the help of the Holy Spirit.[12] There is a growth in insight into the realities and words that are being passed on. This comes about in various ways. It comes through the contemplation and study of believers who ponder these things in their hearts (cf. *Lk.* 2:19 and 51). It comes from the intimate sense of spiritual realities which they experience. And it comes from the preaching of those who have received, along with their right of succession in the episcopate, the sure charism of truth. Thus, as the centuries go by, the Church is always advancing towards the plenitude of divine truth, until eventually the words of God are fulfilled in her.

1026 The sayings of the Holy Fathers are a witness to the life-giving presence of this Tradition, showing how its riches are poured out in the practice and life of the Church, in her belief and her prayer. By means of the same Tradition the full canon of the sacred books is known to the Church and the holy Scriptures themselves are more thoroughly understood and constantly actualized in the Church. Thus God, who spoke in the past, continues to converse with the spouse of his beloved Son. And the Holy Spirit, through whom the living voice of the Gospel rings out in the Church—and through her in the world—leads believers to the full truth, and makes the Word of Christ dwell in them in all its richness (cf. *Col.* 3:16).

1027 9. Sacred Tradition and sacred Scripture, then, are bound closely together, and communicate one with the other. For both of them, flowing out from the same divine well-spring, come together in some fashion to form one thing, and move towards the same goal. Sacred Scripture is the speech of God as it is put down in writing under the breath of the Holy Spirit. It transmits it to the successors of the apostles to that, enlightened by the Spirit of truth, they may faithfully preserve, expound and spread it abroad by their preaching. Thus it comes about that the Church does not draw her certainty about all revealed truths from the holy Scriptures alone. Hence, both Scripture and Tradition must be accepted and honoured with equal feelings of devotion and reverence.[13]

10. Sacred Tradition and sacred Scripture make up a single sacred deposit of the Word of God, which is entrusted to the Church. By adhering to it the entire holy people, united to its pastors, remains always faithful to the teaching of the apostles, to the brotherhood, to the breaking of bread and the prayers (cf. *Acts* 2:42 Greek). So, in maintaining, practicing and professing the faith that has been handed on there should be a remarkable harmony between the bishops and the faithful.[14] 1028

But the task of giving an authentic interpretation of the Word of God, whether in its written form or in the form of Tradition,[15] has been entrusted to the living teaching office of the Church alone.[16] Its authority in this matter is exercised in the name of Jesus Christ. Yet this Magisterium is not superior to the Word of God, but is its servant. It teaches only what has been handed on to it. At the divine command and with the help of the Holy Spirit, it listens to this devotedly, guards it with dedication and expounds it faithfully. All that it proposes for belief as being divinely revealed is drawn from this single deposit of faith. 1029

It is clear, therefore, that, in the supremely wise arrangement of God, sacred Tradition, sacred Scripture and the Magisterium of the Church are so connected and associated that one of them cannot stand without the others. Working together, each in its own way under the action of the one Holy Spirit, they all contribute effectively to the salvation of souls. 1030

Chapter III

SACRED SCRIPTURE: ITS DIVINE INSPIRATION AND ITS INTERPRETATION

1031 11. The divinely revealed realities, which are contained and presented in the text of sacred Scripture, have been written down under the inspiration of the Holy Spirit. For Holy Mother Church relying on the faith of the apostolic age, accepts as sacred and canonical the books of the Old and the New Testaments, whole and entire, with all their parts, on the grounds that, written under the inspiration of the Holy Spirit (cf. *Jn.* 20:31; 2 *Tim.* 3:16; 2 *Pet.* 1:19-21; 3:15-16), they have God as their author, and have been handed on as such to the Church herself.[17] To compose the sacred books, God chose certain men who, all the while he employed them in this task, made full use of their powers and faculties[18] so that, though he acted in them and by them,[19] it was as true authors that they consigned to writing whatever he wanted written, and no more.[20]

1032 Since, therefore, all that the inspired authors, or sacred writers, affirm should be regarded as affirmed by the Holy Spirit, we must acknowledge that the books of Scripture, firmly, faithfully and without error, teach that truth which God, for the sake of our salvation, wished to see confided to the sacred Scriptures.[21] Thus "all Scripture is inspired by God, and profitable for teaching, for reproof, for correction and for training in righteousness, so that the man of God may be complete, equipped for every good work" (2 *Tim.* 3:16-17, Gk. text).

1033 12. Seeing that, in sacred Scripture, God speaks through men in human fashion,[22] it follows that the interpreter of sacred Scriptures, if he is to ascertain what God has wished to communicate to us, should carefully search out the meaning which the sacred writers really had in mind, that meaning which God had thought well to manifest through the medium of their words.

1034 In determining the intention of the sacred writers, attention must be paid, *inter alia*, to "literary forms for the fact is that truth is differently presented and expressed in the various types of historical writing, in prophetical and poetical texts," and in other forms of literary expression. Hence the exegete must look for that meaning which the sacred writer, in a determined situation and given the circumstances of his time and culture, intended to express and did in fact express, through the medium of a contemporary literary form.[21] Rightly to understand what the sacred author wanted to affirm in his works, due attention must be paid both to the customary and characteristic patterns of perception, speech and narrative which prevailed at the age of the sacred writer, and to the conventions which the people of his time followed in their dealings with one another.[24]

1035 But since sacred Scripture must be read and interpreted with its divine authorship in mind,[25] no less attention must be devoted to the content and unity of the whole of Scripture, taking into account the Tradition of the entire Church and the analogy of faith, if we are to derive their true meaning from the sacred texts. It is the task of exegets to work, according to these rules, towards a better understanding and explanation of the meaning of sacred Scripture in order that their research may help the Church to form a firmer judgment. For, of course, all that has been said about the manner of interpreting Scripture is ultimately subject to the judgment of the Church which exercises the divinely conferred commission and ministry of watching over and interpreting the Word of God.[26]

1036 13. Hence, in sacred Scripture, without prejudice to God's truth and holiness, the marvellous "condescension" of eternal wisdom is plain to be seen "that we may come to know the ineffable loving-kindness of God and see for ourselves how far he has gone in adapting his language with thoughtful concern for our nature."[27] Indeed the words of God, expressed in the words of men, are in every way like human language, just as the Word of the eternal Father, when he took on himself the flesh of human weakness, became like men.

Chapter IV

THE OLD TESTAMENT

1037 14. God, with loving concern contemplating, and making preparation for, the salvation of the whole human race, in a singular undertaking chose for himself a people to whom he should entrust his promises. By his covenant with Abraham (cf. *Gen.* 15:18) and, through Moses, with the race of Israel (cf. *Ex.* 24:8), he did acquire a people for himself, and to them he revealed himself in words and deeds as the one, true, living God, so that Israel might experience the ways of God with men. Moreover, by listening to the voice of God speaking to them through the prophets, they had daily to understand his ways more fully and more clearly, and make them more widely known among the nations (cf. *Ps.* 21:28-29; 95: 1-3; *Is.* 2:1-4; *Jer.* 3:17). Now the economy of salvation, foretold, recounted and explained by the sacred authors, appears as the true Word of God in the books of the Old Testament, that is why these books, divinely inspired, preserve a lasting value: "For whatever was written in former days was written for our instruction, that by steadfastness and the encouragement of the Scriptures we might have hope" (*Rom.* 15:4).

1038 15. The economy of the Old Testament was deliberately so orientated that it should prepare for and declare in prophecy the coming of Christ, redeemer of all men, and of the messianic kingdom (cf. *Lk.* 24:44; *Jn.* 5:39; 1 *Pet.* 1:10), and should indicate it by means of different types (cf. 1 *Cor.* 10: 11). For in the context of the human situation before the era of salvation established by Christ, the books of the Old Testament provide an understanding of God and man and make clear to all men how a just and merciful God deals with mankind. These books, even though they contain matters imperfect and provisional, nevertheless show us authentic divine teachings.[28] Christians should accept with veneration these writings which give expression to a lively sense of God, which are a storehouse of sublime teaching on God and of sound wisdom on human life, as well as a wonderful treasury of prayers; in them, too, the mystery of our salvation is present in a hidden way.

16. God, the inspirer and author of the books of both Testaments, in his wisdom has so brought it about that the New should be hidden in the Old and that the Old should be made manifest in the New.[29] For, although Christ founded the New Covenant in his blood (cf. *Lk.* 22:20; 1 *Cor.* 11:25), still the books of the Old Testament, all of them caught up into the Gospel message,[30] attain and show forth their full meaning in the New Testament (cf. *Mt.* 5:17; *Lk.* 24:27; *Rom.* 16:25-26; 2 *Cor.* 3:14-16) and, in their turn, shed light on it and explain it. 1039

Chapter V

THE NEW TESTAMENT

17. The Word of God, which is the power of God for salvation to everyone who has faith (cf. *Rom.* 1:16), is set forth and displays its power in a most wonderful way in the writings of the New Testament. For when the time had fully come (cf. *Gal.* 4:4), the Word became flesh and dwelt among us full of grace and truth (cf. *Jn.* 1:14). Christ established on earth the kingdom of God, revealed his Father and himself by deeds and words; and by his death, resurrection and glorious ascension, as well as by sending the Holy Spirit, completed his work. Lifted up from the earth he draws all men to himself (cf. *Jn.* 10:32, Gk. text), for he alone has the words of eternal life (cf. *Jn.* 6:68). This mystery was not made known to other generations as it has now been revealed to his holy apostles and prophets by the Holy Spirit (cf. *Eph.* 3:4-6, Gk. text), that they might preach the Gospel, stir up faith in Jesus Christ and the Lord, and bring together the Church. The writings of the New Testament stand as a perpetual and divine witness to these realities. 1040

18. It is common knowledge that among all the inspired writings, even among those of the New Testament, the Gospels have a special place, and rightly so, because they are our 1041

principal source for the life and teaching of the Incarnate Word, our Saviour.

1042 The Church has always and everywhere maintained, and continues to maintain, the apostolic origin of the four Gospels. The apostles preached, as Christ had charged them to do, and then, under the inspiration of the Holy Spirit, they and others of the apostolic age handed on to us in writing the same message they had preached, the foundation of our faith: the fourfold Gospel, according to Matthew, Mark, Luke and John.[31]

1043 19. Holy Mother Church has firmly and with absolute constancy maintained and continues to maintain, that the four gospels just named, whose historicity she unhesitatingly affirms, faithfully hand on what Jesus, the Son of God, while he lived among men, really did and taught for their eternal salvation, until the day when he was taken up (cf. *Acts* 1:1-2). For, after the ascension of the Lord, the apostles handed on to their hearers what he had said and done, but with that fuller understanding which they, instructed by the glorious events of Christ and enlightened by the Spirit of truth,[32] now enjoyed.[33] The sacred authors, in writing the four Gospels, selected certain of the many elements which had been handed on, either orally or already in written form, others they synthesized or explained with an eye to the situation of the churches, the while sustaining the form of preaching, but always in such a fashion that they have told us the honest truth about Jesus.[34] Whether they relied on their own memory and recollections or on the testimony of those who "from the beginning were eyewitnesses and ministers of the Word," their purpose in writing was that we might know the "truth" concerning the things of which we have been informed (cf. *Lk.* 1:2-4).

1044 20. Besides the four Gospels, the New Testament also contains the Epistles of St. Paul and other apostolic writings composed under the inspiration of the Holy Spirit. In accordance with the wise design of God these writings firmly establish those matters which concern Christ the Lord, formulate more and more precisely his authentic teachings, preach the saving power of Christ's divine work and foretell its glorious consummation.

For the Lord Jesus was with his apostles as he had promised (cf. *Mt.* 28:20) and he had sent to them the Spirit, the Counsellor who would guide them into all the truth (cf. *Jn.* 16:13). 1045

Chapter VI

SACRED SCRIPTURE IN THE LIFE OF THE CHURCH

21. The Church has always venerated the divine Scriptures as she venerated the Body of the Lord, in so far as she never ceases, particularly in the sacred liturgy, to partake of the bread of life and to offer it to the faithful from the one table of the Word of God and the Body of Christ. She has always regarded, and continues to regard the Scriptures, taken together with sacred Tradition, as the supreme rule of her faith. For, since they are inspired by God and committed to writing once and for all time, they present God's own Word in an unalterable form, and they make the voice of the Holy Spirit sound again and again in the words of the prophets and apostles. It follows that all the preaching of the Church, as indeed the entire Christian religion, should be nourished and ruled by sacred Scripture. In the sacred books the Father who is in heaven comes lovingly to meet his children, and talks with them. And such is the force and power of of the Word of God that it can serve the Church as her support and vigor, and the children of the Church as strength for their faith, food for the soul, and a pure and lasting fount of spiritual life. Scripture verifies in the most perfect way the words: "The Word of God is living and active" (*Heb.* 4:12), and "is able to build you up and to give you the inheritance among all those who are sanctified" (*Acts* 20:32; cf. *1 Th.* 2:13). 1046

22. Access to sacred Scripture ought to be open wide to the Christian faithful. For this reason the Church, from the very beginning, made her own the ancient translation of the Old Testament called the Septuagint; she honors also the other Eastern translations, and the Latin translations, especially that which is called the Vulgate. But since the Word of God must be readily available at all times, the Church, with motherly concern, sees to it that suitable and correct translations are made into various languages, especially from the original 1047

texts of the sacred books. If it should happen that, when the opportunity presents itself and the authorities of the Church agree, these translations are made in a joint effort with the separated brethren, they may be used by all Christians.

1048 23. The spouse of the incarnate Word, which is the Church, is taught by the Holy Spirit. She strives to reach day by day a more profound understanding of the sacred Scriptures, in order to provide her children with food from the divine words. For this reason also she duly fosters the study of the Fathers, both Eastern and Western, and of the sacred liturgies. Catholic exegetes and other workers in the field of sacred theology should zealously combine their efforts. Under the watchful eye of the sacred Magisterium, and using appropriate techniques they should together set about examining and explaining the sacred texts in such a way that as many as possible of those who are ministers of the divine Word may be able to distribute fruitfully the nourishment of the Scriptures of the People of God. This nourishment enlightens the mind, strengthens the will and fires the hearts of men with the love of God.[35] The sacred Synod encourages those sons of the Church who are engaged in biblical studies constantly to renew their efforts, in order to carry on the work they have so happily begun, with complete dedication and in accordance with the mind of the Church.[36]

1049 24. Sacred theology relies on the written Word of God taken together with sacred Tradition, as on a permanent foundation. By this Word it is most firmly strengthened and constantly rejuvenated, as it searches out, under the light of faith, the full truth stored up in the mystery of Christ. Therefore, the "study of the sacred page" should be the very soul of sacred theology.[37] The ministry of the Word, too—pastoral preaching, catechetics and all forms of Christian instruction, among which the liturgical homily should hold pride of place—is healthily nourished and thrives in holiness through the Word of Scripture.

1050 25. Therefore, all clerics, particularly priests of Christ and others who, as deacons or catechists, are offically engaged in the ministry of the Word, should immerse themselves in the Scriptures by constant sacred reading and diligent study. For it must not happen that anyone becomes "an empty preacher of the Word of God to others, not being a hearer of the Word in his own heart,"[38] when he ought to be sharing the boundless riches of the divine Word with the faithful committed to his care, especially in the sacred liturgy. Likewise, the sacred Synod forcefully and specifically exhorts all the Christian faithful, especially those who live the religious life, to learn "the surpassing knowledge of Jesus Christ" (*Phil.* 3:8) by frequent reading of the divine Scriptures. "Ignorance of the Scriptures is ignorance of Christ."[39] Therefore, let them go gladly to the sacred text itself, whether in the sacred liturgy, which is full of the divine words, or in devout reading, or in such suitable exercises and various other helps which, with the approval and guidance of the pastors of the Church, are happily spreading everywhere in our day. Let them remember, however, that prayer should accompany the reading of sacred Scripture, so that a dialogue takes place between God and man. For, "we speak to him when we pray; we listen to him when we read the divine oracles."[40]

1051 It is for the bishops, "with whom the apostolic doctrine resides"[41] suitably to instruct the faithful entrusted to them in the correct use of the divine books, especially of the New Testament, and in particular of the Gospels. They do this by giving them translations of the sacred texts which are equipped with necessary and really adequate explanations. Thus the children of the Church can familiarize themselves safely and profitably with the sacred Scriptures, and become steeped in their spirit.

1052 Moreover, editions of sacred Scripture, provided with suitable notes, should be prepared for the use of even non-Christians, and adapted to their circumstances. These should be prudently circulated, either by pastors of souls, or by Christians of any rank.

1053 26. So may it come that, by the reading and study of the sacred books "the Word of God may speed on and triumph" (*2 Th.* 3:1) and the treasure of Revelation entrusted to the Church may more and more fill the hearts of men. Just as from constant attendance at the eucharistic mystery the life of the Church draws increase, so a new impulse of spiritual life may be expected from increased veneration of the Word of God, which stands forever" (*Is.* 40:8; cf. *1 Pet.* 1:23-25).

GAUDIUM ET SPES
Selections from
Pastoral Constitution
on the Church in the Modern World
December 7, 1965

THE SITUATION OF MAN IN THE WORLD TODAY

Hope and anguish

At all times the Church carries the responsibility of reading the signs of the time and of interpreting them in the light of the Gospel, if it is to carry out its task. In language intelligible to every generation, she should be able to answer the ever recurring questions which men ask about the meaning of this present life and of the life to come, and how one is related to the other. We must be aware of and understand the aspirations, the yearnings, and the often dramatic features of the world in which we live. An outline of some of the more important features of the modern world forms the subject of the following paragraphs.

1055 Ours is a new age of history with critical and swift upheavals spreading gradually to all corners of the earth. They are the products of man's intelligence and creative activity, but they recoil upon him, upon his judgments and desires, both individual and collective, upon his ways of thinking and acting in regard to people and things. We are entitled then to speak of a real social and cultural transformation whose repercussions are felt too on the religious level.

1056 A transformation of this kind brings with it the serious problems associated with any crisis of growth. Increase in power is not always accompanied by control of that power for the benefit of man. In probing the recesses of his own mind man often seems more uncertain than ever of himself: in the gradual and precise unfolding of the laws of social living, he is perplexed by uncertainty about how to plot its course.

In no other age has mankind enjoyed such an abundance of wealth, resources and economic well-being; and yet a huge proportion of the people of the world is plagued by hunger and extreme need while countless numbers are totally illiterate. At no time have men had such a keen sense of freedom, only to be faced by new forms of slavery in living and thinking. There is on the one hand a lively feeling of unity and of compelling solidarity of mutual dependence, and on the other a lamentable cleavage of bitterly opposing cams. We have not yet seen the last of bitter political, social, and economic hostility, and racial and ideological antagonism, nor are we free from the spectre of a war of total destruction. If there is a growing exchange of ideas, there is still widespread disagreement about the meaning of the words expressing our key concepts. There is lastly a painstaking search for a better material world, without a parallel spiritual advancement. 1057

Small wonder then that many of our contemporaries are prevented by this complex situation from recognizing permanent values and duly applying them to recent discoveries. As a result they hover between hope and anxiety and wonder uneasily about the present course of events. It is a situation that challenges men to reply; they cannot escape. 1058

Deep-seated changes

5. The spiritual uneasiness of today and the changing structure of life are part of a broader upheaval, whose symptoms are the increasing part played on the intellectual level by the mathematical and natural sciences (not excluding the sciences dealing with man himself) and on the practical level by their repercussions on technology. The scientific mentality has wrought a change in the cultural sphere and on habits of 1059

thought, and the progress of technology is now reshaping the face of the earth and has its sights set on the conquest of space.

1060 The human mind is, in a certain sense, broadening its mastery over time—over the past through the insights of history, over the future by foresight and planning. Advances in biology, psychology, and the social sciences not only lead man to greater self-awareness, but provide him with the technical means of molding the lives of whole peoples as well. At the same time the human race is giving more and more thought to the forecasting and control of its own population growth.

1061 The accelerated pace of history is such that one can scarcely keep abreast of it. The destiny of the human race is viewed as a complete whole, no longer, as it were, in the particular histories of various peoples: now it merges into a complete whole. And so mankind substitutes a dynamic and more evolutionary concept of nature for a static one, and the result is an immense series of new problems calling for a new endeavor of analysis and synthesis.

Changes in the social order

1062 6. As a result the traditional structure of local communities—family, clan, tribe, village, various groupings and social relationships—is subjected to ever more sweeping changes. Industrialization is on the increase and has raised some nations to a position of affluence, while it radically transfigures ideas and social practices hallowed by centuries. Urbanization too is on the increase, both on account of the expanding number of city dwellers and the spread of an urban way of life into rural settings. Recent more efficient mass media are contributing to the spread of knowledge and the speedy diffusion far and wide of habits of thought and feeling, setting off chain reactions in their wake. One cannot underestimate the effect of emigration on those who, for whatever reason, are led to undertake a new way of life. On the whole, the bonds uniting man to his fellows multiply without ceasing, and "socialization" creates yet other bonds, without, however, a corresponding personal development, and truly personal relationships "personalization." It is above all in countries with advanced standards of economic and social progress that these developments are evident, but there are stirrings for advancement afoot among peoples eager to share in the benefits of industrialization and urbanization. Peoples like these, especially where ancient traditions are still strong, are at the same time conscious of the need to exercise their freedom in a more mature and personal way.

Changes in attitudes, morals and religion

7. A change in attitudes and structures frequently calls accepted values into question. This is true above all of young people who have grown impatient at times and, indeed, rebellious in their distress. Conscious of their own importance in the life of society, they aspire to play their part in it all the sooner. 1063

As regards religion there is a completely new atmosphere that conditions its practice. On the one hand people are taking a hard look at all magical world-views and prevailing superstitions and demanding a more personal and active commitment of faith, so that not a few have achieved a lively sense of the divine. On the other hand greater numbers are falling away from the practice of religion. In the past it was the exception to repudiate God and religion to the point of abandoning them, and then only in individual cases; but nowadays it seems a matter of course to reject them as incompatible with scientific progress and a new kind of humanism. In many places it is not only in philosophical terms that such trends are expressed, but there are signs of them in literature, art, the humanities, the interpretation of history and even civil law: all of which is very disturbing to many people. 1064

Imbalances in the world of today

8. The headlong development of the world and a keener awareness of existing inequalities make for the creation and 1065

aggravation of differences and imbalances. On the personal level there often arises an imbalance between an outlook which is practical and modern and a way of thinking which fails to master and synthesize the sum total of its ideas. Another imbalance occurs between concern for practicality and the demands of moral conscience, not to mention that between the claims of group living and the needs of individual reflection and contemplation. A third imbalance takes the form of conflict between specialization and an overall view of reality.

1066 On the family level there are tensions arising out of demographic, economic and social pressures, out of conflicts between succeeding generations, and out of new social relationships between the sexes.

1067 On the level of race and social class we find tensions between the affluent and the underdeveloped nations; we find them between international bodies set up in the interests of peace and ambitions of ideological indoctrination along with national or block expansionism. In the midst of it all stands man, at once the author and the victim of mutual distrust, animosity, conflict and woe.

Broader aspirations of mankind

1068 9. Meanwhile there is a growing conviction of mankind's ability and duty to strengthen its mastery over nature and of the need to establish a political, social, and economic order at the service of man to assert and develop the dignity proper to individuals and to societies.

1069 Great numbers of people are acutely conscious of being deprived of the world's goods through injustice and unfair distribution and are vehemently demanding their share of them. Developing nations like the recently independent states are anxious to share in the political and economic benefits of modern civilization and to play their part freely in the world, but they are hampered by their economic dependence on the rapidly expanding richer nations and the ever widening gap between them. The hungry nations cry out to their affluent neighbors; women claim parity with men in fact as well as of rights, where they have not already obtained it; farmers and workers insist not just on the necessities of life but also on the opportunity to develop by their labor their personal talents and to play their due role in organizing economic, social, political, and cultural life. Now for the first time in history people are not afraid to think that cultural benefits are for all and should be available to everybody.

These claims are but the sign of a deeper and more widespread aspiration. Man as an individual and as a member of society craves a life that is full, autonomous, and worthy of his nature as a human being; he longs to harness for his own welfare the immense resources of the modern world. Among nations there is a growing movement to set up a worldwide community. 1070

In the light of the foregoing factors there appears the dichotomy of a world that is at once powerful and weak, capable of doing what is noble and what is base, disposed to freedom and slavery, progress and decline, brotherhood and hatred. Man is growing conscious that the forces he has unleashed are in his own hands and that it is up to him to control them or be enslaved by them. Here lies the modern dilemma. 1071

Man's deeper questionings

10. The dichotomy affecting the modern world is, in fact, a symptom of the deeper dichotomy that is in man himself. He is the meeting point of many conflicting forces. In his condition as a created being he is subject to a thousand shortcomings, but feels untrammeled in his inclinations and destined for a higher form of life. Torn by a welter of anxieties he is compelled to choose between them and repudiate some among them. Worse still, feeble and sinful as he is, he often does the very thing he hates and does not do what he wants.[1] And so he feels himself divided, and the result is a host of discords in social life. Many, it is true, fail to see the dramatic nature of this state of affairs in all its clarity for their vision is in fact blurred by materialism, or they are prevented from even thinking about it by the wretchedness 1072

of their plight. Others delude themselves that they have found peace in a world-view now fashionable. There are still others whose hopes are set on a genuine and total emancipation of mankind through human effort alone and look forward to some future earthly paradise where all the desires of their hearts will be fulfilled. Nor is it unusual to find people who having lost faith in life extol the kind of foolhardiness which would empty life of all significance in itself and invest it with a meaning of their own devision. Nonetheless, in the face of modern developments there is a growing body of men who are asking the most fundamental of all questions or are glimpsing them with a keener insight: What is man? What is the meaning of suffering, evil, death, which have not been eliminated by all this progress? What is the purpose of these achievements, purchased at so high a price? What can man contribute to society? What can he expect from it? What happens after this earthly life is ended?

1073 The Church believes that Christ, who died and was raised for the sake of all,[2] can show man the way and strengthen him through the Spirit in order to be worthy of his destiny: nor is there any other name under heaven given among men by which they can be saved.[3] The Church likewise believes that the key, the center and the purpose of the whole of man's history is to be found in its Lord and Master. She also maintains that beneath all that changes there is much that is unchanging, much that has its ultimate foundation in Christ, who is the same yesterday, and today, and forever.4 And that is why the Council, relying on the inspiration of Christ, the image of the invisible God, the firstborn of all creation,[5] proposes to speak to all men in order to unfold the mystery that is man and cooperate in tackling the main problems facing the world today.

CHRIST THE NEW MAN

1074 22. In reality it is only in the mystery of the Word made flesh that the mystery of man truly becomes clear. For Adam, the first man, was a type of him who was to come,[6] Christ the Lord, Christ the new Adam, in the very revelation of the mystery of the Father and of his love, fully reveals man to himself and brings to light his most high calling. It is no wonder, then, that all the truths mentioned so far should find in him their source and their most perfect embodiment.

He who is the "image of the invisible God" (*Col.* 1:15),[7] is himself the perfect man who has restored in the children of Adam that likeness to God which had been disfigured ever since the first sin. Human nature, by the very fact that it was assumed, not absorbed, in him, has been raised in us also to a dignity beyond compare.[8] For, by his incarnation, he, the son of God, has in a certain way united himself with each man. He worked with human hands, he thought with a human mind. He acted with a human will,[9] and with a human heart he loved. Born of the Virgin Mary, he has truly been made one of us, like to us in all things except sin.[10] 1075

As an innocent lamb he merited life for us by his blood which he freely shed. In him God reconciled us to himself and to one another,[11] freeing us from the bondage of the devil and of sin, so that each one of us could say with the apostle: the Son of God "loved me and gave himself for me" (*Gal.* 2:20). By suffering for us he not only gave us an example so that we might follow in his footsteps,[12] but he also opened up a way. If we follow this path, life and death are made holy and acquire a new meaning. 1076

Conformed to the image of the Son who is the firstborn of many brothers,[13] the Christian man receives the "first fruits of the Spirit" (*Rom.* 8:23) by which he is able to fulfil the new law of love.[14] By this Spirit, who is the "pledge of our inheritance" (*Eph.* 1:14), the whole man is inwardly renewed, right up to the "redemption of the body" (*Rom.* 8:23). "If the Spirit of him who raised Jesus from the dead dwells in you, he who raised Christ Jesus from the dead will give life to your mortal bodies also through his Spirit who dwells in you" (*Rom.* 8:11).[15] The Christian is certainly bound both by need and by duty to struggle with evil through many afflictions and to suffer death; but, as one who has been made a partner in the paschal mystery, and as one who has been configured to the death of Christ, he will go forward, strengthened by hope, to the resurrection.[16] 1077

1078 All this holds true not for Christians only but also for all men of good will in whose hearts grace is active invisibly.[17] For since Christ died for all,[18] and since all men are in fact called to one and the same destiny, which is divine, we must hold that the Holy Spirit offers to all the possibility of being made partners, in a way known to God, in the paschal mystery.

1079 Such is the nature and the greatness of the mystery of man as enlightened for the faithful by the Christian revelation. It is therefore through Christ, and in Christ, that light is thrown on the riddle of suffering and death which, apart from his Gospel, overwhelms us. Christ has risen again, destroying death by his death, and has given life abundantly to us[19] so that, becoming sons in the Son, we may cry out in the Spirit: Abba, Father![20]

CHRIST: ALPHA AND OMEGA

1080 45. Whether it aids the world or whether it benefits from it, the Church has but one sole purpose—that the kingdom of God may come and the salvation of the human race may be accomplished. Every benefit the people of God can confer on mankind during its earthly pilgrimage is rooted in the Church's being "the universal sacrament of salvation,"[21] at once manifesting and actualizing the mystery of God's love for men.

1081 The Word of God, through whom all things were made, was made flesh, so that as a perfect man he could save all men and sum up all things in himself. The Lord is the goal of human history, the focal point of the desires of history and civilization, the center of mankind, the joy of all hearts, and the fulfilment of all aspirations.[22] It is he whom the Father raised from the dead, exalted and placed at his right hand, constituting him judge of the living and the dead. Animated and drawn together in his Spirit we press onwards on our journey towards the consummation of history which fully corresponds to the plan of his love: "to unite all things in him, things in heaven and things on earth" (*Eph.* 1:10).

The Lord himself said: "Behold, I am coming soon, bringing my recompense, to repay every one for what he has done. I am the alpha and the omega, the first and the last, the beginning and the end" (*Apoc.* 22:12-13). 1082

Solemn Profession of Faith by Pope Paul VI at the Closing of the Year of Faith June 30, 1968

With this solemn liturgy We end the celebration of the 19th centenary of the martyrdom of the holy Apostles Peter and Paul, and thus close the Year of Faith. We dedicated it to commemoration of the holy Apostles in order that We might give witness to Our steadfast will to *keep undefiled the deposit*[1] of the faith which they transmitted to Us, and that We might strengthen Our desire to live by it in the historical circumstances in which the Church finds herself in her pilgrimage in the midst of the world.

1084 We feel it Our duty to give public thanks to all who responded to Our invitation by bestowing on the Year of Faith a splendid fruitfulness through the deepening of their personal adherence to the Word of God, through the renewal in various communities of the profession of faith, and through the testimony of a Christian life. To Our brothers in the episcopate especially, and to all the faithful of the holy Catholic Church, We express Our appreciation and We grant Our blessing.

1085 Moreover, We deem that We must fulfill the mandate entrusted by Christ to Peter, whose successor We are, though the least in merit; namely, *to confirm Our brothers*[2] in the faith. With the awareness, certainly, of Our human weakness, yet with all the strength impressed on Our spirit by such a command, We shall accordingly make a profession of faith, pronounce a creed which, without being strictly speaking a dogmatic definition, repeats in substance—with some developments called for by the spiritual condition of our time—the creed of Nicaea, the creed of the immortal Tradition of the holy Church of God.

1086 In making this profession, We are aware of the disquiet which disturbs some of the convictions of men today with regard to the faith. They do not escape the influence of a profoundly changing world, in which so many certainties are being denied or disputed. We see even Catholics allowing themselves to be seized by a kind of passion for change and novelty. The Church, most assuredly, always has the duty to carry on the effort to study more deeply and to present in a manner ever better adapted to successive generations the unfathomable mysteries of God, rich for all in the fruits of salvation. But at the same time the greatest care must be taken, while fulfilling the indispensable duty of research, to do no injury to the teachings of Christian doctrine. For that would give rise, as is unfortunately seen in these days, to disturbance and perplexity in many faithful souls.

1087 It is important in this respect to recall that, beyond scientifically verified phenomena, the intellect which God has given us reaches *that which is*, and not merely the subjective expression of the structures and development of consciousness; and on the other hand, that the task of interpretation—of hermeneutics—is to try to understand and extricate, while respecting the word expressed, the meaning conveyed by a test, and not to refashion this meaning in some manner, in accordance with arbitrary hypotheses.

1088 But above all, We place our unshakable confidence in the Holy Spirit, the soul of the Church, and the source of every true progress in truth and charity and theological faith, upon which rests the life of the Mystical Body. We know that souls await the word of the Vicar of Christ, and We respond to that expectation with the instructions which We regularly give. But today We are given an opportunity to make a more solemn utterance.

1089 On this day, chosen by Us to close the Year of Faith, on this feast of the blessed Apostles Peter and Paul, We have wished to offer to the living God the homage of a profession of faith. And as once at Caesarea Philippi the Apostle Peter spoke on behalf of the Twelve to make a true confession, beyond human opinions, of Christ as Son of the living God, so today his humble successor, pastor of the universal Church, on behalf of all the People of God, raises his voice to give a firm witness to the divine truth entrusted to the Church to be announced to all nations.

1090 We have wished Our profession of faith to be to a high degree complete and explicit, in order that it may respond in a fitting way to the need for light felt by so many faithful souls, and by all those in the world, to whatever spiritual family they belong, who are in search of the truth.

1091 To the glory of God Most Holy and of Our Lord Jesus Christ, trusting in the aid of the Blessed Virgin Mary and of the holy Apostles Peter and Paul, for the profit and edification of the Church, in the name of all the pastors and all the faithful, We now pronounce this profession of faith, in full spiritual communion with all of you, beloved brothers and sons.

1092 We believe in one only God, Father, Son and Holy Spirit, Creator of things visible, such as this world in which our transient life passes; of things invisible, such as the pure spirits which are also called angels;[3] and Creator in each man of his spiritual and immortal soul.

1093 We believe that this only God is absolutely one in His infinitely holy essence as also in all His perfections, in His omnipotence, His infinite knowledge, His providence, His will and His love. *He is He who is,* as He revealed to Moses;[4] and He is *love*, as the Apostle John teaches us:[5] so that these two names, Being and Love, express ineffably the same divine reality of Him who has wished to make Himself known to us, and who, *dwelling in light inaccessible,*[6] is in Himself above every name, above everything and above every created intellect. God alone can give us right and full knowledge of this reality by revealing Himself as Father, Son and Holy Spirit, in whose eternal life we are called by grace to share, here below in the obscurity of faith and after death in eternal light.

The mutual bonds which eternally constitute the Three Persons, who are each one and the same Divine Being, are the blessed inmost life of God Thrice Holy, infinitely beyond all that we can conceive in human measure.[7] We give thanks to the Divine Goodness, however, that many believers can testify with us before men to the Unity of God, even though they do not know the mystery of the Most Holy Trinity. 1094

We believe then in the Father, who eternally begets the Son; in the Son, the Word of God, who is eternally begotten; in the Holy Spirit, the uncreated Person who proceeds from the Father and the Son as their eternal Love. Thus in the Three Divine Persons, *coeternal and coequal,*[8] the life and beatitude of God perfectly One superabound and are consummated in the supreme excellence and glory proper to uncreated Being, so that thus *there should be venerated unity in the Trinity and Trinity in the unity.*[9] 1095

We believe in Our Lord Jesus Christ, who is the Son of God. He is the Eternal Word, born of the Father before time began, and one in substance with the Father, *homoousious to Patri,*[10] and through Him all things were made. He was incarnate of the Virgin Mary by the power of the Holy Spirit, and was made man: equal therefore to the Father according to His divinity, and inferior to the Father according to His humanity,[11] and Himself one, not by some impossible confusion of His natures, but by the unity of His person.[12] 1096

He dwelt among us, full of grace and truth. He proclaimed and established the kingdom of God and made us know the Father. He gave us His new commandment to love one another as He loved us. He taught us the way of the Beatitudes of the Gospel: poverty in spirit, meekness, suffering borne with patience, thirst after justice, mercy, purity of heart, will for peace, persecution suffered for justice' sake. 1097

Under Pontius Pilate He suffered, the Lamb of God bearing on Himself the sins of the world; and He died for us on the cross, saving us by His redeeming Blood. He was buried, and rose on the third day of His own power, raising us by His Resurrection to that sharing in the divine life which is grace. He ascended to heaven, and He will come again, this 1098 time in glory, to judge the living and the dead: each according to his merits—those who have responded to the love and kindness of God going to eternal life, those who have refused them to the end going to the fire that is not extinguished.

1099 And His kingdom will have no end.

1100 We believe in the Holy Spirit, who is Lord and Giver of life, who is adored and glorified together with the Father and the Son. He spoke to us by the prophets; He was sent by Christ after His Resurrection and His Ascension to the Father. He illuminates, vivifies, protects and guides the Church; He purifies the Church's members, provided that they do not shun His grace. His action, which penetrates to the inmost soul, enables man to respond to the call of Jesus: Be perfect as your heavenly Father is perfect.

1101 We believe that Mary is the Mother, who remained ever a Virgin, of the Incarnate Word, our God and Saviour Jesus Christ,[13] and that she was, in consideration of the merits of her Son, redeemed in a more sublime manner,[14] preserved immune from all stain of original sin,[15] and by the gift of grace far surpasses all other creatures.[16]

1102 Joined by a close and indissoluble bond to the mystery of the Incarnation and Redemption,[17] the Blessed Virgin Mary, the Immaculate, was raised body and soul to heavenly glory at the end of her earthly life,[18] and was made like her risen Son in anticipation of the future lot of all the just; and We believe that the Blessed Mother of God, the New Eve, Mother of the Church,[19] continues in heaven her maternal role with regard to Christ's members, cooperating with the birth and growth of divine life in the souls of the redeemed.[20]

1103 We believe that in Adam all have sinned, which means that the original offense committed by him caused human nature, common to all men, to fall to a state in which it bears the consequences of that offense, and which is not the state in which it was at first in our first parents, established as they were in holiness and justice, and in which men knew neither evil nor death. It is human nature so fallen, stripped of the grace that clothed it, injured in its own natural powers and subjected to the dominion of death, that is transmitted to all men, and it is in this sense that every man is born in sin. We therefore hold, with the Council of Trent, that original sin is transmitted with human nature, *not by imitation but by propagation,* and that it is thus *proper to everyone.*[21]

We believe that Our Lord Jesus Christ, by the sacrifice of the cross, redeemed us from original sin and all the personal sins committed by each one of us, so that, in accordance with the word of the Apostle, "*where the offense has abounded, grace has abounded yet more.*"[22] 1104

We believe in one Baptism instituted by Our Lord Jesus Christ for the remission of sins. Baptism should be administered even to little children not yet able to be guilty of any personal sin, in order that, though born deprived of supernatural grace, they may be reborn *of water and the Holy Spirit* to the divine life in Christ Jesus.[23] 1105

We believe in one, holy, catholic and apostolic Church, built by Jesus Christ on that rock which is Peter. She is the Mystical Body of Christ; at the same time a visible society instituted with hierarchical organs, and a spiritual community; the Church on earth, the pilgrim People of God here below, and the Church filled with heavenly blessings; the seed and the first fruits of the kingdom of God, through which the work and the sufferings of Redemption are continued throughout human history, and which looks for its perfect accomplishment beyond time in glory.[24] 1106

In the course of time, the Lord Jesus forms His Church by means of the Sacraments flowing from His abundance.[25] By these she makes her members participants in the mystery of the Death and Resurrection of Christ, in the grace of the Holy Spirit who gives her life and movement.[26] She is therefore holy, though she has sinners in her midst, because she herself has no other life but that of grace: it is through living by her life that her members are sanctified; it is through removing themselves from her life that they fall into sins and disorders that prevent the radiation of her sanctity. This is why she suffers and does penance for these offenses, of which she has the power to heal her children through the Blood of Christ and the gift of the Holy Spirit. 1107

Heiress of the divine promises and daughter of Abraham according to the Spirit, through that Israel whose Scriptures 1108 she lovingly guards, and whose Patriarchs and Prophets she venerates; founded upon the Apostles and transmitting from century to century their ever-living words and their powers as pastors in the successor of Peter and the bishops in communion with him; perpetually assisted by the Holy Spirit, she has the charge of guarding, teaching, explaining and spreading the truth which God revealed in a somewhat veiled manner by the Prophets, and fully and absolutely through the Lord Jesus. We believe all that is contained in the word of God written or handed down, and that the Church proposes for belief as divinely revealed, whether by a solemn judgment or by the ordinary and universal magisterium.[27] We believe in the infallibility enjoyed by the successor of Peter when he teaches *ex cathedra* as pastor and teacher of all the faithful,[28] and which is assured also to the episcopal body when it exercises with him the supreme magisterium.[29]

1109 We believe that the Church founded by Jesus Christ and for which He prayed is indefectibly one in faith, worship and the bond of hierarchical communion. In the bosom of this Church, the rich variety of liturgical rites and the legitimate diversity of theological and spiritual heritages and special disciplines, far from injuring her unity, make it more manifest.[30]

1110 Recognizing also the existence of numerous elements of truth and sanctification outside the organism of the Church of Christ, which belong to her as her own and tend to Catholic unity,[31] and believing in the action of the Holy Spirit—who stirs up in the heart of Christ's disciples the desire for this unity[32]—We hope that the Christians who are not yet in the full communion of the one Church will at last be united in one flock with one shepherd.

1111 We believe that the Church is necessary for salvation, because Christ, who is the sole Mediator and Way of salvation, renders Himself present for us in His Body which is the Church.[33] But the divine design of salvation embraces all men; and those who without fault on their part do not know the Gospel of Christ and His Church, but seek God sincerely, and endeavor under the influence of grace to do His will as recognized through the promptings of their conscience, can, in a number known only to God, obtain salvation.[34]

We believe that the Mass, celebrated by the priest representing the person of Christ by virtue of the power received through the Sacrament of Orders, and offered by him in the name of Christ and the members of His Mystical Body, is the Sacrifice of Calvary rendered sacramentally present on our altars. We believe that as the bread and wine consecrated by the Lord at the Last Supper were changed into His Body and His Blood which were to be offered for us on the cross, so the bread and wine consecrated by the priest are changed into the Body and Blood of Christ enthroned gloriously in heaven, and We believe that the mysterious presence of the Lord, under the appearance of those elements which seem to our senses the same after as before the Consecration, is a true, real and substantial presence.[35] 1112

Christ cannot be thus present in this Sacrament except by the change into His Body of the reality itself of the bread and the change into His Blood of the reality itself of the wine, leaving unchanged only the properties of the bread and wine which our senses perceive. This mysterious change is very appropriately called by the Church *transubstantiation*. Every theological explanation which seeks some understanding of this mystery must, in order to be in accord with Catholic faith, maintain that in the reality itself, independently of our mind, the bread and wine have ceased to exist after the Consecration, so that it is the adorable Body and Blood of the Lord Jesus that from then on are really before us under the sacramental species of bread and wine,[36] as the Lord willed it, in order to give Himself to us as food and to associate us with the unity of His Mystical Body.[37] 1113

The unique and indivisible existence of Christ the Lord glorious in heaven is not multiplied, but is rendered present by the Sacrament in the many places on earth where Mass is celebrated. Thus we have that *mystery of faith* and of Eucharistic riches, to which we must without any exception assent. And this existence remains present, after the Sacrifice, in the Blessed Sacrament which is, in the tabernacle, the living heart of each of our churches. And it is our very sweet duty to 1114 honor and adore in the Blessed Host, which our eyes see, the Incarnate Word whom they cannot see, and who, without leaving heaven, is made present before us.

1115 We confess that the kingdom of God begun here below in the Church of Christ is not of this world, whose form is passing, and that its proper growth cannot be confounded with the progress of civilization, of science or of human technology; but that it consists in an ever more profound knowledge of the unfathomable riches of Christ, an ever stronger hope in eternal blessings, an ever more ardent response to the love of God, and an ever more generous bestowal of grace and holiness among men.

1116 But it is this same love which induces the Church to concern herself constantly about the true temporal welfare of men. Without ceasing to recall to her children that they have not here a lasting dwelling, she also urges them to contribute, each according to his vocation and his means, to the welfare of their earthly city, to promote justice, peace and brotherhood among men, to give their aid freely to their brothers, especially to the poorest and most unfortunate.

1117 The deep solicitude of the Church, the Spouse of Christ, for the needs of men, for their joys and hopes, their griefs and efforts, is therefore nothing other than her great desire to be present to them, in order to illuminate them with the light of Christ and to gather them all in Him, their only Savior. This solicitude can never mean that the Church conform herself to the things of this world, or that she lessen the ardor of her expectation of her Lord and of the eternal kingdom.

1118 We believe in life eternal. We believe that the souls of all those who die in the grace of Christ—whether they must still be purified in purgatory, or whether from the moment they leave their bodies Jesus takes them to paradise as He did the good thief—are the People of God in the eternity beyond death, which will be finally conquered on the day of resurrection when these souls will be reunited with their bodies.

1119 We believe that the multitude of those gathered around Jesus and Mary in paradise form the Church of heaven, where in eternal beatitude they see God as He is,[38] and where they also, in different degrees, are associated with the holy angels in the divine rule exercised by Christ in glory, interceding for us and helping our weakness by their brotherly care.[39]

We believe in the communion of all the faithful of Christ, those who are pilgrims on earth, the dead who are attaining their purification, and the blessed in heaven, all together forming one Church; and We believe that in this communion the merciful love of God and His saints is ever listening to our prayers, as Jesus told us: Ask and you will receive.[40] Thus it is with faith and in hope that We look forward to the resurrection of the dead, and the life of the world to come. 1120

Blessed be God Thrice Holy. Amen. 1121

Address of Pope Paul VI
to a General Audience
January 13, 1971

Our brief and very simple thoughts are today directed to Christians—that is, to those who do not reject the name but claim it as an essential feature of their personality and culture. But in this shapeless multitude of Christians we may roughly distinguish two main currents, running in opposite directions. One tends to dilute the meaning of the name Christian. Those belonging to this current attach the name as little as possible to their personal life; they empty it (demythologize it, they say today) as much as possible of its original religious and theological content, and keep only certain features which have become basic to civil usage. They accept certain general values which are useful for defining, developing and benefiting man as such—values like dignity, privacy, liberty, sociability, hope, and so on. In other words, they are content with a Christianity that is noble and human, if you will, but vague and open to every sort of personal and provisional interpretation. It is said that we are all Christians, but we might add: each in his own way.

1123 The other current, on the contrary, tends to acknowledge in Christianity a character of considerable commitment to important realities. It recognizes a doctrine, a way of life, a religion, a membership in the Church, a mystery of communion with God and, finally, a personal relationship of faith, hope and love with Christ, the historical Christ of the Gospels, Christ the Savior, whose words and grace the Church preserves and dispenses. This is a personal relationship with the Paschal Christ, who associates every authentic believer with the palingenesis of His Redemption; with the living, heavenly Christ who is present and invisible, who influences the destinies of every man and of mankind, and who will come one day, that day of the final conflagration of history. Today, as always, Christians are walking on a slope: toward a descending Christianity, nominal and evanescent, on the one hand; but toward a rising Christianity on the other—toward the living, personal and real Christ.

1124 We naturally want to belong to this second movement, which is truer, though also harder; it goes toward Jesus Christ, our living and true Lord—He who is sufficient and necessary for giving full and genuine meaning to our existence, He who shows Himself to be the more indispensable and weighty for our world of today, the more this world seeks to forget Him, to exclude Him, to make Him meaningless.

1125 An overpowering desire then arises in us who are followers in the spirit of sincerity and consistency—a desire to get near to this Jesus, to know Him, to see Him. There is in the Gospel an episode which is barely mentioned but full of significance. The evangelist John mentions it in his account of Jesus' entry into Jerusalem in a deliberately public and popular manner, surrounded by the acclaiming, rejoicing crowd, which finally recognized Him as the Son of David, the Messiah. The episode is recounted as follows:

1126 "Now there were certain Gentiles among those who had gone up to worship on the feast. These therefore approached Philip, who was from Bethsaida of Galilee, and asked him, saying, 'Sir, we wish to see Jesus.' "[1] To see Jesus: This is the constant desire of people of goodwill who have been reached by some remarkable news about the mysterious personage upon whom so much restless curiosity and so many loving hopes are centered.

1127 If only we might see Him! If only we could form a faithful image of Him! We who are immersed in the so-called "civilization of the image" would naturally make every claim to fill our gaze with the physical appearance of our Master and Savior. We sometimes think that if we had this good fortune, at least this incentive, we would be more inclined to believe in Him and follow Him, as was the case with those who were spectators in the historical events of the Gospel. But the Gospel itself speaks a word which disappoints our avid wish, and points out to us the now sole and secure way of faith: "Blessed are they who have not seen, and yet have believed."[2] Yes, we must content ourselves with meeting Jesus by way of this delicate and not always easy process of knowledge which is called faith, and which does not exclude, but rather demands rational study of Revelation.

1128 But the psychology of faith needs some representation or image. The history of Christianity tells us that, once they had overcome the Jewish law against representation of living things (made for fear of temptations to idolatry), the faithful tried to sketch Christ's image. At first He was represented as an indistinct person in some Gospel scene (the shepherd, for example), then as a human face (as in the catacombs of Commodilla), then in the priestly features proper to Byzantine paintings; and afterward came all that imagination arising from piety and art which still provides us with Jesus' features, depicted in accordance with the concept our mind has formed of Him.[3] Perhaps the singular image upon the Holy Shroud might deserve special study. But the fact is that "trustworthy sources say absolutely nothing about Jesus' physical features."[4] We are like blind people before a friend. Good and artistic religious iconography helps us to make up for the lack of an actual representation of Him.

1129 But our thoughts go on: Was Jesus handsome? Was He ugly? Such queries mount up as we turn to passages in the Bible which refer to Him and mention one or another feature of the Messiah. They tell us that He was "fairer than the sons of men,"[5] but that He was also "the man of sorrows," who "has no beauty or comeliness."6 If we turn to the Gospel, we find Him transfigured: "His face shone as the sun."7 And we also find Him disfigured: "Jesus therefore came forth"—from the governor's palace—"wearing the crown of thorns and the purple cloak. And Pilate said to them, 'Behold the man!' "[8]

1130 But then? Shall we content ourselves with going through the various Gospel scenes, from the Crib to Calvary, to the

Mount of Olives and the Ascension, asking masters of portraiture to satisfy our loving desire to see His features? This is done, and it is a good thing, for is not "the Bible of the poor," which used to be spoken of, just such an artistic presentation of Jesus and His life? But praise be to those who help us, through these same images, to make a further step.

1131 What kind of a step? A step toward the real Christ, the Christ of faith, the Christ who mirrors the invisible godhead by means of His visibility, as the Christmas Preface reminds us: "While we acknowledge Him to be God seen by men, we may be drawn by Him to the love of things unseen." And let us also remember Christ's own revealing words: "Who sees me sees also the Father."[9] That is, we are authorized to discover God in Jesus![10] Are we aware of what this means? We are on the threshold of the supreme beauty.[11]

1132 What is beauty?[12] Oh, what a long reply would be needed to this elementary question! What flights we should have to make in order to get beyond the often deceptive levels of degraded, tangible, merely aesthetic beauty, so as to reach the level of resplendent truth. That is beauty—the beauty of dazzling Being, of the diaphanous form of full and perfect life! We will say only that Christ is beauty, human and divine beauty, the beauty of reality, truth and life: "The life was the light."[13]

1133 It is not a mythical or mystical emphasis which makes Us cry out this definition of Him; it is the testimony We owe to the Gospel. It is a testimony which We owe to you, brothers and children, you who are urged by the spirit of our time to go looking for the "type," the model, the perfect man. Christ is the "type," the archetype, the prototype of mankind.[14] Remember this. With Our apostolic blessing.

Address of Pope Paul VI
to a General Audience
January 27, 1971

The Christian, who wants to be a follower of Christ, who feels the necessity of getting close to Him through the bonds of authenticity and certainty, will always have an instinctive need to see Him. This is so because he is a man, and especially a man of our time, which lives so much by visual images. The Christian would like to know what Jesus Christ looked like—in features, in carriage and as a person. We have said this before, but the wish is sill there; and it returns when questions arise about the true inspiration of His message and about the duty to conform our conduct to His teaching. Isn't this desire always present in the people of the Gospel? Take Zacchaeus, for example, as described by St. Luke: "He sought to see who Jesus was"; but since he was too short to see Him through the crowd, he climbed into a sycamore tree and there he saw—or rather, was seen by— the Lord, who called him and told him to come down, because He wished to be his guest that day.[1]

1135 But we do not share the good fortune of Jesus' contemporaries, who saw Him with their own eyes.[2] Nor has this been the fortune of any humans born since His time. Even as early as the end of the second century, St. Irenaeus, Bishop of Lyons, gave a warning that the corporeal images of Jesus which had been in circulation till then were apocryphal.[3] St. Augustine stated categorically that "we are quite ignorant" of what Jesus' bodily appearance was like, just as we do not know what our Lady looked like.[4] We must form a picture from elements common to human nature and from the imaginative reflections that come to mind from information about Him acquired through reading the Gospel and believing His word. Art and devotion help in this difficult formulation.

This picture is not vain fantasy. Our effort is meritorious and, in a sense, indispensable for anyone who wants to have a concrete and faithful concept of Christ, one which is ideal but without mythical artificiality. 1136

Let us ask ourselves: how do we picture Christ Jesus to ourselves? That is to say, what characteristic aspect comes to light in the Gospel? What does Jesus seem to be like at first sight? Once again, His own words help us: "I am meek and humble of heart."[5] Jesus wishes to be regarded thus, to be seen in this way. And if we could see Him, that is how He would look, even though the vision of Him which the Apocalypse presents fills His heavenly form with shape and light.[6] This characteristic of sweetness, goodness and above all, meekness, is essential. When we ponder it, we perceive that it both reveals and conceals a fundamental mystery about Christ—the mystery of the Incarnation, of the humble God. 1137

This mystery governs all Christ's life and mission: "The humble Christ is the center of Christology," said St. Augustine.[7] It imbues the whole of the Gospel's teaching in relation to us: "What else does it teach, if not this humility? . . . . In this humility we are able to draw near to God," the Doctor of Hippo also said.[8] And does not St. Paul use a term which suggests the absolute when he tells us that Christ "emptied" Himself: *semetipsum exinanivit?*[9] Jesus is the good man above all, and that is why He descended to the lowest rung of the human ladder. He became a baby, He became poor, He became a sufferer, a victim, so that none of His brothers among mankind might feel He was above or distant from him; He placed Himself at the feet of all. He is for all; He belongs to all—indeed to each of us individually. As St. Paul says: "He loved *me* and gave himself up for me."[10] 1138

So it is no wonder that the iconography of Christ has always sought to express this mildness, this extreme goodness. 1139

Mystical understanding of Him came to contemplate His heart and to make veneration of the Sacred Heart the fervent and symbolic center of Christian devotion and activity for us moderns, concerned as we are with feelings and psychology, and always oriented toward the metaphysics of love.

1140 But now an objection arises, especially today. Is this picture of Christ, who personifies His own preaching—namely, the beatitudes of poverty, meekness and non-resistance[11]—is this the true Christ? Is He the Christ for us? Where is Christ the Pantocrator, the strong Christ, the King of kings, the Lord of lords;[12] Where is the reforming Christ,[13] the polemical Christ, the Christ of contestation[14] and anathemas?[15] Where is the liberating Christ, the Christ of violence?[16] Isn't there talk today of the Christianity of violence and the theology of revolution?

1141 After so much talk of peace, the temptation to violence as the supreme assertion of liberty and maturity, as the sole means of reform and redemption, is so strong that people speak of the theology of violence and revolution. And the facts, or at least the tendencies to have recourse to "established disorder," often correspond to such exciting theories. Thus there is an attempt to have Christ on one's side, in order to justify certain disorderly, demagogic and rebellious attitudes by appealing to His words and attitudes.

1142 Many people say these things. We Ourself have referred to this on other occasions. We have just one piece of advice for now. When we consider this alleged contradiction between the picture of a meek and gentle Christ, the Good Shepherd, the Christ crucified for love, and the picture of a virile and severe Christ, indignant and contentious, we must reflect well and see how things are in the original documents, the Gospels, the New Testament, authentic and consistent Tradition, and in their genuine interpretation. It seems to Us that we have a duty to pay honest attention to all this, especially to Christ's complex personality. He was certainly both strong and mild at the same time, just as He was God and man at the same time. Then we should consider the true reaction—certainly not a political or anarchical one—which Christ's reforming energy inspires in this fallen and corrupt world. In other words, we should consider the real hopes which He offers mankind.

We shall then see that the figure of Christ also presents—without altering the charm of His merciful gentleness—an aspect which is grave and strong—formidable, if you like—when dealing with cowardice, hypocrisy, injustice and cruelty, but never detached from a sovereign aura of love. 1143

Love alone makes Him the Savior. And only through the ways of love can we approach Him, imitate Him, and bring Him into our souls and into the ever dramatic vicissitudes of human history. 1144

Yes, we shall be able to see Him, who has lived among us and has shared our earthly lot in order to bring His Gospel of salvation to the world and prepare us for this fullness of salvation. We shall see Him "full of grace and truth."[17] 1145

Faith and love are the eyes that now enable us to see Him to a certain extent—to see Him in this life. 1146

Address of Pope Paul VI
to a General Audience
February 3, 1971

If only we could see Christ, many people say today, that would be enough to get a real idea of Him for ourselves—if only we could see Him. Accustomed as we are to know and sum up everything in very brief, practical, nominal and tangible formulas, we would like to have the satisfaction of getting to know Him by looking at Him directly, immediately, with a secret and rash hope of being able to judge, measure and define Him in this way; of being able to decide eventually whether or not to accept Him, and to determine finally what attitude to assume in His regard.

1148 This attitude, as We said on another occasion, was that of Jesus' contemporaries: Who is this problem man? Is He just someone like everybody else?[1] Is He a prophet?[2] One who leads people astray?[3] The Son of David?[4] And they all wanted to read His identity in His face. Remember the episode in the synagogue at Nazareth, when Jesus returned there at the beginning of His public life, and read out Isaiah's prophecy about the Messiah? St. Luke tells us that "the eyes of all were gazing on him"[5]—first in admiration, then in indignation, finally in anger, when Jesus said, "This Scripture is being fulfilled before your very eyes."

1149 As for us, we cannot see Him, yet we have some general knowledge of Him. What features, what characteristics spring to mind when we try to imagine Him? We still ask: Who was He, and what was He like? Let us begin by excluding features which usually mark remarkable men. He was not rich. The Lord said of Himself, "The foxes have dens, and the birds of the air have nests; but the Son of Man has nowhere to lay his head."[6] He was not renowned for His culture, and His fellow townspeople were amazed that He was so wise and eloquent. "Is not this the carpenter, the son of Mary?" they asked.[7] He was not a politician, a demagogue, an agitator. Jesus rejected the devil's temptation of an offer to repay a moment's servile obeisance with the kingdoms of the world and their glory.[8] And after multiplying the loaves, He fled from the enthusiastic crowd which wished to make Him king.[9]

1150 He was no soldier, captain, man-of-arms, such as many expected the Messiah to be, a vindicator and liberator of the Jewish people. He was not even a zealot, a revolutionary, a challenger of Roman rule in the land. When they insidiously put the burning question to Him, whether it was right to pay taxes to Caesar, He replied: "Render to Caesar the things that are Caesar's, and to God the things that are God's."[10] Who, then, is Jesus? At any rate, what did Jesus look like? What was His face like, His bodily appearance? What kind of activity makes Him known to us?

1151 To this question, which takes us into the field of the Gospel, it seems we can answer that He appeared as a prophet.[11] Do you picture Him as a prophet? A prophet is a man who utters wise and mysterious oracles about future hidden destinies. But he is especially a man who hears and announces divine messages. He has the key to God's secrets. He is the herald of a Word greater than human measure.[12] Thinking of Jesus as the man of the Word of God takes us quite a distance into the mystery of His person—but there our exploration has to stop.

1152 But an easier question arises spontaneously. What message did the prophet Jesus bring? We must go back to the beginning of His preaching, which is linked with that of John the Baptist, the precursor. Both the one and the other had the same prophetic theme: "Repent," John exclaimed, "for the kingdom of heaven is at hand."[13] "Repent," Jesus preached immediately afterwards, "for the kingdom of heaven is at hand."[14] Here we ought to examine this coincidence of words, and draw a comparison between John and Jesus. But another theme now draws our attention—the great theme of the kingdom of heaven, or the kingdom of God, which lies at the heart of Christ's preaching. Perhaps we have not thought about it enough.

1153 It is obvious that in the course of these very brief and simple remarks, We cannot give you an idea of the "kingdom" proclaimed by Jesus. The study of this subject would lead us to understand something of the history of Israel and of the tension engendered in the Jewish people at the time of Christ by their eager and impatient expectation of this kingdom's establishment. In the mind of the people it was to consist in a political liberation, in power and glory, brought about by a miraculous person, the "anointed" of God, the triumphant Messiah. Kingdom and Messiah are the two points to be studied in order to grasp the drama of the Gospel. It is up to you to do this.

1154 For the moment We will remark here that Christ takes the prophetic term kingdom, and makes His own (as a matter of fact, it is as the King of the Jews that He will be condemned to the death of the Cross[15]); but He changed its meaning profoundly. The kingdom of heaven which Christ announces, inaugurates and personifies in Himself, is the marvelous design of God. It is the new religious blueprint; it is, as St. Paul says, "the mystery which has been hidden for ages and generations, but now is clearly shown."[16] It is the economy of mercy and of grace which Christ opens to those who believe in Him. It is the Church, the sign and instrument of the kingdom in the process of realization; it is the beginning of a dynamic promise that will guide the steps of humanity toward the final vision in God of eternal life.

1155 Oh, how much there is to meditate on in this theme of the kingdom, so simple and so many-sided, so accessible to the human mind, so fruitful and such a force for renewal! It has become a part of the world's history and touches every individual conscience; and it is crystallized in the words and person of Jesus. Yes, Jesus is the prophet of the kingdom of God. He has come, and His kingdom is at hand. He is the one who possesses, proclaims and bestows on mankind the true, all-embracing and incomparable answer. He is the Teacher, Shepherd and Savior.

1156 Have you never noticed that the more advanced men are, the more fanatically they search for the man who sums up in himself the ideal of humanity, and who expresses in himself the norm of life, respect for all the values, the hope of a new destiny? Our own history is there to prove it—but alas, with such foolish enthusiasm, such servile humiliation, such desperate and at times tragic disappointments. The age-old dream continues: I am seeking the man.

1157 Very well then, if we honestly fix our minds on Jesus, with simple faith and awakening love, He will stand out before us, grace and resplendent, freeing us and holding us captive. And again today, for us children of this heady and disheartening age, the crucial discovery of the first two disciples will be repeated: "We have found the Messiah (which interpreted is the Christ)."[17]

1158 That is the wish We have for each one of you—that you may find Christ. With Our apostolic blessing.

Address of Pope Paul VI
to a General Audience
February 10, 1971

In these familiar weekly conversations since Christmas, We have been attempting to share with Our visitors—as though more to stimulate curiosity than for the purpose of study—some ideas about Jesus, His physical appearance, His personality, His moral profile. A great deal remains to be said, but much has been gained already if we are alert to the fascination of this theme. This is why We return to it again. We want to offer you two lines of thought by way of summary. We urge each of you to look into your Christian conscience, schooled in our Catholic faith, and search for the answers to two questions: Who was Jesus? What did Jesus do?

1160 His personality and His works: these are two great themes. But the very fact that they exceed all our measurements ought to attract, not disconcert us. So let us turn our attention this time to that first stimulating question: Who was Jesus?

1161 Let us begin by noting at once that this question lies at the very heart of the Gospel. We might say that the story which the Gospel tells is woven entirely around this question of Jesus' real identity: Who is Jesus? "Is he not the carpenter's son?"[1] That is how public opinion viewed Him. Better informed persons knew something about His home background: "Is this not the son of Mary?"[2] Scarcely had He appeared on the public scene when John the Baptist saw Him approaching the Jordan, and exclaimed, "Behold the Lamb of God".[3]

This was a strange title, which perceived in Jesus a victim predestined for a redemptive sacrifice. The evangelist records the continuation of the precursor's testimony which, from these beginnings, concluded: "This is the Son of God."[4] John was to repeat his cry the next day: "Behold the Lamb of God."[5] One of the disciples, Andrew, was the first to understand the message, and he expressed it in other words when he met his brother Simon Peter and said: "We have found the Messiah."[6]

1162 Even then Jesus was shrouded in mystery: In short, who is this young, mysterious prophet? From prison, John sent his own disciples to find out, in order to teach them, perhaps also to entrust them to the new Master. They asked Him: "Art thou he who is to come, or shall we look for another?"[7] Curiosity was spreading, causing tension and disquiet, and Jesus Himself took up the question. Do you recall the celebrated conversation He had with His disciples near Caesarea Philippi? He certainly did not question them merely to get information, but rather to have them clarify the idea they had formed of Him, and to declare according to their new knowledge the faith which God had given them concerning His mysterious personality.

1163 "Who do men say that the Son of Man is?" He asked, referring to Himself. They gave various accounts of rumors about Him, and then came the great question: "And you, who do you say that I am?" This was instantly followed by Peter's impetuous reply, inspired by God the Father: "Thou are the Christ, the Son of the living God."[8]

1164 This marvelous definition is the joy of believers, a problem for exegetes, the torment and target of unbelievers. This was crowned by two subsequent confirmations. One was the reply of Jesus Himself, setting the eternal seal upon the truth revealed: "Blessed are thou, Simon son of Jona"–John–"for flesh and blood has not revealed this to thee"–that is, you did not learn this by the natural way of knowledge–"but my Father in heaven. And I say to thee, thou art Peter . . ."[9] What a beautiful comment St. Leo the Great made when he put the following words into Christ's mouth: "As the Father has manifested to thee My divinity, so I make known thy excellence to thee."[10]

1165 The other confirmation was given at the Transfiguration of Jesus, which occurred at night six days later, on the mountain, while a voice spoke from a bright cloud: "This is my beloved Son, with whom I am well pleased; hear him."[11]

1166 Following this line of thought we come to the Gospel of St. John. He was no less historical than the others, but he had a doctrinal and spiritual purpose which caused his whole account to be taken up with the question of Jesus' identity as a person and in His work. It would be most interesting at this point to draw up a list of the titles used in the Gospel to designate Jesus. Each title might be the object of study and, even more, of ecstatic meditation. Jesus, the Master, the Son of David, is called the water which slakes thirst,[12] the bread from heaven,[13] the light of the world,[14] the door of salvation,[15] the good shepherd,[16] the resurrection and the life,[17] the way, the truth, and the life,[18] and so on.[19]

1167 This brings us to the closing stage of Jesus' temporal life, the decisive moment of His trial before the religious authorities. He was declared to be "liable to death,"[20] because when the Jewish high priest put Him on oath to say in the name of the living God whether "thou are the Christ, the Son of God,"[21] Jesus answered affirmatively: "Thou hast said it."

1168 And how many other affirmations[22] and testimonies we would have to collect,[23] were it not that the dominant fact of the Resurrection embraced and confirmed them all, and gave faith in the divinity of Christ to the infant Church and subsequent tradition. Will faith finally succeed in giving a definitive reply to that question which cannot be shrugged off: Who is Jesus? Can it do this by adhering strictly to historical data, but with that clearsightedness which comes from the Spirit and that courage which comes from love?

1169 Let us listen once again to one of the loftiest voices which speak to us in the New Testament, that of John: "In the beginning was the Word . . . and the Word was God . . . and the Word was made flesh and dwelt among us."[24] He is God, the Son of God with us. Let us listen to St. Paul: "He is the image of the invisible God."[25]

1170 In the joy of having reached the summit of the definition of Christ, perhaps we shall experience a sense of dizziness as if we were blinded, as if we no longer understood. Is it not Jesus, whom we recognize as the Christ and acknowledge to be the Son of God, to be God like the Father—isn't it He who gave us proof of a baffling inferiority? He Himself said, "The Father is greater than I."[26] Don't we continually encounter passages in the Gospels where Jesus prays?[27] Do we not hear His anguished cry from the Cross: "My God, my God, why hast thou forsaken me?"[28] And do we not see Him dead, like any other mortal? In other words, do we not see in Him a being who unites in Himself the human and the divine? Yes, it is exactly so.

1171 The definition of Christ arrived at by the three early Church Councils of Nicaea, Ephesus and Chalcedon gives us the infallible dogmatic formula: one single person, one single ego, living and operating in two natures, divine and human.[29] Is this a difficult formula? Yes, indeed. Or rather we should say, it is ineffable; but it is suited to our capacity for expressing the overwhelming mystery of the Incarnation in simple words and in analogical concepts—that is, concepts which are exact, but alway sinferior to the reality they express.

1172 Here let us close, happy, strong and steadfast in the truth, whose infallible charism is enjoyed by the Church and by this chair, which We unworthily occupy. Let us end here, resolving to live in ourselves that mystery of the Incarnation into which we have been led by Baptism and faith; resolving to live it by believing, praying, working, hoping, loving and exclaiming: "For me to live is Christ."[30] We are ready to explore—and, with God's grace, to experience—that other mystery of Christ which also concerns us totally: the Redemption.

1173 Here let us close and fearlessly face the storm of the opposing Christologies unleashed against our Catholic faith—those of the last century especially, and of today, our own century of light and darkness. Let us admire the extremely erudite effort of modern learning to investigate Christ and His person, His history and the evidence about Him, and let us learn to study more ourselves. But we should be watchful, even distrustful, as we see school succeed school; as we observe that the enormous erudition of so many teachers is usually permeated with some hypothesis, prejudice or questionable philosophy which, when joined with the wealth of knowledge which they have accumulated, often leads to shipwreck in invincible doubt or radical and irrational denial.[31]

1174 If we are vigilant and trusting, "who shall separate us from the love of Christ?"[32] Let us sing our Creed! With Our apostolic blessing.

Address of Pope Paul VI to a General Audience February 17, 1971

In the wake of the Christmas feasts (which will soon be followed by the Lent and Easter cycle), We have been looking into Our knowledge of Christ, contenting Ourself with dwelling briefly on some striking aspects of His extraordinary person. And now, at the conclusion of this simple study, We want to try to answer an important question, using concepts that We suppose are within everyone's reach.

1176 What was the purpose of Jesus' life? Did it have an intention, a design, a goal? What did Jesus, the Son of God and Mary, do by entering and operating in this world? The question takes on immense and mysterious proportions if we are already informed about Jesus' being, that is, if we know who He was. The question arises spontaneously and urgently: Why?

1177 Viewing the history of the Lord intuitively and as a whole, We can answer: the first and most evident reason for Christ's life is the proclamation of His word. He came to preach the Gospel. Christ's presence in the world is characterized by the truth which He proclaims. His life is God's word to mankind. This word finds confirmation in the miracles performed by Christ; it finds the instrument for its diffusion and for its permanence in time in the choice and investiture of the Apostles, who were given the task of guiding and instructing

Christ's followers; of forming the Church, the human and historical complement, the new People of God.

1178 Is this all? Have we observed and listened carefully? Let us see. We cannot disregard, in the first place, the tragic end of Christ's earthly life, the drama of His death on the Cross. Nor can we overlook an extraordinary fact, which gives exceptional significance to this drama: Jesus knew that He would die in this way. No hero knows the fate that awaits him. No mortal can measure the time he still has to live, or know how much and what suffering he will have to bear.

1179 But Jesus did know. Can we imagine the psychology of a man who clearly foresees a moral and physical martyrdom, such as Jesus bore? On several occasions, at moments of complete awareness, He foretold His Passion to His disciples. The Gospel narrative is full of these prophetic confidences, which show Jesus' heart-rending foreknowledge of the fate that awaited him.[1] He knew "His hour." This matter of "His hour" would be an extremely interesting meditation for penetrating a little into Christ's mind. The evangelist John dedicates frequent valuable indications to it.[2] Christ, it could be said, has continually before Him the clock of future time, and of present time in reference to the mysterious cycles of events seen by God. The prophecies of the past and the future are an open book before His divine eyes.[3]

1180 Jesus was willing. The voluntary character of Christ's Passion is seen from so many of His Gospel testimonies. When, for example, He predicted to His disciples that it would be necessary to go to Jerusalem, to suffer greatly and be killed there, and Peter protested and wanted to dissuade Him from accepting this fate, Jesus reproved him severely.[4] He repeated the reproof when Peter, at Gethsemane, wished to defend Him with his sword: "Put up thy sword into the scabbard. Shall I not drink the cup that the Father has given me?"[5] Let us recall further what the evangelist Mark reports: "For the Son of Man has not come to be served but to serve, and to give his life as a ransom for many."[6]

1181 If we reflect on this vocation of Jesus, a vocation of pain and sacrifice, we can imagine some features of Christ's face. One of the apocryphal books supposed that Jesus never laughed;[7] He sometimes wept;[8] and we readily imagine Him smiling sweetly on children.[9] But what inner suffering Jesus bore all His life as a foretaste of His imminent Passion: this can be realized from the scene at Gethsemane.[10] Yet He was not a stoic; He was not sad. He was poised in an inward and higher communion with His Father.[11]

1182 And we can notice some distinctive features of His moral character, of His heart: Jesus was kind with a divine kindness;[12] He had understanding of the pain and distress of others.[13] He was able to comprehend, forgive and rehabilitate; His meetings with sinners are well known. Jesus has been magnificently understood and defined, in contemporary Christological discussion, as "the man for others." That is so. And St. Paul—that is, all the theology of the New Testament and of Catholic Tradition—had a deep insight into the secret of Jesus' earthly life, the reason, the purpose of the Incarnation, and tells us in what form and to what extent Jesus was for others: "Christ died for our sins according to the Scriptures."[14]

1183 Jesus came to the world for us and for our salvation. This is what Jesus did: He saved us. He was called just that, Jesus, which means Savior. And He saved us by becoming a victim for our Redemption. This is the mystery of abasement of the man Jesus that merges with the mystery of the sublimation of the man Jesus which is the Incarnation. It enters into the most important truths of the Christian theological system, that is, into the eternal plan, fully revealed only with Christ, of God's love for us;[15] into the tremendous and obscure but indispensable dogma, as Pascal said.[16] For without this mystery, we could know nothing about ourselves. It enters into the sacrificial value of the Lord's Passion, which is universal and replaces the expiation that would otherwise be due from us which would be impossible for us.

1184 Here we have the final and total work of Christ, the Redemption. The Redemption enters into human destinies in such a way as to establish a possible, free and highly auspicious personal relationship of each of us with our Lord Jesus Christ: "Christ loved me and gave himself up for me," St. Paul proclaimed[17]—for me. Here, beloved brothers and sons,

Christian life begins for each of us, a life of love, which comes to us. Light, fire, blood of Christ, in the Spirit; and love, which goes out from us, as it can, with all its strength, toward Christ and in search of our brothers, always in the Spirit. Amen.

Declaration of the Sacred Congregation for the Doctrine of the Faith
March 8, 1972

The mystery of the Son of God made man, and the mystery of the Most Holy Trinity, both pertaining to the Most Holy Trinity, both pertaining to the innermost substance of Revelation, must be, in their authentic truth, the source of light for the lives of Christians. But because some recent errors undermine these mysteries, the Sacred Congregation for the Doctrine of the Faith has determined to reaffirm and safeguard the belief in them that has been handed down to us.

1186 Jesus Christ, while dwelling on this earth, manifested in various ways, by word and deed the adorable mystery of His person. After being made "obedient to death,"[1] He was divinely exalted in His glorious resurrection, as was fitting for the Son "through whom all things"[2] were made by the Father. Of Him St. John solemnly proclaimed: "in the beginning was the Word, and the Word was with God; and the Word was God. . .And the Word was made flesh."[3]

1187 The Church has reverently preserved the mystery of the Son of God made man, and "in the course of the ages and centuries"[4] has propounded it for belief in a more explicit way. In the Creed of Constantinople, which is still recited today during the Eucharistic celebration, the Church proclaims her faith in "Jesus Christ, the only begotten Son of God, born of the Father before all ages, . . . who for us men and for our salvation, . . . was made man."[5] The Council of Chalcedon decreed for belief that the Son of God according to His divinity was begotten of the Father before all ages, and according to His humanity was born in time of the Virgin Mary.[6] Moreover, this Council spoke of one and the same Christ the Son of God as a "person" or *hypostatis,* but used the term "nature" to denote His divinity and His humanity. Using these terms, it taught that both His natures, divine and human, together belong-without confusion, unalterably, indivisibly and inseparable—to the one person of our Redeemer.[7]

1188 In the same way, the Fourth Lateran Council taught for belief and profession that the Son of God, coeternal with the Father, was made true man and is one person in two natures.[8] This is the Church, clearly expressed in many Second Vatican Council, holding to the constant tradition of the whole Church, clearly expressed in many passages.[9]

1189 Opinions which hold that it has not been revealed and made known to us that the Son of God subsists from all eternity in the mystery of the Godhead, distinct from the Father and the Holy Spirit, are in open conflict with this belief. The same is true of opinions which should abandon the notion of the one person of Jesus Christ begotten in His divinity of the Father before all ages, and born in His humanity of the Virgin Mary in time; and, lastly, of the assertion that the humanity of Christ existed not as being assumed into the external person of the Son of God, but existed rather of itself as a person, and therefore that the mystery of Jesus Christ consists only in the fact that God, in revealing Himself, was present in the highest degree in the human person Jesus.

1190 Those who think in this way are far removed from true belief in Christ, even when they maintain that the special presence of God in Jesus results in His being the supreme and final expression of Divine Revelation; nor do they come back to true belief in Christ's divnity by adding that Jesus can be called God because God is supremely present in what they call His human person.

1191 Once the mystery of the divine and eternal person of Christ the Son of God is abandoned, the truth respecting the Most Holy Trinity is also undermined, and with it the truth regarding the Holy Spirit who proceeds eternally from the Father and the Son, or from the Father through the Son.[10] Therefore, in view of recent errors, some points concerning the belief in the Most Holy Trinity, and especially in the Holy Spirit, should be recalled to mind.

1192 The Second Epistle to the Corinthians concludes with this admirable expression: "The grace of our Lord Jesus Christ, and the charity of God, and the fellowship of the Holy Spirit be with you all."[11] The commission to baptize, recorded in St. Matthew's Gospel, names the Father, the Son and the Holy Spirit as the three pertaining to the mystery of God, and it is in their name that the new faithful must be reborn.[12] Lastly, in St. John's Gospel, Jesus speaks of the coming of the Holy Spirit: "When the Advocate has come, whom I will send you from the Father, the Spirit of truth who proceeds from the Father, he will bear witness concerning me."[13]

1193 Following Divine Revelation, the magisterium of the Church, to which alone is entrusted "the task of authentically interpreting the word of God, whether written or handed down,"[14] acknowledges in the Creed of Constantinople "the Holy Spirit, the Lord and giver of live, . . . who together with the Father and the Son is adored and glorified."[15] In like manner, the Fourth Lateran Council taught that it is to be believed and professed "that there is but one true God, . . . Father and Son and Holy Spirit: three persons indeed, but one essence. . . : the Father proceeding from none, the Son from the Father alone, and the Holy Spirit equally from both, without beginning, always and without end."[16]

1194 The opinion that Revelation has left us uncertain about the eternity of the Trinity, and in particular about the eternal existence of the Holy Spirit as a person in God distinct from the Father and the Son, deviates from the faith. It is true that the mystery of the Most Holy Trinity was revealed to us in the economy of salvation, and most of all in Christ Himself, who was sent into the world by the Father and together with the Father sends the life-giving Spirit to the People of God. But by this Revelation there is also given to believers some knowledge of God's intimate life, in which "the Father who generated, the Son who is generated, and the Holy Spirit who proceeds" are "consubstantial and co-equal, alike omnipotent and co-eternal."[17]

1195 What is expressed in the above-mentioned conciliar documents concerning the one and same Christ the Son of God, begotten before the ages in His divine nature, and also concerning the eternal persons of the Most Holy Trinity, belongs to the immutable truth of the Catholic faith.

1196 This certainly does not prevent the Church, in her awareness of the progress of human thought, from considering it her duty to have these mysteries continually examined by contemplation of the faith and theological examination, and to have them fully expounded in up-to-date terminology. But while the necessary duty of investigation is being pursued, diligent care must be taken that these profound mysteries are not interpreted in a sense other than that in which "the Church has understood and understands them."[18]

1197 The unimpaired truth of these mysteries is of the greatest moment for the whole Revelation of Christ because they pertain to its very core in such a way that, if they are undermined, the rest of the treasure of Revelation is adulterated. The truth of these same mysteries is of no less concern to the Christian way of life because nothing so effectively manifests the charity of God, to which the whole of Christian life should be a response, as does the Incarnation of the Son of God, our Redeemer,[19] and also because "through Christ, the Word made flesh, man might have access in the Holy Spirit to the Father and come to share in the divine nature."[20]

1198 With regard to the truths which the present declaration is safeguarding, it is up to the pastors of the Church to see that there is unity on the part of their people in professing the faith, especially on the part of those who, by the magisterium's mandate, teach the sacred sciences or peach the Word of God. This function of the bishops belongs to the office divinely committed to them "of keeping pure and entire" "the deposit of faith" in communion with Peter's successor, and "of proclaiming the Gospel unceasingly."[21] By reason of this same office they are bound not to permit ministers of the Word of God, deviating from the way of sound doctrine, to transmit it corrupt or incomplete.[22] The people entrusted to the care of the bishops, who "are responsible for them before God,"[23] enjoy the "inalienable and sacred right to receive the word of God, the whole word of God, which the Church has unfailing studied more and more deeply."[24]

Christians, then—and theologians above all, because of their important office and necessary function in the Church—must make faithful profession of the mysteries which this declaration reaffirms. In like manner, by the movement and illumination of the Holy Spirit, the Church's sons must hold fast to the whole doctrine of the faith under the leadership of their pastors and of the pastor of the universal Church.[25] 1199

"Thus there is a single common effort by the bishops and the faithful to hold onto the heritage of faith and to practice and profess it."[26] 1200

The Supreme Pontiff by divine Providence Pope Paul VI, in an audience granted to the undersigned Prefect of the Sacred Congregation for the Doctrine of the Faith on February 21, 1972, ratified and confirmed this declaration for safeguarding from certain recent errors the belief in the mysteries of the Incarnation and of the Most Holy Trinity, and ordered it to be published. 1201

Given at Rome, from the offices of the Sacred Congregation for the Doctrine of the Faith, on the 21st day of February, the feast of St. Peter Damian, in the year of our Lord 1972. 1202

Homily of Pope Paul VI on the 16th Centenary of St. Athanasius' Death May 6, 1973

"This is the day the Lord has made; let us be glad and rejoice in it." We readily repeat this liturgical acclamation prompted by the feast of Easter on this present occasion, when We are profoundly moved by the presence of Patriarch Shenouda III—who is himself honored by the title of "Pope" of the venerable and very ancient coptic Church, which has its center at Alexandria, Egypt.

1204 Here is one who is head of a Church still officially separated from Us and for centuries absent from the celebration of communal prayer with this Church of Rome. But he heads a Church which traces its origin back to the evangelist Mark, whom St. Peter calls his son;[1] a Church which had in St. Athanasius—the 16th centenary of whose blessed death we are celebrating today—the invincible defender of our common Nicene faith, that is, faith in the divinity of our Lord Jesus Christ. This faith was proclaimed under divine inspiration by Simon, son of John, who was therefore transformed by Christ Himself into the unchanging Peter and made by Him the foundation of the whole Church.

1205 Patriarch Shenouda is here, and he has come expressly and spontaneously to tie again the bonds of love,[2] in happy anticipation of that perfect unity of the Spirit[3] which—following the recent Second Ecumenical Vatican Council- We are striving humbly and sincerely to restore. He is here with Us and with this great gathering of the faithful at the

Apostle Peter's tomb. How could We fail to rejoice and to invite all of you, sons and daughters of this Roman Catholic Church, to praise the Lord with Us on this extraordinary day?

1206 We see that the book of the Church's history—in which the mysterious hand of the Lord chiefly guides men's hands to write there "new things and old"[4]—opens before us age-old pages and others which are still blank and ready to record events which will—God willing!—be happier ones, examples of God's merciful providence in the life of the Church, which is still a pilgrim in time. How could We fail to greet this great and honored brother from afar who is so close to Us today? We greet the visitor and guest here at Our altar, united with Our pontifical prayer, and We also welcome his large and distinguished delegation.

1207 The reading from the holy Gospel[5] which we have just heard invites us to reflect on the fundamental theme of our faith—the Resurrection of our Lord Jesus Christ. St. Paul says: "If you confess with your lips that Jesus is Lord and believe in your heart that God raised him from the dead, you will be saved."[6] It seems that this Gospel narrative of the Mass we are celebrating intends to attest the reality of the fact of Christ's Ressurection as an objective historical reality, proved even by the direct tangible experience of the senses, although it pertains to a supernatural order. It seems likewise to want to stimulate us to draw our indomitable, most lively faith directly from observation of this extraordinary reality. This faith is like that of Thomas, the positive man of criticism, doubt and verification, with his still resounding words: "My Lord and my God!"[7]

1208 How appropriate is today's liturgical reflection, celebrating as it does the glorious memory of St. Athanasius, the intrepid, undaunted defender of the faith! St. Athanasius is a Father and Doctor of the universal Church, and thus merits our common remembrance.

1209 It seems to Us that the best way to commemorate a saint who made an extraordinary contribution to the Church's life at a decisive moment of her history when heretics denied the very consubstantial divinity of the Word and hence of

Christ, is by reflecting on the heritage he has left us, the witness of faith in his life and thought.

1210 When we consider his life, we find a believer solidly gounded on evangelical faith, a convinced defender and champion of truth, ready to endure every calumny, persecution and violence. He spent 20 of the 46 years of his episcopate in repeated exile; this very city of Rome sheltered him for three years of his second exile (April, A.D. 339 to October, A.D. 346), in the time of Pope Julius (A.D. 337-352).

1211 Always, everywhere and before all men, before the powerful and those in error, he professed faith in the divinity of Jesus Christ, true God and true man, so that the Eastern liturgical tradition describes him as a "column of the true faith"[8] and the Catholic Church numbers him among the Doctors of the Church.

1212 He was indeed a man of the Church. A vigilant and attentive pastor, he dedicated his entire life to the service of the Church —not only his own Church of Alexandria, but the whole Church. Everywhere he brought the warmth of his faith, the edifying example of his strictly consistent life and the call to prayer which he had learned from the monks of the desert, among whom he was several times obliged to take refuge.

1213 The divinity of Christ is the central point of St. Athanasius' preaching to the men of his time, who were tempted by the Arian crisis. The definition of the first Ecumenical Council of Nicaea (A.D. 325)—according to which Jesus Christ is the Son of God, of the same substance as the Father, true God from true God—was the constant landmark of his teaching. Only if one accepts this doctrine can one speak of redemption, salvation and the reestablishment of communion between man and God. Only the Word of God redeems perfectly; without the Incarnation, man would remain in the state of corrupt nature, from which penance itself could not free him.[9]

1214 Freed by Christ from corruption and saved from death, man is reborn to new life and once more acquires the pristine image of God, in which he had been created in the beginning and which sin had corrupted. "The Word of God," declares

St. Athanasius, "came Himself so that, being the image of the Father, He might create man anew in the image of God."[10]

St. Athanasius develops this theology, centering it on redeemed man's sharing in the very life of God through Baptism and sacramental life. He even declares, in a forceful expression, that the Word of God "became man so that we might be divinized."[11] 1215

This new creation restores what sin had compromised: the knowledge of God and a radical change of moral life. 1216

Jesus Christ reveals the Father to us and makes Him knowable: "The Word of God became visible with a body so that we might be able to form an idea of the invisible Father."[12] 1217

From this new knowledge of God follows the need for moral renewal. St. Athanasius strongly urges it: "Whoever wants to understand the things of God must purify himself in his way of life and resemble the saints by the similarity of his own actions so that, united with them in the conduct of his life, he may be able to understand what has been revealed to them by God."[13] 1218

Thus we are brought to the center of the Christian event: redemption through the work of Jesus Christ; the radical renewal of man with his restoration to the image and likeness of God; restored communion of life between man and God, which is also expressed in a profound change of conduct. 1219

This is the sublime message which St. Athanasius the Great today addresses to us also: to be strong in faith and consistent in the practice of the Christian life, even at the cost of grave sacrifices. It is up to us to accept this message, to ponder it, examine it closely and carry it out in our lives. 1220

Through the prayers of St. Athanasius, Father and Doctor of the Church, may God grant that we too, in our time, be able worthily to confess that Jesus Christ is Lord and Savior of the world. 1221

We would like, in closing, to speak to the faithful whom We see here. Members of the Roman parish of St. Athanasius, We are happy to see you present for this great ceremony. We welcome all of you and ask you to take Our greetings and 1222 blessing to the entire parish community. We urge you especially to honor the memory of the great patron of your parish, St. Athanasius. How can you honor him? You do so by commemorating his life and professing his faith; by loving Christ, the eternal Word of God, Son of God and Son of Man, our Teacher and Savior; and by a sincere, faithful commitment to Christ's Church and a practical charity toward our neighbor. Are We understood? We impart Our special blessing to all of you and to your parish priest.

Address of Pope Paul VI
to a General Audience
February 6, 1974

The thought of Christmas is still in our minds and that is quite natural. If, in celebrating Christmas, we have really understood that we have met God made man—like one of us—who came with the intention of drawing near to us, seeking us, taking on human form in order to speak to us, to enter into our life's destiny, to save us, then we cannot but pause and attribute to this meeting a decisive importance for our own lives.

1224 Let us think carefully about the meaning of this meeting with Christ, and in particular about what it really involves for us. Let us consider it in the context of the great religious plan offered to world history. Without leaving heaven and forsaking the attributes of His eternal divinity, the God of mystery enters the changing scene of time.[1] He who is infinite takes on the limits of *kenosis*, that is to say, He empties Himself.[2] He is ineffable, yet He clothes Himself in our visible flesh.[3] He is inaccessible, yet He reveals Himself to little ones;[4] He makes Himself available to human society[5] in order to raise our lowly earthly life to a supernatural level[6] and thereby change mankind's fate from perdition to unexpected good fortune. How can we remain indifferent and forgetful of all this?

1225 If, upon reflection, we also discover that this plan concerns us personally, that it is wholly centered on each of us, it becomes our personal drama. It endows us inwardly with an extraordinary wealth of gifts, the gifts of the Holy Spirit; and it offers us a free but formidable choice regarding the kind of life we want to live: are we Christians or not? That is to say, are we Christians or are we, in the last analysis, insignificant beings deprived of eternal hope? If we encounter Christ on life's difficult path, can we remain indifferent?

1226 The encounter with Christ! Let us recall it from the Gospel narrative, which symbolically mirrors our whole human life. Certainly there is, in this context, the indifference and even hostility of many Gospel personages who react to meeting Christ with materialistic blindness and deafness, or even with suspicious malice and crafty opposition, resolved to do away with His troublesome presence.[7]

1227 But there are those who realize on meeting Jesus that they are in the presence of a wonderful, incomparable Man, and they recognize Him at once for what He is. Andrew is the first to reveal it to his brother Simon (later to be called Peter): "We have found the Messiah."[8] The meeting is a decisive one; it becomes a vocation which Jesus will formulate precisely and which in this first stage is common to all of us—the Christian vocation.

1228 This name challenges, marks and transforms us deeply. We are Christians. It is a controversial name. The early generation felt at first its unpleasant implications;[9] then came discrimination and danger.[10] But then it soon became a fine, glorious name for believers, for the faithful.[11] It was to become the specific name for all of Christ's followers.[12] We received this name at Baptism, when we become Christians.

1229 Let us keep this fact clearly in mind. There at Baptism, we met Christ. It was a sacramental, vital, regenerating meeting. It was our true Christmas. Now then, what does such a meeting with Christ involve? Again the Gospel teaches us: it involves following Him. It involves a style of life, a binding commitment, an inestimable fortune.[13]

1230 Here, in a nutshell, we have everything. Here we have the consistency of our life, faithfulness to our religious profession, the unique character of our mode of existing in the world, the obligation of our moral witness. Here also we have the source of our capacity for superhuman virtues, inner strength in all earthly trouble, the driving force of our missionary and social charity.

To be Christians! We will just repeat what We wrote in Our first Encyclical *Ecclesiam Suam*: 1231

"Those who are baptized and by this means incorporated into Christ's Mystical Body, His Church, must attach the greatest importance to this event. They must be acutely aware of being raised to higher status, of being reborn to a supernatural life, there to experience the happiness of being God's adopted sons, the special dignity of being Christ's brothers, the blessedness, the grace and the joy of the indwelling of the Holy Spirit. 1232

"They have indeed been called to a new kind of life, but they have lost nothing of their own humanity except the unhappy state of original sin. Rather, the humanity in them is now capable of bearing the fairest flowers of perfection and the most precious and holiest of fruits."[14] 1233

We repeat this while thinking again of the recent Christmas feast, of our meeting with Christ, of our being reborn in Baptism and called to perennial renewal. The announcement of the Holy Year reminds us of all this and invites us to achieve it. 1234

Address of Pope Paul VI
to a General Audience
February 13, 1974

Once more, for the last time, We are going to talk about Christmas. We would not like this feast to have been celebrated without leaving traces in the minds of those who have participated wholeheartedly in it. What traces? Well, veneration of such mystery should have left a hundred traces of every kind among our spiritual impressions—ranging from well known ones of human poetry to others of historical reflection or religious sentiment. Christmas is an inexhaustible source of themes for our piety, moral education, theological investigation and mystical contemplation. Today let us dwell upon a single consequence which we would like to derive from that ever memorable feast, and which arouses in us an unfilled need rather than a sense of restful satisfaction.

1236 What is it, then? It is an obvious and apparently very simple thing: we would like to know Jesus, who was born, whom we have admired and venerated in the manger, in whose honor we offered three Masses on Christmas Day; to know the One who was in some way the reason for our various domestic celebrations and greetings; the One whose coming into the world has marked a special date in the calendar. But do we know Him, the center of the feast?

1237 Who is Jesus? We intend no offense to anyone by asking this question, because We take it for granted that you all know the catechism definition: He is the Son of God made

Man. All of you have abundant information about Him, derived from the Gospel narrative and theological notions, perhaps also from devotional or artistic images. So far so good, and We think this is normal in anyone who bears the name of Christian.

1238 But a first characteristic, fundamental note of our knowledge of Jesus Christ is this: if we really know Him we realize that we do not know Him enough. What we know about Him doesn't satisfy our need, our duty of intellectual knowledge; instead it stimulates, excites and enkindles this need and duty. We all feel invited—almost logically, spiritually compelled—to get to know Him better, to form a clearer, more concrete, more complete idea of Him. The new curiosity no longer leaves us in peace; it plagues us with the relentless, insatiable question: who is Jesus?

1239 Hence, beloved brothers and sons, there is a second point concerning our knowledge of the Lord Jesus: this knowledge is gradual. Not only is it not exhausted in a mere sensible image—a picture, a Gospel scene, a biographical account; but if this knowledge is really impressed on our spirit in some way, it arouses the desire to identify it better, to probe it more deeply, to verify its meaning and content. It becomes a problem; in short, who is this Jesus?

1240 Each of you will remember how this investigation arose among Jesus' own contemporaries. Especially after some miracle of His, the question would recur: "Who, then, is this, that he commands even the winds and the sea, and they obey him?"[1] You will recall that Jesus Himself started a kind of inquiry among His disciples, as the Evangelist Matthew tells us: "Now Jesus, having come into the district of Caesarea Philippi, began to ask his disciples, saying 'Who do men say the Son of Man is?' "[2] Opinions differed. This was an indication that Jesus' revelation of Himself did indeed allow something of the extraordinary to appear and transpire, but not without covering it with a human veil that was not always transparent to everyone. Even Mary and Joseph "were marvelling at the things spoken concerning him";[3] and they did not understand everything about this mysterious child.[4] Even His fellow townsmen in Nazareth viewed Him with amazement and suspicion, not knowing exactly who He was.[5]

1241 One would think that Jesus liked to be incognito. The whole Gospel of John is full of this haunting problem regarding the essential identity of the Master's personality.[6] Around this problem the drama of His Passion takes place, with its double trial, religious and civil. The former leads to His confession that He is the Messiah, the Son of God, and the latter to His admission that He is the King of the Jews. Then comes the inconceivable epilogue of His Resurrection, which transcends the understanding of the immediate witnesses, so that they merit the risen Christ's reproach: "O foolish ones and slow of heart to believe in all that the prophets have spoken!"[7]

1242 Jesus is a mystery. We will never be able to explore this mystery enough or to fathom it completely. Knowledge of Him has finally had to be transformed into faith, that is, into a superrational knowledge; this knowledge is absolutely certain, but it is based on evidences that partly lie outside our experimental control. But these evidences have the force of conviction because after all they are divine, and they require from us that wider way of knowing—with the mind and heart, without understanding everything because there is too much to understand—and that is precisely what we call faith.

1243 Jesus must be studied with all the power of our capacity of understanding (and Love's capacity of understanding exceeds that of pure intelligence). So it was for the Church: she thought it over, studied and discussed it; she had for herself the light of the Holy Spirit; and with centuries of very cautious, faithful labor, she succeeded in formulating the doctrine that is exact but always limitless and opening on the mystery of our Lord Jesus Christ: who He was, what He did for us, how He gives and will give Himself to us.

1244 We call this central chapter of our religion "Christology." At present other chapters, such as the one on "ecclesiology" (so much studied by the Council) and the one on "pneumatology"—that is, concerning the doctrine on the Holy Spirit—claim our study and our spiritual life. But let us not close the book of our doctrine on Christ the Lord, as if He were already well known to each of us. We must open this book again; we must keep it always ready for attentive reflection and passionate contemplation. "For to me to live is Christ," St. Paul says.[8]

1245 And then we must be jealous custodians of it and not let ourselves be taken by surprise by learned opinions outside the Church's school, these are often prejudiced in method or content, and claim to give a new interpretation (a hermeneutics), one that ultimately destroys the true theology concerning the Christ of our Christmas.

1246 We would be tempted to discuss with you this subtle modern controversy about our living, true Christ, and We would have liked to suggest some good books for you to read. But We see that this is not the time or the place; besides, you can easily do this for yourselves. Look for some books on Christ, beginning with a new, methodical and devout reading of the holy Gospel.

References

QUAS PRIMAS, Encyclical Letter of Pope Pius XI on the Feast of Christ the King, December 11, 1925.

1 *Eph.* iii. 9.

2 *Dan.* vii. 13, 14

3 *Num.* xxiv. 19.

4 *Ps.* ii.

5 *Ps.* xliv.

6 *Ps.* lxxi.

7 *Isa.* ix. 6, 7.

8 *Jerem.* xxiii. 5.

9 *Dan.* vii. 13, 14.

10 *Zach.* ix. 9.

11 *Luke* i. 32, 33.

12 *Matt.* xxv. 31-40.

13 *John* xviii, 37.

14 *Matt.* xxviii. 18.

15 *Apoc.* i. 5.

16 *Apoc.* xix. 16.

17 *Heb.* i. 2.

18 cf. *1 Cor.* xv. 25.

19 In Luc. x.

20 *1 Peter* i. 18, 19.

21 *1 Cor.* vi. 20.

22 *1 Cor.* vi. 15.

23 Conc. Trid. Sess. vi. Can. 21.

24 *John* xiv. 15; xv. 10.

25 *John* v. 22.

26 Hymn for the Epiphany.

27 Enc. *Annum Sanctum,* May 25, 1899

28 *Acts.* iv. 12.

29 St. Aug., *Ep. ad Macedonium*, iii.

30 Enc. *Ubi Arcano.*

31 *1 Cor.* vii. 23.

32 Enc. *Annum Sanctum,* May 25, 1899.

33 Sermo 47, *de Sanctis.*

Letter Ephesinam Synodum to Cardinal Sincero, December 25, 1930.

1 *Luke* 1:48.

LUX VERITATIS, Encyclical Letter of Pope Pius XI on the Light of Truth, December 25, 1931.

1 *Matt.* vii, 20.

2 *John* xv, 6.

3 Letter to the Most Eminent Cardinals, B. Pompili and A. Sincerdo, d. 25 Dec., 1930, Acta Ap. Sedis, Vol. XXIII, pp. 10-12.

4 Ephes. iv,13-16.

5 Mansi, Conciliorum Amplissima Collection IV, c. 1007; Schwartz, Acta Concilorum Oecumenicorum 1, 5. p. 408.

6 Mansi, l.c., IV, 1011.

7 Mansi, 1.c., IV, 1015.

8 Mansi, 1.c., IV, 1034 sq.

9 Migne, P.L., 50, 463; IV, 1019 sq.

10 Mansi, 1.c., IV, 1291.

11 Mansi, 1.c., IV, 1292.

12 Mansi, 1.c., IV, 1287.

13 Mansi, 1.c., IV, 1292.

14 Mansi, 1.c., IV, 556.

15 Mansi, 1.c., IV, 1290.

16 Conc. Vatic., sess. IV, cap. 2.

17 Mansi, 1.c., IV, 1295.

18 Mansi, 1.c., IV, 1287.

19 Mansi, 1.c., IV, 1287.

20 Mansi, 1.c., IV, 1294 sq.

21 Mansi, 1.c., IV, 1287 sq.

22 Epist. 190, Corpus scriptorum ecclesiasticorum latinorum, 57, p. 159 sq.

23 Mansi, 1.c., VI, 124.

24 Mansi, 1.c., VI, 351-354

25 Migne, P.L., 77, 478; cfr. Mansi, 1.c., IX, 1048.

26 Mansi, 1.c., IV, 891.

27 *Matt.* iii, 17; xvii, 5. 2 *Peter* I, 17.

28 *Matt.* ix, 2-6. *Luke* v, 20-24. vii, 48, al.

29 *Matt.* viii, 3. *Mark* xiv, 1. *Luke* v, 13. *John* ix, al.

30 *John* xi, 43. *Luke* vii, 14 al.

31 *Rom.* viii, 29.

32 *Isaias* liii, 5. *Matt. viii, 17.*

33 Summ. Theol. 111,11,2.

34 *Matt.* xvi, 14.

35 Roman Missal.

36 1 *John* iv, 3.

37 1 *Cor.* xii, 12.

38 Ephes. iv, 16.

39 Encycl. *Mortalium Animos.*

40 Mansi, 1.c., IV, 1290.

41 *Luke* ii, 34.
42 *Acts* iv, 12.
43 Mansi, 1.c., IV, 891.
44 Ephes. vii, 18-20.
45 Ephes. vii, 18-20.
46 De Carne Christi, 17 P.L. II, 781.
47 Mansi, l.c., IV, 599.
48 Theol. III, a.6.
49 *Matt.* i, 6.
50 *Rom.* viii, 29.
51 Encycl. *Octobri Mense Adventante*, Sept. 1891.
52 Encycl. s.c.
53 Mansi, 1.c., IV, 891.
54 Encycl. *Casti Connubii*, Dec., 1930.
55 Encycl. *Divini Illus Magistrii*, Dec., 1929.
56 Litt. Apost. *Neminem fugit*, Jan., 1892.
57 *Phil.* iv, 7.

MYSTICI CORPORIS, Encyclical Letter of Pope Pius XII on the Mystical Body of Christ and Our Union in It with Christ, June 29, 1943.

1 Cf. *Col.* 1, 24.
2 *Acts*, XX, 28.
3 Cf. *1 Peter*, IV, 13.
4 Cf. *Eph.*, II, 21-22; *I Peter*, II, 5.
5 Sessio III, *Const. de fide cath.*, c. 4.
6 *Rom.*, V, 20.
7 Cf. *II Peter*, I, 4.
8 *Eph.* II, 3.
9 *John*, III, 16.
10 Cf. *John*, I, 12.
11 Cf. Vat. Council, *Const. de Eccl.*, prol.
12 Cf. *ibidem*, *Const. de fide cath.*, c. 1

13 *Col.*, I, 18.

14 *Rom.* XII, 5.

15 Cf. *A. S. S.*, XXVIII, p. 710.

16 *Rom.*, XII, 4.

17 *I Cor.*, XII, 13.

18 Cf. *Eph.* IV, 5.

19 Cf. *Matth.*, XVIII, 17.

20 Cf. *Matth.*, IX, 11; *Mark*, II, 16; *Luke*, XV, 2.

21 August., *Epist.*, CLVII, 3, 22: Migne, *P. L.*, XXXIII, 686.

22 August., *Serm.*, CXXXVII, 1: Migne, *P. L.*, XXXVIII, 754.

23 Encycl. *Divinum Illud;* A. A. S., XXIX, p. 649.

24 *John*, XVII, 18.

25 Cf. *Matth.*, XVI, 18-19.

26 *John*, XV, 15; XVII, 8 and 14.

27 Cf. *John*, III, 5.

28 Cf. *Gen.*, III, 20.

29 Ambrose, *In Luc*, II, 87: Migne, *P. L.*, XV, 1585.

30 Cf. *Matth.*, XV, 24.

31 Cf. St. Thos., I-II, q. 103, a. 3, ad 2.

32 Cf. *Eph.*, II, 15.

33 Cf. *Col.*, II, 14.

34 Cf. *Matth.*, XXVI, 28; *I Cor.*, XI, 25.

35 Leo the Great, *Serm.*, LXVIII, 3: Migne, *P. L.*, LIV, 374.

36 Jerome and Augustine, *Epist.* CXII, 14 and CXVI, 16: Migne, *P. L.*, XXII, 924 and 943; St. Thos., I-II, q. 103, a. 3, ad 2; a. 4, ad 1; Council of Flor. *pro Jacob.:* Mansi, XXXI, 1738.

37 Cf. *II Cor.*, III, 6.

38 Cf. St. Thos., III, q. 42, a. 1.

39 Cf. *De pecc. orig.*, XXV, 29: Migne, *P. L.*, XLIV, 400.

40 Cf. *Eph.*, II, 14-16.

41 Cf. *Acts.* II, 1-4.

42 Cf. *Luke*, III, 22; *Mark*, I, 10.

43 *Col.*, I, 18.

44 Cf. *Eph.*, IV, 16; *Col.*, II, 19.

45 *Col.*, I, 15.

46 *Col.*, I, 18; *Apoc.*, I, 5.

47 *I Tim.*, II, 5.

48 Cf. *John*, XII, 32.

49 Cf. Cyr. Alex., *Comm. in Ioh.* I, 4: Migne, *P.G.*, LXXIII, 69; St. Thos., I, q. 20, a. 4, ad 1.

50 *Hexaem.*, VI, 55: Migne, *P. L.*, XIV, 265.

51 Cf. August., *De agon. Christ.*, XX, 22: Migne, *P. L.*, XL, 301.

52 Cf. St. Thos., I, q. 22, a. 1-4.

53 Cf. *John*, X, 1-18; *I Peter*, V, 1-5.

54 Cf. *John*, VI, 63.

55 *Proverbs*, XXI, 1.

56 Cf. *I Peter*, II, 25.

57 Cf. *Acts*, VIII, 26; IX, 1-19; X, 1-7; XII, 3-10.

58 *Phillipp.*, IV, 7.

59 Cf. Leo XIII, *Satis Cognitum:* A. S. S. XXVIII, 725.

60 *Luke*, XII, 32.

61 Cf. *Corp. Iur. Can.*, Extr. comm., I, 8, 1.

62 Gregory the Great, *Moral.*, XIV, 35, 43: Migne, *P. L.*, LXXV, 1062.

63 Cf. Vat Council, *Const. de Eccl.*, Cap. 3.

64 Cf. *Cod. Iur. Can.*, can. 329, 1.

65 *I Paral.*, XVI, 22; *Ps.*, CIV, 15.

66 Cf. *I Peter*, V, 3.

67 Cf. *I Tim.*, VI, 20.

68 Cf. *Ep. and Eulog.*, 30: Migne, *P. L.*, LXXVII, 933.

69 *I Cor.*, XII, 21.

70 *John*, XV, 5.

71 Cf. *Eph.*, IV, 16, *Col.*, II, 19.

72 *Comm. in Ep. ad Eph.*, Cap. 1, lect.8; *Hebr.*, II, 16-17.

73 *Phillipp.*, II, 7.

74 Cf. *II Peter*, I, 4.

75 Cf. *Rom.*, VIII, 29.

76 Cf. *Col.*, III, 10.

77 Cf. *I John*, III, 2.

78 *Col.*, I, 19.

79 Cf. *John* XVII, 2.

80 *Col.*, II, 3.

81 Cf. *John*, I, 14-16.

82. Cf. *John*, I, 18.

83 Cf. *John*, III, 2.

84 Cf. *John*, XVIII, 37.

85 Cf. *John*, VI, 68.

86. Cf. August., *De cons. evang.*, I, 35, 54; Migne, *P. L.*, XXXIV, 1070.

87 Cf. *Hebr.*, XII, 2.

88 Cf. Cyr. Alex., *Ep. 55 de Symb.:* Migne, *P. G.*, LXXVII, 293.

89 Cf. *John*, XV, 5.

90 Cf. St. Thos., III, q. 64, a. 3.

91 *Eph.*, IV, 7.

92 *Eph.*, IV, 16; cf. *Col.*, II, 19.

93 Cf. *De Rom. Pont.*, I, 9; *De Concil*, II, 19.

94 Cf. *I Cor.*, XII, 12.

95 Cf. *Acts*, IX, 4; XXII, 7; XXVI, 14.

96 Cf. Greg. Nyss., *De vita Moysis:* Migne, *P. G.*, XLIV, 385.

97 Cf. *Serm.*, CCCLIV, 1: Migne, *P. L.*, XXXIX, 1563.

98 Cf. *John*, XVII, 18, and XX, 21.

99 Cf. Leo XIII, *Sapientiae Christianae:* A. S. S., XXII. 392; *Satis Cognitum: ibidem*, XXVIII, 710.

100 *Rom.*, VIII, 9; *II Cor.*, III, 17; *Gal.*, IV, 6.

101 Cf. *John*, XX, 22.

102 Cf. *John*, III, 34.

103 Cf. *Eph.*, I, 8; IV, 7.

104 Cf. *Rom.*, VIII, 14-17; *Gal.*, IV, 6-7.

105 Cf. *II Cor.*, III, 18.

106 A. S. S., XXIX, p. 650.

107 *Gal.*, II, 20.

108. Cf. Ambrose, *De Elia et ieiun.*, 10, 36-37, et *In Psalm.* 118, *serm.* 20, 2: Migne, *P. L.*, XIV, 710 et XV, 1483.

109 *Eph.*, V, 23.

110 *John*, IV, 42.

111 Cf. *1 Tim.*, IV, 10.

112 *Acts.* XX, 28.

113 *Enarr. in Ps.*, LXXXV, 5; Migne, *P. L.*, XXXVII, 1085.

114 Clem. Alex., *Strom.*, VII, 2; Migne, *P. G.*, IX, 413.

115 *I Cor.*, III, 23; Pius XI, *Divini Redemptoris:* A. A. S., 1937, p. 80.

116. *De Verritate*, q. 29, a. 4, c.

117 Cf. Leo XIII, *Sapientiae Christianae:* A. S. S., XXII, p. 392.

118 Cf. Leo. XIII *Satis Cognitum:* A. S. S., XXVIII, p. 724.

119 Cf. *Ibidem*, p. 710.

120 Cf. *Ibidem*, p. 710.

121 Cf. *Ibidem*, p. 710.

122 St. Thos., *De Veritate*, q. 29, a. 4, ad 9.

123 Vat. Council, Sess. IV, *Const. dogm. de Eccl.*, prol.

124. *Col.*, I, 13.

125 Vat. Council, Sess. III, *Const. de fide Cath.*, Cap. 3.

126 *Philipp.*, II, 8.

127. *John*, XX, 22.

128 *John*, XX, 21.

129 *Luke*, X, 16.

130. Cf. Vat Council, Sess. III, *Const. de fide Cath.*, Cap. 3.

131 *Serm.*, XXI, 3: Migne. *P. L.*, LIV, 192-193.

132 Cf. August., *Contra Faust.*, 21, 8: Migne, *P. L.*, XLII, 392.

133 Cf. *Eph.*, V, 22-23; *John*, XV. 1-5; *Eph.*, IV, 16.

134 *Col.*, I, 18.

135 Cf. *Enarr. in Ps.*, XVII, 51, and SC, II, 1: Migne, *P. L.*, XXXVI, 154, and XXXVII, 1159.

136 *John*, XVII, 21-23.

137 *Apoc.*, V, 12-13.

138 Cf. *John*, XIV, 16 and 26.

139 *Eph.*, IV, 5. 140.

140 Cf. *John*, XVII, 3.

141 *I John*, IV, 15.

142 *II Cor.*, IV, 13.

143 Cf. *Gal.*, II, 20.

144 Cf. *Eph.*, III, 17.

145 Cf. *Hebr.*, XII, 2.

146 *Tit.*, II, 13.

147. Cf. *Hebr.*, XIII, 14.

148 *Eph.*, IV, 4.

149 Cf. *Col.*, I, 27.

150 *I John*, IV, 16.

151 *John*, XIV, 28.

152 *John*, XV, 9-10.

153 *I John*, IV, 20-21.

154 *Rom.*, XII, 5.

155 *I Cor.*, XII, 25.

156 *Serm.* XXIX: Migne, *P. L.*, LVII, 594.

157 Cf. St. Thos., *Comm. in Ep. ad Eph.*, Cap. II, lect. 5.

158 *Rom.*, VIII, 9-10.

159. Cf. St. Thos., *Comm. in Ep. ad Eph.*, Cap. I, lect. 8.

160 Cf. St. Thos., I, q. 43, a. 3.

161 Sess. III, *Const. de fide Cath.*, Cap. 4.

162 Cf. *Divinum Illud:* A. S. S., XXIX, p. 653.

163 *Mal.*, I, 11.

164 Cf. *Didache*, IX, 4.

165 Cf. *Rom.*, VIII, 35.

166 Cf. *Eph.*, V, 22-23.

167 *Ps.*, LXXXIII, 12.

168 *Expos. Evang. sec. Luc.*, IV, 49: Migne, *P. L.* XV, 1626.

169 *Gal.*, II, 20.

170 *I Cor.*, XV, 10.

171 Cf. St. Thos., II-II, q. 83, a. 5 et 6.

172 *I Tim.*, II, 5.

173 Cf. St. Thos., *De Veritate*, q. 29, a. 4, c.

174 *John*, XIV, 14.

175 *Apoc.*, V, 13.

176 *Ps.*, CXXXVI, 5-6.

177 *Eph.*, II, 20; *I Peter,* II, 4-5.

178 Cf. *II Cor.*, XI, 14.

179 Cf. *II Cor.*, X, 5.

180 Cf. *Hebr.*, XIII, 17.

181 *I Cor.*, XII, 22-23.

182 Cf. Decree of Holy Office, 2 Dec. 1940: A. A. S., 1940, p. 553.

183 Cf. *Gen.*, IV, 10.

184 Cf. *Rom.*, XII, 5; *I Cor.*, XII, 25.

185 Cf. *I Cor.*, XII, 26.

186 Cf. *Luke,* X, 33-37.

187 Cf. *Luke,* VI, 27-35; *Matth.*, V. 44-48.

188 Cf. *Eph.*, III, 18.

189 Cf. *Luke,* XXII, 32.

190 Cf. *John,* XVII, 9-19.

191 Cf. *John,* XVII, 20-23.

192 Cf. *Matth.*, IX, 38; *Luke,* X, 2.

193 *John,* XVII, 21.

194 Cf. Litt. enc. *Summi Pontificatus:* A. A. S., 1939, p. 419.

195 Iren., *Adv. Haer.*, IV, 33, 7: Migne, *P. G.*, VII, 1076.

196 Cf. Pius IX, *Iam Vos Omnes,* 13 Sept. 1868: Act. Conc. Vat., C. L. VII, 10.

197 Cf. Gelas, I, *Epist.* XIV: Migne, *P. L.*, LIX, 89.

198 Cf. August. *In Ioann, Ev. tract.*, XXVI, 2: Migne, *P. L.*, XXX, 1607.

199 Cf. August., *Ibidem.*

200 *Hebr.*, XI, 6.

201 Vat. Council, *Const. de fide Cath.*, Cap. 3.

202 Cf. Leo XIII, *Immortale Dei:* A. S. S. XVIII, pp. 174-175; Cod. Iur. Can., c. 1351.

203 Cf. August., *Ibidem.*

204 *Is.*, XXXII, 17.

205 Cf. *I Tim.*, II, 2.

206 Cf. *Wis.*, VI, 23.

207 *Ibidem*, VI, 4-10.

208 *John*, XIII, 1.

209 Cf. *Acts*, XX, 28.

210 *Rom.*, VI, 5.

211 *II Tim.*, II, 11.

212 Cf. *Col.*, I, 24.

213 Cf. *Serm.*, LXIII, 6: LXVI, 3: Migne, *P. L.*, LIV, 357 and 366.

214 *In Ps.*, 118, XXII, 30: Migne, *P. L.*, XV, 1521.

215 *Office for Holy Week.*

216 St. Thos., III, q. 30, a. 1, c.

217 *John*, II, 11.

218 *Col.*, I, 24.

219 Cf. *Vesper hymn of Office of the Sacred Heart.*

220 Cf. Pius X, *Ad Diem Illum:* A. S. S., XXXVI, p. 453.

ORIENTALIS ECCLESIÆ DECUS, Encyclical Letter of Pope Pius XII on St. Cyril, Patriarch of Alexandria, April 9, 1944.

1 Ep. 12, 4: Migne, 50, col. 467.

2 Ep. 13, 2: *ib.*, 471.

3 Ep. 25, 7: *ib.*, 552.

4 Cf. Mansi, VI, 953, 956-7; VII, 9.

5 Cf. *Ep. ad Imp, Theodosium:* Migne *P.L.*, 54, col. 891.

6 Cf. Mansi, IX, 231 sq.

7 Cf. Mansi, X, 1076 sq.

8 Cf. Mansi, XI, 270 sq.

9 Cf. *ib.*, 262 sq.

10 *A.A.S.*, XXIII (1931), pp. 493 sq.

11 Cf. *In Joannem*, lib. x: Migne, *P.G.*, 74, col. 419.

12 Ep. 10; Migne, *P.G.*, 77, col. 78.

13 Ep. 9: *ib.*, 62.

14 Ep. 10: *ib.*, 70.

15 Ep. 9: *ib.*, 63.

16 Ep. 1: *ib.*, 14.

17 Ep. 55: *ib.*, 202-203.

18 Ep. 61: *ib.*, 325.

19 Cf. Ep. 9: *ib.*, 322.

20 Cf. Ep. 57: *ib.*, 322.

21 Ep. 58: *ib.*, 322.

22 Ep. 18: *ib.*, 123-126.

23 Cf. Ep. 9: *ib.*, 62.

24 Ep. 39: *ib.*, 175.

25 Ep. 39: *ib.*, 175.

26 Ep. 33: *ib.*, 161.

27 Ep. 39: *ib.*, 174.

28 Ep. 11: *ib.*, 79.

29 Cf. *Ep. ad Cyrillum: ib.*, 90.

30 Mansi, IV, 1287.

31 *Apol. ad Theodos.*: Migne, *P.G.*, 76, col, 482.

32 Ep. 22: *P.L.*, 50, col. 542-543.

33 Ep. 40: Migne, *P.G.*, 77, col. 202.

34 Ep. 4, 1-2: Migne, *P.L.*, 50, col. 561.

35 Ep. 5, 1, 3, 5: *ib.*, 602-604.

36 Ep. 44: *P.G.*, 77, col. 226.

37 Ep. 49: *ib.*, 254.

HAURIETIS AQUAS, Encyclical Letter of Pope Pius XII on Devotion to the Sacred Heart, May 15, 1956.

1 *Is.*, 12, 3.

2 *Jas.* 1, 17.

3 *Jn.* 7, 37-39.

4 Cf. *Is.* 12, 3; *Ez.* 47, 1-12; *Za.*. 13, 1; *Ex.* 17, 1-7; *Nm.* 20, 7-13; I *Cor.* 10, 4; *Ap.* 7, 17; 22, 1.

5 *Rom.* 5, 5.

6 I. *Cor.* 6, 17.

7 *Jn.* 4, 10.

8 Enc. *Annum Sacrum*, May 25, 1899: A.L., Vo. 19, 1900, pp. 71, 77-78.

9 Enc. *Miserentissimus Redemptor*, May 8, 1928: A.A.S., 20, 1928, p. 167.

10 Cfr. Enc. *Summi Pontificatus*, October 20, 1939: A.A.S. 31, 1939, p. 415.

11 Cfr. A.A.S., 32, 1940, p. 276: 35, 1943, p. 470; 37, 1945, pp. 263-264; 40, 1948, p. 501; 41, 1949, p. 331.

12 *Eph*. 3, 20-21.

13 *Is*. 12, 3.

14 Council of Ephesus, Can. 8; cfr. Mansi, *Sacrorum Conciliorum Amplis. Collectio*, 4, 1083 C; Second Council of Constantiniople, Can. 9 cfr. *Ibid*. 9, 382 E.

15 Cfr. Encl. *Annum Sacrum*: A.L., vol. 19, 1900, p. 76.

16 Cfr. *Ex*. 34, 27-28.

17 *Dt*. 6, 4-6.

18 *Sum. Theol.*, II-II, q. 2, a. 7: ed. Leon, tom. 8, 1895, p. 34.

19 *Dt*. 32, 11.

20 *Os*. 11, 1, 3-4; 14, 5-6.

21 *Is*. 49, 14-15.

22 *Ct*. 2, 2; 6, 3; 8, 6.

23 *Jn*. I, 14.

24 *Jer*. 31, 3; 31, 33-34.

25 Cf. *Jn*. 1, 29; *Hebr*. 9, 18-28; 10, 1-17.

26 *Jn*. 1, 16-17.

27 *Jn*. 21, 20.

28 *Eph*. 3, 17-19.

29 *Summa Theologica* 3, q. 48, a.2; ed. Leon. tom. 11, 1903, p. 464.

30 Cfr. Enc. *Miserentissimus Redemptor*; A.A.S. 20, 1928, p. 170.

31 *Eph*. 2, 4; *Sum. Theol*. 3, q. 46, a. 1 ad 3; Ad Leon, tom. 11, 1903, p. 436.

32 *Eph*. 3, 18.

33 *Jn*. 4-24.

34 2 *Jn*. 7.

35 Cfr. *Lk*., 1, 35.

36 St. Leo the Great, *Epist. Dogm. "Lectis dilectionis tuae" ad Flavianum Const. Patr.* 13 June, a. 449; cfr. P.L. 54, 763.

37 Council of Chalcedon, a. 451; cfr. Manis. *Op. cit.* 7, 115 B.

38 Pope St. Gleasius, Tract 3: *"Necessarium" Of the Two Natures in Christ*, cfr. A. Thiel, *Letters of the Roman Pontiffs from St. Hilary to Pelagius* II, p. 532.

39 Cfr. St. Thomas *Sum. Theol.* 3, q. 15, a 4; q. 18, a.6; ed. Leon. tom. 11, 1903, p. 189 and 237.

40 Cfr. I *Cor.* 1, 23.

41 *Heb.* 2, 11-14; 17-18.

42 *Apol.* 2, 13; P.G. 6, 465.

43 *Epist.* 261, 3: P.G. 32, 972.

44 *In Joann.* Homil. 63, 2; P.G. 50, 350.

45 *De fide ad Gratianum*, 2, 7, 56; P.L. 16, 594.

46 *Super Matth.* 26, 37; P.L. 26, 205.

47 *Enarr. in Ps.* 87, 3; P.L. 37, 1111.

48 *De Fide Orth.* 3, 6: P.L. 94, 1006.

49 *Ibid.* 3, 20: P.G. 94, 1801.

50 *Sum. Theol.* 1-2, q. 48, a.4; Leon. tom 6, 1891, p. 306.

51 *Col.* 2, 9.

52 Cfr. *Summa. Theol.*, 3, q. 9, a. 1-3; ed. Leon tom 11, 1903, p. 142.

53 Cfr. *Ibid.* 3, q. 33, a. 2, ad 3m; q. 46, a. 6: ed. Leon. tom. 11, 1903, pp. 342, 433.

54 *Tit.* 3, 4.

55 *Mt.* 27, 50; *Jn.* 19, 30.

56 *Eph.* 2, 7.

57 *Heb.* 10, 5-7, 10.

58 *Registr. epist.* lib. IV ep. 31 *ad Theodorum Medicum*; P.L. LXXVII, 706.

59 *Mk.* 8, 2.

60 *Mt.* 23, 37.

61 *Mt.* 21, 13.

62 *Mt.* 26, 39.

63 *Mt.* 26, 50, *Lk.* 22, 48.

64 *Lk.* 23, 28, 31.

65 *Lk.* 23, 34.

66 *Mt.* 27, 46.

67 *Lk.* 23, 43.

68 *Jn.* 19, 28.

69 *Lk.* 23, 46.

70 *Lk.* 22, 15.

71 *Lk.* 22, 19-20.

72 *Mal.*, 1, 11.

73 *De Sancta Virginitate*, VI, P.L. XL, 339.

74 *Jn.* 15, 13.

75 *Jn.* 2, 16.

76 *Gal.* 2, 20.

77 Cfr. S. Thom. *Sum. Theol.* III, q. 19, a. 1: Ed. Leon. Tom. XI, 1903, p. 329.

78 *Sum. Theol. Suppl.* q. 42, a.1 ad 3m; ed. Leon tom. XII, 1906, p. 81.

79 Hymn *ad Vesp. Festi.* SS *mi cordis Iesu.*

80 *Sum. Theol.* III, q. 66 a.3, ad 3m: Leon. Thom. XII, 1906, p. 65.

81 *Eph.* 5, 2.

82 *Eph.* 4, 8, 10.

83 *Jn.* 14, 16.

84 *Col.* 2, 3.

85 *Rom.* 8, 35, 37-39.

86 *Eph.* 5, 25-27.

87 Cfr. 1 *Jn.* 2, 1.

88 *Heb.* 7, 25.

89 *Heb.* 5, 7.

90 *Jn.* 3, 16.

91 St. Bonaventure, Opusa. X: *Vitis mystica*, c. III, N. 5; *Opera Omnia*, Ad. Claras Aquas (Quararchi) 1898, Tom. VIII, p. 164; cfr. S. Thom. *Sum. Theol.* III, 9. 54, a.4: ed Leon Tom XI, 1903, p. 513.

92 *Rom.* 8, 32.

93 Cfr. *Sum. Theol.*, 3, q. 48, a.5: ed. Leon. Tom. 11, 1903, p. 467.

94 *Lk.* 12, 50.

95 *Jn.* 20, 28.

96 *Jn.* 19, 37; *Za.* 12, 10.

97 Cfr. Enc. *Miserentissimus Redemptor*: A.A.S., 20, 1928, pp. 167-168.

98 Cfr. A. Gardellini, *Decreta authentica* 1867, n. 4579, tom. 3, p. 174.

99 Cfr. *Decr. S.C. Rit.* Apud N. Nilles *De rationibus festorum Sacratissirni Cordis Jesu et purissimi Cordis Mariae* 5th edition. Innsbruck, 1885, tom. 1, p. 157.

100 *Eph.* 3, 14, 16-19.

101 *Ti.* 3, 4.

102 *Jn.* 3, 17.

103 *Jn.* 4, 23-24.

104 Innocent XI, Constit, Ap. *Colelestis Pastor*, November 19, 1687; *Bullarium Romanum*, Rome, 1734, 1734, tom. 8, p. 443.

105 *Sum. Theol.* II-II, q. 81 a.3 ad 3m; ed. Leon. tom. 9, 1897, p. 180.

106 *Jn.* 14, 6.

107 *Jn.* 13, 34; 15, 12.

108 *Jer.* 31, 31.

109 *Commet. in Evang. S. Joann.* c. 13, lect. 7, 3, ed. Parmae, 1860, tom. 10, p. 541.

110 *Sum. Theol.* II-II q. 82 a. 1.

111 *Summ. Theol.* I q. 38 a. 2.

112 *Mk.* 12, 30; *Mt.* 22, 37.

113 Cfr. Leo XIII Enc. *Annum Sacrum*: A. Ls., vo. 19, 1900, p. 71 sq.; *Decr. S.C. Rituum* June 28, 1899, in Decr. Auth. 3, x. 3712; Pius XI, Enc. *Miserentissimus Redemptor*: A.A.S. 1928, p. 177 sq.; *Decr. S.C. Rit.* January 29, 1929; A.A.S. 21, 1929, p. 77.

114 *Lk.* 15, 22.

115 *Exposit. in Evang. sec Lucam*, 1, 10, n. 175; P.L. 15, 1942.

116 Cfr. St. Thomas *Sum. Theol.* II-II, q. 34, a.2: ed. Leon tom. 8, 1895, p. 274.

117 *Mt.* 24, 12.

118 Cfr. Enc. *Miserentissimus Redemptor*: A.A.S. 20, 1928, p. 166.

119 *Is.* 32, 17.

120 Enc. *Annum Sacrum*: A. L., vol. 19, 1900, p. 79; *Miserentissimus Redemptor*; A.A.S., 20, 1928, p. 167.

121 *Litt. Apost. quibus Archisodalitas a Corde Eucharistico Jesu ad S. Jochim de Urbe erigitur*, February 17, 1903; A.L. Vo. 22, 1903, p. 307 sq.; cfr, Enc. *Mirae caritatis* May 22, 1902: A.L. vo. 22, 1903, p. 116.

122 St. Albert the Great *De Eucharistia* dist. 6, tr. 1, c. 1: Opera Omnia ed. Borgent, vol. 38, Paris, 1890, p. 358.

123 Enc. Tamisti, A.L. vol. 20, 1900 p. 303.

124 Cfr. A.A.S. 34, 1942, p. 345.

125 Roman Missal *Preface of Jesus Christ the King*.

AETERNA DEI SAPIENTIA, Encyclical Letter of Pope John XXIII Commemorating the Fifteenth Centenary of the Death of St. Leo the Great, Pope and Doctor of the Church, November 11, 1961.

1 *Wisd.* 8:1.

2 Sermon, 12 Oct., 1952, in *Discorsi e Radiomessaggi* XIV, p. 358.

3 *Prov.* 4:18.

4 Cf. Ed. Duchesne, I, 238.

5 Cf. Ep. 31, 4, Migne, PL 54, 794.

6 Migne, PL 59, 9-272.

7 *De Incarn. Domini, contra Nestorium*, lib. VII, prol. PL 50, 9.

8 Migne, PL 55, 21-156.

9 Cf. *ibid.* 54, 757.

10 *Ibid.* col. 759.

11 Ep. 29 *to the Emperor Theodosius*, PL 54, 783.

12 Cf. Ep. 28, PL 54, 756.

13 Cf. Ep. 95, 2, *to the Empress Pulcheria*, PL 54, 943.

14 Cf. *ibid.*

15 Cf. *ibid.*

16 Cf. Ep. 82, 2, *to the Emperor Marcian*, PL 54, 931; Ep. 103 *to the Gallic Bishops*, PL 54, 988-991.

17 Encycl. *Sempiternus Rex*, 8th Sept. 1951, AAS 43 (1951) 625-644.

18 Cf. C. Kirch, *Enchir. fontium hist. eccl. antiquae*, Freiburg in Br., edn. 4, 1923, n. 943.

19 Ep. 104, 3 *to the Emperor Marcian*, PL 54, 955; cf. Ep. 106, *to Anatolius, bishop of Constantinople*, PL 54, 995.

20 Ep. 114, 3 *to the Emperor Marcian*, PL 54, 1022.

21 *Ibid.*

22 Benedict XIV Pont. Max. opera omnia, vol. 18, *Bullarium, tom.* III, part II, Prati 1847, p. 205.

23 1 *Cor.* 12:31.

24 Cf. *John* 21:15-17.

25 Ep. 12, 5 *to the African Bishops*, PL 54, 652.

26 Ep. 80, 1 *to Anatolius, Bishop of Constantinople*, PL 54, 913.

27 Sermon 26, 2 *on the Feast of the Nativity*, PL 54, 213.

28 *Col.* 1:18.

29 Cf. Ep. 165, 2 *to the Emperor Leo*, PL 54, 1157.

30 Cf. *ibid.*

31 Cf. Serm. 22, 2 *on the Feast of the Nativity*, PL 54, 195.

32 Serm. 4, 1, *on the Feast of the Nativity*, PL 54, 149; cf. Serm. 64, 6 *on the Passion*, PL 54, 357; Ep. 69, 4, PL 54, 870.

33 Serm. 66, 2 *on the Passion*, PL 54, 365-366.

34 Serm. 64, 7 *on the Passion*, PL 54, 357.

35 Serm. 24, 6 *on the Feast of the Nativity*, PL 54, 207.

36 Ep. 14, 11 *to Anastasius, bishop of Thessalonica*, PL 54, 676.

37 Serm. 4, 2 *on the Anniversary of his Elevation*, PL 54, 149-150.

38 *Ibid.* col. 151; cf. Serm. 83, 2 *on the Feast of the Apostle Peter*, PL 54, 430.

39 Serm. 4, 3, PL 54, 151-152; cf. Serm. 83, 2, PL 54, 451.

40 Serm. 5, 4 *on the Anniversary of his Ordination*, PL 54, 154.

41 Cf. Serm. 3, 4 *on the Anniversary of his Elevation*, PL 54, 147.

42 Serm. 3, 3 *on the Anniversary of his Elevation*, PL 54, 146; cf. Serm. 83, 3 *on the Feast of the Apostle Peter*, PL 54, 432.

43 Ep. 30 *ad Concil. Milev.*, PL 20, 590.

44 Ep. 13 *to Rufus, bishop of Thessaly*, 11 Mar., 422, in C. Silva-Tarouca S.I. *Epistolarum Romanorum Pontificum collect. Thessal.*, Rome 1937, p. 27.

45 Ep. 14, 1 *to Anastasius, bishop of Thessalonica*, PL 54, 668.

46 Serm. 82, 1 *on the Feast of the Apostles Peter and Paul*, PL 54, 422-423.

47 Serm. 86, 3 *against the heresy of Eutyches*, PL 54, 468.

48 Mansi, *Concil. dimpliss, collect*. VI, p. 913.

49 Ep. 100, 3 *from the Emperor Marcian*, PL 54, 972; Ep. 77, 1 *from the Empress Pulcheria*, PL 54, 907.

50 Ep. 52, 1 *from Theodoret, Bishop of Cyrus*, PL 54, 847.

51 *Menaia tou holou eniautou* III, Rome 1896, p. 612.

52 Migne PG 117, 319.

53 1 *Tim*. 2:5.

54 Cf. Conc. Vat. I, Sess. III, cap. 3 *de fide*.

55 *Heb*. 13:20.

56 Cf. *John* 21:15-17.

57 *Adv. Haer*. I. III, c. 2, n. 2, PG 7, 848.

58 *Ibid*.

59 *John* 17:21.

60 Cf. *John* 11:42.

61 *Ibid*. 10:16.

62 Cf. I *Tim*. 2:5; 1 *John* 2:1.

63 *Ps*. 132:1.

64 Cf. *Phil*. 1:27.

65 Ep. 50, 2 *to the people of Constantinople*, PL 54, 843.

66 *John* 17:11. 20. 23.

67 *Col*. 3:14.

68 Cf. 2 *Cor*. 6:16.

69 Serm. 48, 1, *on Lent*, PL 54, 298-9.

70 Ep. 88, 2 PL 54, 441-442.

71 Ep. 95, 2 *to the Empress Pulcheria*, PL 54, 943.

SACROSANCTUM CONCILIUM, General Principles for the Restoration and Promotion of the Sacred Liturgy, December 4, 1963.

1 Cf. *Is*. 61:1; *Lk*. 4:18.

2 Cf. St. Ignatius of Antioch: *Ad Ephesios,* 7:2.

3 Cf. *1 Tim.* 2:5.

4 *Sacramentarium Veronese* (Leonianium).

5 Easter Preface of the *Roman Missal.*

6 Prayer before Second Lesson of Holy Saturday (*Roman Missal,* before restoration).

7 Cf. *Mk.* 16:15.

8 Cf. *Acts* 26:18.

9 Cf. *Rom.* 6:4; *Eph.* 2:6; *Col.* 3:1; *2 Tim.* 2:11.

10 Cf. *Jn.* 4:23.

11 Cf. *1 Cor.* 2:26.

12 Council of Trent, Session 23: *Decree on the Holy Eucharist,* ch. 5.

13 Council of Trent, Session 22: *Doctrine on the Holy Sacrifice of the Mass*, ch. 2.

14 Cf. St. Augustine, *Tractatus in Ioannem VI,* ch. 1, n. 7.

15 Cf. *Apoc.* 21:2; *Col.* 3:1; *Heb.* 8:2.

16 Cf. *Phil.* 3:20; *Col.* 3:4.

17 Cf. *Jn.* 17:3; *Lk.* 24:27; *Acts* 2:38.

18 Cf. *Mt.* 28:20.

19 Postcommunion for both Masses of Easter Sunday.

20 Collect for Mass of Tuesday of Easter Week.

21 Cf. *2 Cor.* 6:1.

22 Cf. *Mt.* 6:6.

23 Cf. *1 Th.* 5:17.

24 Cf. *2 Cor.* 4:10-11.

25 Secret for Monday of Pentecost Week.

26 St. Cyprian, "*On the Unity of the Catholic Church,*" 7; cf. Letter 66, n. 8, 3.

27 Cf. Council of Trent, Session 22: *Doctrine on the Holy Sacrifice of the Mass*, ch. 8.

28 Cf. St. Ignatius of Antionch: *Magnesians*, 7; *Philadelphians,* 4; *Smyrnaeans*, 8.

LUMEN GENTIUM, The Dogmatic Constitution on the Church, November 21, 1964.

1 Cf. St. Cyprian, *Epist.* 64, 4: *PL* 3, 1017, *CSEL* (Hartel), III B, p. 720. St. Hilary of Poiters, *in Matth.* 23, 6: *PL* 9, 1047. St. Augustine, passim. St. Cyril of Alexandria, *Glaph. in Gen.* 2, 10: *PG* 69, 110A.

2 Cf. St. Gregory the Great, *Hom in Evang.* 19, 1: *PL* 76, 1154B. St. Augustine, *Serm.* 341, 9, 11: *PL* 39, 1499 f. St. John Damascene, Adv Iconocl. 11: *PG* 96, 1357.

3 Cf. St. Irenaeus, *Adv. Haer.* III, 24, 1: *PG* 7, 966B; Harvey 2, 131: ed Sagnard, *Sources Chr.*, p. 398.

4 St. Cyprian, *De Orat. Dom.* 23: *PL* 4, 553; Hartel, IIIA, p. 285. St. Augustine, *Serm.* 71, 20, 33: *PL* 38, 463 f. St. John Damascene, *Adv. Iconocl.* 12: *PG* 96, 1358D.

5 Cf. Origen, *in Matth.* 16, 21: *PG* 13, 1443 C. Tertullian, *Adv. Marc.* 3, 7: *PL* 2, 357 C; *CSEL* 47, 3 p. 386. For liturgical documents, cf. *Sacramentarium Gregorianum: PL* 78, 160B., or C. Mohlberg, *Liber Sacramentorum Romanae Ecclesiae,* Rome, 1960, p. 111, XC: "God, you who establish an eternal dwelling place for Yourself out of every assembly of the saints . . . "; Hymn *Urbs Jerusalem beata* in the monastic breviary, and *Coelestis urbs Jerusalem* in the Roman breviary.

6 Cf. St. Thomas, *Summa Theol.* III, Q. 62, a. 5, ad 1.

7 Cf. Pius XII, Encyc. letter *Mystici Corporis* (June 29, 1943): *AAS* XXXV (1943), 208.

8 Cf. Leo XIII, Encyc. epistle *Divinum illud* (May 9, 1897): ASS XXIX (1896-97), 650. Pius XII, Encyc. letter *Mystici Corporis, op. cit.*, pp. 219-220; Denz. 2288 (3808). St. Augustine, Serm. 268, 2: *PL* 38, 1232, and elsewhere. St. John Chrysostom, *in Eph.* Hom. 9, 3: *PG* 62, 72. Didymus *Alex., Trin.* 2, 1: *PG* 39, 449f. St. Thomas, *in Col.* 1, 18, lect. 5; ed. Marietti, II, n. 46: "As one body is constituted from the unity of the soul, so the Church is constituted from the unity of the Spirit . . . "

9 Leo XIII, Encyc. letter *Sapientiae christianae* (Jan. 10, 1890): *ASS* XXII (1889-90), 392. *Ibid.*, Encyc. epistle *Satis cognitum* (June 29, 1896): *ASS* XXVIII (1895-96), 710 and 724ff. Pius XII, Encyc. letter *Mystici Corporis, op. cit.*, pp. 199-200.

10 Cf. Pius XII, Encyc. letter *Mystici Corporis, op. cit.* pp. 221ff. *Ibid.*, Encyc. letter *Humani generis* (Aug 12, 1950): *AAS* XLI (1950). 571.

11 Leo XIII, Ency. epistle *Satis cognitum, op. cit.*, p. 713.

12 Cf. *Symbolum Apostolicum:* Denz. 6-9 (10-13); *Symb. Nic. Const.:* Denz. 86 (150; coll. *Prof. fidei Trid.:* Denz. 994 and 999 (1862 and 1868).

13 It is called "the holy (catholic, apostolic) Roman Church" in *Prof. fidei Trid., op. cit.,* and Vatican Council I, Sess. III, Dogmatic Constitution *de fide cath.:* Denz. 1782 (3001).

14 St. Augustine, *Civ. Dei,* XVIII, 51, 2: *PL* 41, 614.

MYSTERIUM FIDEI, Encyclical Letter of Pope Paul VI on the Doctrine and Worship of the Holy Eucharist, September 3, 1965.

1 *Constitution on the Sacred Liturgy*, c. 2, n. 47; *AAS* LVI (1964), 113 [Cf. *TPS* IX, 325.].

2 *Jn* 6, 55.

3 Cf. *Jn* 17, 23.

4 Encyc. letter *Mirae caritatis: Acta Leonis XIII*, XXII (1902-1903) 122.

5 *Homily on Matthew*, 82, 4; *PG* 58, 743.

6 *Summa Theol.* III, q. 75, a. 1, c.

7 *In IV Sent.*, dis. X, P. I, art. un., qu. I; *Opera Omnia*, tome IV, Ad Claras Aquas (1889), 217.

8 *Jn* 6, 61-69.

9 St. Augustine, *Against Julian*, VI, 5, 11; *PL* 44, 829.

10 *City of God*, X, 23; *PL* 41, 300.

11 *Dogmatic Constitution on the Catholic Faith*, c. 4.

12 Cf. Council of Trent, *Teaching on the Holy Sacrifice of the Mass*, c. I.

13 Cf. *Ex* 24, 8.

14 *Lk* 22, 19-20; cf. *Mt* 26, 26-28; *Mk* 14, 22-24.

15 *Acts* 2, 42.

16 *Acts* 4, 32.

17 *1 Cor* 11, 23 ff.

18 *1 Cor* 10, 16.

19 Cf. *Mal* 1, 11.

20 Council of Trent, *Doctrine on the Holy Sacrifice of the Mass*, c. 2.

21 *Catecheses*, 23 [*myst.* 5], 8-18; *PG* 33, 1115-1118.

22 Cf. *Confessions* IX, 12, 32; *PL* 32, 777; cf. *ibid.* IX 11, 27; *PL* 32, 775.

23 Cf. *Serm.* 172, 2; *PL* 38, 936; cf. *On the care to be taken of the dead*, 13; *PL* 40, 593.

24 Cf. St. Augustine, *City of God*, X, 6; *PL* 42, 284.

25 Cf. Encyc. letter *Mediator Dei; AAS* XXXIX (1947), 552.

26 Cf. *Dogmatic Constitution on the Church*, c. 2, 11; *AAS* LVII (1965), 15.

27 Cf. *ibid.*, c. 2, n. 10; *AAS* LVII (1965), 14.

28 *Constitution on the Sacred Liturgy*, c. 1, n. 27; *AAS* LVI (1964), 107 [Cf. *TPS* IX, 322.].

29 Cf. Roman Pontifical.

30 Cf. c. 1, n. 7; *AAS* LVI (1964), 100-101.

31 St. Augustine, *On Psalm 85*, 1: *PL* 37, 1081.

32 *Mt* 18, 20.

33 Cf. *Mt* 25, 40.

34 Cf. *Eph* 3, 17.

35 Cf. *Rom* 5, 5.

36 St. Augustine, *Against the Letter of Petiliani*, III, 10, 11; *PL* 43, 353.

37 St. Augustine, *On Psalm 86*, 3; *PL* 37, 1102.

38 *Homily on the Second Epistle to Timothy* 2, 4; *PG* 62, 612.

39 Aegidius Romanus, *Theorems on the Body of Christ*, theor. 50 (Venice, 1521), p. 127.

40 St. Thomas, *Summa Theol.*, IIIa, p. 73, a. 3, c.

41 Cf. Council of Trent, *Decree on the Holy Eucharist*, c. 3.

42 Pius XII, Encyc. letter *Humani Generis; AAS* XLII (1950), 578.

43 *Decree on the Holy Eucharist*, Introduction and c. 2.

44 *Didachè*, 9, 1; F. X. Funk, *Patres Apostolici*, 1, 20.

45 *Epistle to Magnus*, 6; *PL* 3, 1139.

46 *1 Cor* 10, 17.

47 St. Ignatius, *Epistle to the Smyrnians*, 7, 1; *PG* 5, 714.

48 *Commentary on Matthew*, c. 26; *PG* 66, 714.

49 *Decree on the Most Holy Eucharist*, c. 1.

50 Cf. Encyc. letter *Mirae caritatis; Acta Leonis XIII*, XXII (1902-1903), 123.

51 Cf. Council of Trent, *Decree on the Most Holy Eucharist*, c. 4 and canon 2.

52 *Catecheses*, 22, 9 [*myst.* 4] *PG* 33, 1103.

53 *Homily on Judas' betrayal*, 1, 6; *PG* 72, 451.

54 *On Matthew* 26, 27; *PG* 72, 451.

55 *On Mysteries* 9, 50-52; *PL* 16, 422-424.

56 Mansi, *Collectio amplissima Conciliorum*, XX, 524D.

57 Const. *Auctorem fidei*, August 28, 1794.

58 Allocution of September 22, 1956, *AAS* XLVIII (1956), 720 [Cf. *TPS* III, 281-282.].

59 *AAS* LVII (1965), 588-592.

60 *On Psalm 98*, 9; *PL* 37, 1264.

61 *Apostolic Tradition*; ed. Botte, *La Tradition Apostolique de St. Hippolyte*, Muenster (1963), p. 84.

62 *Fragment on Exodus; PG* 12, 391.

63 *On Shows; CSEL* III, 8.

64 *Epistle to Calosyrius; PG* 76, 1075.

65 Cf. Basil, *Epistle 93; PG* 32, 483-486.

66 St. Augustine, *Treatise on John* 26, 13; *PL* 35, 1613.

67 Decree of the Sacred Congregation of the Council, December 20, 1905, approved by St. Pius X; *ASS* XXXVIII (1905), 401.

68 Cf. *Jn* 1, 14.

69 Cf. *Col* 3, 3.

70 *1 Cor* 8, 6.

71 Cf. St. Augustine, *On the literal interpretation of Genesis*, XI, 15, 20; *PL* 34, 437.

72 Cf. *1 Cor* 1, 10.

73 *Lk* 1, 78.

74 *Jn* 6, 48 ff.

75 *Mt* 6, 11.

76 *3 Kgs* 19, 8.

77 *Ps* 77, 25.

78 *Decree on the Most Holy Eucharist*, c. 8.

79 Cf. *Jn* 17, 20-21.

80 Cf. *1 Cor* 10, 17.

81 *C.J.C.*, canon 801.

82 *Epistle to the Philadelphians* 4; *PG* 5, 700.

DEI VERBUM, Dogmatic Constitution on Divine Revelation, November 18, 1965.

1 St. Augustine, *De Catechizandis rudibus*, c. 4, 8: *PL* 40, 316.

2 Cf. *Mt.* 11:27; *Jn.* 1:14 and 17; 14:6; 17:1-32; 2 *Cor.* 3:16 and 4:6; *Eph.* 1:3-14.

3 *Epistle to Diognetus*, c. 7, 4: Funk, *Patres Apostolici*, I, p. 403.

4 First Vatican Council, *Dogm. Const. on Cath. Faith*, c. 3 (on Faith): *Denz.* 189 (3008).

5 Second Council of Orange, can. 7: *Denz.* 180 (377). First Vatican Council, *loc. cit.*: *Denz.* 1791 (3010).

6 First Vatican Council, *Dogm. Const. on Cath. Faith*, c. 2 (on Revelation): *Denz.* 1786 (3005).

7 Ibid.: *Denz.* 1785 and 1786 (3004 and 3005).

8 Cf. *Mt.* 28:19-20 and *Mk.* 16:15. Council of Trent, Session IV, Decree *On the Canonical Scriptures: Denz.* 783 (1501).

9 Cf. Council of Trent, *loc. cit.*: First Vatican Council, Session III, *Dogm. Const on the Catholic Faith*, c. 2 (on Revelation): *Denz.* 1787 (3006).

10 St. Irenaeus, *Adv. Haer.*, III, 3, 1: *PG* 7, 848; Harvey, 2, p. 9.

11 Cf. Council of Nicea II: *Denz.* 303 (602). Council of Constantinople IV, Session X, can. 1: *Denz.* 336 (650-652).

12 Cf. First Vatican Council, *Dogm. Const. on the Catholic Faith*, c. 4 (on Faith and Reason): *Denz.* 1800 (3020).

13 Cf. Council of Trent, Session IV, *Loc. cit.: Denz.* 783 (1501).

14 Cf. Pius XII, Apost. Const. *Munificentissimus Deus*, 1 Nov. 1950: *AAS* 42 (1950) 756, taken along with the words of St. Cyprian, *Epist.* 66, 8; Hartel, III, B, p. 733: "The Church is the people united to its Priests, the flock adhering to its shepherd."

15 Cf. First Vatican Council, *Dogm. Const. on the Catholic Faith*, c. 3 (on Faith): *Denz.* 1972 (3011).

16 Cf. Pius XII, Encycl. *Humani Generis*, 12 Aug. 1950: *AAS* 42 (1950) 568-569: *Denz.* 2314 (3886).

17 Cf. Vatican Council I, *Const. dogm. de fide catholica*, c. 2 (de revelatione): *Denz.* 1787 (3006). *Bibl. Commission*, Decr. 18 June 1915: *Denz.* 2180 (3629); EB 420; Holy Office, *Letter*, 22 Dec. 1923: EB 499.

18 Cf. Pius XII, Encycl. *Divino Affantee Spiritu*, 30 Sept. 1943: *AAS* 35 (1943), p. 314; EB 556.

19 *In* and *by* man: cf. *Heb.* 1:1; 4:7 (*in*); 2 *Sam.* 23:2; *Mt.* 1:22 and *passim* (by); Vatican Council I, *Schema de doctr. cath.*, note 9; Coll. Lac., VII, 522.

20 Leo XIII, Encycl. *Providentissimus Deus*, 18 Nov. 1893: *Denz.* 1952 (3293); EB 125.

21 Cf. St. Augustine, *Gen. ad Litt.*, 2, 9, 20: *PL* 34, 270-271; *Epist.* 82, 3: *PL* 33, 277; *CSEL* 34, 2, p. 354.—St. Thomas. *De Ver.* q. 12, 1. 2, C.—Council of Trent, Session IV, *de canonicis Scripturis: Denz.* 783 (1501)—Leo XIII, Encycl. *Providentissimus*: EB 121, 124, 126-127.—Pius XII, Encycl. *Divino Affante*: EB 539.

22 St. Augustine, *De Civ. Dei*, XVII, 6, 2: *PL* 41, 537: *CSEL* XL, 2, 228.

23 St. Augustine, *De Doctr. Christ.*, III, 18, 26; *PL* 34, 75-76.

24 Pius XII, *loc. cit.: Denz.* 2294 (3829-2830); EB 557-562.

25 Cf. Benedict XV, Encycl. *Spiritus Paraclitus*, 15 Sept. 1920: EB 469. St. Jerome, *In Gal.* 5, 19-21: *PL* 26, 417 A.

26 Cf. Vatican Council I, *Const. dogm. de fide catholica*, c. 2 (de revelatione): *Denz.* 1788 (3007).

27 St. John Chrysostom, *In Gen.* 3, 8 (hom. 17, 1): *PG* 53, 134. *Attemperatio* corresponds to the Greek *synkatabasis.*

28 Pius XI, Encycl. *Mit brennender Sorge*, 14 March 1937: *AAS* 29 (1937), p. 151.

29 St. Augustine, *Quaest. in Hept.* 2, 73: *PL* 34, 623.

30 St.Irenaeus, *Adv. Haer*, III, 21, 3: *PG* 7, 950 (—25, 1: Harvey 2, p. 115). St. Cyril of Jerusalem; *Catech.* 4, 35: *PG* 33, 497. Theodore of Mopsuestia, In Soph. 1, 4-6: *PG* 66, 452D-453A.

31 Cf. St. Irenaeus, *Adv. Haer.* III, 11, 8: *PG* 7, 885; ed. Sagnard, p. 194.

32 Cf. *Jn.* 14:25; 16:13.

33 *Jn.* 2:22; 12-16; cf. 14:26; 16:12-13; 7:39.

34 Cf. The Instruction *Sacra Mater Ecclesia* of the Pontifical Biblical Commission: *AAS* 56 (1964), p. 715.

35 Cf. Pius XII, Encycl. *Divino Afflante*: EB 551, 553, 567. Biblical Commission, Instruction on the Teaching of S. Scripture in Seminaries of Clerics and Religious, 13 May 1950: *AAS* 42 (1950), pp. 495-505.

36 Cf. Pius XII, ibid.: EB 569.

37 Cf. Leo XIII, Encycl. *Providentissimus*: EB 114; Benedict XV, Encycl. *Spiritus Paraclitus:* EB 483.

38 St. Augustine, *Serm.* 179: *PL* 38, 966.

39 St. Jerome, *Comm. in Isaias, Prol.: PL* 24, 17. Cf. Benedict XV, Encycl. *Spiritus Paraclitus:* EB 475-480; Pius XII, Encycl. *Divino Afflante:* EB 544.

40 St. Ambros, *De Officiis ministrorum*, I, 20, 88: *PL* 16, 50.

41 St. Irenaeus, *Adv. Haer.* IV, 32, 1: *PG* 7, 1071; (=49, 2) Harvey, 2, p. 255.

GAUDIUM ET SPES, Selections from Pastoral Constitution on the Church in the Modern World, December 7, 1965.

1 Cf. *Rom.* 7:14 ff.

2 Cf. *2 Cor.* 5:15.

3 Cf. *Acts* 4:12.

4 Cf. *Heb.* 13:8.

5 Cf. *Col.* 1:15.

6 Cf. *Rom.* 5:14. Cf. Tertullian, *De carnis resurrectione*, "For in all the form which was moulded in the clay, Christ was in his thoughts as the man who to be": *PL* 2, 282; *CSEL*, 47, p. 33, 1. 12-13.

7 Cf. *2 Cor.* 4:4.

8 Cf. Council Constantinople II, can. 7: "Neither was God the Word changed into the nature of flesh, nor his flesh changed into the nature of the word"; *Denz.* 219 (428); cf. also Council Constantinople III: "For as his all-holy and immaculate ensouled flesh was not destroyed (*theothesia ouk anèrethé*) by being deified, but persisted in its own state and sphere": *Denz.* 291 (302).

9 Cf. Council Constantinople III: "So also his human will was not destroyed by being deified, but was rather preserved": *Denz.* 291 (556).

10 Cf. *Heb.* 4:15.

11 Cf. *2 Cor.* 5:18-19; *Col.* 1:20-22.

12 Cf. *1 Pet.* 2:21; *Mt.* 16:24; *Lk.* 14-17.

13 Cf. *Rom.* 8:29; *Col.* 3:10-14.

14 Cf. *Rom.* 8:1-11.

15 Cf. *2 Cor.* 4:14.

16 Cf. *Phil.* 3:10; *Rom.* 8:17.

17 Cf. Vatican Council II, Dogmatic Constitution *Lumen Gentium*, ch. 2, n. 16: *AAS* 57 (1965), p. 20.

18 Cf. *Rom.* 8:32.

19 Cf. *Byzantine Easter Liturgy*.

20 Cf. *Rom.* 8:15 and *Gal.* 4:6; cf. also *Jn.* 1:22 and *Jn.* 3:1-2.

21 Dogmatic Constitution *Lumen Gentium* ch. 7, n. 48: *AAS* 57 (1965), p. 53.

22 Cf. Paul VI, *Allocution*, Feb. 1965.

Solemn Profession of Faith by Pope Paul VI at the Closing of the Year of Faith, June 30, 1968.

1 See *1 Tm* 6,20.

2 See *Lk* 22,32.

3 See Dz.-Sch. 3002.

4 See *Ex* 3, 14.

5 See *1 Jn* 4, 8.

6 See *1 Tm* 6,16.

7 See Dz.-Sch. 804.

8 See Dz.-Sch. 75.

9 Ibid.

10 See Dz.-Sch. 150.

11 See Dz.-Sch. 76.

12 Ibid.

13 See Dz.-Sch. 251-252.

14 See *Dogmatic Constitution on the Church,* no. 53 [*TPS* X, 395].

15 See Dz.-Sch. 2803.

16 See *Constitution on the Church*, no. 53 [*TPS* X, 395].

17 See *Constitution on the Church*, nos. 53, 58, 61 [*TPS* X, 395, 396, 397].

18 See Dz.-Sch. 3903.

19 See *Constitution on the Church*, nos. 53, 56, 61, 63 [*TPS* X, 395-96, 397, 398]; see Paul VI, Allocution for closing of the third session of the Second Vatican Council: *AAS* 56, (1964), 1016 [*TPS* X, 138-39]; see Apost. exhortation *Signum Magnum*, Introd. [*TPS* XII, 278-279].

20 See *Constitution on the Church*, no. 62 [*TPS* X, 397-98]; see Paul VI, Apost. exhortation *Signum Magnum*, p. 1, no. 1 [*TPS* XII, 280].

21 See Dz.-Sch. 1513.

22 See *Rom* 5, 20.

23 See Dz.-Sch. 1514.

24 See *Constitution on the Church*, nos. 8 and 5 [*TPS* X, 363-64, 361].

25 See *Constitution on the Church*, nos. 7, 11 [*TPS* X, 362-63, 366-67].

26 See *Constitution on the Sacred Liturgy*, nos. 5, 6 [*TPS* IX, 317-18]; see *Constitution on the Church*, nos. 7, 12, 50 [*TPS* X, 362-63, 367, 392-94].

27 See Dz.-Sch. 3011.

28 See Dz.-Sch. 3074.

29 See *Constitution on the Church*, no. 25 [*TPS* X, 375-76].

30 See *Constitution on the Church*, no 23 [*TPS* X, 374-75]; see *Decree on the Eastern Catholic Churches*, nos. 2, 3, 5, 6 [*TPS* X, 167, 168-69].

31 See *Constitution on the Church*, no. 8 [*TPS* X, 363-64].

32 See *Constitution on the Church*, no. 15 [*TPS* X, 369].

33 See *Constitution on the Church*, no. 14 [*TPS* X, 368-69].

34 See *Constitution on the Church*, no. 16 [*TPS* X, 369-70].

35 See Dz.-Sch. 1651.

36 See Dz.-Sch. 1642, 1651-1654; Paul VI, Encyc. *Mysterium Fidei* [*TPS* X, 309 ff.].

37 See *S. Th.*, III, 73, 3.

38 See *1 Jn* 3, 2; Dz.-Sch. 1000.

39 See *Constitution on the Church*, no. 49 [*TPS* X, 392].

40 See *Lk* 10, 9-10; *Jn* 16, 24.

Address of Pope Paul VI to a General Audience, January 13, 1971.

1 *Jn.* 12, 20-21.

2 *Jn.* 20, 29.

3 Compare the devotion to the visage of Christ connected with Veronica: Dante, *Paradise*, XXXI, 103-108.

4 G. Ricciotti, *Vita di Gesu Cristo*, p. 203 ff.

5 *Ps.* 44, 3.

6 *Is.* 53, 203.

7 *Mt.* 17, 2.

8 *Jn.* 19, 5.

9 *Jn.* 14, 9.

10 See *Jn.* 1, 18.

11 See St. Augustine, *Enarr. in Ps.* 44: *PL* 36, 495.

12 See *S. Th.* I-II, 27, 1, 3.

13 *Jn.* 1, 4.

14 See *Rom.* 8, 29.

Address of Pope Paul VI to a General Audience, January 27, 1971.

1 *Lk.* 19, 1 ff.

2 See *1 Jn.* 1, 1.

3 *Adv. Haereses*, 1, 25: *PG* 7, 685.

4 *De Trinit.* 8, 5: *PL* 42, 952.

5 *Mt.* 11, 29.

6 *Ap.* 1, 12 ff.

7 See portalié, *D. Th. C.* 1, II, 2372.

8 *En. in Ps.* 31, 18: *PL* 36, 270.

9 *Phil.* 2, 7.

10 *Gal.* 2, 20.

11 See *Mt.* 5, 38 ff.

12 See *Ap.* 19, 11 ff.

13 "But I say to you . . ." *Mt.* 5.

14 For example, *Mt.* 5, 20.

15 See *Mt.* 23.

16 See *Mt.* 11, 12.

17 *Jn.* 1, 14.

Address of Pope Paul VI to a General Audience, February 3, 1971.

1 See *Lk.* 4, 22.

2 *Mt.* 16, 14; 21, 11.

3 *Mt.* 27, 63.

4 *Mt.* 21, 9.

5 *Lk.* 4, 20.

6 *Mt.* 8, 20.

7 *Mk.* 6, 3; 1, 27.

8 *Mt.* 4, 8.

9 *Jn.* 6, 15.

10 *Mt.* 22, 21; see O. Cullmann, *Jesus et les revolutionnaires de son temps*, p. 47 ff.

11 See *Mt.* 13, 57; 21, 11; *Lk.* 7, 16; 7, 39; *Jn.* 4, 19; 6, 14; 9, 17; etc.

12 See *Jn.* 7, 16.

13 *Mt.* 3, 2.

14 *Mt.* 4, 17.

15 See *Jn.* 19, 19.

16 *Col.* 1, 26.

Address of Pope Paul VI to a General Audience, February 10, 1971.

1 *Mt.* 13, 55.

2 *Mk.* 6, 3.

3 *Jn.* 1, 29.

4 *Jn.* 1, 34.

5 *Jn.* 1, 36.

6 *Jn.* 1, 41.

7 *Mt.* 11, 3.

8 *Mt.* 16, 13-16.

9 *Mt.* 16, 17-18.

10 *Serm.* 4, 2: *PL* 54, 150.

11 *Mt.* 17, 5; see *2 Pt.* 1, 16 ff.

12 *Jn.* 4, 10.

13 *Jn.* 6, 41.

14 *Jn.* 8, 12.

15 *Jn.* 10, 9.

16 *Jn.* 10, 11.

17 *Jn.* 11, 25.

18 *Jn.* 14, 6.

19 See L. de Grandmaison, *Jesus Christ*, IV, *The Person of Jesus;* L. Sabourin, *Les noms et les titres de Jesus*, Desclée de Brouwer; O. Cullmann, *Christologie du N.T.* (1955).

20 *Mt.* 26, 66.

21 *Mt.* 26, 63.

22 See *Mt.* 11, 26; *Jn.* 8, 52-58; 17, 1-6.

23 See *Mt.* 27, 43; 27, 54; *Jn.* 20, 28.

24 *Jn.* 1, 1 ff.

25 *Col.* 1, 15.

26 *Jn.* 14, 28.

27 See *Lk.* 6, 42.

28 *Mt.* 27, 46.

29 See Denz.-Sch. 290 ff.

30 *Phil.* 1, 21.

31 See M. J. Lagrange, *Le sens du christianisme . . .*; G. Ricciotti, *Vita di Gesú Cristo*, par. 194-224; L. de Grandmaison, *Jesus Christ*; S. Zedda, *I Vangeli e la critica oggi*, Treviso (1965); for recent negative theories: G. de Rosa, "*La secolorizazzione del Cristianesimo*," "*Civiltà Cattolica*" (1970), 2877, 2878.

32 *Rom.* 8, 35.

Address of Pope Paul VI to a General Audience, February 17, 1971.

1 See *Mk.* 8, 31; 9, 31; 10, 33 ff.

2 See *Jn.* 2, 4; 7, 30; 12, 23; 13, 1;17, 1.

3 See Gospel of St. Matthew; *Jn* 13, 18; 15, 25; *Lk.* 24, 25; etc.

4 *Mt.* 16, 21-13.

5 *Jn.* 18, 11; *Heb.* 9, 14.

6 *Mk.* 10, 45; *Is.* 53, 10 ff.

7 See Letter from Lentulus.

8 See *Jn.* 11, 35; *Lk.* 19, 4.

9 *Mk.* 9, 36; 10, 16.

10 *Lk.* 22, 43.

11 See *Jn.* 12, 27-28.

12 See *Mk.* 10, 17-18, 21.

13 *Mt.* 11, 28.

14 *1 Cor.* 15, 3.

15 *Col.* 1, 26.

16 *Penesées,* 434.

17 *Eph.* 5, 2; *Gal.* 2, 20.

Declaration of the Sacred Congregation for the Doctrine of the Faith, March 8, 1972.

1 See *Phil.* 2, 6-8.

2 1 *Cor* 8, 6.

3 *Jn.* 1, 1, 14 (see 1, 18).

4 See Vat. Coun. I, Dogmatic constitution *Dei Filius*, chap. 4; *Conc. Oec. Decr.*, Herder (1962), p. 785; Denz.-Sch. 3020.

5 *Missale Romanum*, Vatican Polyglot Press (1970), p. 389; Denz.-Sch. 150.

6 See Council of Chalcedon, *Definitio; Conc. Oec. Decr.*, p. 62; Denz.-Sch. 301.

7 See ibid. Denz.-Sch. 302.

8 See 4th Lateran Council, Constitution *Firmiter credimus; Conc. Oec. Decr.*, p. 206; Denz.-Sch. 800 f.

9 See Vat. Coun. II, *Dogmatic Constitution on the Church*, nos. 3, 7, 52, 53 [*TPS* X, 360, 362-363, 394-395]; *Dogmatic Constitution on Divine Revelation*, nos. 2, 3 [*TPS* XI, 72-73]; *Pastoral Constitution on the Church in the World of Today*, no. 22 [*TPS* XI, 272-273]; *Decree on Ecumenism*, no. 12 [*TPS* X, 180-181]; *Decree on the Pastoral Office of Bishops in the Church*, no. 1 [*TPS XI*, 181] *Decree on the Missionary Activity of the Church*, no. 3 [*TPS* XI, 410-412]; see also Paul VI, *Credo of the People of God*, no. 11: *AAS* 60 (1968), 437 [*TPS* XIII, 277].

10 See Council of Florence, Bull *Laetentur caeli; Conc. Oec. Decr.*, p. 501 f.; Denz.-Sch. 1300.

11 2 *Cor.* 13, 13.

12 See *Mt.* 28, 19.

13 *Jn.* 15, 26.

14 Vat. Coun. II, *Dogmatic Constitution on Divine Revelation*, no. 10 [*TPS* XI, 76].

15 *Missale Romanum*, loc. cit.; Denz.-Sch. 150.

16 See 4th Lateran Council, Constitution *Firmiter credimus; Conc. Oec. Decr.*, p. 206; Denz.-Sch. 800.

17 Ibid.

18 Vat. Coun. I, Dogmatic Constitution *Dei Filius*, chap. 4, can. 3; *Conc. Oec. Decr.*, p. 787; Denz.-Sch. 3043. See Pope John XXIII, Allocution at opening of Vat. Coun. II: *AAS* 54 (1962), 792 [*TPS* VIII, 212-213], and Vat. Coun. II, *Pastoral Constitution on the Church in the World of Today*, no. 62 [*TPS* XI, 300-301]. See also Paul VI, *Credo of the People of God*, no. 4: *AAS* 60 (1968), 434 [*TPS* XIII, 273].

19 See 1 *Jn.* 4, 9 f.

20 See Vat. Coun. II, *Dogmatic Constitution on Divine Revelation*, no. 2 [*TPS* XI, 72]; see *Eph.* 18; 2 *Pt.* 1, 4.

21 See Paul VI, apost. exhortation *Quinque iam anni: AAS* 68 (1971), 99 [*TPS* XV, 327].

22 See 2 *Tm*, 4, 1-5. See Paul VI, apost. exhortation *Quinque iam anni: AAS* 68 (1971), 103 f. [*TPS* XV, 330-331]. See also Synod of Bishops (1967), *Relatio Commissioni Synodalis constitutae ad examen ulterius peragendum circa opiniones periculosas et atheismum*, II, 3: *De pastorali ratione agendi in exercitio magisterii*, Vatican Polyglot Press (1967), p. 10 f. (*Oss. Rom*., Oct. 30-31, 1967, p. 3).

23 Paul VI, apost. exhortation *Quinque iam anni: AAS* 68 (1971), 103 [*TPS* XV, 330].

24 Ibid.: *AAS* 68 (1971), 100 [*TPS* XV, 327].

25 See vat. Coun. II, *Dogmatic Constitution on the Church*, nos. 12, 15 [*TPS* X, 367, 375-376]; Synod of Bishops (1967), *Relatio Commissionis Synodalis*, II, 4: *De Theologorum opera et responsabilitate*, p. 11 (*Oss. Rom*. loc. cit.).

26 Vat. Coun. II, *Dogmatic Constitution on Divine revelation*, no. 10 [*TPS* XI, 75].

Homily of Pope Paul VI on the 16th Centenary of St. Athanasius' Death, May 6, 1973.

1 1 *Pt.* 5, 13.

2 See *Col.* 3, 14.

3 See *Eph.* 4, 3.

4 See *Mt.* 13, 52.

5 *Lk.* 24, 35-48.

6 *Rom.* 10, 9.

7 *Jn.* 20, 28.

8 *Apolytikion* of May 2.

9 See *De Incarnatione: PG* 25, 144, 119.

10 Ibid.

11 Ibid.

12 Ibid.

13 Ibid.

Address of Pope Paul VI to a General Audience, February 6, 1974.

1 See *Eph.* 1, 10.

2 See *Phil* 2, 7.

3 See 1 *Tim* 3, 16; *Jn* 14, 9.

4 See *Mt.* 11, 26.

5 *Bar.* 3, 38.

6 2 *Pt.* 1, 4.

7 See *Mk.* 3, 6.

8 *Jn* 1, 41.

9 See *Acts* 11, 26; 26, 28.

10 1 *Pt.* 4, 16.

11 See *Jas.* 2,7.

12 See E. Jacquier, *Les Actes . . .*, 351, 352.

13 See E. Neuhaüsler, *Exigence de Dieu et morale chrétienne*, Cerf (1962, 1971), p. 271 ff.

14 See *TPS* X, 255. –Ed.

Address of Pope Paul VI to a General Audience, February 13, 1974.

1 *Lk.* 8, 25.

2 *Mt.* 16, 13.

3 *Lk.* 2, 33.

4 *Lk.* 2, 50.

5 See *Mk.* 6, 2-4.

6 See *Jn* 10, 24: "If thou art the Christ, tell us openly.

7 *Lk.* 24, 25.

8 *Phil.* 1, 21.